Managing for Public Service Performance

Managing for Public Service Performance

How People and Values Make a Difference

Edited by

Peter Leisink
Lotte B. Andersen
Gene A. Brewer
Christian B. Jacobsen
Eva Knies
Wouter Vandenabeele

OXFORD
UNIVERSITY PRESS

OXFORD

UNIVERSITY PRESS

Great Clarendon Street, Oxford, OX2 6DP,
United Kingdom

Oxford University Press is a department of the University of Oxford.
It furthers the University's objective of excellence in research, scholarship,
and education by publishing worldwide. Oxford is a registered trade mark of
Oxford University Press in the UK and in certain other countries

First Edition published in 2021
Impression: 1

Published in the United States of America by Oxford University Press
198 Madison Avenue, New York, NY 10016, United States of America

British Library Cataloguing in Publication Data
Data available

Library of Congress Control Number: 2021930495

ISBN 978-0-19-289342-0

DOI: 10.1093/oso/9780192893420.001.0001

Printed and bound in Great Britain by
Clays Ltd, Elcograf S.p.A.

Preface

This volume is the result of a collective endeavor. The chapters in this volume are authored by researchers who have been engaged for many years in studying parts of the puzzle of public management and public service performance. They know each other's work as they have discussed their research papers at annual conference sessions held by the Study Group on Public Personnel Policies of the European Group for Public Administration. They signed up enthusiastically for the project initiated by the Study Group's conveners of reviewing the state of the art and bringing their insights together.

The purpose of joining forces is twofold. First, we are motivated to contribute to knowledge growth regarding "managing for public service performance." We recognize that knowledge growth will be difficult if researchers continue to use different concepts. Such is the case in this field where some researchers study management systems and others leadership, and where public service performance is understood in many different ways and often without explicit recognition of the various stakeholders' interests. Knowledge growth is also impaired by the organization of science in disciplines, which all have their favorite theoretical perspectives, their own journals, and their own conferences. This compartmentalization discourages the integration of theoretical perspectives and the use of insights from one discipline to compensate for the blind spots of another. This volume builds on the research expertise and perspectives from the fields of public management, leadership, human resource management, and work and organizational psychology. De-compartmentalization was achieved by writing individual draft chapters, having extensive discussions of all chapters in a two-day workshop, and subsequent revised versions that make individual expertise productive for the purpose of describing and explaining public management's contribution to public service performance.

Second, we are motivated to contribute to improving public service performance and increasing the effectiveness of public organizations in achieving the multiple ends they serve. Government, education, and healthcare are essential public services that we focus on because citizens' chances in life critically depend on their quality. The success of public organizations, their public service performance, is continuously affected by societal developments that create social issues, put pressure on existing policies, and invite politicians to instigate policy changes and public management reforms to address these (new) issues and better achieve policy objectives. Our research is committed to establishing a knowledge base, which is useful for public managers when they contribute to public service performance. One practically relevant insight that we elaborate on in this volume is the importance of public managers' people management of the employees they supervise, motivating them through transformational leadership and ensuring that employees fit their job and organizational environment, which creates engagement and willingness to exert themselves on behalf of public service provision.

Aims and Approach

The purpose of contributing to the growth of knowledge of "managing for public service performance" means that this volume has several aims:

- clarifying conceptual issues that are central to the management–performance relationship;
- critically reflecting on assumptions underlying public management and public service performance understandings;
- theoretically explaining direct and indirect relationships between public management and public service performance, making use of generic theoretical models, and specifying relevant public sector variables;
- outlining a research agenda, based on an assessment of the state of the art, including theoretical gaps and methodological limitations.

In order to achieve these aims, this volume takes a multidisciplinary, critical, rigorous, and context-sensitive approach. The volume combines insights and perspectives from the fields of public management, leadership, human resource management, and work and organizational psychology. These disciplines complement each other because they focus on different aspects of management and public service performance, and on different linking mechanisms. In addition, they tend to draw on different theoretical explanations.

The critical approach this volume takes to assumptions underlying public management and public service performance understandings is based on a stakeholder perspective. Related to the multiple ends that public organizations serve, different stakeholders have a legitimate interest in both processes and results. They have different understandings of what is desirable in public service provision. Using this perspective, we critically reflect on which stakeholder interests are included and which are excluded in empirical studies, and whether stakeholders' understandings are measured directly or indirectly. This is one aspect of our critical approach to the modernist assumption of progress through improved managerial control. Another aspect involves our interest in the contextual factors that affect the management–performance relationship, which vary strongly and are affected by societal developments that continue to put pressure on existing policies and call for improving their effectiveness.

Finally, this volume is characterized by a rigorous and context-sensitive approach. A rigorous approach favors generic theoretical models and validated measures. Public administration and management research can benefit from this as public service motivation research has shown. However, rigor requirements may decrease the relevance of research for the public management field. By paying attention to distinctive features of the public sector context, when and where these are relevant for studies to take into account, we try to balance rigor and relevance and contribute to both knowledge growth and the improvement of public services in practice.

Scope and Audience

This volume provides state-of-the-art reviews of research on various aspects of the public management–public service performance relationship. We examine the activities of public managers, their leadership, and human resource strategies, which assist in achieving the multiple ends of public organizations. These ends involve different types of public service performance: organizational and societal outcomes in which various stakeholders have an interest, as well as employee outcomes which relate directly to the public servants who are central to the delivery of public services. This is our subject matter, and its scope is determined by two factors.

First, the authors are experts in the fields of public administration and management, leadership, human resource management, and work and organizational psychology. Research in these disciplines is the basis of the state-of-the-art reviews that the individual chapters present. This multidisciplinary scope is a distinctive and unique feature of this volume.

Second, the international literature, particularly articles published by leading peer-reviewed scientific journals, informs this volume. However, the international literature, to which the authors of this volume contribute, focuses strongly on managing for public service performance in democratic societies. The authors have their academic homes in six European countries, namely Belgium, Denmark, Germany, the Netherlands, Switzerland, and the United Kingdom, as well as in the US, Hong Kong, and Japan. Their institutional environment informs the perspective of their writing and makes this volume most relevant for democratic societies, although we believe, as we explain in Chapters 1 and 4, that our perspective is also relevant for societies that do not fully adhere to democratic principles.

Given this volume's purpose and scope, its primary audience is academic scholars: researchers, students, and lecturers. The state-of-the-art reviews presented by the chapters in this volume are complemented by suggestions for further research, and both provide valid information and inspiration for new studies in our field. Specifically, many chapters discuss the methodological limitations of existing research and outline what kind of research is needed to advance knowledge of the field. Additionally, the systematic literature reviews that several chapters provide are helpful to students new to their field of interest in getting an overview of the subject. This volume also hopes to attract the interest of policy advisors employed by large government organizations who participate in research, for instance, by commissioning research, sitting on supervisory committees, or co-creating knowledge. The chapters in this volume discuss the practical implications of research on their specific topic, which are often based on the experience the authors have as policy advisors themselves. One evidence-based piece of advice for public management practice is that adopting so-called best practices or copying organizations "at the cutting edge of management reform or innovation" is not per se the best way forward for public organizations. Instead, our authors take the public sector context seriously and discuss how insights from the body of knowledge can be adapted to the specific context of public organizations that work hard to improve their public service and create public value.

Acknowledgments

Many people have contributed to what has become this volume. First, we are grateful to our authors. Most authors have participated for many years in the Study Group on Public Personnel Policies of the European Group for Public Administration (EGPA). Its annual meetings provide a platform where researchers present their work-in-progress and discuss this in an open and constructive atmosphere. The research programs the Study Group has hosted over the past decade have influenced our thinking about "managing for public service performance." Individual contributors have benefitted from the feedback provided by the Study Group's colleagues. In addition to this, a dedicated book workshop was held directly following the EGPA Conference in Lausanne, in September 2018. We thank Maxime Dekkers for organizing the workshop. Draft versions of the chapters in this volume were discussed at this workshop with a view to enhancing the quality of the chapters and the overall cohesion of the volume. We are grateful to our authors for participating in the workshop and sharing their knowledge with the aim of producing a top quality volume. We are also grateful for their willingness to engage with editorial suggestions and revise their draft chapters to make their chapters coherent with the volume's approach and overall framework.

We would also like to thank the three anonymous reviewers who were invited by Oxford University Press to comment on our book proposal and sample chapters. Their questions, comments, and suggestions have helped us revise and improve our explanation of this volume's approach and its application by individual chapters. Natasha Elizabeth Perera, who works as a language editor at the Department of Political Science, Aarhus University, took care of the production of the manuscript and did a great job. Thank you. More generally, we would like to thank the Department of Political Science and the Crown Prince Frederik Center for Public Leadership at Aarhus University, Denmark, and the Utrecht University School of Governance, the Netherlands, for their support for this book project. Finally, we would like to thank Jenny King and her colleagues at Oxford University Press for their support throughout the process. We hope that all who have contributed to what has become this volume, and of course the many readers, will be pleased with the outcome.

Contents

List of Figures

List of Tables and Boxes

Tables

Boxes

List of Contributors

Lotte B. Andersen is Professor in the Department of Political Science at Aarhus University, Denmark, and Center Director of the Crown Prince Frederik Center for Public Leadership. Her research interests include leadership, motivation, behavior, and the performance of public and private employees. She has also contributed to research concerning economic incentives and motivation crowding theory. She serves as a PMRA board member, Co-Editor of *PAR*, *IPMJ*, and *PPMG*, and is Co-Chair of the EGPA Study Group on Public Personnel Policies. Her books and articles are listed on her webpage.

Tanachia Ashikali is Assistant Professor of Public Management at the Institute of Public Administration at Leiden University, the Netherlands. Her research expertise includes diversity management, leadership, and inclusion in public organizations, with a focus on quantitative research methods and techniques.

Gene A. Brewer is an internationally recognized scholar of public administration with research interests in governance, public management, and the policy process. He has long served as a faculty member at the University of Georgia in the US and holds secondary appointments at Utrecht University in the Netherlands, KU Leuven in Belgium, and the Institute of Public Affairs in the Republic of Georgia. Dr. Brewer regularly consults for both governmental and nongovernmental organizations internationally.

David Giauque is Associate Professor of the Sociology of Organizations and Public Administrations at the University of Lausanne, Switzerland. His research is mainly dedicated to topics such as HRM in the public sector, comparative public administration, changes and reforms in public organizations and their consequences, as well as motivation and well-being in Swiss public administrations. He has led several research projects funded by the Swiss National Science Foundation and is the author and co-author of numerous scientific books and articles.

Julian Seymour Gould-Williams is Professor of Human Resource Management at Cardiff Business School, Cardiff, the UK. He has many years of experience in researching the effects of HRM practices in local government. More recently, he has considered the role of leadership and other organizational factors that influence employees' work experiences and motivation. He is particularly interested in the motivational drivers of public sector workers and develops theory and measurement to improve the understanding of such drivers. Julian has published in many leading academic journals.

Sandra Groeneveld is Professor of Public Management at the Institute of Public Administration, Leiden University, the Netherlands. Her research interests include the structure and management of public organizations, focusing particularly on questions of representative bureaucracy, diversity management, leadership, and organizational change.

Caroline H. Grøn is Associate Professor in the Crown Prince Frederik Center for Public Leadership at the Department of Political Science, Aarhus University, Denmark. She works on public management and leadership and has published in *Administration & Society*, the *International Review of Administrative Sciences*, the *Review of Public Personnel Administration*, and the *Journal of European Public Policy*.

Annie Hondeghem is Professor in the Faculty of Social Sciences and Director of the KU Leuven Public Governance Institute, Belgium. She is a specialist in public personnel management, equal opportunity and diversity policies, and change management. She currently is working on themes of migration and refugees. Her publications include *Motivation in Public Management: The Call of Public Service* (Oxford University Press, 2008, with J. Perry) and *Leadership and Culture: Comparative Models of Top Civil Servant Training* (Palgrave Macmillan, 2015, with M. Van Wart and E. Schwella).

Christian B. Jacobsen is Associate Professor in the Department of Political Science, Aarhus University, Denmark. His research focuses on management and leadership in public service organizations, employee motivation, and performance. He is Vice-Manager of the Crown Prince Frederik Center for Public Leadership, with responsibility for research activities. Since 2017, he has served as Co-Chair of the EGPA Study Group on Public Personnel Policies. His articles have been published in leading academic journals.

Oliver James is Professor of Political Science at the University of Exeter, UK. His research interests include political and managerial leadership of public organizations, citizen–provider relationships, and organizational reform. Recent publications include *Experiments in Public Management Research* (Cambridge University Press, 2017, with S. Jilke, and G. Van Ryzin).

Ulrich T. Jensen is Assistant Professor in the School of Public Affairs at Arizona State University, USA. His research builds on new and innovative ways to understand the importance of leadership in shaping the motivation and values of public service providers and the performance of their organizations. His research has appeared, among other places, in the *Journal of Public Administration Research and Theory*, *Public Administration Review*, *Public Administration*, and *Social Science & Medicine*.

Anne Mette Kjeldsen is Associate Professor of Public Administration and Management in the Department of Political Science, Aarhus University, Denmark. She serves as Associate Study Director for the Aarhus University Master's Programme in Public Management. Her research focuses on motivation, job satisfaction, and the commitment of frontline public service personnel, as well as distributed leadership and change implementation in the areas of health and social services. Her studies have been published in leading academic journals.

Eva Knies is Professor of Strategic Human Resource Management in the Utrecht University School of Governance, Utrecht, the Netherlands. Her research interests are in the areas of strategic human resource management's contribution to public service performance, public leadership, and sustainable employability. She serves as Co-Chair of the EGPA Study Group on Public Personnel Policies and as Associate Editor of *The International Journal of HRM*. Her website lists her articles in international journals and other publications.

Peter Leisink is Professor Emeritus of Public Administration and Organization Science at the Utrecht University School of Governance, Utrecht, the Netherlands. His research interests include the management and organization of public service organizations, strategic human resource management's contribution to public service performance, leadership, and public service motivation. From 2009 to 2019, he served as Co-Chair of the EGPA Study Group on Public Personnel Policies. His webpage lists his articles and other publications.

Ahmed Mohammed Sayed Mostafa is Associate Professor at Leeds University Business School, Leeds, the UK. His research interests are in the areas of high-performance work systems, leadership and employee well-being, and performance. His research on these topics has been published in journals such as *Public Administration Review*, *Public Management Review*, the *International Journal of Human Resource Management*, and the *Journal of Business Ethics*.

Ayako Nakamura is Assistant Professor at Musashino University, Tokyo, Japan. She is working on the comparative study of government control. Recent publications include "Controlling Risk inside Modern Government: Developing Interval Measures of the Grid-Group Dimensions for Assessing Suicide Risk Control Systems in the English and Japanese Prison Services." *Public Administration 64* (4) (2016), pp. 1077–93.

Poul A. Nielsen is Associate Professor in the Crown Prince Frederik Center for Public Leadership at Aarhus University, Denmark. His research examines performance management systems in politics and public management and focuses on topics such as performance budgeting, responsibility attribution, and organizational learning. He has published research in journals such as the *Journal of Public Administration Research and Theory*, *Public Administration Review*, *Public Administration*, and *Governance*. He received the Academy of Management PNP Division's 2017 Best Journal Article Award.

Sophie Op de Beeck holds a PhD in Social Sciences (KU Leuven) and currently works as a research advisor in the Humanities and Social Sciences Group of KU Leuven, Belgium. Her research interests are situated in the area of public personnel management, more specifically strategic human resource management, the implementation of HR practices, and the role of line managers in personnel issues. In addition, she has specialist expertise in (European) research funding.

Nicolai Petrovsky is Associate Professor in the Department of Public Policy at City University of Hong Kong. His research focuses on public service performance, managerial succession, and citizen–state interactions. Recent publications include "What Explains Agency Heads' Length of Tenure? Testing Managerial Background, Performance, and Political Environment Effects." *Public Administration Review 77* (4) (2017), pp. 591–602 (with O. James, A. Moseley, and G. A. Boyne).

Adrian Ritz is Professor of Public Management at the KPM Center for Public Management at the University of Bern in Switzerland. His research interests focus on public management, administrative reforms, leadership, motivation, and performance in public organizations. He has published in scientific journals such as the *Journal of Public Administration Research and Theory*, *Perspectives on Public Management and Governance*, *Public Administration Review*, *Public Management Review*, and *Human Resource Management*. His co-authored book, *Public Management* (Springer) is in its 6th edition.

Heidi H. Salomonsen is Associate Professor in the Department of Management, Aarhus University, Denmark. Her main research interests include public management and strategic communication in the public sector, in particular, reputation management and leadership communication, as well as relationships between top civil servants, ministers, and political advisers. She has published on those topics in journals such as *Public Administration, Public Administration Review*, the *International Review of Administrative Sciences*, and the *International Journal of Strategic Communication*.

Carina Schott is Assistant Professor at the Utrecht University School of Governance, Utrecht, the Netherlands. She conducts research in the field of public management at the individual level. Specifically, her research concerns the motivation and decision-making processes of public servants and the implications of a changing work environment on the nature of their work. Her research has appeared, among other places, in *Public Management Review, Public Administration*, and the *American Review of Public Administration*.

Trui Steen is Professor of Public Governance and Co-Production of Public Services at KU Leuven, Public Governance Institute, Belgium. She is interested in public organizations and the role of public service professionals. Her research includes topics such as professionalism, public service motivation, citizen participation and co-production of public services, local government, and public sector innovation. She is Co-Chair of the IIAS Study Group on the Co-Production of Public Services. Her work has been published in various scholarly journals.

Bram Steijn is Professor of HRM in the Public Sector in the Department of Public Administration and Sociology, Erasmus University Rotterdam, the Netherlands. He has published on HRM-related issues, such as strategic HRM, quality of work, teamwork, motivation of employees, public service motivation, and policy alienation of public professionals. He is a board member

of the Dutch HRM Network and a member of the editorial board of the *Review of Public Personnel Administration*.

Wouter Vandenabeele is Associate Professor at Utrecht University School of Governance, Utrecht, the Netherlands, and a visiting professor at KU Leuven University, Belgium. His research interests concern the motivation and behavior of public employees, the evolution of public institutions, and innovation in public administration research methods. He has published numerous articles and book chapters on these topics. He is Co-Chair of the EGPA Study Group on Public Personnel Policies and Co-Founder of the Special Interest Group on Public Service Motivation at the IRSPM.

Joris Van der Voet is Associate Professor of Public Management at the Institute of Public Administration, Leiden University, Leiden, the Netherlands, where he coordinates the Public Management program. His research focuses on the behavior of public managers during organizational change. He has a particular interest in the question of how public managers can create innovation in times of financial decline. His research has been published in journals such as *Public Administration, Public Management Review*, and *The American Review of Public Administration*.

Jasmijn Van Harten is Assistant Professor at the Utrecht University School of Governance, Utrecht, the Netherlands. Her research focuses on organizational investments in workers' employability and consequent outcomes. She is also involved in research on the functioning of the top civil service. She has published in international scientific journals such as the *International Journal of Human Resource Management*, the

Journal of Health Organization and Management, and *Personnel Review.*

Nina Van Loon is a policy advisor in the Municipality of Rotterdam in the Netherlands and a guest researcher at the Department of Political Science, Aarhus University, Denmark. Her research interests are the performance of public services and the role of employees in enhancing performance. In particular, she focuses on red tape, public service motivation, and the coping of public professionals. Her articles on these topics have been published in leading international journals.

Brenda Vermeeren is Assistant Professor in the Department of Public Administration and Sociology at Erasmus University Rotterdam, the Netherlands. She is also a senior advisor at ICTU-InternetSpiegel (a program under the Ministry of the Interior and Kingdom Relations, the Netherlands). Her research interests include the relationship between HRM and public performance, the role of line managers in implementing HRM, and the antecedents and effects of multiple job holding. An overview of her publications can be found on her webpage.

Dominik Vogel is Assistant Professor of Public Management at the University of Hamburg, Hamburg, Germany. His research focuses on the motivation of public employees, leadership and human resource management in the public sector, the interaction of citizens with public administrations, and performance management. His research is based on quantitative methods, especially survey research and experimental methods. He is Communication Editor of the *Journal of Behavioral Public Administration.*

1

Introduction

Managing for Public Service Performance:
How People and Values Make a Difference

Peter Leisink, Lotte B. Andersen, Gene A. Brewer,
Christian B. Jacobsen, Eva Knies, and Wouter Vandenabeele

1.1 Introduction

"Managing for public service performance" is a topic that continues to interest politicians, public managers and employees, citizens, and other stakeholders, as well as public management scholars. Just one example of this interest is a study by Thijs et al. (2018) commissioned by the European Union. This study provides a comparative overview of public administration characteristics and performance in twenty-eight EU member states. Its chapter on government capacity and performance deals with topics such as the civil service system and human resource management (HRM), the organization and management of government organizations, and overall government performance. Noting that management matters for public service performance, many studies aim to identify the key factors that contribute to public service performance (e.g. Andrews and Boyne 2010; Andrews et al. 2012; Ashworth et al. 2009; Boyne 2003; Hammerschmid et al. 2016; Pedersen et al. 2019; Walker et al. 2010).

Improving public service performance is an issue, if not increasingly a wicked issue. In many countries across the globe, politicians require public organizations to deal with complex social issues related to globalization, migration, health crises, an aging population, climate change, terrorism, and homeland security. It is up to public servants to deliver on politicians' promises, to achieve the goals of public policy programs set by governments, and to act responsively to the different stakeholders and complex situations with which they are faced. Classic government bureaucracy does not seem equal to these challenges. Thus, a better understanding of what managing for public service performance means and what it requires from public managers and public servants is essential for the success of public policy programs.

For public administration and management research, "managing for public service performance" is also an important issue that raises essential theoretical and empirical questions. Theoretically, the role attributed to public management has

Peter Leisink, Lotte B. Andersen, Gene A. Brewer, Christian B. Jacobsen, Eva Knies, and Wouter Vandenabeele, *Introduction: Managing for Public Service Performance: How People and Values Make a Difference* In: *Managing for Public Service Performance: How People and Values Make a Difference*. Edited by: Peter Leisink, Lotte B. Andersen, Gene A. Brewer, Christian B. Jacobsen, Eva Knies, and Wouter Vandenabeele, Oxford University Press (2021). © Peter Leisink, Lotte B. Andersen, Gene A. Brewer, Christian B. Jacobsen, Eva Knies, and Wouter Vandenabeele.
DOI: 10.1093/oso/9780192893420.003.0001

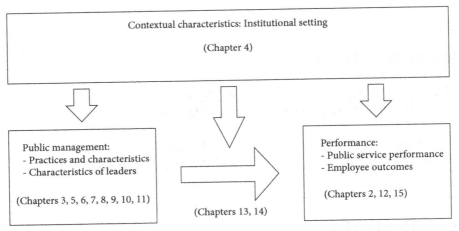

Figure 1.1 Conceptual model of the main concepts examined by the chapters

sparked debate over classic assumptions regarding the politics–administration dichotomy and the public values that (should) guide public servants (Alford 2008; Rhodes and Wanna 2007; 2009). Relatedly, "managing for public service performance" has led to the critical study of the differences between public and private organizations and their implications for management (Rainey 2009). It also raises new issues such as the relevance of context in research (O'Toole and Meier 2015; Pollitt 2013). Empirically, the study of "managing for public service performance" has provided evidence for the positive relationship between management and public service performance. However, the question of *how, when, and where* management makes a meaningful contribution to public service performance has received scant attention. This question can be framed methodologically: What are the key causal variables which include the key mediating and moderating variables? Addressing this question in either form requires a contextual approach.

The contextual approach in this work draws upon O'Toole and Meier (2015). Contextual variables affect the management–performance relationship, and this is illustrated in our conceptual model (Figure 1.1), which structures our overall study. Johns (2006, 386) defines context as "situational opportunities and constraints that affect the occurrence and meaning of organizational behavior as well as functional relationships between variables." Our aim is to describe these situational opportunities and constraints more specifically. Our ideas of what this context entails, in particular, how it relates to institutional characteristics and how this is relevant to management, are discussed in depth in Chapter 4. The present chapter will focus on how the concept is relevant to how public management affects public service performance.

Despite the steadily increasing number of studies on how public management impacts public service performance, the question of what constitutes public service performance remains contested (Talbot 2005). Public service performance is often associated with new public management (NPM) because of its focus on results and use of performance management instruments (Andrews et al. 2016; Pollitt and Bouckaert 2004). Since the mid-1980s, public management reforms across a range of countries in Europe, North America, and Australasia have incorporated an NPM-oriented approach focused on efficiency, results, and innovation. Its distinctiveness from the orientation of classic Weberian bureaucracy is evidenced by the latter's emphasis on hierarchy, compartmentalization, and process, involving legality, rule following, due process, and neutrality rather than outcomes (Kettl 2017; Selden et al. 1999). Thus, the conceptualization of public service performance is an issue in itself.

In addition, how management is understood—the concept and its scope—varies widely. For instance, the Government Performance Project in the US (Ingraham et al. 2003) assumes that government organizations perform well when management runs good management systems. Another line of research focuses on improving leadership (Trottier et al. 2008; Van Wart 2003) and has, to some extent, elaborated on the contribution managers can make to performance through their influence on others. However, public management research has only been modestly interested in how public organizations' human capital can best be managed to achieve organizational goals. Overall, the public management literature has not fully absorbed the findings from the service quality literature (Heskett et al. 1994; Normann 1991; Zeithaml et al. 1990) or the human resource management (HRM) literature (Boxall and Purcell 2016; Jiang and Messersmith 2017), which provides firm evidence on the importance of human resources in delivering, improving, and innovating services.

This summary inspection of the field illustrates that the body of knowledge on "managing for public service performance" consists of contested issues and alternative perspectives, lacks integration, and contains some specific gaps. Thus, the aim of this volume is to clarify the major conceptual and theoretical issues and to provide evidence and commentary on the state of research in this important subject. More specifically, we describe how public managers can manage for public service performance and outline a research agenda, and we point out the practical implications of what we know. We are aware that "managing for public service performance" may convey a modernist assumption of progress through managerial control (Van Dooren and Hoffman 2018), but the aim of this volume is to go beyond this. We argue that there are many different stakeholders with different understandings of what is desirable in public service provision. Put another way, there are multiple public values that compete for attention in public service provision, which creates ambiguity (at best) or conflict (at worst). This latter perspective centering on public values allows us to reflect critically on public management and public service performance.

This chapter maps the field that the chapters in this volume will examine in detail. It does not do so by providing summaries of the individual chapters, but rather by painting a broad-stroke picture of our central argument in order to help the reader navigate through the volume. Section 1.2 elaborates on the contextual approach this volume takes. Subsequently, Section 1.3 describes the characteristics of the public sector context from an institutional perspective that pays attention to both public values and structural features impacting public service provision. Section 1.4 describes the empirical scope of our study. Following this, Section 1.5 explores the state of research, concentrating on public management, public service performance, and the linking mechanisms. This will serve to explain the volume's distinctive characteristics in Section 1.6. This section will also explain the ordering of the volume's chapters and topics and summarize their contributions toward answering the main question that motivates this work: How do public managers make a meaningful contribution to public service performance?

1.2 Time and Place of Public Management and Performance: A Contextual Approach

A readily and broadly accepted definition of management is "a process of getting things done through and with people operating in organized groups" (Koontz 1961, 175). Unfortunately, with a history of concentrating on practical outcomes and normative consequences rather than conceptual clarity, public management is less well defined (Hood 1991). The nomological network of the concept entails notions like public administration, public governance, and public policy, which may create confusion about what public management actually is and how it differs from allied constructs. Further ambiguity is often present because many of these scholarly and professional conceptualizations are based upon their particular ontological, epistemological, and methodological assumptions. A history of the field therefore reads like a patchwork of claims about what you can and cannot do or know in this particular domain (Ongaro 2017; Riccucci 2010).

Nevertheless, public management can—based on the above-mentioned concept of management and the extant literature—be understood as the activities aiming to achieve the multiple ends of public organizations. How these ends and public management's role in achieving them are understood evolves over time (Pollitt 2013). Indeed, one illustration is the very introduction of the term "public management" from the 1970s onwards along with ideological changes in society that have increased the dominance of managerialism (Pollitt and Bouckaert 2004, 9), at least in some countries in Europe, North America, and Australasia.

Noting that public management reforms aimed at helping or forcing public sector organizations to perform better have swept across many Organisation for Economic Co-operation and Development (OECD) countries and elsewhere since the 1980s, Pollitt and Bouckaert (2004) pose the question of what broad forces have been at work in driving and constraining change. They propose a heuristic framework that distinguishes socio-economic forces, political pressures, and features of the administrative system itself, which interact and drive or constrain public management reform, with considerable variation between countries. Their approach resembles an open systems perspective, which sees organizations in constant interaction with their environment.

Pollitt and Bouckaert's conceptual model is a useful framework for mapping how the environment currently impacts public management and public organizations. This is illustrated, for instance, by Lodge and Hood (2012), who argue that the key societal changes affecting OECD states consist of multiple austerities, with financial austerity being compounded by population aging and environmental risk. The environment's turbulence creates uncertainties and issues that challenge public management's capacity to achieve public service performance. Examples of such issues and the public management activities they engender are provided by several chapters in this volume, including Chapter 10: "Managing a Diverse Workforce," Chapter 11: "Leading Change in a Complex Public Sector Environment," and Chapter 15: "Managing Employees' Employability."

Pollitt and Bouckaert's study of public management reforms focuses on processes in a longer time perspective. However, the external environment also affects management's activities and impact on performance in a short time perspective. This is a premise of O'Toole and Meier's (2015) theory of how context affects the management–performance linkage. They see context as consisting of industry, sector, and economy-wide factors as well as other normative and institutional structures and regimes (O'Toole and Meier 2015, 238). They develop a public management context matrix that includes the environmental context (with its complexity, turbulence, munificence, and social capital), the political context (with the separation of powers, federalism, process, and performance appraisal as dimensions), and the internal context (including organizational goals, centralization, and professionalization). The hypotheses they develop explain how specific contextual factors will influence public management activities and their contributions to performance.

However, O'Toole and Meier (2015) pay less attention to public values. These can be regarded as an institutional feature of the public sector context, which interact with several other contextual variables. Chapter 4 elaborates on the public sector context as an institutional environment. In our view, institutions are not limited to the features as described by O'Toole and Meier. Rather, institutions are persistent structures situated at various levels above the individual; they are based on common values and influence behavior (Peters 2000). The value component is as important as the structural component, and the interaction between values and structures guides our analysis. "Publicness" is a case in point of an institution that impacts public management. What "publicness" involves varies between settings, and this will be explained by analyzing the public values that are salient in a particular setting.

This perspective on context can also be used to explain this volume's focus on public service in democratic societies. Our institutional perspective is drawn from the literature that mainly comes from and is most relevant in democratic societies. This focus states that characteristics of democratic societies frame—and, in a sense, restrict—our analysis. For instance, the interdependent and complex institutional environment in democratic societies enhances robustness, buffers external shocks, and does not permit sudden top-down policy changes. The normative assumption inherent in liberal democracy—i.e. its explicit attention to stakeholder structures—is that this will likely lead to better performance. We believe that our perspective is also relevant for systems that do not fully adhere to democratic principles because applying this perspective will facilitate a more complete reflection on the institutional environment and its impact.

1.3 Going Inside the Institutional Perspective: The Public Sector Context

The way in which governments react to societal challenges is dependent on their institutional characteristics and involves their structures and their normative and cultural–cognitive elements. These three elements, which are central to the institutional perspective (Scott 2001), are interrelated. The different modes of governance (Andersen et al. 2012) and reform paradigms (Van de Walle et al. 2016) illustrate this interrelatedness of institutional elements. The structural element is represented by organizational designs, such as hierarchy, market, and network. The normative and cultural–cognitive elements are represented by the particular public values that specify the principles on which governments, governance modes, and policies are based (Bozeman 2007).

Van de Walle et al. (2016) distinguish the Weberian paradigm based upon hierarchy and legality from the NPM paradigm, which emphasizes efficiency, performance, and innovation. They describe NPM as a response, starting with the Thatcher and Reagan governments in the 1980s, to the perceived weaknesses of bureaucratic structures. NPM was mainly concerned with the introduction of market-like mechanisms and business management logic into the public sector. However, NPM has had negative effects in terms of increasing fragmentation, coordination challenges, and a weakened public service ethos that has led to the emergence of a new paradigm. Various labels are used for this new paradigm, which include neo-Weberianism, network governance, and new public governance, and which emphasizes coordination, effectiveness, and outcomes as key characteristics. Van de Walle et al. (2016, 3) observe that the succession of reform paradigms has led to "successive layers of reforms sedimenting within public administrations" and increasing their complexity and variety.

Andersen et al. (2012) aim to link public values to a typology of modes of governance. The four modes of governance they distinguish are: (1) hierarchical governance based on classic Weberian bureaucracy; (2) clan governance based on norms of a relevant group such as a profession; (3) network governance based on balancing interests and including different societal interests in government and policy; and (4) market governance based on the idea of utilizing the market as an allocative mechanism. Theoretically, the literature associates different public values to these modes of governance. Andersen et al. (2012) add to this by asking Danish public managers to evaluate the importance of public values in relation to the governance modes. One important finding is the clustering of public values into seven components: (1) the public at large; (2) rule abidance; (3) budget keeping; (4) professionalism; (5)

balancing interests; (6) efficient supply; and (7) user focus. Another important result is that these value components can be linked to the four governance modes. The values of professionalism and balancing interests are negatively related, indicating that the clan/professional and network governance modes differ most regarding who should decide (the relevant group of professionals versus all societal groups involved). Also, rule abidance and user focus are negatively related, implying a value conflict between hierarchy and the market. Finally, there appear to be value differences between organizations that perform different tasks within the public sector. For example, public managers in regulative/administrative organizations regard rule abidance and balancing interests as more important than public managers in service delivery organizations, who regard professionalism and user focus as more important.

These studies highlight the importance of including the public sector context in our study of managing for public service performance. The public values that inform public service performance may differ significantly between types of organizations and between types of governance modes. Furthermore, the institutional characteristics of certain public sector contexts may enable certain kinds of public management behaviors while constraining others. The kind of publicness of an institutional context is arguably a central feature to take into account, for instance, when studying the relationship between public values and public service motivation (PSM) of employees or the impact of a structural feature such as red tape on the job performance of public employees. What publicness entails in structural, normative, and cultural–cognitive terms is thus part of this study (addressed in Chapter 4).

It is important to recognize that the institutional context is a determinant as well as an outcome of actors' behaviors (Ongaro 2017). On the one hand, the prevailing public values influence the value preferences and actions of the actors, and, on the other, values are (re)produced by actors' actions (Andersen et al. 2012; Vandenabeele et al. 2013). Values seen in this institutional perspective are an important feature of this volume, as signaled by its subtitle "how values make a difference." The other part of the subtitle refers to "how people make a difference." This view resonates with Pfeffer's (1998) emphasis on "putting people first" and can be considered a generic feature of HRM, which holds for the public and private sectors alike. By combining this starting point with "how values make a difference," we aim to highlight the interrelatedness of the important role people play in public service provision and the public sector context.

1.4 Public Services: The Scope of This Volume

The concept of public services refers to services provided, ordered, and/or mainly financed by government for its citizens, corporate actors, and society as a whole. This understanding is related to the structural characteristics that are regarded as distinctive of public organizations (Rainey 2009), namely, government ownership, funding, and political authority/oversight. Typical public organizations, which exhibit all three characteristics, include government ministries. However, there is institutional variation across countries regarding these criteria, which is illustrated by the example of healthcare: While the National Health Service in the United Kingdom is public according to all three formal criteria, healthcare in the Netherlands is provided by organizations that are legally private bodies charged with a public task.

There are economic and political reasons for having specific kinds of services provided by public organizations instead of by the market (see Rainey 2009). Services are provided by public organizations when these services, once provided, benefit everyone and society as a whole (e.g. national defense and education). Governments also regulate market activities and market externalities when markets themselves are unable or unwilling to do so, such as in the case of the environmental consequences of market activity. In addition, there are political reasons for providing publicly funded services that stem from human dignity or human rights, for instance, in the case of homeless people or asylum seekers.

Thijs et al. (2018, 7–8) use structural criteria when they describe public employment in the EU member states. The broadest concept of public sector employment, labeled as producing "services of general interest," includes 29.7 percent of the EU workforce and comprises private sector employment in areas such as education and health. A second, slightly narrower concept of public sector employment excludes private sector employment in these areas and covers employment in the three mainly publicly funded sectors of public administration, health, and education. This concept differs from the situation in many non-EU countries where health and education are considered part of public administration. Following this second definition, 25 percent of total employment pertains to public sector employment in the twenty-eight EU member states. The third and strictest definition using the label of "government/public administration" excludes health and education. Government employment represents 6.9 percent of the workforce in the twenty-eight EU member states.

For a look beyond the European Union, we turn to the OECD. The OECD (2017) uses the concept of general government employment, which covers employment in all levels of government (central, state, local, and social security funds) and includes core ministries, agencies, departments, and non-profit institutions that are controlled by public authorities. *Government at a Glance 2017* (OECD 2017) concludes that the size of general government employment varies significantly among OECD countries. Nordic countries such as Denmark, Norway, and Sweden report the highest general government employment levels, reaching almost 30 percent of total employment. On the other hand, OECD countries from the Asian region have low levels of public employment, amounting to only around 6 percent of Japan's total employment and 7.6 percent of Korea's total workforce (OECD 2017, 90). Anglo-American countries fall in between, with general government employment representing around 15 percent of total employment. For instance, the US reports 15 percent, Great Britain 17 percent, and Canada 18 percent.

In this volume, we will concentrate on public administration, health, and educational services. Health and education fall within the scope of this work, irrespective of countries' traditions to consider them as part of public administration or as sectors in and of themselves.

1.5 Literature Review: Defining Key Concepts

1.5.1 Managing

The idea of drawing a sharp distinction between leadership and management has been criticized on various grounds. Nevertheless, studies in the field of public management and public service performance tend to concentrate on management or on leadership, and only a few studies try to combine the two explicitly (Andrews and Boyne 2010; Knies et al. 2018b).

Management capacity has been the central independent variable in an influential line of research on government performance (Ingraham et al. 2003). The underlying assumption is that when a government's systems—including capital, financial, information technology, and human resources management systems—work well, the government will be effective and perform well. Putting good management systems in place is regarded as the responsibility of public managers. In addition, public managers need a strong orientation toward performance, including performance-orientated strategic planning and measurement as a basis for policy-making and management. This line of research continues to inform studies of public management and the management systems that are seen as tools to affect performance (Andrews and Boyne 2010; Andrews et al. 2012; Melton and Meier 2017; Nielsen 2014). Many studies in this line of research focus on internal management and individual organizations. Other studies concentrate on boundary-spanning management practices such as networking with external stakeholders and more complex organizational configurations such as implementation structures and networks (e.g. Agranoff 2007; Andrews et al. 2012; Meier et al. 2007; Provan and Milward 2001).

There is also a line of research that understands "managing" as leadership activities. For instance, Andrews and Boyne (2010) combine their interest in managerial capacity with leadership and assume that executive managers' leadership skills help to coordinate management systems and link them to performance. Following Van Wart's (2003) call to study leadership in the public sector context, some studies have examined public managers' leadership styles and described them as transformational or transactional (Jensen et al. 2016), often linking these styles to leadership effectiveness (Trottier et al. 2008) or organizational outcomes (Jacobsen and Andersen 2015; Oberfield 2014; Sun and Henderson 2017). Other leadership studies have developed concepts of public sector leadership (Fernandez et al. 2010; Tummers and Knies 2016), relying to some extent on Yukl's (2012) taxonomy of leadership behavior. The lack of consensus in the study of managerial and leadership activities is further illustrated by the fact that activities such as setting challenging goals, building trust, and stimulating employee participation are studied as internal management activities by some (e.g. Favero et al. 2016) and as transformational leadership by others (e.g. Jensen et al. 2016).

Knies et al. (2016) note that many studies understand managing for public service performance as referring to activities by executive or senior managers. Studies of middle and frontline managers are rare (Brewer 2005; Knies et al. 2018b). This gap in the public management literature is conspicuous as frontline managers are considered vital in the service management and HRM literatures. The service management literature argues that "at the moment of truth" when the service provider and service customer meet, the skills, motivation, and tools of the frontline employee largely determine whether the expectations of the client will be met (Normann 1991, 16–17; Zeithaml et al. 1990). In other words, service quality is essentially the result of individual or small group performance. Hence, personnel management at the frontline of service delivery is considered a key factor in service performance (Normann 1991). As a consequence, the importance of the frontline manager looms large (Purcell and Hutchinson 2007). In the HRM literature, Wright and Nishii (2013) have elaborated on the role of line managers in a more general sense by distinguishing between intended HRM practices, which refer to the HRM strategy determined by executive managers, and implemented HRM practices, referring to those that are typically applied by line managers. The authors argue that line managers' implementation is important because it impacts employee perceptions of management intentions and because these perceptions influence employee behavior and ultimately organizational performance.

Taking into account the public sector context, one can understand why lower-level managers have not been studied intensively. The focus of public service practice has not been so much on the individual client or customer but on collective outcomes for citizens and society generally. Furthermore, this latter perspective is the basis of the Weberian bureaucracy model and its adherence to rules and regulations in public service delivery and in internal matters related to finance and personnel management. Given the reliance on rules and procedures, human characteristics and their dynamics were expected to exert very little influence. Some even contended that the very nature of bureaucracy substituted for leadership (Javidan and Waldman 2003). Thus, there was little need or room for an increasing role for line managers as this would conflict with the dominant model of bureaucracy and public personnel management, which was based upon government directives and detailed personnel policy regulations (McGuire et al. 2008; Truss 2008).

Contrary to the selective focus found in much of the current literature, this work will pay attention to both management and leadership activities and combine insights from different disciplines. Chapters 3 and 5 will examine the management and leadership literatures extensively and draw on research from several disciplines. This volume will also study managers at different levels in the hierarchy who are involved in the public service delivery process. Thereby, we strive for a more comprehensive understanding of the contribution managers make to public service performance, both directly and indirectly through the employees they supervise and through various organizational processes. We will also distinguish between different management and leadership activities because they may contribute to public service performance in different ways (Park and Rainey 2008; Ritz 2008; Vermeeren et al. 2014). An example of different leadership activities can illustrate this point. On the one hand, transformational leadership is known to be positively related to employees' PSM (Vandenabeele 2014; Wright et al. 2012), the use of performance information (Moynihan et al. 2012; Sun and Henderson 2017), and employees' organizational citizenship behaviors (Bottomley et al. 2016). On the other hand, initiating structure, which is a supervisor's task-related leadership behavior (Yukl 2012), has a strong impact on subordinates' job performance (Rowold et al. 2014). What this example also shows is that studying management requires us to examine the public employees whose attitudes and behaviors are impacted by management and leadership activities, and through whose job performance unit-level and organizational performances are achieved.

1.5.2   Public Service Performance

Performance is the core of public management. One of the first accounts in this domain was written by Woodrow Wilson (1887), who equated performance with mere efficiency (Halachmi and Bouckaert 1993). Over time, the literature on public service performance has grown, paralleling the growing interest in NPM. Gradually, conceptualizations of performance in the public sector have become more complex. However, an early observation still holds: "performance is a difficult concept to define and measure. Stakeholders often disagree about which aspects are most important" (Brewer and Selden 2000, 685). The diversity of opinion is also reflected in different approaches to measurement. Brewer and Selden (2000) proposed a multidimensional concept of performance that distinguishes between internal and external accomplishments on the administrative values of efficiency, effectiveness, and fairness. Another multidimensional conceptualization was proposed by Boyne (2002) in his study of local government performance. He distinguished between outputs, efficiency, outcomes/effectiveness, responsiveness, and democratic outcomes. Both conceptualizations have informed other studies (e.g. Andrews and Boyne 2010; Boyne et al. 2006; Kim 2005). These studies have developed measures of performance for different public services provided by, for example, schools, municipalities, and federal ministries or national agencies. However, the diversity of performance criteria in existing studies continues unabated. In fact, a review of performance based on research published in ten public administration journals argues that there are at least six distinctions in performance criteria (Andersen et al. 2016).

Organizational performance in HRM studies (e.g. Boxall and Purcell 2016) is no longer understood as financial performance only, which suited the earlier focus of most HRM research on private organizations, but as also including employee outcomes. HRM studies have developed an understanding of employee outcomes that is broader than Boyne's (2002) staff satisfaction, which he regards as an aspect of the performance dimension "responsiveness." Drawing on work and organizational psychology, HRM studies examine various aspects of employee well-being, which involve physical, psychological, and social well-being (Van de Voorde et al. 2012). HRM studies in the public sector have examined a variety of employee outcomes, such as job satisfaction (Steijn 2008), affective commitment (Mostafa et al. 2015), work engagement (Borst et al. 2019), and resigned satisfaction and burnout (Giauque et al. 2012; Van Loon et al. 2015).

Public management studies' conceptualization of public service performance refers primarily to organizational and societal outcomes (Van Dooren et al. 2010). To be clear, we will refer to this latter understanding when using the concept of public service performance, and we will use the term "employee outcomes" to refer to outcomes that are specific to employees as relevant stakeholders.

Parallel to the ongoing research interest in public service performance, there is a growing interest in the concept of public value creation (e.g. Alford et al. 2017; Hartley et al. 2019) following seminal work by Moore (1995; 2013). This raises the question of how the two are related. We will touch on this issue here and provide further discussion in Chapter 2. Moore (1995) sees the primary responsibility of public managers as using operational resources to satisfy the public's aspirations and concerns—as voiced by an authorizing environment—and undertaken to create particular public value outcomes. However, the definition and measurement of public value itself are not very clear. Moore (2013) proposes a public value account that suggests concrete measures to recognize the value that an agency produces and the costs it incurs. How public value is operationalized depends on the public service context. The achievement of collectively valued social outcomes might include mission achievement (e.g. enhancing democracy, protecting the natural environment, and moving welfare clients to independence), client satisfaction, or attaining justice and fairness (e.g. providing access for all welfare clients and ensuring equitable distribution of services). This operationalization resembles the development of concrete measures for the multiple dimensions of public service performance of different public organizations (Boyne et al. 2006). However, the concept of public value goes beyond public service performance in that public value theory involves the recognition of multiple stakeholders and public debate about what is seen as valuable to society and to the public sphere (Hartley et al. 2019). While public service performance consists of aggregated individual preferences for what is considered good performance, public value creation requires public debate about what adds value to a fair and just society (Hartley et al. 2019). Clearly, public service performance research may benefit from public value theory by paying explicit attention to different stakeholders and to the public values to which stakeholders refer in weighing certain outcomes (see Chapter 2).

1.5.3 Linking Mechanisms

Public management research has invested much effort in studying the impact of public management on performance and paying some attention to external and internal contextual factors (e.g. Andrews and Boyne 2010; Andrews et al. 2012; Meier et al. 2017). Public management studies have paid less attention to the linking mechanisms between frontline and organizational-level performance.

HRM research has extensive interest in the mechanisms that link HRM and leadership to unit-level and organizational-level performance outcomes. The main premise is that HRM and line managers' implementation of HRM policies affect employees' perceptions of HRM, impacting their attitudes and behaviors and ultimately helping to determine individual and organizational performance. Jiang et al. (2012) offer a theoretical explanation for these linking mechanisms. Based on social exchange theory, the authors argue that by investing in employees through HRM, an organization signals that it values its employees and cares about their well-being. This creates feelings of obligation and a psychological contract among employees, instilling the need to reciprocate and engage in behavior that supports organizational goals. In addition, Jiang et al. (2012) use the resource-based theory to argue that HRM affects employees' competencies (knowledge, skills, and abilities), enabling them to contribute to performance. Boxall and Purcell (2016) add that HRM contributes to performance if HRM practices are well integrated and aim to influence not only employees' abilities and motivation but also their opportunities to perform well. The validity of these mechanisms linking HRM and performance has been demonstrated in the public sector (Messersmith et al. 2011). Early studies of HRM in the public sector showed the impact of various mediating variables, including employees' trust and job satisfaction (Gould-Williams 2003). Later studies have added insights about the mediating role of, for instance, person–job and person–organization fit (Steijn 2008; Van Loon et al. 2017).

One specific link in the public management–public service performance chain is the individual employee's job performance. Wright and Nishii's (2013) multilevel framework regards organizational performance as building on unit/team and ultimately individual performance. However, while individual job performance presumably contributes to organizational performance, studies find that antecedents of job performance do not influence organizational performance (see Chapter 14 for an example involving PSM as an antecedent). Chapters in Part II of this volume generally deal with organizational performance, and chapters in Part III take an interest in job performance and the factors that influence this.

Given the dearth of public management studies of the mechanisms that link public managers' activities to public service performance and employee outcomes, it is obvious that we have much to gain by taking a multidisciplinary approach that draws from scholarship on public management, leadership, HRM, and work and organizational psychology research.

1.6 Our Approach

This chapter has introduced the topic of managing for public service performance and the approach this volume takes to study this topic. Summarizing the distinctive characteristics, our approach can be described as:

- *multidisciplinary*: combining insights and perspectives from the fields of public management, leadership, HRM, and work and organizational psychology;
- *critical*: moving from an instrumental approach toward a broader understanding of public managers' and employees' activities affecting public service performance, including consideration of the stakeholders involved in this process and the different public values they hold; and
- *context-sensitive*: examining the validity of generic insights relative to public sector characteristics that impact public service performance.

This latter characteristic deserves some further elaboration. This chapter discussed the public sector context that impacts the management–performance relationship. Adding contextual variables to the study of "managing for public service performance" increases its relevance for the public sector context. However, doing so can decrease the generalizability of the results along with the opportunity to compare the results with studies conducted in other contexts and specifically in private sector contexts. That is why Knies et al. (2018a, 8) regard contextualization as a balancing act between rigor and relevance. However, they argue that increasing the relevance through contextualization does not inevitably cause a loss of rigor. First, claims that variables are distinctive of the public sector context and should be included in research should themselves be evidence-based. Second, public sector studies should explain the level of contextualization required for their study after considering its effect on the rigor and relevance of their study. For instance, as Knies et al. (2018a, 6) explain, framing the relevance of the research question for public sector organizations and highlighting how this context differs from those in mainstream studies amount to a basic level of contextualization that will hardly affect a study's generalizability. However, adding public sector-specific variables to the model or adjusting generic measures to fit the public sector context amounts to an advanced level of contextualization and will affect a study's generalizability to non-public sector contexts more profoundly. Therefore, the approach this volume takes to the study of "managing for public service performance" will be context-sensitive on the basis of evidence supporting the relevance and measurement of contextualization. In this, we aim to move the state of the art beyond a mere best-practice approach—which mainly identifies successful practices to apply them elsewhere—to a more contextualized best-fit approach (Purcell 1999). This means that we try not just to identify what works but also to reflect on what works where and why.

The outline of this volume is based on the major components of the public management–performance framework (see Figure 1.1). Figure 1.1 visualizes the main components schematically; the individual chapters add rich details to the conceptualization of the variables and their relationships. Overall, the volume consists of three parts. Part I introduces the key concepts and elaborates on the institutional setting of different public services. Part II focuses on public managers' characteristics and practices in "managing for public service performance." The chapters draw mainly on management, leadership, and HRM perspectives. The chapters in this part concentrate on the organizational level, understanding public service performance as referring primarily to organizational and societal outcomes, and pay attention to the macro and organizational context. Part III of the volume adds to this by concentrating on the linking mechanisms at the micro level and deals with employees' attitudes and behaviors, public service motivation, and person–environment fit as well as employee outcomes. Related to the focus on micro-level mechanisms, these chapters add insights from work and organization psychology to management and leadership perspectives.

On the left-hand side of the conceptual model, the main independent variable is represented by public management. Chapter 3 offers a conceptual introduction to people management based on strategic HRM and leadership literatures. Subsequent chapters included in Part II offer reviews of the contribution to public service performance made by leadership (Chapter 5). the qualities of effective public managers (Chapters 6 and 7), performance management (Chapter 8), and the various types of human resource management systems (Chapter 9), as well as two specific public leaders' roles included in the concept of "integrated public leadership" (Fernandez et al. 2010), namely, diversity management (Chapter 10) and change leadership (Chapter 11).

On the right-hand side of the conceptual model, the dependent variables are presented. The concept of public service performance is examined in Chapter 2, which also reviews how studies include stakeholders in public service performance measures. Employee outcomes are also featured explicitly as a dependent variable. Chapter 12 offers a general overview of employee outcomes and the organizational and job characteristics that affect them. Other chapters in Part III cover various aspects of employee well-being as well as employees' employability (Chapter 15).

The institutional setting of public services is the main topic of Chapter 4. It provides insights about the idea of publicness as an institutional characteristic and its relationship with management and behavior in public institutions. Subsequent chapters add to this by examining the contextual features that are relevant to their topic. The chapters in Part II pay more attention to contextual characteristics on the sectoral and organizational levels, such as governance paradigms and public service logics. The chapters in Part III pay more attention to contextual characteristics at the job and individual level, such as red tape and public service motivation.

The chapters in Part III examine mechanisms at the micro level that link public management and public service performance. Specific attention is given to the impact of public value conflicts on public professionals and their behaviors (Chapter 13) and to PSM and individual job performance (Chapter 14).

This conceptual model has the heuristic purpose of helping to integrate the answers that individual chapters give to our overall question of how management makes a meaningful contribution to public service performance. The comprehensive answer to this question is summarized in Section 16.2 of the concluding chapter. Chapter 16 also provides directions for future research and outlines the implications of our insights for public organizations' efforts to create public value.

References

Agranoff, R. 2007. *Managing within Networks: Adding Value to Public Organizations.* Washington, DC: Georgetown University Press.

Alford, J. 2008. "The Limits to Traditional Public Administration, or Rescuing Public Value from Misrepresentation." *The Australian Journal of Public Administration 67* (3): pp. 357–66.

Alford, J., S. Douglas, K. Geuijen, and P. 't Hart. 2017. "Ventures in Public Value Management: Introduction to the Symposium." *Public Management Review 19* (5): pp. 589–604.

Andersen, L., T. Beck Jørgensen, A. Kjeldsen, L. Pedersen, and K. Vrangbaek. 2012. "Public Values and Public Service Motivation: Conceptual and Empirical Relationships." *The American Review of Public Administration 43* (3): pp. 292–311.

Andersen, L., A. Boesen, and L. Pedersen. 2016. "Performance in Public Organizations: Clarifying the Conceptual Space." *Public Administration Review 76* (6): pp. 852–62.

Andrews, R., P. Bezes, G. Hammerschmid, and S. Van de Walle. 2016. "Conclusion: A Kaleidoscope of Administrative Reforms in Europe." In *Public Administration Reforms in Europe: The View from the Top*, edited by G. Hammerschmid, S. Van de Walle, R. Andrews, and P. Bezes, pp. 273–80. Cheltenham: Edward Elgar.

Andrews, R., and G. Boyne. 2010. "Capacity, Leadership, and Organizational Performance: Testing the Black Box Model of Public Management." *Public Administration Review 70* (3): pp. 443–54.

Andrews, R., G. Boyne, K. Meier, L. O'Toole, and R. Walker. 2012. "Vertical Strategic Alignment and Public Service Performance." *Public Administration 90* (1): pp. 77–98.

Ashworth, R., G. Boyne, and T. Entwistle. 2009. *Public Service Improvement: Theories and Evidence.* Oxford: Oxford University Press.

Borst, R., P. Kruyen, and C. Lako. 2019. "Exploring the Job Demands–Resources Model of Work Engagement in Government: Bringing in a Psychological Perspective." *Review of Public Personnel Administration 39* (3): pp. 372–97.

Bottomley, P., A. Mostafa, J. Gould-Williams, and F. Léon-Cázares. 2016. "The Impact of Transformational Leadership on Organizational Citizenship Behaviours: The Contingent Role of Public Service Motivation." *British Journal of Management 27* (2): pp. 390–405.

Boxall, P., and J. Purcell. 2016. *Strategy and Human Resource Management.* 4th ed. London: Palgrave Macmillan.

Boyne, G. 2002. "Concepts and Indicators of Local Authority Performance: An Evaluation of the Statutory Frameworks in England and Wales." *Public Money & Management 22* (2): pp. 17–24.

Boyne, G. 2003. "Sources of Public Service Improvement: A Critical Review and Research Agenda." *Journal of Public Administration Research and Theory 13* (3): pp. 367–94.

Boyne, G., K. Meier, L. O'Toole, and R. Walker. 2006. *Public Service Performance.* Cambridge: Cambridge University Press.

Bozeman, B. 2007. *Public Values and Public Interest: Counter-Balancing Economic Individualism.* Washington, DC: Georgetown University Press.

Brewer, G. 2005. "In the Eye of the Storm: Frontline Supervisors and Federal Agency Performance." *Journal of Public Administration Research and Theory 15* (4): pp. 505–27.

Brewer, G., and S. Selden. 2000. "Why Elephants Gallop: Assessing and Predicting Organizational Performance in Federal Agencies." *Journal of Public Administration Research and Theory 10* (4): pp. 685–711.

Favero, N., K. Meier, and L. O'Toole. 2016. "Goals, Trust, Participation, and Feedback: Linking Internal Management with Performance Outcomes." *Journal of Public Administration Research and Theory 26* (2): pp. 327–43.

Fernandez, S., Y. Cho, and J. Perry. 2010. "Exploring the Link between Integrated Leadership and Public Sector Performance." *The Leadership Quarterly 21*: pp. 308–23.

Giauque, D., A. Ritz, F. Varone, and S. Anderfuhren-Biget. 2012. "Resigned but Satisfied: The Negative Impact of Public Service Motivation and Red Tape on Work Satisfaction." *Public Administration 90* (1): pp. 175–93.

Gould-Williams, J. 2003. "The Importance of HR Practices and Workplace Trust in Achieving Superior Performance: A Study of Public Sector Organizations." *International Journal of Human Resource Management 14* (1): pp. 28–54.

Halachmi, A., and G. Bouckaert. 1993. "The Challenge of Productivity in a Changing World." *International Review of Administrative Sciences 59* (1): pp. 5–10.

Hammerschmid, G., S. Van de Walle, R. Andrews, and P. Bezes. 2016. *Public Administration Reforms in Europe: The View from the Top.* Cheltenham: Edward Elgar.

Hartley, J., A. Sancino, M. Bennister, and S. Resodihardjo. 2019. "Leadership for Public Value: Political Astuteness as a Conceptual Link." *Public Administration 97* (2): pp. 239–49.

Heskett, J., T. Jones, G. Loveman, W. Sasser, and L. Schlesinger. 1994. "Putting the Service–Profit Chain to Work." *Harvard Business Review 72* (2): pp. 164–74.

Hood, C. 1991. "A Public Management for All Seasons?" *Public Administration 69* (1): pp. 3–19.

Ingraham, P., P. Joyce, and A. Donahue. 2003. *Government Performance: Why Management Matters.* Baltimore, MD: Johns Hopkins University Press.

Jacobsen, C., and L. Andersen. 2015. "Is Leadership in the Eye of the Beholder? A Study of Intended and Perceived Leadership Practices and Organizational Performance." *Public Administration Review 75* (6): pp. 829–41.

Javidan, M., and D. A. Waldman. 2003. "Exploring Charismatic Leadership in the Public Sector: Measurement and Consequences." *Public Administration Review 63* (2): pp. 229–42.

Jensen, U., L. Andersen, L. Bro, A. Bøllingtoft, T. Eriksen, A. Holten, C. Jacobsen, J. Ladenburg, P. Nielsen, H. Salomonsen, N. Westergard-Nielsen, and A. Würtz. 2016. "Conceptualizing and Measuring Transformational and Transactional Leadership." *Administration & Society 51* (1): pp. 3–33.

Jiang, K., D. Lepak, J. Hu, and J. Baer. 2012. "How Does Human Resource Management Influence Organizational Outcomes? A Meta-Analytic Investigation of Mediating Mechanisms." *Academy of Management Journal 55* (6): pp. 1264–94.

Jiang, K., and J. Messersmith. 2017. "On the Shoulders of Giants: A Meta-Review of Strategic Human Resource Management." *International Journal of Human Resource Management 29* (1): pp. 6–33.

Johns, G. 2006. "The Essential Impact of Context on Organizational Behavior." *Academy of Management Review 31* (2): pp. 386–408.

Kettl, D. 2017. *Politics of the Administrative Process.* 7th ed. Thousand Oaks, CA: Sage.

Kim, S. 2005. "Individual-Level Factors and Organizational Performance in Government Organizations." *Journal of Public Administration Research and Theory 15* (2): pp. 245–61.

Knies, E., P. Boselie, J. S. Gould-Williams, and W. V. Vandenabeele. 2018a. "Strategic Human Resource Management and Public Sector Performance: Context Matters." *International Journal of Human Resource Management*, pp. 1–13. https://doi.org/10.10 80/09585192.2017.1407088.

Knies, E., C. Jacobsen, and L. Tummers. 2016. "Leadership and Organizational Performance: State of the Art and Research Agenda." In *Routledge Companion to Leadership*, edited by J. Storey, J. Denis, J. Hartley, D. Ulrich, and P. 't Hart, pp. 404–18. London: Routledge.

Knies, E., P. Leisink, and S. Kraus-Hoogeveen. 2018b. "Frontline Managers' Contribution to Mission Achievement: A Study of How People Management Affects Thoughtful Care." *Human Service Organizations: Management, Leadership & Governance 42* (2): pp. 166–84.

Koontz, H. 1961. "The Management Theory Jungle." *Academy of Management Journal 4* (3): pp. 174–88.

Lodge, M., and C. Hood. 2012. "Into an Age of Multiple Austerities? Public Management and Public Service Bargains across OECD Countries." *Governance 25* (1): pp. 79–101.

McGuire, D., L. Stoner, and S. Mylona. 2008. "The Role of Line Managers as Human Resource Agents in Fostering Organizational Change in Public Services." *Journal of Change Management 8* (1): pp. 73–84.

Meier, K., L. O'Toole, G. Boyne, and R. Walker. 2007. "Strategic Management and the Performance of Public Organizations: Testing Venerable Ideas against Recent Theories." *Journal of Public Administration Research and Theory 17* (3): pp. 357–77.

Meier, K., A. Rutherford, and C. Avellaneda. 2017. *Comparative Public Management: Why National, Environmental, and Organizational Context Matters.* Washington, DC: Georgetown University Press.

Melton, E., and K. Meier. 2017. "For the Want of a Nail: The Interaction of Managerial Capacity and Human Resource Management on Organizational Performance." *Public Administration Review 77* (1): pp. 118–30.

Messersmith, J., P. Patel, D. Lepak, and J. Gould-Williams. 2011. "Unlocking the Black Box: Exploring the Link between High-Performance Work Systems and Performance." *Journal of Applied Psychology 96* (6): pp. 1105–18.

Moore, M. 1995. *Creating Public Value: Strategic Management in Government.* Cambridge, MA: Harvard University Press.

Moore, M. 2013. *Recognizing Public Value.* Cambridge, MA: Harvard University Press.

Mostafa, A., J. Gould-Williams, and P. Bottomley. 2015. "High-Performance Human Resource Practices and Employee Outcomes: The Mediating Role of Public Service Motivation." *Public Administration Review 75* (5): pp. 747–57.

Moynihan, D., S. Pandey, and B. Wright. 2012. "Setting the Table: How Transformational Leadership Fosters Performance Information Use." *Journal of Public Administration Research and Theory 22* (1): pp. 143–64.

Nielsen, P. 2014. "Performance Management, Managerial Authority, and Public Service Performance." *Journal of Public Administration Research and Theory 24* (2): pp. 431–58.

Normann, R. 1991. *Service Management: Strategy and Leadership in Service Business.* 2nd ed. Chichester: John Wiley & Sons.

Oberfield, Z. 2014. "Public Management in Time: A Longitudinal Examination of the Full Range of Leadership Theory." *Journal of Public Administration Research and Theory 24* (2): pp. 407–29.

OECD. 2017. *Government at a Glance 2017.* Paris: OECD Publishing.

Ongaro, E. 2017. *Philosophy and Public Administration: An Introduction.* Cheltenham: Edward Elgar.

O'Toole, L. J., and K. Meier. 2015. "Public Management, Context and Performance: In Quest of a More General Theory." *Journal of Public Administration Research and Theory 25* (1): pp. 237–56.

Park, S., and H. Rainey. 2008. "Leadership and Public Service Motivation in U.S. Federal Agencies." *International Public Management Journal 11* (1): pp. 109–42.

Pedersen, M., N. Favero, V. Nielsen, and K. Meier. 2019. "Public Management on the Ground: Clustering Managers Based on Their Behavior." *International Public Management Journal 22* (2): pp. 254–94.

Peters, B. G. 2000. *Institutional Theory in Political Science: The New Institutionalism.* Cheltenham: Edward Elgar.

Pfeffer, J. 1998. *The Human Equation: Building Profits by Putting People First.* Boston, MA: Harvard Business School Press.

Pollitt, C. 2013. *Context in Public Policy and Management: The Missing Link?* Cheltenham: Edward Elgar.

Pollitt, C., and G. Bouckaert. 2004. *Public Management Reform: A Comparative Analysis.* 2nd ed. Oxford: Oxford University Press.

Provan, K., and H. Milward. 2001. "Do Networks Really Work? A Framework for Evaluating Public-Sector Organizational Networks." *Public Administration Review 61* (4): pp. 414–23.

Purcell, J. 1999. "Best Practice and Best Fit: Chimera or Cul-de-Sac?" *Human Resource Management Journal 9* (3): pp. 26–41.

Purcell, J., and S. Hutchinson. 2007. "Front-Line Managers as Agents in the HRM–Performance Causal Chain: Theory, Analysis and Evidence." *Human Resource Management Journal 17* (1): pp. 3–20.

Rainey, H. 2009. *Understanding and Managing Public Organizations*. San Francisco, CA: Jossey-Bass.

Rhodes, R., and J. Wanna. 2007. "The Limits to Public Value, or Rescuing Responsible Government from the Platonic Guardians." *The Australian Journal of Public Administration 66* (4): pp. 406–21.

Rhodes, R., and J. Wanna. 2009. "Bringing the Politics Back In: Public Value in Westminster Parliamentary Government." *Public Administration 87* (2): pp. 161–83.

Riccucci, N. 2010. *Public Administration: Traditions of Inquiry and Philosophies of Knowledge*. Washington, DC: Georgetown University Press.

Ritz, A. 2008. "Public Service Motivation and Organizational Performance in Swiss Federal Government." *International Review of Administrative Sciences 75* (1): pp. 53–78.

Rowold, J., L. Borgmann, and K. Bormann. 2014. "Which Leadership Constructs are Important for Predicting Job Satisfaction, Affective Commitment, and Perceived Job Performance in Profit versus Nonprofit Organizations?" *Nonprofit Management & Leadership 25* (2): pp. 147–64.

Scott, W. 2001. *Institutions and Organizations*. Thousand Oaks, CA: Sage.

Selden, S., G. Brewer, and L. Brudney. 1999. "Reconciling Competing Values in Public Administration: Understanding the Administrative Role Concept." *Administration & Society 31* (2): pp. 171–204.

Steijn, B. 2008. "Person–Environment Fit and Public Service Motivation." *International Public Management Journal 11* (1): pp. 13–27.

Sun, R., and A. Henderson. 2017. "Transformational Leadership and Organizational Processes: Influencing Public Performance." *Public Administration Review 77* (4): pp. 554–65.

Talbot, C. 2005. "Performance Management." In *The Oxford Handbook of Public Management*, edited by E. Ferlie, L. Lynn, and C. Pollitt, pp. 491–517. Oxford: Oxford University Press.

Thijs, N., G. Hammerschmid, and E. Palaric. 2018. *A Comparative Overview of Public Administration Characteristics and Performance in EU28*. Brussels: European Commission.

Trottier, T., M. Van Wart, and X. Wang. 2008. "Examining the Nature and Significance of Leadership in Government Organizations." *Public Administration Review 68* (2): pp. 319–33.

Truss, C. 2008. "Continuity and Change: The Role of the HR Function in the Modern Public Sector." *Public Administration 86* (4): pp. 1071–88.

Tummers, L., and E. Knies. 2016. "Measuring Public Leadership: Developing Scales for Four Key Public Leadership Roles." *Public Administration 94* (2): pp. 433–51.

Vandenabeele, W. 2014. "Explaining Public Service Motivation: The Role of Leadership and Basic Needs Satisfaction." *Review of Public Personnel Administration 34* (2): pp. 153–73.

Vandenabeele, W., P. Leisink, and E. Knies. 2013. "Public Value Creation and Strategic Human Resource Management: Public Service Motivation as a Linking Mechanism." In *Managing Social Issues: A Public Values Perspective*, edited by P. Leisink, P. Boselie, M. Van Bottenburg, and D. Hosking, pp. 37–54. Cheltenham: Edward Elgar.

Van de Voorde, K., J. Paauwe, and M. Van Veldhoven. 2012. "Employee Well-Being and the HRM–Organizational Performance Relationship: A Review of Quantitative Studies." *International Journal of Management Reviews* 14 (4): pp. 391–407.

Van de Walle, S., G. Hammerschmid, R. Andrews, and P. Bezes. 2016. "Introduction: Public Administration Reforms in Europe." In *Public Administration Reforms in Europe: The View from the Top*, edited by G. Hammerschmid, S. Van de Walle, R. Andrews, and P. Bezes, pp. 2–11. Cheltenham: Edward Elgar.

Van Dooren, W., G. Bouckaert, and J. Halligan. 2010. *Performance Management in the Public Sector*. London: Routledge.

Van Dooren, W., and C. Hoffmann. 2018. "Performance Management in Europe: An Idea Whose Time Has Come and Gone?" In *The Palgrave Handbook of Public Administration and Management in Europe*, edited by E. Ongaro and S. Van Thiel, pp. 207–25. London: Palgrave Macmillan.

Van Loon, N., W. Vandenabeele, and P. Leisink. 2015. "On the Bright and Dark Side of Public Service Motivation: The Relationship between PSM and Employee Wellbeing." *Public Money & Management* 35 (5): pp. 349–56.

Van Loon, N., W. Vandenabeele, and P. Leisink. 2017. "Clarifying the Relationship between Public Service Motivation and In-Role and Extra-Role Behaviors: The Relative Contributions of Person–Job and Person–Organization Fit." *American Review of Public Administration 47* (6): pp. 699–713.

Van Wart, M. 2003. "Public Sector Leadership Theory: An Assessment." *Public Administration Review 63* (2): pp. 214–28.

Vermeeren, B., B. Kuipers, and B. Steijn. 2014. "Does Leadership Make a Difference? Linking HRM, Job Satisfaction, and Organizational Performance." *Review of Public Personnel Administration 34* (2): pp. 174–95.

Walker, R., G. Boyne, and G. Brewer. 2010. *Public Management and Performance: Research Directions*. Cambridge: Cambridge University Press.

Wilson, W. 1887. "The Study of Administration." *Political Science Quarterly 2* (2): pp. 197–222.

Wright, B., D. Moynihan, and S. Pandey. 2012. "Pulling the Levers: Transformational Leadership, Public Service Motivation and Mission Valence." *Public Administration Review 72* (2): pp. 206–15.

Wright, P., and L. Nishii. 2013. "Strategic HRM and Organizational Behavior: Integrating Multiple Levels of Analysis." In *HRM and Performance: Achievements and Challenges*, edited by J. Paauwe, D. Guest, and P. Wright, pp. 97–110. Chichester: Wiley.

Yukl, G. 2012. "Effective Leadership Behavior: What We Know and What Questions Need More Attention." *Academy of Management Perspectives 26* (4): pp. 66–85.

Zeithaml, V., A. Parasuraman, and L. Berry. 1990. *Delivering Quality Service: Balancing Customer Perceptions and Expectations*. New York: Free Press.

PART I

KEY CONCEPTS AND
THE PUBLIC SECTOR CONTEXT

2

Stakeholders, Public Value(s), and Public Service Performance

Lotte B. Andersen, Gene A. Brewer, and Peter Leisink

2.1 Introduction

Public services are ordered and/or mainly financed by government and delivered to citizens, corporate actors, and society as a whole. Many different constituencies have a stake in public service delivery, including citizens as taxpayers and clients, businesses, the media, employer and employee unions, civil society organizations, and many others. The term "stakeholders" refers to "any group or individual who can affect or is affected by the achievement of the organization's objectives" (Freeman 1984, 46). Stakeholders typically have different views on and preferences for what is desirable in public service provision, which are tantamount to public values.

These values, how they are understood and weighed by stakeholders, and how they infuse the process of public service provision, are influenced by the broader social, economic, and political context. Thus, the period of austerity policies following the economic crisis in 2008 saw governments emphasizing the economy and efficiency dimensions of public service performance. The subsequent economic recovery revived public debate on the quality of public services. The aging population raises the question of sustainable quality of care. Flows of immigrants raise questions regarding the sustainability of human rights values because these are increasingly perceived by host country citizens as causing pressure on social service systems and posing threats to national security. New technologies can be game-changers as e-government, social media, and Big Data revolutionize public service delivery but also raise thorny privacy and accessibility issues. These broader developments set the stage for an ongoing debate among various stakeholders on the scope and level of the public services they desire from public organizations. This is where the debate about public service performance evolves into a debate about what adds value to the public sphere, a fair and just society which considers long-term and minority views (Benington 2011).

The diversity of opinions among different stakeholders tends to be accommodated by the multiple ends that public organizations are ordered to serve by the authorizing

Lotte B. Andersen, Gene A. Brewer, and Peter Leisink, *Stakeholders, Public Value(s), and Public Service Performance* In: *Managing for Public Service Performance: How People and Values Make a Difference.* Edited by: Peter Leisink, Lotte B. Andersen, Gene A. Brewer, Christian B. Jacobsen, Eva Knies, and Wouter Vandenabeele, Oxford University Press (2021).

environment. This multiplicity in turn makes it hard to assess their public service performance, where performance can be seen as an actual achievement relative to intended achievements (Jung 2011, 195). Where stakeholders disagree on the outcomes they regard as valuable to society—i.e. the public value to be created as well as how public service providers should operate—researchers cannot help but focus on stakeholders and their preferences when analyzing public service performance.

The external context, the ongoing social changes, and the different values that stakeholders emphasize, influence governments and public organizations, depending on the prevalent governance paradigm. Governance paradigms consist of institutional templates, crude policies, operational strategies, and desired programs. They prescribe how public service provision should be structured and how it should operate. Governance paradigms co-exist and compete, and they can help us understand the relationship between public values and public service performance (Torfing et al. 2020). Table 2.1 presents an overview of some of today's important paradigms, which we further describe below.

Weberian *bureaucracy* emphasizes process rather than outcomes, and its two key governance mechanisms are hierarchy and formal rules. Key values are loyalty and neutrality, and the goal-setting process is top-down from politicians to administrators, who are depicted as neutral technocrats. In contrast, *professional rule* is based on specialized, theoretical knowledge in the relevant occupations (e.g. physicians) combined with the relevant norms of those occupations. This makes professional quality the key value in this paradigm, while the most important governance mechanism is adherence to professional norms. A third paradigm is *new public management* (NPM), which emphasizes incentives, market mechanisms, customer focus, and managerial discretion, based upon private sector practices. NPM emphasizes efficient service delivery and places a strong focus on user/customer satisfaction.

Table 2.1 Overview of the discussed governance paradigms

Governance paradigm	Key mechanisms: through which means is high performance achieved?	Key values: what is seen as desirable?
Bureaucracy	Hierarchy and formal rules	Neutral and loyal implementation of political goals
Professional rule	Relevant occupation's knowledge and norms	Professional quality
New public management (NPM)	Incentives and market mechanisms	Customer/user satisfaction and efficiency
Neo-Weberian state (NWS)	Centralized coordination based on values and data about citizens	Citizen-friendliness and representative democracy
New public governance (NPG)	Networks and inclusion of all types of societal actors, including co-creation	Collaboration with surrounding society and horizontal coordination
Public value management	Focus on public value creation and generation of political support	Seeking public interest

Turning to the new governance paradigms, the *neo-Weberian state* (NWS) revitalizes old virtues (such as representative democracy) combined with more coherent service provision through centralized coordination and increased citizen-friendliness (Pollitt and Bouckaert 2017). The argument is that service provision should be informed by analytical insights based on data about citizens' needs and behaviors (Ejersbo and Greve 2014). In *new public governance* (NPG), inclusion of the surrounding society is both a governance mechanism and a key value seen as desirable in itself. Horizontal coordination is seen as a way to counter the silos created by hierarchies, professions, and narrow vertical managerial responsibilities. Additionally, new public governance emphasizes intra-organizational networks as an important delivery mechanism (Osborne 2006), and the same is true for *public value management* (Stoker 2006). Public value management is not yet a coherent paradigm, but key governance mechanisms appear to include a constant focus on public value creation and active generation of political support. This paradigm sees public service provision as very different from private sector operations. The emphasis on values is shared with the neo-Weberian state paradigm. Denhardt and Denhardt (2011) promote seven principles that could synthesize these two paradigms: (1) serve citizens, not customers; (2) seek the public interest; (3) value citizenship and public service above entrepreneurship; (4) think strategically, act democratically; (5) recognize that accountability is not simple; (6) serve, rather than steer; and (7) value people, not just productivity. The governance paradigms listed in Table 2.1 can be used to understand the links between stakeholders, public values, and public service performance, and this serves the core purpose of this chapter.

In Section 2.2, we present the theoretical perspectives on public value (Moore 1995) and public values (Beck Jørgensen and Bozeman 2007), which are somewhat different but related concepts. We also elaborate on how we see their nexus and relationship to public service performance. Section 2.3 uses these insights to examine the public service performance literature based on nine illustrative studies. Much public administration scholarship neglects the stakeholders despite their seminal role in defining good performance in democratic political systems (Amirkhanyan et al. 2014; Boyne et al. 2006; Song and Meier 2018). We have, therefore, selected studies that explicitly pay attention to stakeholders. The final section (Section 2.4) discusses normative implications.

2.2 Key Concepts in Public Management Research: Public Value(s) and Public Service Performance

Public value, public values, and public service performance are connected: If we do not understand what is deemed desirable, we cannot discuss how public managers can make the best use of the public assets that are entrusted to them. The literature based on Moore's (1995) book on public value creation focuses on public value in the singular, meaning the outcomes which are seen as valuable to society and the activities by public managers for adding value. In contrast, the literature based on the work of Beck Jørgensen and Bozeman (2007) sees public values as widely held preferences for how society should be governed and public services delivered. After a discussion and comparison of these traditions (see also Hartley et al. 2019a), we relate them to our understanding of public service performance.

2.2.1 The Concept of Public Value

Moore (1995) describes value creation as managing public sector enterprises in ways that increase value to the public in both the short and the long run. Basically, public organizations produce value when they improve "the quality of individual and collective life for citizens" (Moore 2013, 8). But what improves our lives? In his 2013 sequel to the 1995 book, Moore (2013, 111–14) answers this question by developing a public value account "that can identify the value the enterprise intended to produce, what it actually produced, and the costs incurred along the way." A government organization's public value account "has to speak to concerns for large, abstract, public values such as the public good and the pursuit of justice but also has to be sufficiently specific, concrete and measurable to recognize the value that the agency produces and the costs it incurs" (Moore 2013, 112). Moore argues (2013, 3) that what makes social outcomes valuable is that "the wider 'public', that has tacitly agreed to be taxed and regulated to produce the desired social result, values [the outcome]. This suggests that in the public sector, the relevant 'customer' is a collective public (local, regional or national) acting through the imperfect processes of representative democracy..." Thus, for instance, the public value account of the police includes, on one hand, the costs of using state authority, and on the other, reducing crime as well as creating positive experiences for those who have encounters with the police.

In the process of public value creation, managers have a crucial role. Moore acknowledges that public organizations have many stakeholders with divergent preferences but argues that it is possible to move from initial disagreement on values to a framework that continually changes as external ideas of what is valuable change. The keywords here are trust (between the public manager and the relevant politicians), imagination (of how value can be created in new ways), and openness to feedback (from the relevant part of the external environment). The literature acknowledges that decisions about what part of the environment is most relevant are highly normative questions and are often left to the public managers' discretion. The argument is that public managers have an active role in helping to "create and guide networks of deliberation and delivery and help maintain and enhance the overall effectiveness, accountability, and capacity of the system" (Bryson et al. 2014, 446). Here, responsiveness to elected officials, citizens, and an array of other stakeholders is emphasized. The argument is that public managers both need to have discretion and need to be constrained by law and democratic/constitutional values (Bryson et al. 2014,

446). Moore (2013, 9) shares this view and sees the core problem of creating accountability for government performance as constituted by "the procedural question of
what actors (working through what processes) could legitimize a particular concept
of public value and the substantive question of which particular values this legitimate actor would choose." Note how Moore connects public value and public values
in this statement.

Moore is not the only public administration scholar discussing public value in the
singular. Other definitions of the concept draw upon his ideas. Benington (2011)
extends Moore's understanding by conceptualizing public value as involving the
activities, services, outputs, and outcomes which the public values most, as well as
what adds value to the public sphere (see Hartley et al. 2019a). This second dimension of public value signals that public value cannot be equated with the aggregated
individual choices of members of the public. The dimension of "adding value to the
public sphere" involves the recognition that various stakeholders are likely to express
divergent values and interests, which ideally are debated in the public sphere, leading to some degree of agreement, or which require judgments by elected politicians,
public servants, or community leaders, with a view to what fits a fair and just society
that considers longer-term and minority views (Hartley et al. 2019a; 2019b). Bryson
et al. (2014, 448) develop a similar view of public value as "producing what is either
valued by the public, is good for the public, including adding to the public sphere, or
both, as assessed against various public value criteria." Recent contributions also
begin to combine the "public value" and "public values" literatures, and we therefore
turn to the latter approach.

2.2.2 The Concept of Public Values

The public values (plural) literature is largely based on Beck Jørgensen and Bozeman's
(2007) work. They draw attention to values as ideals, coined as principles, to be followed in the public sector when producing a service and regulating citizens and
business firms. The public values literature insists that the desirable, not only the
desired, is important, and public values thus *provide direction* to public employees
rather than *drive action* (Andersen et al. 2013; Brewer 2013; Vandenabeele et al.
2013). In other words, public values can convey strategic direction about the desired
ends of public policy, as well as generate motivation and commitment to achieve
those ends. Public values are considered important because they are expected to
shape our perceptions of reality, give identity to individuals as well as organizations,
guide behavior, give meaning to public service, and help maintain communities and
societies (cf. Kluckhohn 1962; Lawton and Rose 1994; Maguire 1998). According to
Bozeman (2007, 13), public values specify "the rights, benefits and prerogatives to
which citizens should (and should not) be entitled; the obligations of citizens to
society, the state and one another; and the principles on which governments and
policies should be based."

The last (institutional) element in Bozeman's definition is important because it indicates that public values can be seen as the basic building blocks of the public sector (Beck Jørgensen 1999, 581). Beck Jørgensen and Bozeman (2007) identified seventy-two public values, which indicates a considerable breadth in the total public values universe. To reduce complexity, they classify seven value constellations: (1) the public sector's contribution to society; (2) transformation of interests to decisions; (3) relationships between administrators and politicians; (4) relationships between public administrators and their environment; (5) intra-organizational aspects of public administration; (6) behaviors of public sector employees; and (7) relationships between public administration and the citizens. Each value constellation focuses on certain aspects of the public sector that the value in question is related to or is directed toward.

Andersen et al. (2013) add to the public values approach by relating values to modes of governance. They find that in governance practice, values are not harmoniously arranged as most public organizations exhibit more than one mode of governance. This means that value conflicts are a recurrent phenomenon.

2.2.3 Connecting Public Value Creation to Public Values

There are differences as well as similarities between public value creation and public values approaches. Both see public value as referring to "objective states of the world that can be measured" (Bryson et al. 2014, 449). One illustration is Moore's (2013) public value account. Both also suggest that public values are important in propelling efforts for transforming the state into a better form.

The most important difference is that Moore, unlike Bozeman, assumes a hierarchy of values in which effectiveness and efficiency take priority over justice and fairness. This assumption is illustrated by Moore's (2013, 42) argument that "because state authority is often engaged in the operations of public agencies, another evaluative frame becomes relevant. We ask not only whether the organization has acted efficiently and effectively but also whether it has acted justly and fairly." In his 2013 book, Moore makes a case for the use of process measures and not only outcome measures. However, priority is taken by efficiency, which is included in his public value account as "[the] use of collectively owned assets and associated costs," and effectiveness, which is included as "[the] achievement of collectively valued social outcomes." Still, the argument is that certain features of process can have value apart from their instrumental worth in producing desired outcomes.

The two approaches are also complementary and connected. As Bryson et al. (2014, 48) and Vandenabeele et al. (2013, 41) argue, public values act as criteria to assess or as reasons for valuing what is valued by the public and good for them. One could argue that the public values that are important in a political/administrative system (i.e. the public values approach) must be identified in order to devise ways to achieve those values and assess the actual value created (i.e. the public value creation approach). In other words, one cannot create public value without understanding public values. This view incorporates Benington's (2011, 50) point that public value is defined in a deliberative democratic process in which competing public values and stakeholder interests can be expressed and debated. Based on this understanding, we turn to another related concept.

2.2.4 The Concept of Public Service Performance

Over the past few decades of public management reforms, researchers have directed their efforts toward conceptualizing and measuring public service performance. Andersen et al. (2016a, 852) define performance very broadly as the actual achievement of a unit relative to its intended achievements, such as the attainment of goals and objectives. Public service performance is generally considered to be an elusive, complex, and ambiguous concept. Many authors (e.g. Andrews et al. 2006) do not attempt to define the concept but note that performance is multifaceted because public organizations are required to address a range of goals and subsequently focus attention on the measurement of performance dimensions. In his study of local government, Boyne (2002) conceptualized public service performance as multidimensional, including outputs, efficiency, effectiveness, responsiveness, and democratic outcomes. This multidimensional understanding of public service performance is now widely accepted, but opinions differ on many issues such as the operationalization of performance dimensions, the use of subjective or objective measures, and how stakeholders prioritize or weigh the various performance dimensions (Andrews et al. 2006; Knies et al. 2018; Walker et al. 2010). This diversity of opinions has been mapped by Andersen et al. (2016a), who argue that the conceptual space for public performance can be clarified by focusing on six distinctions representing various characteristics of performance criteria. The first distinction concerns our central question about stakeholders, which we elaborate on below. The other distinctions refer to other characteristics of performance criteria, including their formality, subjectivity, type of process focus, type of product focus, and unit of analysis. These six distinctions are useful for evaluating what is included—or left out—in the study of public service performance.

Adopting a stakeholder perspective raises the central question of who decides what good performance is. This question is central because public organizations have multiple stakeholders with diverse views on what constitutes good performance. In this respect, the inclusion of multiple stakeholders' views on performance draws on the notion of public value creation as contested because of the multiple publics with diverse views and interests (Hartley et al. 2019a). However, using the stakeholder distinction in our analysis of public service performance reflects only the question of who decides about activities and outcomes constituting actual good performance, but it does not engage with the further issue of which stakeholders are included in the public debate on what adds value to the public sphere. The further question of how multiple priorities are weighed up and how stakeholders derive their performance evaluations from a longer-term perspective on public value cannot usually be examined by survey studies.

We distinguish between three degrees of stakeholder inclusion in research: (1) no attempt to include stakeholder perspectives in the assessment of performance; (2) indirect inclusion; and (3) direct inclusion. The latter is the strongest inclusion because stakeholder interests are expressed by the stakeholders themselves. Indirect inclusion happens when researchers include criteria that they expect to reflect stakeholder interests. Thus, the percentage of classes taught in universities by persons with PhD degrees can, for example, be assumed to reflect a student interest in having research-based education, but without explicit information on students' views, this may only reflect what university administrators think students want.

2.3 Stakeholder Understandings in Public Service Performance Research: Illustrative Examples

This section illustrates the importance of stakeholders, performance criteria, and public values by reviewing nine illustrative studies in public service performance research. It is not a mapping exercise that describes the indicators used in various studies because this has already been done (Andersen et al. 2016a; Walker and Andrews 2015). Instead, we discuss substantive performance criteria in specific studies, their treatment of the multiplicity of stakeholders, and their reference to public values. Our selection of the nine studies is discussed in Section 2.3.1, followed by sections for the three functional sectors studied (Sections 2.3.2–2.3.4) and a summary comparison (Section 2.3.5).

2.3.1 Selection of Studies

We look at performance in schools, environmental regulation, and local authorities/municipalities that represent important public services that can be compared across nations (Van der Wal et al. 2008) and that are affected by the societal developments that spark public debate over public policy and services as mentioned in Section 2.1. In addition, the three functional sectors represent distributive (education) and regulative (environmental regulation) policy types as well as multipurpose entities (local authorities/municipalities[1]) that generate public service performance and involve multiple stakeholders, which is our main interest. We will examine how the

---

[1] In addition, central government policy instruments are often managed regionally and implemented locally, mingling their vertical dimension. Their horizontal dimension is also blurred because policy domains often overlap and interact, and some policies have impacts on other domains. For example, poverty reduction programs may affect health and education policy outcomes, as well as tax revenues and expenditures. These characteristics also tend to increase and/or complicate the number of stakeholder groups, public value(s), and performance elements.

performance criteria used in these studies are related to the various governance paradigms mentioned in Section 2.1. These studies come from articles published in the *Journal of Public Administration Research and Theory* in the last ten years. They include a multi-stakeholder approach, and they contain an empirical analysis of public service performance. Three articles were selected in each functional area in an attempt to achieve geographic and author diversity. Table 2.2 summarizes the key points in relation to this chapter's concepts and thus prepares for the comparison in Section 2.3.5.

2.3.2 Schools

Education is a popular policy area in public administration (O'Toole and Meier 2011, 14). There are several reasons for this. First, education is a large public service in many countries. Second, Meier and O'Toole's (2001; 2002; 2003) panel data project in Texas school districts has set an example for several years. Third, student test scores provide a comparable performance measure across organizational units and over time. The findings from Texan schools are already well-known in the field, and most articles were published before our investigated time span; hence, we include three articles from other contexts.

Favero et al. (2016) examine the relationship between internal management and educational performance for more than 1,100 schools in the New York City school system over a three-year period. The authors define performance as student academic achievement measured by state standardized tests (an index based on English and math scores). It follows from the context that state-level administrative and political decision makers are the stakeholders who set this criterion. Yet Favero et al. (2016, 338) acknowledge that "the stakeholders of public school systems typically care about more than standardized examination scores, and so do those who manage the schools." Accordingly, the authors also explore parental satisfaction, student attendance, the official education progress report, school violence, and teacher turnover. However, they distinguish between "the core educational function" and other "additional valued outputs and outcomes" (Favero et al. 2016, 341), following O'Toole and Meier's approach and paying "particular attention to performance in terms of effectiveness," which is "the extent to which policy objectives are being achieved" (O'Toole and Meier 2011, 2). Our interpretation is that the key value of Favero et al.'s (2016) study is that policy objectives should be achieved, which is consistent with the bureaucracy and neo-Weberian state paradigms, while the secondary values of user satisfaction and teacher turnover reflect elements of NPM and professional rule. Some aspects of performance are measured by directly surveying the stakeholder concerned.

Turning to the Andersen et al. (2016b) article, the performance criterion is students' academic achievements in Danish public schools. The additional insights come from the different measures of this criterion that correspond to different stakeholders' views. Here, the authors distinguish between internal stakeholders (teachers

Table 2.2 Overview of use of concepts in illustrative articles

	Stakeholder(s) mentioned in articles	Specific performance criteria in articles	Key public values reflected in articles (our interpretation)	Related to governance paradigms' key values
Schools				
Favero et al. 2016	State-level political and administrative decision-makers supplemented by parents, students, and teachers	New York City students' academic achievement in state standardized tests, parental satisfaction, and teacher turnover	Policy objectives should be achieved for individual students, but it is also seen as desirable that users are satisfied and teachers stay	Bureaucracy NWS NPM
Andersen et al. 2016a	Internal (teachers) and external (examiners and administrative and political decision makers) stakeholders	Danish students' academic achievement measured in final exams, yearly marks, and teacher self-reported contributions	Policy objectives should be achieved for individual students, but professional quality is also seen as desirable, given focus on teachers and external examiners	Bureaucracy NWS Professional rule
Song and Meier 2018	Decision makers (highest priority, given that official test scores are seen as most important), parents, students, and teachers	Seoul students' academic achievement supplemented by satisfaction with school quality, student learning, educational facilities, and safety	Policy objectives should be achieved for schools and individual students. Users should be satisfied, and professionals should perceive high quality in the organization.	Bureaucracy NWS Professional rule NPM
Environmental regulation				
Zhan et al. 2014	Environmental policy implementation officers (and their perceptions of pressures from other stakeholders) and enterprise executives	Environmental enforcement effectiveness in Guangzhou, China	Policy objectives should be achieved through enforcement effectiveness based on collaboration with other government agencies	Bureaucracy NWS NPG
Heckman 2012	State officials and external stakeholders, e.g. reporters and citizen watchdog groups, as included in administrative data	American states' air pollution control outcomes	Policy objectives (reduction of pollution) should be achieved at state level through good management practice as seen by societal actors	Bureaucracy NWS NPM

	Stakeholder(s) mentioned in articles	Specific performance criteria in articles	Key public values reflected in articles (our interpretation)	Related to governance paradigms' key values
Darnall et al. 2010	Environmental facility managers (and their perceptions of pressures from other stakeholders)	Efficiency in US manufacturing facilities (importance of savings due to environmental practice)	Indirect contribution to government policy objectives	-
Local authorities				
Brewer and Walker 2010	External stakeholder (Audit Commission) assessment of various performance dimensions supplemented by internal management assessment	Multidimensional performance in English local authorities (quality, efficiency, effectiveness, equity, responsiveness, etc.)	Performance should include dimensions that relate to all relevant stakeholders	Bureaucracy NWS NPM NPG
Yang 2009	Internal stakeholders' assessments of honest reporting with regard to elected officials, media, public and citizen groups, and employees	Process criterion of performance for Taipei (Taiwan) government units: honest performance reporting	Performance should be reported honestly as a cornerstone of integrity and transparency	Bureaucracy NWS
Pérez-López et al. 2015	Taxpayers and private firms based on the goal of market efficiency	Cost-efficiency in Spanish local governments	Public service provision should be efficient	NPM

and their self-reported contributions to students' academic achievements and the marks they give students for the year's work) and external stakeholders (external examiners who make evaluations on behalf of national decision-makers based on standardized criteria). The findings suggest that institutionalization of the assessment (e.g. standardization based on professional norms) can be a way to ensure consistency. Andersen et al. (2016b, 76) thus argue that if the professions are willing to combine the official policy goals with their professional norms, the resulting criterion can be considered a key public value. This approach combines elements from the bureaucracy, neo-Weberian state, and professional rule paradigms. Inclusion of the stakeholder perspective is both direct (for teachers' perceptions of performance) and indirect (based on the assumption that children and parents are interested in academic achievement).

Song and Meier (2018) combine three different surveys and archival data on secondary education in Seoul, Korea, to analyze how students' academic achievement is associated with parents', students', and teachers' judgments of school quality. They find that parents, students, and teachers provide similar assessments of school performance and that their assessments are aligned with archival performance measures (especially for high-performing schools). Song and Meier (2018) discuss the question of whether different stakeholders should be canvassed if their assessments are similar. They urge caution in generalizing too widely. One reason is that academic performance is especially important for attaining higher positions in Korean society, making agreement important for all stakeholders. Uniformity in the Korean educational system should also be considered because comparable tests are critical for all students' futures. Furthermore, parents and students in Seoul City are informed by their schools of the school's mean scores as well as their own child's score. Having this knowledge may homogenize different stakeholders' perspectives on school quality. Interestingly, parents and students are more responsive to information about school performance than about individual student performance, implying that citizens may prioritize the former. Again, inclusion of a stakeholder perspective on performance is both direct and indirect.

Despite the different contexts for the three studies of school performance (New York City, Denmark, and Seoul, Korea), their focus is very similar. The key public value is to achieve policy objectives as measured by student test scores, which is key in the bureaucracy and neo-Weberian state paradigms. However, all three articles also examine at least one other type of stakeholder understanding of school performance, consistent with aspects of professional rule and NPM.

2.3.3 Environmental Regulation

In the policy area of environmental regulation, several published studies include stakeholders' value preferences when measuring performance. The following three articles study different units of analysis and different contexts.

Zhan et al. (2014) conducted extensive surveys and interviews with environmental regulators and business executives in the city of Guangzhou, China. The authors trace the transformation of China's policy implementation process from a centralized, top-down effort to one that is more decentralized and inclusive of local stakeholders. They distinguish between vertical stakeholders (from the central and provincial governments) and horizontal stakeholders (the municipal government and various local societal groups), arguing that both types can exert demands and provide political support. There have been vast changes in the past decade in the level of support from and relative influence of these different stakeholders. Specifically, support from the central government and the public increased over time, but not from the local government and regulated industries. In terms of performance criteria, the focus is on environmental enforcement effectiveness and thus on official goal attainment. Still, the authors discuss the perceptions of street-level bureaucrats and private firms, including these stakeholder perspectives at least indirectly. The focus on formalism, centralism, and goal attainment places the article in the bureaucratic and neo-Weberian state paradigms, but the authors also emphasize collaboration with other government agencies, and such horizontal coordination is a key value in new public governance.

In another study, Heckman (2012) analyzed the impact of management quality, spending, problem severity, and political factors on American states' air pollution control outcomes. His measures are robust and include several well-known archival measures such as the Government Performance Project (GPP) scores for the fifty states. Some measures reflect the value preferences and viewpoints of stakeholder groups indirectly. An interesting insight is that the selection of performance measures has notable effects on the findings. Specifically, a model that uses aggregate pollution levels to measure performance does not show any impact of management quality on pollution, while a model that uses the estimated reduction in pollution emissions as the performance standard shows substantive impact. This highlights the importance of selecting performance measures that clearly and fully capture relevant stakeholders' goals. The study exemplifies an indirect stakeholder inclusion. In terms of key public values, the article supplements the desirability of achieving policy objectives with the desirability of good management practice in itself, reflecting a combination of aspects of the neo-Weberian state and NPM paradigms.

In the third study concerning business' environmental practices, Darnall et al. (2010) differentiate between primary stakeholders (value chain and management stakeholders) and secondary stakeholders (environmental and community, regulatory, and industry stakeholders). They observe that some businesses participate in voluntary environmental programs (VEPs) to address the problem that stakeholders who seek to reward or punish businesses for their environmental behavior often cannot look inside these organizations and assess their internal policies and operations. Participation in VEPs may signal willingness to exceed minimum environmental requirements. The key public value in this article is that public organizations should enable private firms to go beyond compliance with environmental commitment and be efficient in doing it. Drawing on data from nearly 300 organizations, the authors find that managers who recognize the importance of stakeholder influences on their businesses' environmental practices are more likely to participate in VEPs. They also find that organizations with strong efficiency goals are more likely to participate in VEPs because their managers anticipate cost savings from minimizing waste.

This study by Darnall et al. deviates from the other two studies that focus on the achievement of policy objectives as the key public value relating to the bureaucracy and neo-Weberian state paradigms. Instead, Darnall et al. (2010) focus on financial business performance combined with environmental commitment. Both Darnall et al. (2010) and Zhan et al. (2014) include other stakeholders through questions about these stakeholders' pressures. Substantive value preferences from other stakeholders are included only by Heckman (2012), based on survey data of these stakeholders. A key difference between studies from schools and environmental services is that private firms are seen as more important stakeholders in the latter.

2.3.4 Local Authorities/Municipalities

The Cardiff-based researchers' datasets (e.g. Andrews and Boyne 2010; Boyne 2002) have been widely used to study performance in English local authorities. The article by Brewer and Walker (2010) is based on these datasets. An interesting aspect of local authorities as multipurpose entities is that the broader economic conditions such as recessions are especially important because of the broad tasks of local authorities. While Brewer and Walker (2010) control statistically for resource constraints, the other two articles actively address crisis as a potential contextual factor.

Brewer and Walker's (2010) article has a clear stakeholder perspective. They emphasize that performance is a multidimensional construct that covers many concerns such as quality, efficiency, effectiveness, responsiveness, and equity, and that perspectives on what constitutes high levels of performance vary across stakeholder groups. The authors distinguish between internal stakeholders (e.g. senior managers and frontline staff) and external stakeholders (e.g. voters, regulators, and service users). Studying a representative sample of 100 English local authorities, they use data from the Comprehensive Performance Assessment developed by the UK Audit Commission under the Blair Labour Party government. Six performance dimensions are assessed, largely based upon surveys, site visits, inspections, and archival data. The surveys included surveys of citizens and employees speaking for themselves on various aspects of service performance. Dimensions such as responsiveness and equity, which relate to citizens' and clients' value preferences, are evaluated by the Audit Commission, and these measures are complemented with corresponding surveys of local authority managers to mount empirical studies. The article highlights the importance of the stakeholder perspective, showing that there is variation between performance as reported by managers and performance as reported by the Audit Commission, which is an external body. In line with the multidimensional performance criteria, relevant stakeholders' demands and preferences are taken into account, and mostly in a direct way. As such, this understanding of performance might well correspond with the official policy goals of the bureaucracy and the neo-Weberian state paradigms but also of NPM.

In Yang's (2009) study, stakeholders are treated as recipients of performance information. Given that the inclusion of this perspective is based on the author's assumptions about the stakeholders' interests, it is indirect. Yang focuses on a process performance criterion, namely whether performance reporting in government units in Taipei (the capital of Taiwan) is honest. Specifically, honest performance reporting captures the degree of perceived honest communication with four stakeholder groups: elected officials, the media, the public and citizen groups, and employees. The assessment of honesty in performance reporting comes from surveys of managers, performance specialists, and regular administrators from the units of twelve district governments. The results show that employees and middle managers do not score the level of honest performance reporting by top managers as very high (Yang 2009, 93–4). The results also indicate wide support for the importance of stakeholder participation in performance assessment. Yang (2009) argues that stakeholder participation has positive effects on honest performance reporting and on government performance because external stakeholders provide frames of reference that differ from those of organizational members. In terms of public values, the key message in this article seems related to the bureaucracy and neo-Weberian state paradigms, suggesting that performance should be reported honestly, both because honesty is desirable in itself and because it contributes to integrity, transparency, and goal attainment in public service provision.

Contributing directly to the discussion of performance in the reverberations of crisis, Pérez-López et al. (2015) investigate whether new public management (NPM) delivery forms improved the efficiency of Spanish local governments both before and during the global recession of 2008. In the context of heightened budgetary and financial constraints on local government, new ways of managing public services were sought using the NPM delivery forms. These efforts brought new stakeholders to the fore as private organizations became more important due to public–private partnerships, mixed firms, and contracting out. Using cost efficiency as their performance criterion, the authors show that the creation of agencies, contracting out, and inter-municipal cooperation reduced cost efficiency. However, during the global recession, the adoption of mixed firms contributed to higher levels of cost efficiency. The central public value is efficiency as in NPM.

The three studies differ in how local government performance is understood and which stakeholders are included. In the Brewer and Walker (2010) study, multiple dimensions of performance are used, some of which relate to external stakeholders, while the study by Pérez-López et al. (2015) considers only cost efficiency as a performance criterion. Yang (2009) studies honest performance reporting, which can be considered a process criterion of public service performance, in this case, seen from the perspectives of four internal and external stakeholder groups.

2.3.5 A Comparative Analysis of Public Service Performance Studies Focusing on Stakeholders

As Table 2.2 suggests, there is great variation between the performance criteria in these articles, except that all school articles, two environmental articles, and at least one local authority article (Brewer and Walker 2010) include official goal attainment. The variation manifests itself in several ways: a multidimensional/composite (Brewer and Walker 2010) versus a single dimension measure of performance (Pérez-López et al. 2015); outcome measures such as student test scores (e.g. Favero et al. 2016) versus process measures such as performance reporting honesty (Yang 2009); and performance assessments based on administrative data (Heckman 2012) and based on several sources including stakeholder self-reports (Andersen et al. 2016b). From a stakeholder perspective, we welcome a multidimensional public service performance concept and the use of performance measures that relate to specific stakeholders' value preferences and that measure these value preferences directly by surveying the stakeholder concerned. This notion of what a stakeholder perspective involves is met by just over half the studies we examined even though we selected studies that paid explicit attention to stakeholders. Limitations of the articles we studied include that authors present performance information they assume is relevant for specific stakeholders but without asking these stakeholders themselves, and that some studies do not study stakeholder value preferences but stakeholder pressures as perceived by officials or managers (Darnall et al. 2010; Zhan et al. 2014).

Most of the nine articles reflect several public values. Exceptions are Zhan et al.'s (2014) singular focus on enforcement effectiveness and Pérez-López et al.'s (2015) focus on efficiency. Table 2.2 suggests that six public values are important across the nine studies: (1) achieving policy objectives; (2) honest performance reporting; (3) professional quality; (4) user satisfaction; (5) efficiency; and (6) inclusion of societal actors' values. These values are linked to specific governance paradigms discussed in Section 2.1. Achieving policy objectives is an important value, especially in the classic bureaucracy and neo-Weberian state governance paradigms. This links back to hierarchy as a governance mechanism and the emphasis on representative democracy, as in the neo-Weberian state paradigm. These paradigms also support honest performance reporting (in the Yang 2009 article). Professional quality, and therefore the relevance of professional rule, can be identified in several articles (Andersen et al. 2016b; Song and Meier 2018). User satisfaction clearly comes from new public management (Favero et al. 2016 and Song and Meier 2018 are good examples). Prioritizing the desirability of efficient public service provision also comes from new public management, and that is central in Pérez-López et al. (2015). Brewer and Walker's (2010) insistence that all relevant stakeholders' perspectives should be taken seriously goes some way to reflecting tendencies from new public governance and public value management because several stakeholders were surveyed and their preferences included.

Our analysis of these nine studies contributes to public management research by showing how researchers can (re)conceptualize public service performance as a more inclusive topic in which stakeholders' values are considered explicitly. The lessons drawn from this exercise are, nonetheless, illustrative and not comprehensive or conclusive. Different stakeholder groups and new public values may emerge in other cases.

2.4 Conclusion

So what does it mean to approach public value(s) and public service performance from a stakeholder perspective? A stakeholder perspective involves the need to focus intently on what people value and how public services affect them. It emphasizes the need to incorporate the views and interests of *multiple* stakeholders in performance research, if possible by direct measures of stakeholders' views and otherwise by indirect measures that refer to stakeholders' interests as understood by others. The requirements of a stakeholder perspective set a challenging agenda to public management researchers, but one which could make research more relevant and useful to society. One reason is that research can assist public organizations to more explicitly discuss public value creation by focusing on different stakeholder understandings of which public values are important and how these values should be prioritized. Another reason is that research can help public organizations reduce the risk of overlooking important aspects of public service performance. Finally, the stakeholder approach we have described comports with democracy and debate in the public sphere, a central element in Benington's (2011) concept of public value.

Some portrayals of public administrators see them as neutrally competent technocrats who are restricted to ministerial duties (as in Wilson [1887] 1997) or as entrepreneurial risk-takers who break through bureaucracy and operate as entrepreneurs (as in some new public management descriptions, e.g. Barzelay 1992). Seen from a stakeholder perspective, public administrators can be portrayed as experts who exercise judgment and make consequential decisions in identifying relevant public values and creating public value when they generate public service performance. Stakeholders' priorities can differ within and between stakeholder groups, and each configuration of interests should receive due attention. In addition, some stakeholders may be more concerned about collective interests than their individual interests when they prioritize public value creation as collectively valued social outcomes—as Song and Meier (2018) revealed. Taking a stakeholder perspective will help research shed more light on how public managers can contribute in a meaningful way to the creation of public service performance and public value.

References

Amirkhanyan, A. A., H. J. Kim, and K. T. Lambright. 2014. "The Performance Puzzle: Understanding the Factors Influencing Alternative Dimensions and Views of Performance." *Journal of Public Administration Research and Theory* 24 (1): pp. 1–34.

Andersen, L. B., T. Beck Jørgensen, A. M. Kjeldsen, L. H. Pedersen, and K. Vrangbæk. 2013. "Public Service Motivation and Public Values: Conceptual and Empirical Relationships." *American Review of Public Administration 36* (3): pp. 126–36.

Andersen, L. B., A. Boesen, and L. H. Pedersen. 2016a. "Performance in Public Organizations: Clarifying the Conceptual Space." *Public Administration Review 76* (6): pp. 852–62.

Andersen, L. B., E. Heinesen, and L. H. Pedersen. 2016b. "Individual Performance: From Common Source Bias to Institutionalized Assessment." *Journal of Public Administration Research and Theory 26* (1): pp. 63–78.

Andrews, R., and G. Boyne. 2010. "Capacity, Leadership and Organizational Performance: Testing the Black Box Model of Public Management." *Public Administration Review 70* (3): pp. 443–54.

Andrews, R., G. Boyne, and R. Walker. 2006. "Subjective and Objective Measures of Organizational Performance: An Empirical Exploration." In *Public Service Performance*, edited by G. A. Boyne, K. J. Meier, L. O'Toole, and R. M. Walker, pp. 14–34. Cambridge: Cambridge University Press.

Barzelay, M. 1992. *Breaking through Bureaucracy: A New Vision of Managing in Government*. Oakland, CA: University of California Press.

Beck Jørgensen, T. 1999. "The Public Sector in an In-Between Time: Searching for New Public Values." *Public Administration 77* (3): pp. 565–84.

Beck Jørgensen, T., and B. Bozeman. 2007. "Public Values: An Inventory." *Administration & Society 39* (3): pp. 354–81.

Benington, J. 2011. "From Private Choice to Public Value." In *Public Value: Theory and Practice*, edited by J. Benington and M. Moore, pp. 31–51. Basingstoke: Palgrave Macmillan.

Boyne, G. A. 2002. "Concepts and Indicators of Local Authority Performance: An Evaluation of the Statutory Frameworks in England and Wales." *Public Money & Management 22* (2): pp. 17–24.

Boyne, G. A., K. J. Meier, L. O'Toole, and R. M. Walker. 2006. *Public Service Performance*. Cambridge: Cambridge University Press.

Bozeman, B. 2007. *Public Value and Public Interest: Counterbalancing Economic Individualism*. Washington, DC: Georgetown University Press.

Brewer, G. A. 2013. "Public Management Contributions for Improving Social Service Performance: Public Values, Public Service Motivation, and Rule Functionality." In *Managing Social Issues: A Public Values Perspective*, edited by P. L. M. Leisink, P. Boselie, M. Van Bottenburg, and D. M. Hosking, pp. 19–36. Cheltenham: Edward Elgar.

Brewer, G. A., and R. M. Walker. 2010. "The Impact of Red Tape on Governmental Performance: An Empirical Analysis." *Journal of Public Administration Research and Theory 20* (1): pp. 233–57.

Bryson, J. M., B. Crosby, and L. Bloomberg. 2014. "Public Value Governance: Moving beyond Traditional Public Administration and the New Public Management." *Public Administration Review 74* (4): pp. 445–56.

Darnall, N., M. Potoski, and A. Prakash. 2010. "Sponsorship Matters: Assessing Business Participation in Government- and Industry-Sponsored Voluntary Environmental Programs." *Journal of Public Administration Research and Theory 20* (2): pp. 283–307.

Denhardt, J. V., and R. B. Denhardt. 2011. *The New Public Service: Serving, Not Steering.* 3rd ed. Armonk, NY: M. E. Sharpe.

Ejersbo, N., and C. Greve. 2014. *Moderniseringen af den offentlige sektor.* Copenhagen: Akademisk Forlag.

Favero, N., K. J. Meier, and L. J. O'Toole. 2016. "Goals, Trust, Participation, and Feedback: Linking Internal Management with Performance Outcomes." *Journal of Public Administration Research and Theory 26* (2): pp. 327–43.

Freeman, R. E. 1984. *Strategic Management: A Stakeholder Approach.* Marshfield, MA: Pitman Publishing, Inc.

Hartley, J., S. Parker, and J. Beashel. 2019b. "Leading and Recognizing Public Value." *Public Administration 97* (2): pp. 264–78.

Hartley, J., A. Sancino, M. Bennister, and S. Resodihardjo. 2019a. "Leadership for Public Value: Political Astuteness as a Conceptual Link." *Public Administration 97* (2): pp. 239–49.

Heckman, A. C. 2012. "Desperately Seeking Management: Understanding Management Quality and Its Impact on Government Performance Outcomes under the Clean Air Act." *Journal of Public Administration Research and Theory 22* (3): pp. 473–96.

Jung, C. S. 2011. "Organizational Goal Ambiguity and Performance." *International Public Management Journal 14* (2): pp. 193–217.

Kluckhohn, C. 1962. "Values and Value-Orientations in the Theory of Action: An Exploration in Definition and Classification." In *Toward a General Theory of Action,* edited by T. Parsons and E. A. Shils, pp. 388–433. Cambridge, MA: Harvard University Press.

Knies, E., P. Leisink, and S. Kraus-Hoogeveen. 2018. "Frontline Managers' Contribution to Mission Achievement: A Study of How People Management Affects Thoughtful Care." *Human Service Organizations: Management, Leadership & Governance 42* (2): pp. 166–84.

Lawton, A., and A. G. Rose. 1994. *Organisation and Management in the Public Sector.* London: Pitman.

Maguire, M. 1998. "Ethics in the Public Service: Current Issues and Practice." In *Ethics and Accountability in a Context of Governance and New Public Management,* edited by A. Hondeghem, pp. 23–34. Amsterdam: IOS Press.

Meier, K. J., and L. J. O'Toole. 2001. "Managerial Strategies and Behavior in Networks: A Model with Evidence from US Public Education." *Journal of Public Administration Research and Theory 11* (3): pp. 271–94.

Meier, K. J., and L. J. O'Toole. 2002. "Public Management and Organizational Performance: The Effect of Managerial Quality." *Journal of Policy Analysis and Management 21* (4): pp. 629–43.

Meier, K. J., and L. J. O'Toole. 2003. "Public Management and Educational Performance: The Impact of Managerial Networking." *Public Administration Review 63* (6): pp. 689–99.

Moore, M. H. 1995. *Creating Public Value: Strategic Management in Government.* Cambridge, MA: Harvard University Press.

Moore, M. H. 2013. *Recognizing Public Value.* Cambridge, MA: Harvard University Press.

Osborne, S. P. 2006. "The New Public Governance?" *Public Management Review 8* (3): pp. 377–87.

O'Toole, L. J., and K. J. Meier. 2011. *Public Management: Organizations, Governance, and Performance.* Cambridge: Cambridge University Press.

Pérez-López, G., D. Prior, and J. L. Zafra-Gómez. 2015. "Rethinking New Public Management Delivery Forms and Efficiency: Long-Term Effects in Spanish Local Government." *Journal of Public Administration Research and Theory 25* (4): pp. 1157–83.

Pollitt, C., and G. Bouckaert. 2017. *Public Management Reform: A Comparative Analysis—Into the Age of Austerity.* 4th ed. Oxford: Oxford University Press.

Song, M., and K. J. Meier. 2018. "Citizen Satisfaction and the Kaleidoscope of Government Performance: How Multiple Stakeholders See Government Performance." *Journal of Public Administration Research and Theory.* Online first. https://doi.org/10.1093/jopart/muy006.

Stoker, G. 2006. "Public Value Management: A New Narrative for Networked Governance?" *American Review of Public Administration 36* (1): pp. 41–57.

Torfing, J., L. B. Andersen, C. Greve, and K. K. Klausen. 2020. *Public Governance Paradigms: Competing and Co-Existing.* Cheltenham: Edward Elgar.

Vandenabeele, W., P. Leisink, and E. Knies. 2013. "Public Value Creation and Strategic Human Resource Management: Public Service Motivation as a Linking Mechanism." In *Managing Social Issues: A Public Values Perspective,* edited by P. L. M. Leisink, P. Boselie, M. Van Bottenburg, and D. M. Hosking, pp. 37–54. Cheltenham: Edward Elgar.

Van der Wal, Z., A. Pekur, and K. Vrangbæk. 2008. "Public Sector Value Congruence among Old and New EU Member-States? Empirical Evidence from the Netherlands, Denmark and Estonia." *Public Integrity 10* (4): pp. 317–33.

Walker, R. M., and R. Andrews. 2015. "Local Government Management and Performance: A Review of Evidence." *Journal of Public Administration Research & Theory 25* (1): pp. 101–33.

Walker, R. M., G. A. Boyne, and G. A. Brewer. 2010. *Public Management and Performance: Research Directions.* Cambridge: Cambridge University Press.

Wilson, W. [1887] 1997. "The Study of Administration." In *Classics of Public Administration,* edited by J. Shafritz and A. Hyde, pp. 14–26. 4th ed. Fort Worth, TX: Harcourt Brace.

Yang, K. 2009. "Examining Perceived Honest Performance Reporting by Public Organizations: Bureaucratic Politics and Organizational Practice." *Journal of Public Administration Research and Theory 19* (1): pp. 81–105.

Zhan, X., C. W.-H. Lo, and S.-Y. Tang. 2014. "Contextual Changes and Environmental Policy Implementation: A Longitudinal Study of Street-Level Bureaucrats in Guangzhou, China." *Journal of Public Administration Research and Theory 24* (4): pp. 1005–35.

3
People Management
Integrating Insights from Strategic Human Resource Management and Leadership

Christian B. Jacobsen and Eva Knies

3.1 Introduction

The central issue in this chapter is people management in public organizations. The notion that people management is crucial for goal attainment is grounded in the resource-based view (Barney 1991) which states that organizations' value-adding, rare, inimitable, and non-substitutable resources can contribute to their sustained competitive advantage. One of the important resources—or even perhaps the most important resource—in public organizations consists of the talents, skills, abilities, and motivations of public service employees. Given that most public organizations are labor-intensive, managing employees is therefore a core task in public management.

The discipline of public management is, nonetheless, a broader field, which involves anything from making organization-wide strategic decisions to giving instructions to individual employees, and it involves general policies as well as individualized communication and support. People management involves both strategic human resource management (SHRM) and leadership. We regard SHRM as the management of people and their work aimed at achieving organizational goals, as performed by managers on different levels and not only by HR specialists (Boxall and Purcell 2011, 7). Leadership can be understood as "the process of influencing others to understand and agree about what needs to be done and how to do it, and the process of facilitating individual and collective efforts to achieve shared objectives" (Yukl 2013, 23). Leadership and SHRM are organizational processes that are both aimed at goal attainment.

These processes are closely related, interdependent, and intertwined both conceptually and practically. For example, HRM can involve pay systems, recruitment policies, and human resource development strategies, whereas leadership can involve individual leaders' decisions and justifications of payment decisions, actual recruitment decisions, and specific decisions on training recipients and content. In this chapter, we specifically focus on internal management processes, although we

Christian B. Jacobsen and Eva Knies, *People Management: Integrating Insights from Strategic Human Resource Management and Leadership* In: *Managing for Public Service Performance: How People and Values Make a Difference.* Edited by: Peter Leisink, Lotte B. Andersen, Gene A. Brewer, Christian B. Jacobsen, Eva Knies, and Wouter Vandenabeele, Oxford University Press (2021). © Christian B. Jacobsen and Eva Knies. DOI: 10.1093/oso/9780192893420.003.0003 acknowledge that public management can have an external focus as well. An important insight in this chapter is that effective people management depends on the "translation" of formal policies and practices to employees. Public managers are a crucial actor in this respect, bringing policies to life and shaping employees' perceptions of people management. We acknowledge that not only formal leaders can act as people managers, but employees can as well (e.g. see the literature on shared and distributed leadership). However, in this chapter, we will mainly focus on formal leaders. We refer to Chapters 5 and 11 for a deeper discussion of distributed leadership.

One challenge in understanding both the functioning and consequences of HRM and leadership in public organizations is that the chain from policies and other general initiatives to actual execution by managers can be long. This chapter will focus on five key aspects related to HRM and leadership in public service organizations. In doing so, we systematically draw on both the general HRM and leadership bodies of literature and specify these insights to the public sector context whenever possible. This goes beyond the instrumental use of different literatures but serves the purpose of demonstrating what the two bodies of literature can add to each other. First, we will briefly present the historical move from personnel management to HRM and leadership. Second, we will discuss the distinction between external and internal management and set the focus on internal management here. Third, we will discuss how the literature has moved from a focus on top management levels to the role of middle managers and frontline leaders (e.g. Jacobsen and Andersen 2015; Knies and Leisink 2014), who are closer to the actual implementation of policies and therefore responsible for turning general policies into results. Fourth, we will discuss how HRM policies and leadership are mutually dependent. Thus, leaders in public organizations rely on HRM policies to gain leverage in their attempts to coordinate and direct employees toward goal attainment, but the implementation of HRM is also dependent on leadership (Purcell and Hutchinson 2007). Fifth, we will discuss how HRM and leadership begin with intentions about content and goals but ultimately rely for their effect on the perceptions of frontline employees who take directions from managers and execute public policies (Wright and Nishii 2013). The chapter concludes with a discussion of the relevance of HRM and leadership for goal attainment and some suggestions for practice and future research.

3.2 From Personnel Management to HRM and Leadership

The theoretical understanding and actual application of people management have changed over time. The interest in personnel management developed with the move from scientific management theories to the human relations and human resource traditions almost a century ago. The Hawthorne studies are one example that clearly demonstrated how workers, compared with other input factors such as financial capital or technological assets, often respond surprisingly differently to management processes due to social psychological processes. This puts the perspective on employee resources, needs, and motives as vital for understanding organizational behavior. Nonetheless, personnel management was still characterized by relatively collective, standardized approaches aimed at achieving employee well-being. Since then, people management approaches have become more individualized, flexible, and aimed at goal attainment next to employee well-being (Boyne et al. 1999). In the HRM literature, this shift has been labeled "from personnel management to Human Resource Management," and it is characterized by a move from a focus on short-term, ad hoc goals to a longer-term strategic understanding of people management. A related important shift is the one from HR specialists being in the lead to an integrated understanding of people management where line managers are primarily responsible (Guest 1987). At the same time, the leadership literature increasingly focused on the integration of multiple approaches to effective leadership, the contingencies of leadership in relation to both workers and context, and value creation rather than leader actions or employee outcomes only (Van Wart 2013).

3.3 Internal Management from a Leadership and HRM Perspective

The literatures on leadership and HRM both distinguish between external aspects of management directed at an organization's environment and internal aspects directed at members of the organization. This chapter mainly focuses on internal management, which has gained increasing attention in the public management literature (e.g. Favero et al. 2016), but we acknowledge that external aspects are important as well for understanding internal management.

Leadership is described as an influencing process, where leaders through both internally and externally oriented behaviors strive to facilitate shared understanding and agreement on organizational inputs, processes, and goals. External leadership is often associated with leader behaviors such as networking, external monitoring and representation, and buffering or exploiting the external environment, whereas a dominant leadership taxonomy describes internal leadership as task-oriented, relations-oriented, and change-oriented (Yukl 2013). In public organizations, external orientation is an important leadership task, given that the external environment is characterized by features such as political governance, multiple stakeholders, organizational interdependence, and turbulence (Tummers and Knies 2016). However, since our focus here is on personnel management, we will consider the specific features of public organizations as important contextual variables that shape how leaders behave internally (Boyne 2002; Oberfield 2014). This topic is discussed in more detail in Chapter 5, which explains how the external environment affects how leadership can be exerted internally.

The HRM literature has a long-standing tradition of looking at aspects of internal management, i.e. the management of people and their work aimed at achieving organizational goals (Boxall and Purcell 2011). Vertical and horizontal alignment are key concepts in the literature dealing with effective HRM. Vertical alignment refers to fitting the HRM strategy to the overall organizational strategy. Horizontal alignment refers to the degree of internal coherence and consistency between an organization's HR practices (Gratton and Truss 2003). Another type of alignment or fit that is distinguished in the literature is external fit, i.e. the fit between internal HR policy and practices to a range of possible external contingencies. Although it is acknowledged that the market and institutional contexts raise issues that have an impact on an organization's HRM, the external context has been studied less frequently compared to the internal contingencies (Paauwe 2004). Moreover, whenever the impact of the external context is the subject of study, the main focus is often on mapping the context and exploring how HRM has adapted to changes in context rather than analyzing consistency in internal and external elements, the link to performance, or the way managers actively deal with the environment (Guest 1997).

3.4   Multilevel Analysis of Managerial Action

Most public organizations are large, and people management involves a multitude of decision makers across levels, functions, and units. The orthodox role of the public manager is to loyally implement general policies and programs, and hierarchical decision-making is dominant. This was the view of traditional public administration, and while new public management stressed leader autonomy, that view also placed the manager in a clear hierarchical setting. However, it is increasingly acknowledged that the performance of public organizations involves creating public value (Moore 1995), and that managers are not only accountable upwards but also responsible for managing outwards to the public and downwards to operational lines (Williams and Shearer 2011, 1372). This places public managers in a strategic role where they need to balance a strategic triangle between public value outcomes, the authorizing environment, and their operational capability (Moore 1995). Hence, the key priority for public managers is to create value demanded by the public, but in order to attain this goal, they need support from political entities, and their success is contingent on their organization's capabilities (Moore and Khagram 2004). Public managers are, therefore, confronted with dilemmas in terms of reconciling potentially conflicting demands from various stakeholders, including superiors, employees, and citizens. This links to the complex performance demands placed on public managers (see Chapter 5), and it begs the question of how the decisions of managers at various levels can be studied.

In terms of studying the behavior of public leaders, a recent review found that public leadership studies either apply a micro-level approach, which focuses on the decisions of individual leaders, or a multilevel approach, which focuses on management systems as a form of social organizations (Vogel and Masal 2015). A dominant part of micro-level public leadership research has its roots in generic leadership research and seeks to import widely applied general leadership theories and approaches into public management research. The best-known approach is perhaps transformational leadership theory, which builds on the expectation that the individual leader has the potential to transform their organization through inspiration, stimulation, and role-modeling behavior (Jensen et al. 2016).

Numerous studies have investigated how transformational leadership and its counterpart, transactional leadership, matter for aspects such as motivation, commitment, and performance (e.g. Bellé 2014; Oberfield 2014; Wright et al. 2012). In addition, Yukl's generic integrated leadership framework has been applied in several studies of public organizations in order to understand the relevance of the leaders' attention to tasks, relations, change, and the external environment (e.g. Fernandez et al. 2010). Thus, many studies within this line of research focus on leadership styles and their effectiveness, whereas the leadership context tends to be neglected or at least downplayed. Although many studies discuss the relevance of the public setting and the individual leader as part of a public system, these elements are rarely actively studied; instead, general leadership competencies are the focal point (Van Wart 2013). An exception is the study by Tummers and Knies (2016), which explicitly focuses on the development of a public leadership scale with attention to specific public competencies such as accountability, rule-following, and political loyalty. However, this specific focus on *public* leadership is rare, and scholars have called for leadership studies that pay more attention to the specific features of the public sector (Vogel and Masal 2015).

The public management literature also encompasses approaches that pay attention to the multiple levels of public management and with a more explicit focus on the public sector. These studies also address leadership. For example, studies on organizational publicness have developed a framework for understanding how public and private organizations can be distinguished in terms of ownership, funding, and control (see also Chapters 1 and 4) and how this matters for public management (Bozeman 1987; Perry and Rainey 1988). However, specific studies of leadership in this tradition are relatively sparse, and only a few studies have systematically investigated leadership differences across sectors (e.g. Boyne 2002; Hansen and Villadsen 2010). Perhaps the most widely applied approach with a multilevel perspective focuses on collaborative leadership, where the leadership role is explicitly defined in relation to the leaders' environment (O'Leary and Vij 2012). According to this view, public organizations are confronted with political conflicts, wicked problems, and scarce resources, which emphasize governance, network, and collaboration for understanding the conditions for public leadership. Public leadership is, therefore, characterized by concerted effort and typically emerges informally and with little attention to hierarchical divisions (Crosby and Bryson 2014).

Whereas leadership research has traditionally focused on the individual leader, the HRM literature has traditionally been dominated by a systems approach. From the mid-1990s onwards, many studies have examined the effects of HR policies and practices (such as pay systems, recruitment policies, or performance management) on organizational performance, without paying much attention to the notion of HR implementation and the actors responsible for that. The independent variable in most of these HRM–performance studies is the presence of HR practices in an organization, which is then linked to several outcome variables. Huselid's (1995) study was one of the first to examine the effects of HR practices on turnover, productivity, and corporate financial performance. Subsequently, similar studies were conducted using various samples of employees in different organizational, sectoral, and national contexts. These studies were included in several meta-analyses (e.g. Combs et al. 2006). Most of these studies used HR directors or senior managers as respondents of their surveys based upon the idea that these stakeholders can overview and report on the HR practices in their organizations. In this approach, HR directors and senior/top managers are considered the main actors responsible for the design and implementation of HR practices. This implies a top-down implementation of HR practices. As such, there is hardly any attention given to the role that lower-level managers play and the impact of their actions.

This began to change in the mid-2000s. It was acknowledged that studying the effects of HRM on organizational outcomes requires a multilevel perspective with attention on the mechanisms linking HRM and performance. The role that managers play in implementing HR practices was one of the topics that gained attention, along with team processes and employee attitudes and behaviors, among others (Jiang et al. 2013). The first wave of research focused on the devolution of HR responsibilities from HR departments to those managers responsible for the daily supervision of employees (e.g. Perry and Kulik 2008; Whittaker and Marchington 2003). The main questions addressed were:

- To what extent are HR responsibilities devolved to the line?
- Is devolution a threat, an opportunity, or a partnership?

Once it was established that line managers play an important role in HR implementation in most organizations (Brewster et al. 2015; Larsen and Brewster 2003), research interests shifted to understanding their role perceptions, actual people management activities, and the enabling and hindering factors that influence their activities (for an elaborate overview, see Chapter 7 of this volume).

The increasing interest in line managers' HR responsibilities and activities does not imply that other stakeholders are overlooked. On the one hand, there is a body of literature studying different HR "delivery channels" such as HR shared service centers and HR professionals (Farndale et al. 2010). On the other hand, some authors acknowledge that managers at various hierarchical levels play different roles in the design and implementation of HR policies and practices. Generally, it is assumed that top or senior managers are primarily responsible for designing HR policies that are in line with the organizational strategy (Gratton and Truss 2003) and for setting the conditions for effective HR implementation by lower-level managers. Middle and frontline managers are assumed to be responsible for actual HR implementation as they are in close proximity to the employees they supervise (Stanton et al. 2010). There is, in sum, increasing research attention on line managers' activities in the HRM literature (e.g. Guest and Bos-Nehles 2013). However, most of these studies are conducted in private organizations, with some notable public sector exceptions (e.g. Knies et al. 2018b; Op de Beeck 2016; Vermeeren 2014). The role of top managers in enacting HR policies and practices is generally acknowledged but little studied in the HRM literature (Trullen et al. 2016). Top managers are studied more often in the leadership and public management bodies of literature; however, their role in HR implementation is overlooked there.

3.5 Combining Leadership and the Implementation of Human Resource Management

HRM and leadership have generally been studied separately, but as we will argue, they are closely related and interdependent. Here, we will discuss the concept of people management, which is defined as "managers' implementation of HR practices and their leadership behavior in supporting the employees they supervise at work" (Knies et al. 2020, 712). People management refers to general approaches relevant to managing employees in public organizations but also to more specific approaches such as performance management, which is discussed in further detail in Chapter 8, and diversity management, which is the topic of Chapter 10. Here, we will discuss the general conceptualization of people management in more detail.

The concept of people management was originally coined by Purcell and Hutchinson (2007) who argue that managers play a crucial role in shaping employees' perceptions of HRM through their implementation of HR practices and their leadership activities. Purcell and Hutchinson advocate that although leadership and HRM are traditionally two rather separate academic disciplines, insights from the two bodies of literature need to be integrated to understand the impact managers have on employees' attitudes, behaviors, and performance (Wright and Boswell 2002). This echoes Guest (2011, 7), who states that "advocates of the influence of leadership will tell us that it is good leadership that makes a difference; and leadership will have an impact on the content and practice of HRM as well as on management activities." Purcell and Hutchinson (2007, 3–4) observe a "symbiotic relationship" between leadership and HR implementation: "FLMs [frontline managers] need well designed HR practices to use in their people management activities in order to help motivate and reward employees and deal with performance issues and worker needs. The way FLMs enact these practices will be influenced by their leadership behavior." This implies that the implementation of HR practices will be attuned to managers' leadership behaviors, and both must be oriented to support the individual employees the manager supervises (Knies et al. 2020, 709). The assumption underlying the concept of people management is that managers have at least some discretion in enacting HRM, depending on the level of formalization of their organization's HR policies. The variability in people management activities is linked to the quality of the relationship between managers and their employees (leader–member exchange, LMX; Graen and Uhl-Bien 1995), which is likely to influence employees' perceptions of HRM. More specifically, Purcell and Hutchinson (2007, 17) argue that both the quality of the LMX relationship and the extent to which a manager is seen as a people manager contribute to the strength of the HRM system.

Following the conceptualization by Purcell and Hutchison (2007), Knies et al. (2020) developed a systematic definition and operationalization of people management. The authors show that people management consists of two components that can each be broken down in two sub-dimensions. For the implementation of HR practices, two levels of implementation are distinguished: general practices and tailor-made arrangements (Guest 2007). With regard to the leadership behavior of line managers, two focal points are distinguished: the support of employees' commitment and the support of employees' career development (Knies and Leisink 2014). These four sub-dimensions serve as the basis for their scale development. Based on a Study 1/Study 2 design, Knies et al. (2020) provide empirical evidence for the reliability and validity of their people management measure. The concept of people management thus has both functional and relational sides.

The implementation of HR practices has mainly been studied by HRM scholars. From that perspective, three important notions help us understand the symbiotic nature of the relationship between HRM implementation and leadership. First, in the literature on HR practices, a distinction is made between assessing the presence, coverage, and intensity of HR practices (Boselie et al. 2005). In the first case, the presence of HR practices is determined by using a dichotomous variable (present/not-present). While this type of measure was used frequently in early HRM–performance studies, it is now considered rather simplistic. Measuring the coverage of HR practices—i.e. the proportion of the workforce covered by certain HR practices—provides more information. According to Boselie et al. (2005), the most "sophisticated" indicator is one that measures the intensity of HR practices, i.e. the degree to which an individual employee is exposed to the practices. Focusing on the intensity of HR practices implies that there is potential variation in the way HR practices are applied to different employees, highlighting the role line managers and their leadership play in "delivering" HR practices.

Second, from the literature on HRM devolution (Brewster et al. 2015; Larsen and Brewster 2003), we learned that "the notion of line management accepting greater responsibility for HRM within employing organizations is now received wisdom" (Larsen and Brewster 2003, 228). It is no longer the HR department or HR manager that is primarily responsible for the implementation of HR practices, but rather those managers who oversee the primary processes in the organization. This implies variation between the HR practices applied to and perceived by employees because different managers are responsible for HR implementation. However, Brewster et al.

(2015) show that context matters: In larger organizations, HR responsibilities are less often devolved to managers. The same holds true for organizations with high union density and organizations with a more strategic HRM function. Moreover, the type of economy determines the devolution of HR responsibilities to managers; the Nordic countries show the highest devolvement, liberal market economies the lowest, and coordinated market economies are in the middle. This implies that in contexts where we find the most devolution, the impact of leadership on employees' perceptions of people management will be the greatest.

Third, from the literature on HR attributions (Nishii et al. 2008), we learned that HR practices are not received and perceived as "value free." That is, employees make assumptions regarding why certain HR practices are implemented by management. The assumptions can be either commitment-oriented (e.g. aimed at service quality or employee well-being) or control-oriented (e.g. aimed at cost reduction or employee exploitation). The former have a positive effect on employees' attitudes and behaviors, and the latter a negative effect. This implies that it matters not only what is implemented (content) but also how it is implemented (process). These insights underscore the importance of managers' behaviors in relation to their employees.

This view on the importance of managers in shaping employee understandings of general systems is also increasingly prominent in the leadership literature. In a study of the implementation of a general management system in Danish schools, Mikkelsen et al. (2015) found that the school principals' actions were decisive for employee perceptions of the system. If the principals used a command and control style of implementation rather than dialogue and suggestions, the teachers were much more likely to see the management system as a means for control rather than for professional support. This was important because teachers who perceived the management system as control also had significantly lower intrinsic motivation to comply with the system. Hence, these findings support the expectation that leader behavior affects employee motivation (specifically, crowding out intrinsic motivation) when general systems are being implemented. Andersen et al. (2018) also show that school leaders' use of verbal rewards can generate understanding and acceptance among teachers for a general reform. Thus, in the implementation of a nationwide reform, the study finds that the principals' use of verbal rewards is positively associated with the teachers' perception that the government initiative is supportive rather than controlling.

3.6 The Importance of Intended Policy as Well as Its Implementation and Perception

Both organizations and individual managers/leaders engage in a number of practices meant to increase goal attainment. However, their intentions do not always result in goal attainment. Wright and Nishii (2013) developed a model for implementing

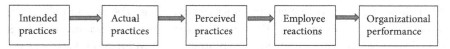

Figure 3.1 Process model of HRM and leadership practices
Source: Based on Wright and Nishii (2013).

HRM that can help us understand why policies can fail to deliver on their promises. This model has also been used by leadership scholars (e.g. see Jacobsen and Andersen 2015).

The model is shown in Figure 3.1. At the outset is the intended practices. Any HR practice or leadership behavior begins with intentions and decisions, which are believed to effectively elicit the desired employee responses (Wright and Nishii 2013). The intended practices are typically both ambitious and idealized, and the practices are intended to solve actual problems. Intended practices are necessary for actual practices, but the actual practices delivered by managers are often likely to differ from how they were intended. Both leadership and HRM practices often face constraints of time, resistance, or scarce resources, which can lead to compromises or less ambitious or even different plans that depart from intentions (e.g. Knies and Leisink 2014; Van Waeyenberg and Decramer 2018). Next, the actual practices are received by members of the organization (i.e. perceived practices), who often differ in psychological profile, organizational experience, and professional background. Therefore, actual practices can be perceived differently by various observers within an organization. That is, actual practices are perceived and interpreted subjectively by each employee (Wright and Nishii 2013), and the effects of a given practice are likely to differ across members of the organization, even those supervised by the same manager. Furthermore, employees' perceptions are likely to differ from the intended practice in the sense that they, on average, perceive the practice differently from how it was actually intended. Employee perceptions of practices are important because they affect how employees respond to the practice. That is, employees are likely to react to a practice based on what they think it is and not what it actually is. If a leader engages in visionary leadership and the employee does not understand or accept the vision, the employee is not likely to respond to it. Employee reactions are ultimately important because employee inputs are a vital factor in most public service organizations. Especially in people-changing organizations (compared to people-processing organizations), such as schools and hospitals, the delivered services are highly reliant on employees' actions, which are therefore also decisive for performance.

The model by Wright and Nishii (2013) is a generic model outlining the mechanisms that link formal policies to organizational performance. Although originally developed by scholars who are mainly interested in HRM in the private sector, the model can also be applied to a public sector context (Knies et al. 2018a), although it might need some contextualization to fit the distinctive context of the public sector. Based on the model by Wright and Nishii, Vandenabeele et al. (2013, 48) developed a model entitled "public value creation," which can serve as a contextualized alternative for the general HRM value chain. This model creates a bridge between the public management discipline, on the one hand, and the HRM discipline, on the other, by building on the HRM process model (Wright and Nishii 2013), the notions of public value (Moore 1995), public values (Beck Jørgensen and Bozeman 2007), and institutional theory (Scott 1995), among others.

The model has also been used to describe how leadership is planned, enacted, and perceived in public organizations (Jacobsen and Andersen 2015). In relation to leadership, the difference between intended and perceived practices has mainly been studied in the framework of self–other agreement (Yammarino and Atwater 1997). Although there is some discussion whether leader self-ratings reflect intended or self-perceived leadership—i.e. whether they are based on planned or enacted leadership—the model is useful for understanding discrepancies between what leaders think they do, when they exert leadership, and how their leadership is picked up by others, particularly their employees. Empirical studies suggest that leaders generally over-rate their own leadership relative to employees, but the studies also confirm the importance of the relationship between leader and employee ratings. If leaders rate their leadership much higher than their employees do, it signals low levels of self-awareness and ability to deliver leadership. In contrast, leaders can agree with their employees about leadership but only if there is agreement that the leader is actually performing as a leader and is expected to improve employee and organizational outcomes (Yammarino and Atwater 1997).

Leader self-reports have been widely applied in studies of public leaders, but recent studies find that follower-reported leadership practices are more closely related to organizational outcomes such as performance than intended or actual/implemented practices are. In a study of upper secondary schools in Denmark, Jacobsen and Andersen (2015) find only weak correlations between leadership ratings made by principals and teachers. They also find that only teacher-perceived leadership is positively correlated with organizational performance (school value added to final grades). Favero et al. (2016) investigated 1,100 New York schools and found that employee-rated leadership is closely related to organizational performance. These findings are in line with the Wright and Nishii (2013) model and highlight the fact that leadership is much more effective when it is visible to frontline employees who deliver services. However, the leadership literature is sparse in terms of explaining when and how leadership is successfully transmitted to employees—i.e. how intentions are transformed into actual leadership, and when actual leadership is visible to employees.

In the HRM literature, Wright and Nishii's (2013) model is the guiding conceptual framework for many studies. However, empirical research on intended, implemented, and perceived practices and links between these three elements in particular "is still in its infancy" (Piening et al. 2014, 546). While employee perceptions are being studied, they are often isolated from intended or implemented HR practices. Yet empirical research provides us with two important insights. First, various studies have shown that there are indeed gaps between intended, implemented, and perceived HR practices. For example, Zhu et al. (2013) show that there are "alignment issues between managers and employees with regard to HR practices," specifically related to their knowledge of HR practices, their experiences with HR practices, and their perceptions of HR effectiveness. Managers tend to be more positive than the employees they supervise (see also Knies 2012). As in the leadership literature, Makhecha et al. (2018) found a weak relationship between manager-rated and employee-rated HR systems. The second conclusion that can be drawn from empirical studies is that HR practices only bring about the desired employee outcomes and result in performance when they are consistently experienced by employees in intended ways (Kehoe and Wright 2013; Khilji and Wang 2006). To put it differently: Employee perceptions matter. These findings highlight that it is important to make a distinction between intended, implemented, and perceived practices and that rhetoric and reality can be two different things.

Contrary to the leadership literature, there are some HRM studies that provide provisional insights into the question of how intended HR practices are turned into implemented and perceived HR practices (Makhecha et al. 2018; Piening et al. 2014). Piening et al. (2014) studied the gaps and linkages between intended, implemented, and perceived HR practices in the context of health and social services organizations. They were particularly interested in the mechanisms underlying the relationships between the three different elements. More specifically, they sought to identify the conditions under which congruency between intended, implemented, and perceived HR practices occurs.

In their results, the authors distinguish between an implementation gap (between intended and implemented HR practices) and an interpretation gap (between implemented and perceived HR practices). They found that organizational ability to leverage resources is crucial in translating intended into implemented HR practices. This refers to "the extent to which an organization is able to configure its financial, structural, and personnel resources to form HR capabilities that support the implementation of HRM" (Piening et al. 2014, 557). A necessary condition for translating intended into implemented HR practices is the need for agreement among HR decision makers about the intended HR practices. Regarding the interpretation gap, they found that employees' expectations regarding HRM play an essential role in the link between implemented and perceived HR practices. Employees form expectations about their organization's intentions based on previous experiences with HR practices in the organization. This implies that lower employee expectations are the result of lower organizational investments in the past. High expectations increase the importance of HR practice implementation for shaping employees' perceptions.

Makhecha et al. (2018) conducted a similar study into the gaps between intended, implemented, and perceived practices in a private sector context (a hypermarket chain). The authors found that the gap between intended and implemented HR practices is the result of the different adaption of HR practices by implementers, such as managers, regarding content, process, and intent. That is, managers are active agents who shape the implemented HR practices according to their own ideas.

According to Makhecha et al. (2018), the gap between implemented and perceived HR practices is shaped by the delivery of HR practices by managers, on the one hand, and by employees' own abilities and motives, on the other. An important element highlighted in their research is the "intent perspective." Both managers and employees have ideas about the intent behind HR practices (either intended or implemented). These ideas influence their perceptions of practices, and as a result, shape their responses to it. This mechanism links to the concept of HR attributions, which suggests that employees make assumptions about the reason why management adopts certain HR practices, and these assumptions have consequences for employees' attitudes and behaviors (Nishii et al. 2008).

3.7 Conclusion

HRM and leadership are central concepts and are closely related in the understanding of people management. However, as research topics, they are rarely integrated, and respective lines of research have developed along parallel lines. Both bodies of literature increasingly see the importance of managerial behaviors directed internally for goal attainment. In the HRM literature, the importance of HRM implementation has been increasingly recognized. A parallel understanding is emerging in the public management literature, but the empirical evidence primarily comes from HRM studies. The internal focus has received attention in the public leadership literature as well, and while public leaders have traditionally been regarded as burdened, restrained, and poorly incentivized to lead, recent studies underline their importance for creating value for society and citizens. One line of research emphasizes that the strategies of individual leaders matter, whereas another line of research stresses that concerted leadership efforts matter for the success or failure of public service provision. In future studies, internal management needs to receive more systematic research attention in the public management literature. One way to begin this research agenda is to gain insights from the HRM literature, where questions of internal management have been extensively studied in recent years. Furthermore, studies need to develop stronger theories about *public* leadership, which takes the specific characteristics of public organizations at various levels into consideration.

Another insight from the literature is that managers at different hierarchical levels have an impact on goal attainment. However, top-level and lower-level managers have different responsibilities when it comes to leadership and HRM, and this could be acknowledged more clearly in the literature. Current studies tend to use a "one-size-fits-all" approach to studying both leadership and HRM, although the challenges confronting top-level and frontline managers—and the tasks they perform—are very different. Understanding HRM and leadership practices requires theories that specify the various contexts and tasks in more detail. There is great potential for increased research attention on lower-level managers (frontline and middle managers) since they often have different understandings and approaches to implementing

HR practices compared with top-level managers, and their impact on how leadership and HRM are realized in service provision seems undeniable. At the same time, we call for better understandings of how people management at lower levels is shaped by the individual manager's characteristics and demands from both superiors and the recipients of services.

Another insight is that there is a close relationship between leadership and HRM, which can be thought of as two sides of the same coin. The best outcomes (e.g. goal attainment) will be realized when HR policies are well designed and implemented by competent and motivated leaders (Purcell and Hutchinson 2007). This has been shown in the few studies that focus on both HRM and leadership, but more studies are needed to derive theories about the mutual dependencies between HRM and leadership. The study of people management can benefit from a better integration of the leadership and HRM bodies of literature, which have too long been regarded as separate topics.

Finally, it has been shown that in relation to both leadership and HRM, it is important to make a distinction between intended, implemented, and perceived practices. Research within both fields shows that there is typically an immense difference between how HRM and leadership are intended, how these are practiced, and how these are perceived by employees. Moreover, employee perceptions affect a range of outcomes such as employee well-being and organizational performance. This insight is important because in labor-intensive production processes, HRM and leadership depend on how employees perceive their practices. If employees see leadership or HRM much less positively than how it was intended, they are likely to show limited response, and if they perceive them as negative, they may act counter to what was intended. More research is needed into the question of when and how leadership and HRM are successfully transmitted to employees, how intentions are transformed into actual behavior, and how leadership and HRM become visible to employees.

Based on existing knowledge about HRM and leadership at different levels in public organizations, the literature can also offer important advice for the practice of people management. First, internal management should be high on the agenda in public organizations because both HRM and leadership studies find that although the external environment is demanding for public organizations, attention to internal aspects more directly shapes employee and organizational outcomes. Also, managers on different levels (but particularly lower-level managers) need to be selected, appraised, trained, and the like with their people management role in mind. The best people managers are those who are able and motivated to perform their people management responsibilities and are not necessarily the best professionals, who are often promoted to managerial positions. Finally, since employee perceptions influence employee attitudes and behaviors, it is important to monitor their experiences regarding leadership and HRM on a continuous basis. This provides input for evidence-based management, which is likely to make a difference for society and users.

References

Andersen, L. B., S. Boye, and R. Laursen. 2018. "Building Support? The Importance of Verbal Rewards for Employee Perceptions of Governance Initiatives." *International Public Management Journal 21* (1): pp. 1–32.

Barney, J. 1991. "Firm Resources and Sustained Competitive Advantage." *Journal of Management 17* (1): pp. 99–120.

Beck Jørgensen, T., and B. Bozeman. 2007. "Public Values: An Inventory." *Administration and Society 39* (3): pp. 354–81.

Bellé, N. 2014. "Leading to Make a Difference: A Field Experiment on the Performance Effects of Transformational Leadership, Perceived Social Impact, and Public Service Motivation." *Journal of Public Administration Research and Theory 24* (1): pp. 109–36.

Boselie, P., G. Dietz, and C. Boon. 2005. "Commonalities and Contradictions in HRM and Performance Research." *Human Resource Management Journal 15* (3): pp. 67–94.

Boxall, P., and J. Purcell. 2011. *Strategy and Human Resource Management*. 3rd ed. Basingstoke: Palgrave Macmillan.

Boyne, G. 2002. "Public and Private Management: What's the Difference?" *Journal of Management Studies 39* (1): pp. 97–122.

Boyne, G., M. Poole, and G. Jenkins. 1999. "Human Resource Management in the Public and Private Sectors: An Empirical Comparison." *Public Administration 77* (2): pp. 407–20.

Bozeman, B. 1987. *All Organizations Are Public: Bridging Public and Private Organizational Theories*. San Francisco, CA: Jossey-Bass.

Brewster, C., M. Brookes, and P. J. Gollan. 2015. "The Institutional Antecedents of the Assignment of HRM Responsibilities to Line Managers." *Human Resource Management 54* (4): pp. 577–97.

Combs, J., Y. Liu, A. Hall, and D. Ketchen. 2006. "How Much Do High-Performance Work Practices Matter? A Meta-Analysis of Their Effects on Organizational Performance." *Personnel Psychology 59* (3): pp. 501–28.

Crosby, B., and J. M. Bryson. 2014. "Public Integrative Leadership." In *The Oxford Handbook of Leadership and Organizations*, edited by D. V. Day, pp. 57–72. Oxford: Oxford University Press.

Farndale, E., J. Paauwe, and P. Boselie. 2010. "An Exploratory Study of Governance in the Intra-Firm Human Resources Supply Chain." *Human Resource Management 49* (5): pp. 849–68.

Favero, N., K. Meier, and L. O'Toole. 2016. "Goals, Trust, Participation, and Feedback: Linking Internal Management with Performance Outcomes." *Journal of Public Administration Research and Theory 26* (2): pp. 327–43.

Fernandez, S., Y. Cho, and J. Perry. 2010. "Exploring the Link between Integrated Leadership and Public Sector Performance." *The Leadership Quarterly 21* (2): pp. 308–22.

Graen, G. B., and M. Uhl-Bien. 1995. "Relationship-Based Approach to Leadership: Development of Leader–Member Exchange (LMX) Theory of Leadership over 25

Years: Applying a Multi-Level Multi-Domain Perspective." *The Leadership Quarterly 6* (2): pp. 219–47.

Gratton, L., and C. Truss. 2003. "The Three-Dimensional People Strategy: Putting Human Resources Policies into Action." *Academy of Management Perspectives 17* (3): pp. 74–86.

Guest, D. E. 1987. "Human Resource Management and Industrial Relations." *Journal of Management Studies 24* (5): pp. 503–21.

Guest, D. E. 1997. "Human Resource Management and Performance: A Review and Research Agenda." *The International Journal of Human Resource Management 8* (3): pp. 263–76.

Guest, D. E. 2007. "HRM: Towards a New Psychological Contract?" In *The Oxford Handbook of Human Resource Management*, edited by P. Boxall, J. Purcell, and P. Wright, pp. 128–46. Oxford: Oxford University Press.

Guest, D. E. 2011. "Human Resource Management and Performance: Still Searching for Some Answers." *Human Resource Management Journal 21* (1): pp. 3–13.

Guest, D. E., and A. Bos-Nehles. 2013. "HRM and Performance: The Role of Effective Implementation." In *HRM and Performance: Achievements and Challenges*, edited by J. Paauwe, D. Guest, and P. Wright, pp. 79–96. Chichester: Wiley.

Hansen, J. R., and A. Villadsen. 2010. "Comparing Public and Private Managers' Leadership Styles: Understanding the Role of Job Context." *International Public Management Journal 13* (3): pp. 247–74.

Huselid, M. A. 1995. "The Impact of Human Resource Management Practices on Turnover, Productivity, and Corporate Financial Performance." *Academy of Management Journal 38* (3): pp. 635–72.

Jacobsen, C. B., and L. B. Andersen. 2015. "Is Leadership in the Eye of the Beholder? A Study of Intended and Perceived Leadership Practices and Organizational Performance." *Public Administration Review 75* (6): pp. 829–41.

Jensen, U. T., L. B. Andersen, L. L. Bro, A. Bøllingtoft, T. L. M. Eriksen, A. Holten, C. B. Jacobsen, J. Ladenburg, P. A. Nielsen, H. H. Salomonsen, N. Westergård-Nielsen, and A. Würtz. 2016. "Conceptualizing and Measuring Transformational and Transactional Leadership." *Administration & Society 51* (1): pp. 3–33.

Jiang, K., R. Takeuchi, and D. P. Lepak. 2013. "Where Do We Go from Here? New Perspectives on the Black Boxes in Strategic Human Resource Management Research." *Journal of Management Studies 50* (8): pp. 1448–80.

Kehoe, R. R., and P. M. Wright. 2013. "The Impact of High-Performance Human Resource Practices on Employees' Attitudes and Behaviors." *Journal of Management 39* (2): pp. 366–91.

Khilji, S. E., and X. Wang. 2006. "'Intended' and 'Implemented' HRM: The Missing Linchpin in Strategic Human Resource Management Research." *The International Journal of Human Resource Management 17* (7): pp. 1171–89.

Knies, E. 2012. "Meer waarde voor en door medewerkers: een longitudinale studie naar de antecedenten en effecten van peoplemanagement [Balanced Value Creation: A Longitudinal Study of the Antecedents and Effects of People Management]." Doctoral dissertation. Utrecht University, Utrecht, the Netherlands.

Knies, E., P. Boselie, J. Gould-Williams, and W. Vandenabeele. 2018a. "Strategic Human Resource Management and Public Sector Performance: Context Matters." *The International Journal of Human Resource Management*, pp. 1–13. https://doi.org/10.10 80/09585192.2017.1407088.

Knies, E., and P. Leisink. 2014. "Linking People Management and Extra-Role Behavior: Results of a Longitudinal Study." *Human Resource Management Journal 24* (1): pp. 57–76.

Knies, E., P. Leisink, and S. Kraus-Hoogeveen. 2018b. "Frontline Managers' Contribution to Mission Achievement: A Study of How People Management Affects Thoughtful Care." *Human Service Organizations: Management, Leadership & Governance 42* (2): pp. 166–84.

Knies, E., P. Leisink, and R. Van de Schoot. 2020. "People Management: Developing and Testing a Measurement Scale." *The International Journal of Human Resource Management 31* (6): pp. 705–36.

Larsen, H., and C. Brewster. 2003. "Line Management Responsibility for HRM: What Is Happening in Europe?" *Employee Relations 25* (3): pp. 228–44.

Makhecha, U. P., V. Srinivasan, G. N. Prabhu, and S. Mukherji. 2018. "Multi-Level Gaps: A Study of Intended, Actual and Experienced Human Resource Practices in a Hypermarket Chain in India." *The International Journal of Human Resource Management 29* (2): pp. 360–98.

Mikkelsen, M. F., C. B. Jacobsen, and L. B. Andersen. 2015. "Managing Employee Motivation: Exploring the Connections between Managers' Enforcement Actions, Employee Perceptions, and Employee Intrinsic Motivation." *International Public Management Journal 20* (2): pp. 183–205.

Moore, M. 1995. *Creating Public Value: Strategic Management in Government*. Cambridge, MA: Harvard University Press.

Moore, M., and S. Khagram. 2004. "On Creating Public Value: What Businesses Might Learn from Government about Strategic Management." Corporate Social Responsibility Initiative Working Paper No. 3. Harvard University, Cambridge, MA.

Nishii, L. H., D. P. Lepak, and B. Schneider. 2008. "Employee Attributions of the 'Why' of HR Practices: Their Effects on Employee Attitudes and Behaviors, and Customer Satisfaction." *Personnel Psychology 61* (3): pp. 503–45.

Oberfield, Z. W. 2014. "Public Management in Time: A Longitudinal Examination of the Full Range of Leadership Theory." *Journal of Public Administration Research and Theory 24* (2): pp. 407–29.

O'Leary, R., and N. Vij. 2012. "Collaborative Public Management: Where Have We Been and Where Are We Going?" *American Public Administration Review 42* (5): pp. 507–22.

Op de Beeck, S. 2016. "HRM Responsibilities in the Public Sector: The Role of Line Managers." Doctoral dissertation. Faculty of Social Sciences, KU Leuven, Leuven, Belgium.

Paauwe, J. 2004. *HRM and Performance: Achieving Long Term Viability*. Oxford: Oxford University Press.

Perry, E. L., and C. T. Kulik. 2008. "The Devolution of HR to the Line: Implications for Perceptions of People Management Effectiveness." *The International Journal of Human Resource Management 19* (2): pp. 262–73.

Perry, J. L., and H. G. Rainey. 1988. "The Public–Private Distinction in Organization Theory: A Critique and Research Strategy." *Academy of Management Review 13* (2): pp. 182–201.

Piening, E. P., A. M. Baluch, and H. G. Ridder. 2014. "Mind the Intended-Implemented Gap: Understanding Employees' Perceptions of HRM." *Human Resource Management 53* (4): pp. 545–67.

Purcell, J., and S. Hutchinson. 2007. "Frontline Managers as Agents in the HRM–Performance Causal Chain: Theory, Analysis and Evidence." *Human Resource Management Journal 17* (1): pp. 3–20.

Scott, W. R. 1995. *Institutions and Organizations*. Thousand Oaks, CA: Sage.

Stanton, P., S. Young, T. Bartram, and S. G. Leggat. 2010. "Singing the Same Song: Translating HRM Messages across Management Hierarchies in Australian Hospitals." *The International Journal of Human Resource Management 21* (4): pp. 567–81.

Trullen, J., L. Stirpe, J. Bonache, and M. Valverde. 2016. "The HR Department's Contribution to Line Managers' Effective Implementation of HR Practices." *Human Resource Management Journal 26* (4): pp. 449–70.

Tummers, L. G., and E. Knies. 2016. "Measuring Public Leadership: Developing Scales for Four Public Leadership Roles." *Public Administration 94* (2): pp. 433–51.

Vandenabeele, W. V., P. Leisink, and E. Knies. 2013. "Public Value Creation and Strategic Human Resource Management: Public Service Motivation as a Linking Mechanism." In *Managing Social Issues: A Public Values Perspective*, edited by P. Leisink, P. Boselie, M. Van Bottenburg, and D. M. Hosking, pp. 37–54. Cheltenham: Edward Elgar.

Van Waeyenberg, T., and A. Decramer. 2018. "Line Managers' AMO to Manage Employees' Performance: The Route to Effective and Satisfying Performance Management." *The International Journal of Human Resource Management 29* (2): pp. 3093–114.

Van Wart, M. 2013. "Administrative Leadership Theory: A Reassessment after 10 Years." *Public Administration 91* (3): pp. 521–43.

Vermeeren, B. 2014. "HRM Implementation and Performance in the Public Sector." Doctoral dissertation. Erasmus University Rotterdam, Rotterdam, the Netherlands.

Vogel, R., and D. Masal. 2015. "Public Leadership: A Review of the Literature and Framework for Future Research." *Public Management Review 17* (8): pp. 1165–89.

Whittaker, S., and M. Marchington. 2003. "Devolving HR Responsibility to the Line: Threat, Opportunity or Partnership?" *Employee Relations 25* (3): pp. 245–61.

Williams, I., and H. Shearer. 2011. "Appraising Public Value: Past, Present, and Futures." *Public Administration 89* (4): pp. 1367–84.

Wright, B. E., D. P. Moynihan, and S. K. Pandey. 2012. "Pulling the Levers: Transformational Leadership, Public Service Motivation, and Mission Valence." *Public Administration Review 72* (2): pp. 206–15.

Wright, P., and W. R. Boswell. 2002. "Desegregating HRM: A Review and Synthesis of Micro and Macro Human Resource Management Research." *Journal of Management 28* (3): pp. 247–76.

Wright, P., and L. H. Nishii. 2013. "Strategic HRM and Organizational Behavior: Integrating Multiple Levels of Analysis." In *HRM and Performance: Achievements and*

Challenges, edited by J. Paauwe, D. Guest, and P. Wright, pp. 97–110. Chichester: Wiley.

Yammarino, F., and L. Atwater. 1997. "Do Managers See Themselves as Others See Them? Implications of Self–Other Rating Agreement for Human Resource Management." *Organizational Dynamics 25* (4): pp. 35–44.

Yukl, G. 2013. *Leading in Organizations*. Harlow: Pearson.

Zhu, C. J., B. K. Cooper, D. Fan, and H. De Cieri. 2013. "HR Practices from the Perspective of Managers and Employees in Multinational Enterprises in China: Alignment Issues and Implications." *Journal of World Business 48* (2): pp. 241–50.

4

An Institutional Perspective on Public Services

Managing Publicness, Identities, and Behavior

Nina Van Loon and Wouter Vandenabeele

4.1 Introduction

If random individuals are asked to mention a public service, they will intuitively provide an answer. They may mention a police department or a municipality. However, the answer in some countries may be "hospital" or "school," while individuals from other parts of the world may argue these services are private. It may become even more confusing when these people start to argue about whether the organization should be part of the public *sector* or whether it should be an organization that is publicly *funded*. Others may argue that this is not important as long as the organization has a public *aim* or fulfills a societal *need*. This chapter aims to delineate what public service means in an organizational context. Moreover, we discuss how publicness and the differences between public services can influence the behavior of organizational members.

Section 4.2 will first provide an overview of various perspectives of publicness. We will frame publicness as an important institutional characteristic of public institutions and discuss how to distinguish public from private organizations. Then, this differentiation in perspectives of publicness is not only applied to distinguish between public and non-public institutions but also to distinguish between public institutions themselves. Next, we will discuss the institutional dynamics and how individual characteristics and behavior can be meshed with institutional features. Here, concepts of identity and fit play an important role. In Section 4.4, the framework that has been developed illustrates the relevance of institutions as a crucial contextual element which influences behavior within a public service organization. Finally, in Section 4.5, practical and research implications of our institutional perspective are discussed.

Nina Van Loon and Wouter Vandenabeele, *An Institutional Perspective on Public Services: Managing Publicness, Identities, and Behavior* In: *Managing for Public Service Performance: How People and Values Make a Difference*. Edited by: Peter Leisink, Lotte B. Andersen, Gene A. Brewer, Christian B. Jacobsen, Eva Knies, and Wouter Vandenabeele, Oxford University Press (2021). © Nina Van Loon and Wouter Vandenabeele. DOI: 10.1093/oso/9780192893420.003.0004

4.2   A Multidimensional Perspective on Publicness

Despite the intuitive answers of individuals regarding what public services are, distinguishing public from private is complicated as, first, publicness should be seen as a multidimensional concept, and second, what is seen as public is context-dependent.

When asked to define a public service, it is likely that individuals refer to different criteria. For example, one may point to the ownership of the organization, distinguishing between governmental or private ownership (Bozeman 1987). Others may point to the source of funding and argue that organizations that are not owned but fully subsidized by the government should also be seen as public (Bozeman 1987; Rainey 2009). Another argument may be based on the mission of the organization when one argues that if an organization aims to contribute to society, it must be a public service (Antonsen and Beck Jørgensen 1997; Bozeman 2007). In the literature, multiple dimensions feature to determine the publicness of services, such as ownership, funding, or values. These dimensions relate to different aspects of the institutional nature of services (March and Olsen 1989; Scott 2001). Here, we use institutional theory to explain the complexity of defining public service.

Institutions consist of elements such as rules and norms, which shape routines, common practices, and shared meanings, and can be seen as relatively persisting phenomena (Scott 2001). Institutions can be seen as social phenomena that regulate, and to a certain extent, standardize behavior (March and Olsen 1989). We can distinguish between structural, normative, and cultural–cognitive elements of institutions (Scott 2001). Rules but also buildings are examples of structural elements as they provide structure to the institution. For example, a church and its rules form important elements of the Catholic institution. Normative elements are values and expectations. In that same Catholic institution, priests are expected to remain unmarried and devote their life entirely to the church. Such normative elements are often less visible but can, nevertheless, play an important part in determining the behavior of individuals (Perry 2000; Thornton and Ocasio 2008). Finally, cultural–cognitive elements are, for example, beliefs and symbols. Bringing it back to the Catholic Church again, the crucifix is an important and powerful symbol, but so are many other symbols which illustrate the underlying values. Institutions can, hence, have many different forms and arise at various levels of life.

An important feature of institutions is that they are relatively resistant to change. This can be attributed to the self-reinforcing mechanisms found in institutions, which strive to maintain points of punctuated equilibria (Krasner 1984). These are starting points of a long period of stability, and this is what institutions strive for through various mechanisms. Mahoney (2000) identified four of such mechanisms: (1) a balance of power that favors the current institutional make-up; (2) the existence of legitimacy for institutional practices; (3) a favorable cost–benefit balance

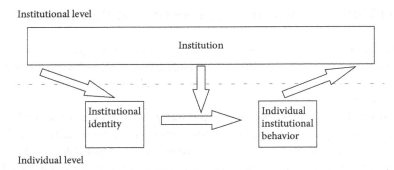

Figure 4.1 Institutional dynamics at the individual and institutional level

(it would entail more costs than benefits to induce change); and (4) the functionality of practices. Disrupting any of these will open a window of opportunity for change, and conversely, if not disrupted, great change will not occur, explaining why institutions are often more persistent than expected.

Individuals interact with many different institutions on a daily basis. These institutions structure their behavior, and at the same time, individuals form and constantly reshape those same institutions. For instance, political structures determine how individuals behave, but with each electoral cycle, this political structure can be adjusted or changed by citizens (March and Olsen 1989; Thornton and Ocasio 2008). When we try to describe the influence of institutions on individuals, we can look at the *institutional context* of particular individuals, which is comprised of all institutions with which these individuals interact. Within the literature, some scholars focus on macro-level institutions, such as countries or political systems. Others focus on societal values and groups at the meso-level. Here, we focus on the micro-level of institutions, which entails interaction between institutions and individual behaviors (see Figure 4.1). The institutional environment stretches over various levels, ranging from macro to micro-institutions, all of which are interdependently interconnected and influence one another.

Looking at the institutional context raises the thorny issue of the concept of context itself. Different traditions in management and public management take the role of context into account in varying ways. By determining the expectations, rules, routines, and norms, the institutional context influences the behavior of an individual (Greenwood et al. 2010; Scott 2001; Thornton and Ocasio 2008). This is the perspective taken here, and it offers a different conceptualization of context than Johns' (2006) and also a broader one than what has been customary in other traditions in public management (O'Toole and Meier 2015; Pollitt and Bouckaert 2004; see also Chapter 1). Our conceptualization combines various insights, as we will explain. This will allow us to provide more insights into the actual dynamics of leadership, management, and performance in public service organizations.

4.2.1 Approaches to Publicness Seen from an Institutional Perspective

Various public administration scholars have aimed to disentangle the concept of publicness as an institutional characteristic of public services. We will use the institutional perspective to discuss several main approaches that aid us in understanding the nature of public services.

Bozeman (1987) boldly claimed that *all organizations are public*, arguing that each organization is funded, owned, or controlled by society to a certain extent. Even the most private companies are regulated by public authority and rules and are often partly dependent on public funding (e.g. for research or innovation) to survive. Moreover, he argues that there are many private organizations that fulfill a societal need. He argues that it is, therefore, impossible to regard publicness or privateness as a dichotomy. Instead, publicness should be seen as a multidimensional concept. Three dimensions are distinguished.

First, ownership, which can be private, governmental, and many different forms in-between such as non-profit foundations or public–private partnerships. Second, publicness is determined by the degree to which the organization depends on public funding. Schools may be privately owned but fully funded by government, as is the case in the Netherlands. According to Bozeman (1987), such a dependency on public funds makes it likely that these services will be subject to societal pressures to a higher degree than organizations that are funded privately. Third, the degree to which organizations are controlled by public authority determines the publicness of the organization (Haque 2001; Koppenjan 2005). In the US, some prison facilities have been privatized, but they are still subject to strict public regulation. Hence, according to Bozeman (1987), we should speak of organizations providing public services that differ in degree of publicness based on their ownership, funding, and public authority. In his analysis, Bozeman (1987; 2007) focuses on what we would call structural elements of institutions as determining the publicness of organizations. He focuses on the organizational characteristics and regulatory elements of organizations that make them more or less public. This perspective leads to the conclusion that an organization or service can be seen as public when it is publicly funded, publicly owned, and subject to public authority to a high degree.

Antonsen and Beck Jørgensen (1997) take a different approach by focusing on the values that define publicness, thereby focusing on normative and cultural–cognitive elements that shape the publicness of services (Beck Jørgensen and Bozeman 2007; Moynihan et al. 2011; Rainey and Bozeman 2000). From a cultural–cognitive perspective, publicness is about the values that an organization relates to and the mission of the organization. Publicness is about whether the organization plays a role in upholding important public values such as equity, legitimacy, and responsiveness (Antonsen and Beck Jørgensen 1997). Beck Jørgensen and

Bozeman (2007) distinguish various categories of public values (see Chapter 2). For example, there are public values relating to a public administration's contribution to the public good and regarding the relationship with citizens, which includes responsiveness. From the perspective of public values as the most important driver of publicness, organizational ownership or authority (economic or political) is not relevant. It is the values the organization stands for that determine whether it can be characterized as a public service. This means that companies that are entirely private from a structural perspective can be public when they adhere to public values.

A final perspective on publicness can be derived from the public value framework. This framework derives publicness from the impact of an organization on society (Moore 1995). Public organizations should focus on the impact they have or want to have on society and ask themselves if they have legitimacy and support for their mission as well as the capabilities to reach it. A crucial role has been reserved in this process for public managers, who are the prime actors in creating public value, obtaining legitimacy with the authorizing environment, and building capacity to obtain results (see Chapter 2).

Each of these approaches provides a different focus on how to distinguish publicness. All of these are grounded in an institutional perspective, zooming in on different institutional components (structure, mission, or values, respectively, and function or impact). Although these elements of the institutional context are almost a given, institutions are not a given but can change: Routines can be altered, and values can evolve (Scott 2001). What is seen as public service is dynamic in time and place as we can see differences between countries and eras in what is considered a public service. Before the twentieth century, healthcare was considered a private service in many countries, relying on charitable foundations or upper-class citizens to provide these services to poor people unable to pay for them. After a period of expanding welfare states in which healthcare was a public service, we can now see a development toward the privatization of healthcare services. Other services that were seen as typically public until recently, such as postal services or telecom, have been privatized in various countries (Haque 2001). On the other hand, for years, banks have been claiming that they were not providing public services, but when the context changed and the Great Financial Crisis evolved, some banks proved too big to fail and were considered to be public from a structural perspective at least. These examples show that public services are not a stable phenomenon: Societies think differently over time regarding whether services are public. The line between public and private has, over the years, also become more fluid due to public–private partnerships, privatization, and private companies such as social enterprises aiming to contribute to society (Moynihan et al. 2011; Rainey and Bozeman 2000). Moreover, there are large differences between countries regarding what they see as public. Whereas hospital services are part of the public sector in some countries, they are not in other countries. While schools are public organizations in many Nordic countries, they are private in the Netherlands and the US (albeit fully publicly funded).

Hence, when referring to public services, this should always be placed within a specific time and place.

This section has shown how scholars have different perspectives on publicness and public services. It shows that what is a public service is context-dependent, heavily influenced by the institutional environment. However, we have provided some insight into institutional elements that play a role in determining publicness. This can be used to describe and analyze the public nature of specific services.

4.3 Differences in Publicness between Public Services

The discussion above shows that because of multiple foci, of which often only one is taken into account, much ambiguity exists with regard to the concepts of public sector or public service. Even within what would be considered the public sector or public services, major differences can be found between organizations. For example, would we argue that schools and government agencies are similar? When we speak of the public sector or public services in too general terms, this conceals the amalgam or patchwork of organizations that these broad terms actually entail. Public service organizations share certain similarities but are also distinct in several important ways (Perry and Rainey 1988; Rainey 2009). Below, the same foci as above are applied to examine the institutional characteristic of publicness further.

A first important difference between public services is the degree of public authority to which they are subject. Whether public service organizations are under scrutiny not only depends on the nature of the service but also on the political climate or even the salience of the service in society at a given moment. For example, the relative autonomy of schools can suddenly be limited when a major scandal with spending public funds is discovered. An organization that is scrutinized thoroughly will likely be subject to stronger institutional forces determining behavior within the organization (Haque 2001).

Second, public services differ in the values to which they adhere (Antonsen and Beck Jørgensen 1997). For example, penitentiary services may place less emphasis on responsiveness to clients than schools. Differences in mission between organizations in a public sector may matter for how they steer or direct the behavior of employees (Van Loon 2017).

Third, the nature of the service may differ between organizations that are publicly owned, funded, or controlled. Some organizations aim to regulate, while others aim to provide services (Kjeldsen 2014; Van Loon et al. 2013). Hasenfeld (1983) distinguished between people-changing and people-processing organizations. People-changing organizations need to build long-term relationships with clients and aim to change the clients they serve. For example, both schools and prisons (in many countries) aim to change the individuals that enter the organization (Hasenfeld 1983; Kjeldsen 2014). People-processing organizations, on the other hand, do not aim to change their clients but change their *status*. They have more single-shot contacts, such as when citizens apply for a construction permit. These are ideal-types and many organizations will be a mix between the two. Municipalities, for example, have some tasks resembling a processing service and others a changing service. However, a dominant nature can often be identified. The processing or changing nature of organizations matters for the way the work is organized and which values and norms are imposed on employees (Van Loon et al. 2015).

4.4   The Relationship between Public Service and Public Service Identities

The interplay of various institutions eventually determines the guise of a public service. This is only the start of our perspective on the role of institutions and their characteristics. The analysis has, until here, focused on the institutional level, but as said before, institutions are constantly being reproduced by individual members (Thornton and Ocasio 2008). Therefore, it is important to also bring the individual level into the equation as an important actor influencing public service.

4.4.1.   Individual Behavior: Institutional Rather Than Rational

In contemporary Western culture, individual liberties seemingly contradict the idea of institutionalized individual behavior, in particular when thinking about behavior in public institutions. Popular conviction has always been that people pursue their own self-interest, be it in business, love, or public affairs. A widespread assumption is that people rationally calculate what is in it for them and subsequently act accordingly (also described as the "economic man"). Nowadays, reference is often made to millennials as being narcissistic (Twenge et al. 2008), but earlier, entire behavioral models were developed assuming that humans were completely rational when deciding on a course of action. A prime example of such an approach is Vroom's (1964) expectancy theory of motivating behavior that stated that people calculate the utility of an action based on its valence (or the value they would attribute to it), rendering a preferred course of action.

However, the presumption that people behave based on rational expectations is as flawed as is the presumption of millennials being narcissistic (Roberts et al. 2010). In fact, the general assumption of the dominance of rational behavior—understood as calculating a course of action based on available alternatives and other sources of information, such as the probability of future events and possible outcomes (Simon 1955)—is more often than not debunked by scientific insights. Simon (1997) developed the term "bounded rationality" for this observation. An important part of the explanation for bounded rationality comes from the psychology of irrationality (Simon 1997), characterized by the predominance of intuition over other types of cognition, the limited processing capacity of human cognition, and other types of cognitive biases (later further developed by Kahneman et al. 2011; Thaler and Sunstein 2009). However, Simon (1997, 111) also pointed to institutions as important sources determining individual behavior: "Human rationality gets its higher goals...from the institutional setting in which it operates and by which it is molded." March and Olsen (1989) have described this as "the logic of appropriateness." According to them, "to act appropriately is to proceed according to the institutionalized practices of a collectivity, based on mutual, and often tacit understandings of what is true, reasonable, natural, right, and good" (March and Olsen 2004, 479). This explains the individual behavior in an institutional environment rather than the "logic of consequence," on which the stereotype of the "economic man" and its rational behavior is based.

4.4.2 Explaining the Mechanism behind Identities and Institutional Behavior

Moving between the institutional and the individual level to unravel the process from institutions to individual behavior, we require a concept that has clear links with both levels. One such concept is "identity" which refers to one's internalized positional designations (Stryker 1980). There is a plethora of interchangeable or related terms such as "self," "self-concept," "social identity," and "role identity." The concept of identity and other related terms have the idea in common that they refer to some kind of socially constructed perception of how one sees oneself in a particular institutionalized situation. On the one hand, this causes identity to be an important explanation of various kinds of individual behavior in institutional situations ("who am I as a child, a parent, an employee, a citizen; and what are the associated values and goals?"). On the other hand, institutions play an important role in forming identities through internalization or socialization (Berger and Luckman [1966] 1991). In this, the concept of identity acts as a bridge between the institutional environment and the reflexive individual and their individual behavior. Figure 4.1 illustrates the dynamics at the institutional and individual level.

The process of socialization (from the perspective of the institution) or internalization (from the perspective of the individual) can be observed from various viewpoints. Socialization into institutional identities partly takes place by responding to the expectations of others (Stryker 1980). In this way, every interaction in a structured or institutional environment is socialization, and it is an ever-continuing process. By taking the role of others through using common symbols or language—carriers of institutions (Scott 2001)—one gets socialized into a particular identity. This "altercasting" (Stryker 1957) transfers the logic of the institution to the individual member, helping the individual to understand what is being expected as a member of that particular institution and internalizing it.

However, not all internalization is equally successful. Ryan and Deci (2012) distinguish between various types of identities, ranging from an externally regulated identity—in which only the necessary information instrumental for operating in a particular institution to reap the benefits of that institution is internalized—over an introjected identity—in which the information for institutional approval is internalized—to an identified identity—in which the logic of an institution is internalized to the extent that this becomes a matter of personal importance. A particular type of identity is an integrated one, which involves that various identities are assimilated reciprocally such that they are all aligned. The degree of internalization depends on the extent to which the basic psychological needs of relatedness (belonging to an environment), autonomy (minimal external control), and competence (conveying information of success) are provided by the institutional environment (Ryan and Deci 2012). Gagné (2003) provides a compelling example in which female gymnasts' identity was leaning more toward identification if their coaches were autonomy supportive, but conversely displayed a more externally regulated identity if their coaches were seen as controlling. This illustrates that one's identity as an institutional member not only depends on the logic of the institution but also on the extent to which an institution provides satisfaction for one's basic psychological needs.

Once internalized to a certain degree, individuals will act upon their institutional identities and consequently behave according to the logic of appropriateness. As a general rule, the values and goals incorporated in a given identity will increase the probability of related behavior. Multiple theories (Ajzen 2005; Bandura 1986; Stryker 1980, to name but a few) posit that internal standards of some sort lead to associated behavior by means of self-regulation, without external pressure or rewards. However, several factors influence how strong this effect will be.

A first set of factors relates to formal characteristics of the identity. The degree of internalization matters substantially. Applying the terminology of self-determination theory (Ryan and Deci 2012), more autonomous types of identities (identification) will demonstrate a stronger link with behavior as opposed to controlled types of identities (externally regulated or introjected). However, it is not only the type of internationalization but also its saliency that determines its impact on behavior (Stryker 1980). The higher placed in the salience hierarchy, the more often an identity will be used as a reference for behavior.

A second set of factors has more to do with the environment in which prospective behavior is to take place. A core tenet of institutional analysis of individual behavior is that the institutional environment is key to what kind of behavior is expected. After all, the logic of appropriateness is limited to the particular institution for which the specified behavior is appropriate. A police officer first and foremost behaves as a police officer when in uniform. Police officers outside their institutional environment may be seen as showing certain—stereotypical—behavior attributed to their "police personality" (such as being overly strict as a parent or having a "bossy" or "tough" nature among friends). The relatively greatest likelihood of finding a police officer behaving like one will be within the boundaries of the related institution.

The explanatory mechanism for this observation lies with the theory of person–environment fit (P–E fit). This is an amalgam of related theories that explains behavior by means of the interaction between the individual characteristics and the environment (Kristof-Brown et al. 2005). Fit is defined as "the congruence, match, similarity, or correspondence between the person and the environment" (Edwards and Shipp 2007, 211). This could be either supplementary fit, referring to similarities between the individual and its environment in terms of values or goals, or complementary fit, when "a weakness or need of the environment is offset by the strength of the individual and vice versa" (Muchinsky and Monahan 1987, 271). The effect of identities on institutional behavior is mainly explained by means of supplementary fit. In any work organization, this could either be fit with the organization in general (person–organization fit), fit with the supervisor or leader (person–supervisor fit), or fit with the team (person–team fit). Such fit is substantially correlated with, for example, job performance or reduced turnover (Hoffman and Woehr 2006; Kristof-Brown et al. 2005; Verquer et al. 2003). Although person–environment fit theory focuses on the organizational context, it is easy to see an analogy with non-"work organization" types of institutions where supplementary fit leads to behavior that is appropriate for a given institutional context, such as in church. However, the multitude of identities and institutions individuals are involved in opens up the possibility of misfit and value conflict between the individual and a given institution. Integrated identities or highly salient but non-fitting identities could cause an individual not to match with the environment in any way. Apart from possible coercive measures from the side of the institution, this will also have a self-regulatory effect as it causes frustration and counterproductive behavior. There are many different types of misfit possible, and these are likely to have different consequences for individual behavior (Edwards 2008).

4.4.3 Behavior in Public Institutions: Management of Individual Behavior as a Link

Public institutions, and in particular public organizations, shape and guide behavior. According to Simon,

> Administrative organizations cannot perhaps claim the same importance as repositories of the fundamental human values as that possessed by older traditional institutions like the family. Nevertheless, with man's growing economic interdependence, and with his growing dependence on the community for essential government services, formal organization is rapidly assuming a role of broader significance than it has ever before possessed. (Simon 1997, 111)

Public institutions can give rise to different identities and behaviors, for example, a soldier's almost physical reaction—such as increased heartbeat or arousal due to pride—when seeing the national flag or a uniform, but also the dress code or lack thereof of civil servants. The part of the self that is associated with public institutions is a complex amalgam. However, not all identity-related elements are of importance for management. Beer et al. (1984) identified different institutional subsystems that are important in managing human assets. For our analysis, four systems have been identified as relevant for management. They entail work systems, reward (or motivational) systems, (a system of) human resources flow, and (a system of) employee influence. These four can be considered sub-institutions at the intra-organizational level as they structure and constrain behavior within the organization. It is interesting to note that they have particular guises when it comes to public institutions.

Considering work systems, a typical governmental organization is depicted as a bureaucracy and has a number of identifying characteristics. Strong hierarchy, division of labor, high levels of formalism in terms of regulation, and written records have always been the trademark of bureaucracy (Weber 1978). Robert Merton (1939) noted early on that there was also an influence on civil servants' behavior, or as he termed it, "personality." He noted that civil servants often lacked flexibility or even demonstrated "trained incapacity" as a result of their membership of public bureaucracies. This has been attributed to "infusing group members with appropriate attitudes and sentiments ... [and] there are definite arrangements in the bureaucracy for inculcating and reinforcing these sentiments" (Merton 1939, 562–3). Although not all public organizations adhere to the ideal-type of the bureaucracy, elements of bureaucratic work systems are often associated with public organizations, for example, for reasons of public control, ownership, or funding. The point is that this sub-institution structures public servants' attitudes and behavior to fit the organization.

Another sub-institution concerns the HR workflow or how personnel and their individual careers are managed. Although various traditions and systems exist in the public sector (Pollitt and Bouckaert 2004), the common foundation is that of an ideal–typical bureaucracy where civil servants are employed for life (Weber 1978). Combined with a pyramidal organizational structure, this results in a career system that is rife with formal selection and promotion procedures. Georgellis et al. (2011) noted longer tenure for public sector employees. Houston (2011) demonstrated that this is not just an institutional arrangement but that government employees also exhibit higher levels of preference for a secure job. Whether this is a selection effect (Buelens and Van den Broeck 2007) or a socialization effect is of little importance as it clearly indicates that individual identity mirrors the institutional system of how human resources are managed. Even with public service bargains being reconsidered (Van der Meer et al. 2013), many traditional elements still remain in place in public organizations.

A third sub-institution of importance in Beer et al.'s (1984) framework is that of employee influence or the systems put in place to create participation. Public organizations have, in recent decades, put an elaborate system in place to ensure employee participation. Collective bargaining rights have been established (Nomden et al. 2003; Riccucci 2011) although these may be differently structured than in the private sector. At the same time, other systems of individual and collective participation were applied (Horton 2003). This is subsequently reflected in how individual behaviors adhere to the institutional arrangements. In the US, union membership steeply increased in the public sector following the acquisition of bargaining rights. Unionization rates in the public sector have been substantially higher in both the US and Europe compared to the private sector (BLS 2020; Scheuer 2011).

A final sub-institution is that of the rewards system, and by extension, the entire associated motivational system. Part of the rewards system concerns compensation aimed at providing extrinsic rewards. Traditionally, bureaucrats were paid a fixed salary in return for their services (Weber 1978). After their career, they received a state pension, which was usually higher than regular pensions. Various reforms tried to introduce more flexible pay systems, not always with great success (Perry et al. 1989; Willems et al. 2006) as public servants have less preference for performance-related pay (Houston 2000). Rewards, however, surpass mere compensation as its main aim is to motivate employees (Beer et al. 1984). This is where another type of public institutional identity, public service motivation, requires attention because it is an important reason why the rewards system and its aim to motivate public servants through financial incentives are problematic (Georgellis et al. 2011; see also Chapter 14).

Although its name refers to motivation, public service motivation has been conceived in such a way that it can be considered a public service identity (Perry and Vandenabeele 2008). First, given its definition as "an individual's predisposition to respond to motives grounded primarily or uniquely in public institutions and organizations" (Perry and Wise 1990, 368), it is clearly related to the concept of identity as applied in this chapter. Likewise, the definition by Vandenabeele (2007, 549) refers to the "belief, values [and] attitudes," which also refer to the components of identity. Second, the definitions by Perry and Wise (1990), Rainey and Steinbauer (1999), and Vandenabeele (2007) refer to institutional elements, explicitly addressing various types of institutions, such as nation, state, or community of people, as a framework of reference. Finally, most measures of public service motivation use some type of value-related construct as its constituting basis. Dimensions such as public interest, public value, self-sacrifice, or compassion are among the most popular operational definitions of public service motivations' dimensions (Kim et al. 2013; Perry 1996; Vandenabeele 2008). These all refer to values that are particular to the institutional environment in which public service motivation is found (Vandenabeele 2011). For all these reasons, public service motivation as applied in contemporary research is as much a motivation as it is an identity.

Public service motivation has been associated with various types of outcomes. However, not all outcomes are equally affected by individual public service motivation levels. Outcomes that are more related to particular public values are more strongly related to employees' public service motivation (Van Loon 2017). For instance, service outcomes (societal added value) and democratic outcomes demonstrate a stronger correlation than other outcomes, such as efficiency, timeliness of service, or individual citizen satisfaction.

This overview of institutional characteristics and associated behavior illustrates the relevance of taking the institutional context, including various sub-institutions, into account when managing for public service performance. Institutional characteristics of the organization influence the effect of public service motivation on performance. In addition, work systems can reduce or foster public service motivation. Likewise, Davis (2013) observed linkages between unionization, red tape, and public service motivation, again creating links between multiple sub-institutions. It is, therefore, only to be expected that other institutional characteristics will also moderate this relationship between public service motivation and performance.

4.5 Institutions, Identities, and Management: Implications for Practice and Research

Our unsurprising conclusion is that good management is not about pushing the correct buttons in the correct order to ensure "getting things done." Management requires sound knowledge of the institutional layout of both the organization and its institutional context, as the interdependence of an institution with its surrounding institutions determines the actual guise of that particular institution. This would explain the failure of, for example, the Belgian Copernic Reform of federal government (Bourgeault and Van Dorpe 2013). An important element was bringing in senior managers from the private sector. However, in only a few years, most of them had left, being unable to navigate the institutional waters of federal government (see Chapter 6).

However, knowledge alone is not sufficient. Management also requires the ability to navigate this complex environment in order to make the right decisions. After all, an institutional perspective claims that institutions both constrain and enable agency (Giddens 1984). This insight is incorporated into the contextual perspective that Paauwe (2004) has presented for strategic human resource management. In this perspective, it is important to align the strategy with the "institutional drivers" from the external environment and with the internal institutional layout. By also identifying the "dominant coalition" and its associated room for maneuver, management will be more successful (Paauwe 2004). By harnessing the right institutional identities and looking for fit, management will obtain the best results, given the institutional environment.

Management is not limited to passively responding to the environment and operating within the "room for maneuver" associated with this layout. Taking into account the interdependent institutional framework, institutions can also actively be changed. However, for this, it does not suffice to change organizational structures or practices. Rather, management should seek to alter the institutional features by responding to, or even creating, windows of opportunity for change. By capitalizing on disruptions of self-reinforcing mechanisms (e.g. the advent of new technology) or by creating them (e.g. changing the power balance by replacing managers), institutions can be changed. These changes will trickle down to the individual level and be internalized. Transformational or charismatic leadership (see Chapters 5, 11, and 13) may be of help in further internalizing these new identities. However, it may be easier to use the existing institutions and pick the "low-hanging fruit" before trying to reach for the sky of fully-fledged institutional change.

An important resource for a management strategy is the availability of sufficient robust and evidence-based knowledge that can be applied in practice. In this respect, a lot of research work remains to be done. Institution- and identity-building are long-term and complex processes, and these processes are not easily mapped and investigated. The fact that multiple identities can intersect and multiple institutions are interdependent complicates the development of a causal chain tremendously. Experiments that fully include these processes are not easily set up, and alternatives such as case study research or survey research—even longitudinal—are lacking in external or internal validity.

Nevertheless, apart from the self-evident strategy of triangulating various results to garner meaningful insights, some alternative strategies present themselves. First, in terms of assessing causal relationships, identifying natural experiments in which change projects were more or less randomly assigned can supplement other, less internally valid strategies to further triangulation. Such natural experiments (Morton and Williams 2008)—e.g. based on differences between different entities in terms of reform or with respect to certain systems that, for some reason, have been "randomly" applied to individuals—could cast additional light on assumed causal relationships. Such natural experiments would cover a longer-term period and would not entail the artificial environment associated with a lab experiment. Second, another strategy addresses the issue of multiple identities. Even outside the realm of public management, such knowledge is scarce (Burke and Stryker 2016). Nevertheless, to fully grasp the complexity of the process in which multiple institutions and their associated identities interact, such knowledge is indispensable. Further research into identity salience—in particular, how to measure this—would be key to understanding this process, for which Burke and Stryker (2016) have provided challenging suggestions.

A lot of work remains to be done, and our knowledge will only incrementally move toward a better understanding of these processes. Therefore, the most important resource is probably an attitude of persistence with respect to developing and applying this knowledge. After all, only this will get us past the stage of reaping the low-hanging fruit.

References

Ajzen, I. 2005. *Attitudes, Personality, and Behavior*. Milton Keynes: Open University Press/McGraw-Hill.

Antonsen, M., and T. Beck Jørgensen. 1997. "The 'Publicness' of Public Organizations." *Public Administration* 75 (2): pp. 337–57.

Bandura, A. 1986. *Social Foundations of Thought and Action.* Englewood Cliffs, NJ: Prentice Hall.

Beck Jørgensen, T., and B. Bozeman. 2007. "Public Values: An Inventory." *Administration & Society 39* (3): pp. 354–81.

Beer, M., B. A. Spector, P. R. Lawrence, D. Q. Mills, and R. Walton. 1984. *Human Resource Management: A General Manager's Perspective.* New York: Free Press.

Berger, P. L., and T. Luckmann. [1966] 1991. *The Social Construction of Reality: A Treatise in the Sociology of Knowledge.* Garden City, NY: Anchor Books.

BLS (Bureau of Labor Statistics). 2020. *Union Members Summary.* Washington, DC: United States Department of Labor. https://www.bls.gov/news.release/union2.nr0.htm.

Bourgault, J., and K. Van Dorpe. 2013. "Managerial Reforms, Public Service Bargains and Top Civil Servant Identity." *International Review of Administrative Sciences 79* (1): pp. 49–70.

Bozeman, B. 1987. *All Organizations Are Public: Bridging Public and Private Organizational Theories.* San Francisco, CA: Jossey-Bass.

Bozeman, B. 2007. *Public Values and Public Interest: Counterbalancing Economic Individualism.* Washington, DC: Georgetown University Press.

Buelens, M., and H. Van den Broeck. 2007. "An Analysis of Differences in Work Motivation between Public and Private Sector Organizations." *Public Administration Review 67* (1): pp. 65–74.

Burke, P. J., and S. Stryker. 2016. "Identity Theory: Progress in Relating the Two Strands." In *New Directions in Identity Theory and Research*, edited by J. E. Stets and R. T. Serpe, pp. 657–81. New York: Oxford University Press.

Davis, R. S. 2013. "Union Commitment and Stakeholder Red Tape: How Union Values Shape Perceptions of Organizational Rules." *Review of Public Personnel Administration 33* (4): pp. 365–83.

Edwards, J. R. 2008. "Person–Environment Fit in Organizations: An Assessment of Theoretical Progress." *Academy of Management Annals 2* (1): pp. 167–230.

Edwards, J. R., and A. J. Shipp. 2007. "The Relationship between Person–Environment Fit and Outcomes: An Integrative Theoretical Framework." In *Perspectives on Organizational Fit*, edited by C. Ostroff and T. A. Judge, pp. 209–58. Mahwah, NJ: Lawrence Erlbaum Associates Publishers.

Gagné, M. 2003. "Autonomy Support and Need Satisfaction in the Motivation and Well-Being of Gymnasts." *Journal of Applied Sport Psychology 15* (4): pp. 372–90.

Georgellis, Y., E. Iossa, and V. Tabvuma. 2011. "Crowding out Intrinsic Motivation in the Public Sector." *Journal of Public Administration Research and Theory 21* (3): pp. 473–93.

Giddens, A. 1984. *The Constitution of Society: Outline of the Theory of Structuration.* Cambridge: Polity Press.

Greenwood, R., A. M. Díaz, S. X. Li, and J. C. Lorente. 2010. "The Multiplicity of Institutional Logics and the Heterogeneity of Organizational Responses." *Organization Science 21* (2): pp. 521–39.

Haque, M. S. 2001. "The Diminishing Publicness of Public Service under the Current Mode of Governance." *Public Administration Review 61* (1): pp. 65–82.

Hasenfeld, Y. 1983. *Human Service Organizations*. Englewood Cliffs, NJ: Prentice-Hall.

Hoffman, B. J., and D. J. Woehr. 2006. "A Quantitative Review of the Relationship between Person–Organization Fit and Behavioral Outcomes." *Journal of Vocational Behavior 68* (3): pp. 389–99.

Horton, S. 2003. "Guest Editorial: Participation and Involvement – The Democratisation of New Public Management?" *International Journal of Public Sector Management 16* (6): pp. 403–11.

Houston, D. J. 2000. "Public-Service Motivation: A Multivariate Test." *Journal of Public Administration Research and Theory 10* (4): pp. 713–28.

Houston, D. J. 2011. "Implications of Occupational Locus and Focus for Public Service Motivation: Attitudes toward Work Motives across Nations." *Public Administration Review 71* (5): pp. 761–71.

Johns, G. 2006. "The Essential Impact of Context on Organizational Behavior." *Academy of Management Review 31* (2): pp. 386–408.

Kahneman, D., D. Lovallo, and O. Sibony. 2011. "Before You Make That Big Decision." *Harvard Business Review 89* (6): pp. 50–60.

Kim, S., W. Vandenabeele, B. E. Wright, L. B. Andersen, F. P. Cerase, R. K. Christensen, C. Desmarais, M. Koumenta, P. Leisink, B. Liu, J. Palidauskaite, L. H. Pedersen, J. L. Perry, A. Ritz, J. Taylor, and P. De Vivo. 2013. "Investigating the Structure and Meaning of Public Service Motivation across Populations: Developing an International Instrument and Addressing Issues of Measurement Invariance." *Journal of Public Administration Research and Theory 23* (1): pp. 79–102.

Kjeldsen, A. M. 2014. "Dynamics of Public Service Motivation: Attraction–Selection and Socialization in the Production and Regulation of Social Services." *Public Administration Review 74* (1): pp. 101–12.

Koppenjan, J. J. F. 2005. "The Formation of Public–Private Partnerships: Lessons from Nine Transport Infrastructure Projects in the Netherlands." *Public Administration 83* (1): pp. 135–57.

Krasner, S. D. 1984. "Approaches to the State: Alternative Conceptions and Historical Dynamics." *Comparative Politics 16* (2): pp. 223–46.

Kristof-Brown, A. L., R. D. Zimmerman, and E. C. Johnson. 2005. "Consequences of Individuals' Fit at Work: A Meta-Analysis of Person–Job, Person–Organization, Person–Group and Person–Supervisor Fit." *Personnel Psychology 58* (2): pp. 281–342.

Mahoney, J. 2000. "Path Dependence in Historical Sociology." *Theory and Society 29* (4): pp. 507–48.

March, J. G., and J. P. Olsen. 1989. *Rediscovering Institutions*. New York: Free Press.

March, J. G., and J. P. Olsen. 2004. "The Logic of Appropriateness." In *The Oxford Handbook of Political Science,* edited by M. Moran, M. Rein, and R. E. Goodin, pp. 689–709. New York: Oxford University Press.

Merton, R. K. 1939. "Bureaucratic Structure and Personality." *Social Forces 18* (4): pp. 560–8.

Moore, M. H. 1995. *Creating Public Value: Strategic Management in Government*. Cambridge, MA: Harvard University Press.

Morton, R. B., and K. C. Williams. 2008. "Experimentation in Political Science." In *The Oxford Handbook of Political Methodology*, edited by J. M. Box-Steffensmeier, H. E. Brady, and D. Collier, pp. 339–56. Oxford: Oxford University Press.

Moynihan, D. P., S. Fernandez, S. Kim, K. M. LeRoux, S. J. Piotrowski, B. E. Wright, and K. Yang. 2011. "Performance Regimes amidst Governance Complexity." *Journal of Public Administration Research and Theory 21* (suppl_1): pp. i141–55.

Muchinsky, P. M., and C. J. Monahan. 1987. "What Is Person–Environment Congruence? Supplementary Versus Complementary Models of Fit." *Journal of Vocational Behavior 31* (3): pp. 268–77.

Nomden, K., D. Farnham, and M. L. Onnee-Abbruciati. 2003. "Collective Bargaining in Public Services." *International Journal of Public Sector Management 16* (6): pp. 412–23.

O'Toole, L. J., and K. J. Meier. 2015. "Public Management, Context, and Performance: In Quest of a More General Theory." *Journal of Public Administration Research and Theory 25* (1): pp. 237–56.

Paauwe, J. 2004. *HRM and Performance: Achieving Long-Term Viability*. Oxford: Oxford University Press.

Perry, J. L. 1996. "Measuring Public Service Motivation: An Assessment of Construct Reliability and Validity." *Journal of Public Administration Research and Theory 6* (1): pp. 5–22.

Perry, J. L. 2000. "Bringing Society In: Toward a Theory of Public Service Motivation." *Journal of Public Administration Research and Theory 10* (2): pp. 471–88.

Perry, J. L., B. A. Petrakis, and T. K. Miller. 1989. "Federal Merit Pay, Round II: An Analysis of the Performance Management and Recognition System." *Public Administration Review 49* (1): pp. 29–37.

Perry, J. L., and H. G. Rainey. 1988. "The Public–Private Distinction in Organization Theory: A Critique and Research Strategy." *Academy of Management Review 13* (2): pp. 182–201.

Perry, J. L., and W. Vandenabeele. 2008. "Behavioral Dynamics: Institutions, Identities, and Self-Regulation." In *Motivation in Public Management: The Call of Public Service*, edited by J. Perry and A. Hondeghem, pp. 56–79. Oxford: Oxford University Press.

Perry, J. L., and L. R. Wise. 1990. "The Motivational Bases of Public Service." *Public Administration Review 75* (1): pp. 53–78.

Pollitt, C., and G. Bouckaert. 2004. *Public Management Reform: A Comparative Analysis*. Oxford: Oxford University Press.

Rainey, H. G. 2009. *Understanding and Managing Public Organizations*. San Francisco, CA: John Wiley & Sons.

Rainey, H. G., and B. Bozeman. 2000. "Comparing Public and Private Organizations: Empirical Research and the Power of the A Priori." *Journal of Public Administration Research and Theory 10* (2): pp. 447–70.

Rainey, H. G., and P. Steinbauer. 1999. "Galloping Elephants: Developing Elements of a Theory of Effective Government Organizations." *Journal of Public Administration Research and Theory 9* (1): pp. 1–32.

Riccucci, N. M. 2011. "Public Sector Labor Relations Scholarship: Is There a 'There,' There?" *Public Administration Review 71* (2): pp. 203–9.

Roberts, B. W., G. Edmonds, and E. Grijalva. 2010. "It Is Developmental Me, Not Generation Me: Developmental Changes Are More Important than Generational Changes in Narcissism—Commentary on Trzesniewski & Donnellan 2010." *Perspectives on Psychological Science 5* (1): pp. 97–102.

Ryan, R. M., and E. L. Deci. 2012. "Multiple Identities within a Single Self: A Self-Determination Theory Perspective on Internalization within Contexts and Cultures." In *Handbook of Self and Identity* edited by M. R. Leary and J. P. Tangney, pp. 225–45. New York: Guildford Press.

Scheuer, S. 2011. "Union Membership Variation in Europe: A Ten-Country Comparative Analysis." *European Journal of Industrial Relations 17* (1): pp. 57–73.

Scott, W. R. 2001. *Institutions and Organizations: Ideas, Interests, and Identities.* Thousand Oaks, CA: Sage.

Simon, H. A. 1955. "A Behavioral Model of Rational Choice." *The Quarterly Journal of Economics 69* (1): pp. 99–118.

Simon, H. A. 1997. *Administrative Behavior: A Study of Decision-Making.* New York: Free Press.

Stryker, S. 1957. "Role-Taking Accuracy and Adjustment." *Sociometry 20* (4): pp. 286–96.

Stryker, S. 1980. *Symbolic Interactionism: A Social Structural Version.* Menlo Park, CA: Benjamin/Cummings Publishing Company.

Thaler, R. H., and C. R. Sunstein. 2009. *Nudge: Improving Decisions about Health, Wealth, and Happiness.* New York: Penguin.

Thornton, P. H., and W. Ocasio. 2008. "Institutional Logics." In *The Sage Handbook of Organizational Institutionalism*, edited by R. Greenwood, C. Oliver, R. Suddaby, and K. Sahlin, pp. 99–128. Thousand Oaks, CA: Sage.

Twenge, J. M., S. Konrath, J. D. Foster, W. K. Campbell, and B. J. Bushman. 2008. "Egos Inflating over Time: A Cross-Temporal Meta-Analysis of the Narcissistic Personality Inventory." *Journal of Personality 76* (4): 875–902.

Vandenabeele, W. 2007. "Toward a Public Administration Theory of Public Service Motivation: An Institutional Approach." *Public Management Review 9* (4): pp. 545–56.

Vandenabeele, W. 2008. "Development of a Public Service Motivation Measurement Scale: Corroborating and Extending Perry's Measurement Instrument." *International Public Management Journal 11* (1): pp. 143–67.

Vandenabeele, W. 2011. "Who Wants to Deliver Public Service? Do Institutional Antecedents of Public Service Motivation Provide an Answer?" *Review of Public Personnel Administration 31* (1): pp. 87–107.

Van der Meer, F. M., C. F. Van den Berg, and G. S. Dijkstra. 2013. "Rethinking the 'Public Service Bargain': The Changing (Legal) Position of Civil Servants in Europe." *International Review of Administrative Sciences 79* (1): pp. 91–109.

Van Loon, N. M. 2017. "Does Context Matter for the Type of Performance-Related Behavior of Public Service Motivated Employees?" *Review of Public Personnel Administration 37* (4): pp. 405–29.

Van Loon, N. M., P. Leisink, and W. Vandenabeele. 2013. "Talking the Talk of Public Service Motivation: How Public Organization Logics Matter for Employees' Expressions of PSM." *International Journal of Public Administration 36* (14): pp. 1007–19.

Van Loon, N. M., W. Vandenabeele, and P. Leisink. 2015. "On the Bright and Dark Side of Public Service Motivation: The Relationship between PSM and Employee Wellbeing." *Public Money & Management 35* (5): pp. 349–56.

Verquer, M. L., T. A. Beehr, and S. H. Wagner. 2003. "A Meta-Analysis of Relations between Person–Organization Fit and Work Attitudes." *Journal of Vocational Behavior 63* (3): pp. 473–89.

Vroom, V. H. 1964. *Work and Motivation.* New York: Wiley.

Weber, M. 1978. *Economy and Society.* Los Angeles: University of California Press.

Willems, I., R. Janvier, and E. Henderickx. 2006. "New Pay in European Civil Services: Is the Psychological Contract Changing?" *International Journal of Public Sector Management 19* (6): pp. 609–21.

PART II
PUBLIC MANAGEMENT AND PUBLIC SERVICE PERFORMANCE

5

Public Managers' Contribution to Public Service Performance

Lotte B. Andersen, Christian B. Jacobsen, Ulrich T. Jensen, and Heidi H. Salomonsen

5.1 Introduction

Do public managers matter for public service performance? The impact of public managers has sometimes been regarded as negligible due to constraints from the political environment, limited goal-setting capabilities, and the vast discretion of frontline employees (Rainey 2014). However, studies suggest that managers can matter a lot for public service performance. Using randomized controlled trials, the public management literature is also gaining more knowledge on how public managers' leadership can affect performance (Knies et al. 2016). Leadership is the process of influencing others to understand and agree about what needs to be done and how to do it, and the process of facilitating individual and collective efforts to achieve shared objectives (Yukl 2013, 23).

In public organizations, managers contribute to performance in a context with multiple and often conflicting performance criteria and many relevant stakeholders. This highlights the role of organizational reputation, both as a separate target for managerial action and as an important factor when we analyze how leadership affects performance. There are also huge differences in the degrees of managerial autonomy, capacity, and ability between different public organizations. The key question in this chapter is how public managers can contribute to public service performance in these different settings.

As discussed in more detail in Chapter 2, performance is relative to its intended achievements as the actual achievement of an organization, taking into account the many aspects that public service delivery often has. As highlighted in Chapter 2, performance criteria in public organizations often go beyond a mere product focus, and there are multiple stakeholders. Several different groups and individuals can affect or are affected by the achievement of the typical public organization's objectives. They expect the organization to deliver certain outputs and achieve specific outcomes, but their understanding of "good performance" is typically much broader

Lotte B. Andersen, Christian B. Jacobsen, Ulrich T. Jensen, and Heidi H. Salomonsen, *Public Managers' Contribution to Public Service Performance* In: *Managing for Public Service Performance: How People and Values Make a Difference.* Edited by: Peter Leisink, Lotte B. Andersen, Gene A. Brewer, Christian B. Jacobsen, Eva Knies, and Wouter Vandenabeele, Oxford University Press (2021). © Lotte B. Andersen, Christian B. Jacobsen, Ulrich T. Jensen, and Heidi H. Salomonsen.
DOI: 10.1093/oso/9780192893420.003.0005

than that. Some performance criteria are directly related to the achievement of changes in the surrounding world: Students should increase their academic skills, patients should get better health, and the environment should be safe for all citizens. In addition to these performance outcome criteria, public organizations are also held accountable for *how* they deliver results. Process matters in the public sector (Andersen et al. 2016), and that is important for how public managers can contribute to public service performance. The association between leadership behavior and organizational performance is therefore seldom deterministic or simple.

The chapter outline is as follows. First, we discuss three critical components—autonomy, capacity, and ability—in achieving high performance through leadership. Whether focusing on goals and objectives, human relations, or distribution of leadership tasks, such behaviors necessitate each of these components. Leaders need the discretion to make meaningful change, have the capacity for reallocating resources, and the abilities to facilitate healthy relationships with and among organizational members. We therefore introduce each of these components before turning our attention to different ways in which managers can contribute to public service performance. Specifically, we focus on leadership behaviors with documented effects on performance and exemplify each of these with insights from recent empirical research. Finally, in Section 5.7, we address how organizational reputation can be both a target for managerial action and an important moderator of the leadership–performance relationship, before turning to a discussion of how leadership training can better equip public managers to contribute to higher public service performance.

5.2 Critical Components in Exerting Public Leadership: Autonomy, Capacity, and Ability

Managerial autonomy, capacity, and ability are critical factors when public managers aim to contribute to public service performance. Our focus below is on how autonomy, capacity, and ability moderate the association between leadership and performance.

Leadership only affects performance when managers actually exert leadership, that is, if they have enough autonomy to act. The reason for starting with the discussion of managerial autonomy is that such discretion in decision-making is a necessary condition for active leadership. Defined as the extent to which a manager can decide independently from political and administrative principals on the choice and use of resources (Verhoest et al. 2004), we argue that higher levels of managerial autonomy can provide a stronger association between leadership and performance. In other words, public managers can contribute more positively to public service performance when they have autonomy, but deficient management can also have more severe negative consequences when the level of managerial autonomy is high.

There are at least two arguments for the expected moderating effect of managerial autonomy (Wynen et al. 2014, 48). First, the managerialist school of thought (Maor 1999) advocates the idea of "business-like government" and expects public managers to behave like private sector managers to be more innovative and entrepreneurial, for example, in combining production factors to create public value and achieve greater performance. Given sufficient managerial autonomy and flexibility, public managers are expected to adopt innovation-oriented behavior that leads to greater service–user orientation and enhanced performance (see also Wynen et al. 2014, 48). Second, autonomy enables public managers to be more flexible toward stakeholders. The argument is that if public managers have autonomy, they will do their utmost to increase organizational performance to obtain legitimacy from important external stakeholders, such as service users and political principals, and thereby safeguard their own existence and future resources by establishing a positive reputation.

As discussed in more detail in Chapter 8, managerial autonomy can be vital to ensure successful implementation of performance management because it allows for local adaptations. Nielsen (2013, 40), for example, finds that two aspects of human resource managerial autonomy moderate the impact on performance, namely, how much discretion managers have in their use of incentives and for recruitment. Without room for local adaptation or customization, public managers cannot initiate performance-improving changes and ensure that performance management and other types of managerial behavior are perceived as supportive by employees (Grøn 2018). Consequently, public managers primarily matter for performance when they have at least some autonomy over the "production process" for public services.

Managerial capacity is another important factor when considering the contributions of public managers to public service performance. The argument is simple: It takes resources to exert leadership and affect performance. Managerial capacity is defined as "available potential for managerial resources to be deployed when needed" (O'Toole and Meier 2010, 341), and it is especially relevant for public organizations in changing or turbulent environments. This is a common characteristic of public organizations, given the conditions described in Chapter 1 in this volume. O'Toole and Meier (2010, 344) argue that managerial capacity can mitigate the impact of environmental shocks. It can give flexibility, spur innovation, and yield higher pay-offs. Capacity in the central office can mean that "one can move a central manager from seeking grants one week to assessing the profitability of food services the next week to an emergency fill-in for a line manager the next" (O'Toole and Meier 2010, 344). This can serve as a buffer to help organizations absorb and survive the effects of shocks and thus facilitate high performance in the long run. Such extra resources might also increase innovation (Nohria and Gulati 1996) and thus also performance (O'Toole and Meier 2010, 345). Similarly, we expect that leadership has a higher chance of affecting performance if managerial capacity is high because of potential resources that can be deployed to support the leadership efforts.

A key part of managerial capacity is managerial systems, conceptualized in the literature as capital management, financial management, human resource management (HRM), and IT management, among others. This includes, for example, risk management structures, arrangements to ensure the best use of resources, measures to prevent sickness or excessive absences, and the existence of performance management systems. Andrews and Boyne (2010) find that the impact of management systems is maximized through integration with effective leadership, which they see as centering on credibility and vision, which implies leading with a clear focus and well-defined goals. Empirically, they score English local governments on "leadership within the organization and its influence on determining priorities," the "clarity of how ambitions will be achieved through robust priority setting," and "realism in relation to how achievable the ambition and priorities are" (Andrews and Boyne 2010, 447). The important point here is that leadership is essential in combination with management systems, and although the investigated leadership is goal-oriented (this concept is discussed further below), there is no reason why this should not apply to other types of leadership.

Managerial ability matters as well. Especially for public service delivery, it is important for managers to navigate in a context that is characterized by public ownership, public funding, and public control/regulation (Bozeman and Bretschneider 1994). As Chapter 6 discusses in much more detail, Petrovsky et al. (2015) argue that outsiders who have little experience in responding to politicians, public funding, and regulatory constraints will find it difficult to lead public organizations and improve their performance. For organizations performing at a high level prior to leadership changes, Petrovsky et al. (2015) expect a performance drop due to the expected lower ability of the new leader to create results in the specific context. Performance will increase when the successor's publicness fit increases, given that this fit captures at least part of the successor's ability to generate performance in the specific organization. For organizations performing at a low level prior to the succession event, the performance increase will be nonlinearly related to the successor's publicness fit (A-formed) so that there is an optimal level of publicness fit. Petrovsky et al. (2015, 228) thus argue that the match can be "too complete" and entail insufficient strategic change, meaning that leaders with middle levels of publicness fit will be better able to introduce needed changes in poorly performing organizations. This argument illustrates our broader claim that managerial ability should be seen in relation to the managerial task and the status of the organization in question.

In sum, we argue that managerial autonomy, capacity, and ability are important when analyzing all types of leadership behavior. However, some types or styles of leadership are more relevant than others for performance, and we have selected three types of leadership behavior to be discussed in Section 5.3. If public managers have enough autonomy, capacity, and general ability, we argue that these types of leadership behavior can increase performance in most public service organizations.

5.3   Selected Types of Leadership with Potential Effects on Public Service Performance

Leaders of public organizations have many possible actions to choose from in the attempt to improve their organization's performance (Day and Antonakis 2012). They can, for example, focus on framing the desires and preferences of elected political officials into local narratives, institutionalize systems for providing feedback or rewards based on employee effort, or build a cohesive culture of collaboration in their organization. While leaders' time and attention are high-demand commodities, we emphasize that the various leadership strategies available are not mutually exclusive. In fact, recent conceptual contributions stress the synergies when integrating multiple strategies for effective leadership in public organizations (Jensen et al. 2016; Tummers and Knies 2016). However, we focus on three broad types of leadership behavior to highlight some of the most important ways through which public managers can increase public service performance.

Based on existing reviews (Orazi et al. 2013; Van Wart 2013; Vogel and Masal 2015), we focus on three types of leadership: (1) goal-oriented leadership; (2) relational leadership; and (3) non-leader-centered leadership. *Goal-oriented leadership* theories argue that clear and appealing visions/goals give direction to employees and make it seem worthwhile for them to pursue specific goals over others. *Relational leadership* emphasizes the ability to create constructive relations in the organization. Examples are servant leadership, leader–member exchange (LMX) theory, and Yukl's (2013) relation-oriented leadership. *Non-leader-centered leadership* includes distributed and shared leadership, and the focus is on leadership initiatives from the employees and on delegation of leadership tasks. The three types of leadership are discussed in more detail below.

Goal-oriented leadership is behavior that is intended to clarify organizational goals and motivate employees to attain those goals (Jensen et al. 2016). The most prominent example is transformational leadership. The argument is that transformational leadership leads to higher performance in public organizations because leaders provide meaning to the job context (Bellé 2014; Oberfield 2012). Although there is debate about how transformational leadership should be conceptualized (e.g. see Van Knippenberg and Sitkin 2013), scholars generally agree that a core element is developing, sharing, and sustaining an organizational vision/mission (Jensen et al. 2016). In terms of goal-setting, transformational leadership directs attention to the ideal, broad, and long-term goals, i.e. the core mission and tasks of an organization, which often constitute the higher purposes of the organization and the work tasks associated with it. Wright et al. (2012) argue that transformational leadership has great potential in public organizations. These organizations have strong service and community-oriented missions, and many of the employees are public service-motivated, suggesting that they are more likely than private sector employees to view their missions as important because of the overlap between organizational goals and their own values.

Goal-oriented leadership also includes transactional leadership. Whereas transformational leadership works through values, meaning, and intrinsic values, transactional leadership is based on an exchange relationship that is expected to appeal to employees' self-interest. Thus, transactional leadership involves more specific goal-setting than transformational leadership and explicit contingencies of potential rewards or sanctions on goal attainment (Jensen et al. 2016). In public organizations, where outcomes are distant and nebulous, the relevant goals may be outputs or actions rather than outcomes for the citizens. Although transactional leadership is meant to appeal to employees' self-interest to attain goals, public managers can still use contingent rewards to support some basic needs that lead to more autonomous types of motivation, such as the need for competence (Jacobsen and Andersen 2017).

Goal-oriented leadership is probably the most investigated type of leadership in the public administration literature, and several studies find a positive association with performance for both transformational and transactional leadership (for an overview, see Knies et al. 2016). Recent experimental work has also confirmed a causal relationship between both transformational and transactional leadership and public service performance (e.g. Bellé 2014; 2015). However, we lack knowledge on the applicability of goal-oriented leadership across contexts and performance criteria. Furthermore, we need more studies of the combined use of different goal-oriented leadership strategies. Although both transformational and transactional leadership are based on seemingly opposite logics, they are not necessarily rival substitutes. In fact, several studies have found that different goal-oriented leadership strategies can be mutually reinforcing (Bass et al. 2003; O'Shea et al. 2009).

Relational leadership aims to foster strong and productive interpersonal relations among organizational members (Fernandez et al. 2010). While goal-oriented leadership focuses on the outcomes of work processes, relational leadership aims to improve the relationships between people in organizations. Relational leadership has received some attention in public management research, which has found a positive association with subjective performance (Fernandez 2008) and indirectly with organizational performance (Fernandez et al. 2010). Whereas relation-oriented leadership (Yukl 2013) focuses broadly on relations within an organization, LMX and servant leadership are examples of relational leadership approaches with a focus on the leader–follower relationship. According to Greenleaf (1970), servant leaders unselfishly attend to their employees' needs, develop them, and thereby serve the needs of society. Servant leadership is positively associated with subjective performance (Newman et al. 2017) and with several antecedents of performance, such as organizational commitment (Miao et al. 2014), organizational citizenship behavior (Schwartz et al. 2016), and innovative behavior (Miao et al. 2018). LMX is affiliated with servant leadership but stresses the importance of the dyadic relationship between leader and follower more explicitly. LMX is typically defined as the quality of the relationship between a leader and an employee (Graen and Uhl-Bien 1995), and debate has centered on whether LMX is a leadership behavior or a result of leadership behaviors. Public management studies have associated LMX with several desired outcomes, such as organizational commitment and work effort (Tummers and Knies 2016), but there are no known studies of the direct relationship between LMX and performance in public organizations.

Leadership is not necessarily leader-centered, which was an insight made already by Barnard (1938). A central tenet in leadership research is that effective leadership depends on the leaders' ability to enable the employees to engage in organizational activities in order to achieve goals. In contrast, approaches that are not leader-centered (such as distributed leadership, shared leadership, and participative leadership) argue that all members of an organization can exert leadership. Especially when the formal leaders are restrained in terms of time, information, and cognitive abilities, employees can fill leadership roles, and formal leaders can also delegate leadership tasks to employees who are not formal leaders. Although these approaches do not agree on the extent that leadership can be (and should be) formalized, they all see leadership as an organizational process in which individuals without formal leadership responsibilities play significant roles in accomplishing leadership tasks. As long as the goals are aligned, distribution of leadership responsibility is expected to make organizational decision-making smoother, flexible, and more appropriate. Fausing et al. (2013) thus argue that sharing leadership responsibility can bring in the ideas, expertise, and skills of multiple individuals. Involvement in decision-making can also be a motivational factor for many employees. Generic research finds that leadership behavior that is not leader-centered is positively associated with team effectiveness (Wang et al. 2014), but most studies that focus on public leadership take a leader-centered perspective, ignoring the important role of followers (Vogel and Masal 2015, 1181). This might be a problem because public employees are more involved in organizational decision-making than private employees in many countries, and we need to know how employees contribute to solving leadership tasks in cooperation with public managers, and what the effects of such distributed responsibilities are. Chapter 11 exemplifies how distributed leadership can be important during organizational change. We focus on leader-centered examples of managers' contributions to performance because we have the most robust knowledge about this perspective.

5.4 Public Managers' Contributions to Public Service Performance: Examples

Goal attainment is a fundamental part of maintaining the mandate provided in social contracts with the public, and researchers have, therefore, focused on public managers' contributions to the attainment of public organizations' goals. In operational terms, scholars have focused on a variety of strategies across different settings, such as local governments, hospitals, and schools. In a series of studies, O'Toole and Meier (2011), for example, demonstrate the sizeable effects of internal management on a range of performance criteria related to student academic achievement in Texas school districts. Some of these findings have been confirmed in other studies

(Amirkhanyan et al. 2018; Andrews et al. 2011; Favero et al. 2016). However, attempts to disentangle the relationship between management and performance in public organizations are ongoing, partly because most existing studies have potential endogeneity problems. What if the managers selected their behavior in response to past performance? What if other factors affected both the behavior of leaders and the performance of their organizations?

In response to these concerns, public management research has recently started to study the impact of exogenous variation in leadership on public service performance. Bellé (2014) thus investigates the impact of a transformational leadership intervention in an Italian hospital. A director of nursing provided a 15-minute talk in which she conveyed the meaningfulness and importance of the project (assembling surgical kits for use in a former war zone). In this randomized controlled trial, nurses who were exposed to the transformational leadership intervention marginally outperformed nurses in the control group (Bellé 2014, 120). Importantly, the effects of the transformational leadership condition were greater when nurses were either (1) exposed to contact with a beneficiary or (2) engaged in a self-persuasion exercise about the importance of assembling the surgical kits. Additionally, these effects were further amplified when nurses reported a strong prosocial motivation to serve other people and society at large (i.e. had a high level of public service motivation). Similarly, Jensen and Bøllingtoft (2017) find that when employee and organization values were congruent in a randomized field experiment, employees of leaders who received a one-year transformational leadership training program reported higher levels of self-rated job performance compared to employees with leaders in the control group. These recent results (using experimental variation in leadership) generally indicate that leadership can have a more substantial—although complex—effect on performance through mediating factors (such as motivation) and/or under certain organizational contingencies (e.g. relational job design and value congruence).

As indicated above, public organizations are not only held accountable for the formal (outcome-related) goals. Process criteria such as transparency, social equity, and fairness also matter, and that brings less traditional types of leadership behavior in focus. Recently, Hassan et al. (2014) linked ethical leadership—such as being an ethical role model to others, treating people fairly, and managing ethics—to lower absenteeism, higher organizational commitment, and higher willingness to report ethics problems in public organizations. The underlying point here is that the complexity of leadership strategies adopted by public managers needs to match the complex performance criteria that public organizations are expected to pursue and attain simultaneously. Public organizations are not only expected to deliver public service outcomes but also services in a responsible, fair, and equitable manner. This requires that public managers integrate a range of behaviors that accommodate a simultaneous focus on clarifying goals and objectives, facilitating a collaborative organizational culture, delegating work tasks, and ensuring the morality of work processes and interaction with beneficiaries.

Consistent with this point, Fernandez et al. (2010) call attention to the *combination* of task, relations, change, diversity, and integrity-oriented leadership. "Integrated leadership" is when these five types of leadership are performed in combination by employees and managers at different levels of the hierarchy. Importantly, findings from US federal sub-agencies indicate that integrated leadership has a positive and sizeable effect on performance (Fernandez et al. 2010). These results support the stakeholder perspective presented in Chapter 2, although the combination of all five types of leadership can be seen as wearing both belt and suspenders. As indirectly suggested by Fernandez et al. (2010, 311), an alternative approach to enhance value for the organization goes through a more specific analysis of the diverse stakeholders and their expectations and potential contributions to the organization. Relation-oriented leadership may, for example, be relatively more important in a hospital, while integrity-oriented leadership may be the most essential aspect of a governmentalized and politicized tax agency. Tax managers may thus have to impose strong demands for legality, fairness, and equitable treatment of citizens to succeed in the eye of key stakeholders, while other leadership behaviors are more important for hospital managers. A stakeholder approach will study the configuration of stakeholders, including their relative importance and understandings of what high performance is.

Such a stakeholder approach would point toward reputation management as an important part of public management, given that a good reputation among stakeholders can be seen as both a contingency with relevance for managers' efforts to increase performance and a result of high performance. Section 5.5 discusses the relationships between management, performance, and organizational reputation.

5.5 Management, Performance, and Reputation

The first step in disentangling the relationships between public organizations' reputation, public managers' behavior, and organizational performance is to observe that public managers actually exert reputation-conscious behavior, including reputation management. This requires a clear conceptualization of reputation management. However, in contrast to the types of leaderships discussed above, the literature on reputation management in general and on public reputation management in particular lacks such a conceptualization enabling robust and systematic empirical validation of its existence, causes, and effects. To address this gap, Pedersen and Salomonsen (2020, 9) suggest defining reputation management as leadership behaviors with the intent to affect the perception by external stakeholders of an organization's reputation. Such intended behaviors include *identification* of stakeholder perceptions and expectations of and to the organization; *communication* to stakeholders to affect the perceptions, including communication reflecting the vision of the organization, its performance, and more; as well as *prioritization* of which stakeholders the communication should be targeting (Pedersen and Salomonsen 2020, 9).

While the two first types of behaviors are inspired by generic definitions of reputation management (Fombrun and Rindova 1998), the third—prioritization—is inspired by bureaucratic reputation theory. Bureaucratic reputation theory argues that given the complexity of stakeholders as well as the complexity of a public organization's reputation, public managers need to prioritize what they communicate and to whom (Carpenter and Krause 2012, 29). Hence, public managers are able to affect external stakeholders' perception of the organization, including perceptions of its performance, by identifying the perceptions held by those actors (e.g. monitoring stakeholders' expressions of the organization in the media, systematic stakeholder analysis, and stakeholder dialogue). They can also communicate their priorities concerning the organizational vision to stakeholders and tell them about organizational performance to affect their future perceptions.

Whether or not public managers' efforts succeed in painting a positive picture of the organization depends on both the managers' (and the rest of the organization's) ability to present the organization in an upbeat way and on how the stakeholders perceive the presentation. Reputation management may be loosely coupled to actual performance, but not necessarily: It is easier to brag about oneself when the underlying performance is good (Christensen and Gornitzka 2017). Similarly, successful reputation management makes it easier to succeed in performance—for example, through attracting more resources or convincing organization members about the importance of the mission and tasks.

The second step in disentangling the relationships between organizational reputations, behaviors of public managers, and organizational performance is to scrutinize these associations both theoretically and empirically. This is exactly what reputation management research is doing right now, and below, we discuss some important insights.

Reputation is "a set of symbolic beliefs about the unique or separable capacities, roles, and obligations of an organization, where these beliefs are embedded in audience networks" (Carpenter 2010, 45). Reputations are perceptions which are formed over time as they develop when multiple stakeholders evaluate the behavior of an organization according to their beliefs or expectations. The question is whether the agency can meet the expectations (Coombs 2007, 164). This means that reputations are either favorable or non-favorable, but rather comparative in nature (Coombs 2007, 164). The point of comparison applied by stakeholders is either evaluations of an organization's behavior and performance vis-à-vis other organizations or evaluations of an organization's past behavior and performance (Coombs 2007, 164). Therefore, reputation—as suggested by bureaucratic reputation theory above—may further be understood as the result of a process in which those beliefs reflect an aggregate evaluation stakeholders make about how well an organization is meeting stakeholder expectations based on its past behaviors (Coombs and Holladay 2010).

For public organizations, the symbolic beliefs may be formed around four different dimensions, reflecting the above-mentioned complexity of a public organization's reputation (Carpenter 2010, 44–6; Carpenter and Krause 2012):

1. *a procedural dimension,* which refers to the extent that the organization is perceived to conform with procedures and legislation;
2. *a technical dimension,* which consists of the perceived "expertise" and professional qualifications of the organization;
3. *a moral dimension* referring to a public organization's perceived ability to meet normative expectations, such as protecting citizens and ensuring transparency; and
4. *a performative dimension* referring to an organization's perceived ability to execute its tasks effectively and the quality hereof, with respect to outcome and output.

Of particular relevance to the subject of this chapter is the performative dimension. Due to the fact that public organizations' reputation relies on different stakeholders' perceptions concerning the organization's effectiveness, quality, morality, and so on (Maor 2015), public leaders must actively manage the reputation(s) of their organization. What stakeholders see is not the reality of the organization but rather an uncertain image of the organization's performance, technical skills, morality, and/or procedural rightness (Carpenter and Krause 2012; Maor 2015). This leaves some leeway for reputation-conscious organizations and their managers to participate strategically in the construction of the stakeholders' perceptions by ensuring that good performance is, in fact, translated into positive perceptions of the organization, or by ensuring that bad performance is not translated into a bad reputation.

The literature names at least three ways that reputation may affect performance and/or the relationship between leadership and performance. First, a positive reputation may facilitate recruiting and retaining high-quality employees who, in turn, increase the capacity of the organization to achieve good performance (Carpenter 2002; Luoma-aho 2007, 124). Second, a positive reputation may enhance motivation and identification for existing employees. Employees are more inclined to identify and feel committed to their organization if it has a positive reputation that reflects back positively on employees (Dukerich et al. 2002; Dutton et al. 1994). A positive reputation held by external stakeholders can function as a mirror for employees to see themselves in a positive light (Dutton and Dukerich 1991). Finally, external stakeholders' perceptions of an organization's reputation matter because a good reputation can insulate organizations from outside (particularly political) interference and thereby enhance autonomy (Carpenter 2002; 2010). As already discussed above, managerial autonomy is very important for the relationship between leadership and performance in public organizations. In sum, a positive reputation can, therefore, boost organizational autonomy and increase managerial autonomy, and this discretion can strengthen the effect of leadership on performance (Carpenter 2002, 491; Carpenter and Krause 2012). A positive reputation can thus be a power resource that public managers can use when negotiating how much autonomy their principal should grant them (Krause and Carpenter 2015).

While reputation management may be performed through other, non-communicative means (Maor 2015), external communication is, as mentioned, a vital part of the reputation management toolkit. However, public managers face several challenges when they use external communication to translate high organizational performance into a positive reputation among prioritized stakeholders. First, public managers often have limited resources (Maor 2015, 30). Especially if managerial capacity is low, their leadership and reputation management skills are expected to be less effective.

Second, confronted with multiple stakeholders with different and potentially conflicting performance criteria (Andersen et al. 2016), public managers must give priority to some stakeholders when communicating about their performance. As noted by Carpenter and Krause (2012, 29), "satisfying some audience subset often means upsetting others or projecting ambiguity." In other words, public managers can be forced to prioritize among stakeholders and also the performative dimension among some performance criteria over others in their communication about performance to external stakeholders. Public managers often prioritize communicating good performance on criteria set by their political sponsors, but this may come at the expense of emphasizing criteria valued by some stakeholders over others. Especially for organizations with many conflicting performance criteria, reputation management is simultaneously necessary and risky for public managers (Maor 2015, 30).

Third, public managers may be constrained by their own views, attitudes, and knowledge (Maor 2015, 30). Affecting external stakeholders' perception of the organization's performance requires that managers are, in fact, knowledgeable on the performance of their organizations. Additionally, their communication to external stakeholders must take the performance information and/or impression already held by these stakeholders into account. Actors on hierarchical levels above public managers often make multiple types of performance information available to stakeholders. Examples are grades for schools, user satisfaction reports for elderly homes, and re-admittance percentages for hospital wards. This can be challenging because public managers may overestimate the performance of their organization relative to more objectively measured performance (Andrews et al. 2010; Meier and O'Toole 2013; Meier et al. 2015). This can become a problem when stakeholders have access to objectively measured performance and can gauge such disparities. Public managers may lose their credibility if they exaggerate organizational results. Furthermore, public managers do not automatically use performance information available for their organization (Moynihan et al. 2012), and this may also bias their communication with external stakeholders, further challenging their credibility.

Summing up, there are good reasons for public managers to consider the reputation of their organizations and actively manage external stakeholders' perception of their organization. However, such leadership behavior may be challenged by traits related to the public sector context per se, as well as by the perceptions and knowledge held by public managers themselves.

5.6 Developing Leaders: How to Acquire Competences to Contribute to Public Service Performance

Public management is highly demanding, and this final part of the chapter therefore addresses the question of how public leaders can increase their ability and learn how to use different leadership strategies in their complex environments. How do we stimulate behaviors that lead to higher performance? How can managers learn to create more public value in public organizations? Addressing these questions, the chapter steps out of the purely analytical role and discusses how public leadership research can proactively contribute to better public service provision through improved leader development, based on robust scientific knowledge about managers' contribution to public service performance.

In a recent study of schools in Houston, Texas, a group of school principals were randomly assigned to either a management training program entailing 300 hours of training on leadership (such as teacher coaching and data-driven instruction) or a control group (Fryer 2017). Following this training program, students from schools with trained principals significantly outperformed their peers at other institutions in the first year. In the second year, the researchers were unable to detect any overall effects on student achievement. This lack of a long-term effect can be at least partially explained by principal turnover, indicating a trade-off between leader development and better performance for individual organizations. If the "higher-skilled" principals simply move to other schools, the training may not imply a welfare loss at the societal level despite failure to realize a performance increase at the local level.

In another study (without random assignment), Seidle et al. (2016) found that a combination of coaching, classroom instruction, feedback, and experiential learning had a significant, positive effect on the leaders' performance. Although the study lacked a control group, it provides strong support for the core elements needed to develop leader capacity and strategic behaviors. Many of these elements are also found in a Danish randomized field experiment on goal-oriented leadership, where they are applied in a systematic training intervention on transformational leadership, transactional leadership, or a combination of the two. Leaders in the control group did not receive any leadership training. Similar to Seidle et al. (2016), the training sessions consisted of classroom instruction, feedback on assignments and case exercises, and experiential learning. While the learning principles are rather implicit in the other studies, the Danish project explicitly explains why a combination of knowledge, reflection, and action is necessary (see Holten et al. 2015 for details). The results from this study show that the leaders in the training program generally became more active leaders in the eyes of their employees compared to leaders from the control group. In a subsample of schools, the study also finds evidence for some positive effects of objectively measured performance.

Taken together, the leadership training studies suggest that it is possible to enhance public managers' competences to contribute to public service performance, but this is far from easy. We *can* stimulate behavior that leads to higher performance, and public managers *can* become better at creating public value in public organizations by participating in training with coaching, classroom instruction, feedback, and experiential learning.

5.7 Conclusion

This chapter demonstrates that research on whether, how, and under what conditions public managers contribute to public service performance is mounting. We highlight research that draws on robust—yet diverse—research designs. While more research is needed on the critical role of public managers, the current snapshot supports the conclusion that public managers—despite facing multiple performance criteria, goals, and constraints from the (political) environments in which they operate—*can* make a difference for the performance of their organizations. More specifically, public managers *do* matter for public service performance.

To qualify the role of public managers and their contribution to public service performance, this chapter has pointed to both novel contextual factors and fundamental components. Regarding the latter, the chapter discusses autonomy, capacity, and ability as three critical components of leadership and puts forward theoretical arguments for why each of these components warrants more attention in future research. For the former, the chapter makes the case for expanding public management research to include less-studied leadership strategies. Next to well-known goal-oriented strategies, inspiration from generic leadership research could fuel more research on the relevance and prevalence of relational and non-leader-centric strategies. Thus, future research endeavors would do well to expand our understanding of the effectiveness of different leadership strategies that might be applied independently or in combination.

Furthermore, the chapter combines recent theorizing on public organizations' reputation and reputation management by arguing that public organizations' reputation may prove to be a vital moderator and a potential performance criterion per se in future research on public management and performance. While public managers already demonstrate an interest in the reputation of their organizations, research is still in its infancy in terms of investigating the organizational reputation per se as well as reputation management's relation to performance.

While the evidence highlighted in this chapter demonstrates that public managers under some conditions can improve public service performance through active leadership, the variety of suggestions for future research reflected here also underscores the many novel paths for public management scholars to pursue. In particular, we encourage a continuation of the emerging pattern to build robust research designs that allow for causal inference while embracing the complexities faced by public managers in leading their organizations in political—and sometimes turbulent—environments.

References

Amirkhanyan, A. A., K. J. Meier, L. J. O'Toole, M. A. Dakhwe, and S. Janzen. 2018. "Management and Performance in US Nursing Homes." *Journal of Public Administration Research and Theory 28* (1): pp. 33–49.

Andersen, L. B., A. Boesen, and L. H. Pedersen. 2016. "Performance in Public Organizations: Clarifying the Conceptual Space." *Public Administration Review 76* (6): pp. 852–62.

Andrews, R., and G. A. Boyne. 2010. "Capacity, Leadership and Organizational Performance: Testing the Black Box Model of Public Management." *Public Administration Review 70* (3): pp. 443–54.

Andrews, R., G. A. Boyne, M. J. Moon, and R. M. Walker. 2010. "Assessing Organizational Performance: Exploring Differences between Internal and External Measures." *International Public Management Journal 13* (2): pp. 105–29.

Andrews, R., G. Boyne, and R. M. Walker. 2011. "The Impact of Management on Administrative and Survey Measures of Organizational Performance." *Public Management Review 13* (2): pp. 227–55.

Barnard, C. 1938. *The Functions of the Executive*. Boston: Harvard Business Review.

Bass, B. M., B. J. Avolio, D. I. Jung, and Y. Berson. 2003. "Predicting Unit Performance by Assessing Transformational and Transactional Leadership." *Journal of Applied Psychology 88* (2): pp. 207–18.

Bellé, N. 2014. "Leading to Make a Difference: A Field Experiment on the Performance Effects of Transformational Leadership, Perceived Social Impact, and Public Service Motivation." *Journal of Public Administration Research and Theory 24* (1): pp. 109–36.

Bellé, N. 2015. "Performance-Related Pay and the Crowding out of Motivation in the Public Sector: A Randomized Field Experiment." *Public Administration Review 75* (2): pp. 230–41.

Bozeman, B., and S. Bretschneider. 1994. "The 'Publicness Puzzle' in Organization Theory: A Test of Alternative Explanations of Differences between Public and Private Organizations." *Journal of Public Administration Research and Theory 4* (2): pp. 197–223.

Carpenter, D. 2002. "Groups, the Media, Agency Waiting Costs, and FDA Drug Approval." *American Journal of Political Science 46* (3): pp. 490–505.

Carpenter, D. 2010. *Reputation and Power: Organizational Image and Pharmaceutical Regulation at the FDA*. Princeton, NJ: Princeton University Press.

Carpenter, D., and G. A. Krause. 2012. "Reputation and Public Administration." *Public Administration Review 72* (1): pp. 26–32.

Christensen, T., and Å. Gornitzka. 2017 "Reputation Management in Complex Environments: A Comparative Study of University Organizations." *Higher Education Policy 30* (1): pp. 123–40.

Coombs, W. T. 2007. "Protecting Organization Reputations during a Crisis: The Development and Application of Situational Crisis Communication Theory." *Corporate Reputation Review 10* (3): pp. 163–76.

Coombs, W. T., and S. J. Holladay. 2010. *PR Strategy and Application: Managing Influence*. Hoboken, NJ: Wiley Blackwell.

Day, D. D., and J. Antonakis. 2012. "Leadership: Past, Present, and Future." In *The Nature of Leadership*, edited by D. D. Day and J. Antonakis, pp. 3–25. 2nd ed. Thousand Oaks, CA: Sage.

Dukerich, J. M., B. R. Golden, and S. M. Shortell. 2002. "Beauty Is in the Eye of the Beholder: The Impact of Organizational Identification, Identity, and Image on the Cooperative Behaviors of Physicians." *Administrative Science Quarterly 47* (3): pp. 507–33.

Dutton, J. E., and J. M. Dukerich. 1991. "Keeping an Eye on the Mirror: Image and Identity in Organizational Adaptation." *Academy of Management Journal 34* (3): pp. 517–54.

Dutton, J. E., J. M. Dukerich, and C. V. Harquail. 1994. "Organizational Images and Member Identification." *Administrative Science Quarterly 39* (2): pp. 239–63.

Fausing, M. S., H. J. Jeppesen, T. F. Jønsson, J. Lewandowski, and M. C. Bligh. 2013. "Moderators of Shared Leadership: Work Function and Team Autonomy." *Team Performance Management: An International Journal 19* (5/6): pp. 244–62.

Favero, N., K. J. Meier, and L. J. O'Toole. 2016. "Goals, Trust, Participation, and Feedback: Linking Internal Management with Performance Outcomes." *Journal of Public Administration Research and Theory 26* (2): pp. 327–43.

Fernandez, S. 2008. "Examining the Effects of Leadership Behavior on Employee Perceptions of Performance and Job Satisfaction." *Public Performance & Management Review 32* (2): pp. 175–205.

Fernandez, S., Y. J. Cho, and J. L. Perry. 2010. "Exploring the Link between Integrated Leadership and Public Sector Performance." *The Leadership Quarterly 21* (2): pp. 308–23.

Fombrun, C., and V. Rindova. 1998. "Reputation Management in Global 1000 Firms: A Benchmarking Study." *Corporate Reputation Review 1* (3): pp. 205–15.

Fryer, Jr., R. G. 2017. "Management and Student Achievement: Evidence from a Randomized Field Experiment." NBER Working Paper No. 23437.

Graen, G. B., and M. Uhl-Bien. 1995. "Relationship-Based Approach to Leadership: Development of Leader–Member Exchange (LMX) Theory of Leadership over 25 Years: Applying a Multi-Level Multi-Domain Perspective." *The Leadership Quarterly 6* (2): pp. 219–47.

Greenleaf, R. K. 1970. *The Servant as Leader*. Indianapolis, IN: The Robert K. Greenleaf Center.

Grøn, C. 2018. "Perceptions Unfolded: Managerial Implementation in Perception Formation." *International Journal of Public Sector Management 31* (6): pp. 710–25.

Hassan, S., B. E. Wright, and G. Yukl. 2014. "Does Ethical Leadership Matter in Government? Effects on Organizational Commitment, Absenteeism, and Willingness to Report Ethical Problems." *Public Administration Review 74* (3): pp. 333–43.

Holten, A. L., A. Bøllingtoft, and I. Wilms. 2015. "Leadership in a Changing World: Developing Managers through a Teaching and Learning Programme." *Management Decision 53* (5): pp. 1107–24.

Jacobsen, C. B., and L. B. Andersen. 2017. "Leading Public Service Organizations: How to Obtain Employees with High Self-Efficacy." *Public Management Review 19* (2): pp. 253–73.

Jensen, U. T., L. B. Andersen, L. Ladegaard, A. Bøllingtoft, T. L. M. Eriksen, A.-L. Holten, C. B. Jacobsen, J. Ladenburg, P. A. Nielsen, H. Salomonsen, N. Westergaard-Nielsen, and A. Würtz. 2016. "Conceptualizing and Measuring Transformational and Transactional Leadership." *Administration & Society 51* (1): pp. 3–33.

Jensen, U. T., and A. Bøllingtoft. 2017. "I Will Work Harder If We Agree! How Value Fit Moderates the Impact of Transformational Leadership on Employee Job Performance." Paper presented at the European Group for Public Administration (EGPA) Annual Conference, Milan, Italy, August 30–September 1, 2017.

Knies, E., C. B. Jacobsen, and L. Tummers. 2016. "Leadership and Organizational Performance: State of the Art and a Research Agenda." In *The Routledge Companion to Leadership*, edited by J. Storey, J. Hartley, J.-L. Denis, P. 't Hart, and D. Ulrich, pp. 404–18. New York: Routledge.

Krause, G. A., and D. Carpenter. 2015. "Transactional Authority and Bureaucratic Politics." *Journal of Public Administration Research and Theory 25* (1): pp. 5–25.

Luoma-aho, V. 2007. "Neutral Reputation and Public Sector Organizations." *Corporate Reputation Review 10* (2): pp. 124–43.

Maor, M. 1999. "The Paradox of Managerialism." *Public Administration Review 59* (1): pp. 5–18.

Maor, M. 2015. "Theorizing Bureaucratic Reputation." In *Organizational Reputation in the Public Sector*, edited by W. Arild and M. Maor, pp. 17–36. London: Routledge.

Meier, K. J., and L. J. O'Toole. 2013. "I Think (I am Doing Well), Therefore I Am: Assessing the Validity of Administrators' Self-Assessments of Performance." *International Public Management Journal 16* (1): pp. 1–27.

Meier, K. J., S. C. Winter, L. J. O'Toole, N. Favero, and S. C. Andersen. 2015. "The Validity of Subjective Performance Measures: School Principals in Texas and Denmark." *Public Administration 93* (4): pp. 1084–101.

Miao, Q., A. Newman, G. Schwartz, and B. Cooper. 2018. "How Leadership and Public Service Motivation Enhance Innovative Behavior." *Public Administration 78* (1): pp. 71–81.

Miao, Q., A. Newman, G. Schwartz, and L. Xu. 2014. "Servant Leadership, Trust, and the Organizational Commitment of Public Sector Employees in China." *Public Administration 92* (3): pp. 727–43.

Moynihan, D. P, S. K. Pandey, and B. E. Wright. 2012. "Setting the Table: How Transformational Leadership Fosters Performance Information Use." *Journal of Public Administration Research and Theory 22* (1): pp. 143–64.

Newman, A., G. Schwartz, B. Cooper, and S. Sendjaya. 2017. "How Servant Leadership Influences Organizational Citizenship Behavior: The Roles of LMX, Empowerment, and Proactive Personality." *Journal of Business Ethics 145* (1): pp. 49–62.

Nielsen, P. A. 2013. *Performance Information in Politics and Public Management: Impacts on Decision Making and Performance.* Aarhus: Politica.

Nohria, N., and R. Gulati. 1996. "Is Slack Good or Bad for Innovation?" *Academy of Management Journal 39* (5): pp. 1245–64.

Oberfield, Z. W. 2012. "Public Management in Time: A Longitudinal Examination of the Full Range of Leadership Theory." *Journal of Public Administration Research and Theory 24* (2): pp. 407–29.

Orazi, D. C., A. Turrini, and G. Valotti. 2013. "Public Sector Leadership: New Perspectives for Research and Practice." *International Review of Administrative Sciences 79* (3): pp. 486–504.

O'Shea, P. G., R. J. Foti, N. M. A. Hauenstein, and P. Bycio. 2009. "Are the Best Leaders Both Transformational and Transactional? A Pattern-Oriented Analysis." *Leadership 5* (2): pp. 237–59.

O'Toole, L. J., and K. J. Meier. 2010. "In Defense of Bureaucracy." *Public Management Review 12* (3): pp. 341–61.

O'Toole, L. J., and K. J. Meier. 2011. *Public Management: Organizations, Governance, and Performance.* Cambridge: Cambridge University Press.

Pedersen, M. Ø, and H. H. Salomonsen. 2020. "Foreign Secretaries and/or Home Secretaries? Linking Transformational Leadership and Reputation Management." Working Paper, available upon request from the authors.

Petrovsky, N., O. James, and G. A. Boyne. 2015. "New Leaders' Managerial Background and the Performance of Public Organizations: The Theory of Publicness Fit." *Journal of Public Administration Research & Theory 25* (1): pp. 217–36.

Rainey, H. G. 2014. *Understanding and Managing Public Organizations.* San Francisco, CA: Jossey-Bass.

Schwartz, G., A. Newman, B. Cooper, and N. Eva. 2016. "Servant Leadership and Follower Job Performance: The Mediating Effect of Public Service Motivation." *Public Administration 94* (4): pp. 1025–41.

Seidle, B., S. Fernandez, and J. L. Perry. 2016. "Do Leadership Training and Development Make a Difference in the Public Sector? A Panel Study." *Public Administration Review* 76 (4): pp. 603–13.

Tummers, L., and E. Knies. 2016. "Measuring Public Leadership: Developing Scales for Four Key Public Leadership Roles." *Public Administration 94* (2): pp. 433–51.

Van Knippenberg, D., and S. B. Sitkin. 2013. "A Critical Assessment of Charismatic-Transformational Leadership Research: Back to the Drawing Board?" *The Academy of Management Annals 7* (1): pp. 1–60.

Van Wart, M. 2013. "Administrative Leadership Theory: A Reassessment after 10 Years." *Public Administration 91* (3): pp. 521–43.

Verhoest, K., B. G. Peters, G. Bouckaert, and B. Verschuere. 2004. "The Study of Organisational Autonomy: A Conceptual Review." *Public Administration and Development 24* (2): pp. 101–18.

Vogel, R., and D. Masal. 2015. "Public Leadership: A Review of the Literature and Framework for Future Research." *Public Management Review 17* (8): pp. 1165–89.

Wang, D., D. A. Waldman, and Z. Zhang. 2014. "A Meta-Analysis of Shared Leadership and Team Effectiveness." *Journal of Applied Psychology 99* (2): pp. 181–98.

Wright, B. E., D. P. Moynihan, and S. K. Pandey. 2012. "Pulling the Levers: Transformational Leadership, Public Service Motivation, and Mission Valence." *Public Administration Review 72* (2): pp. 206–15.

Wynen, J., K. Verhoest, E. Ongaro, S. Van Thiel, and in cooperation with the COBRA Network. 2014. "Innovation-Oriented Culture in the Public Sector: Do Managerial Autonomy and Result Control Lead to Innovation?" *Public Management Review 16* (1): pp. 45–66.

Yukl, G. 2013. *Leadership in Organizations*. Global ed. London: Pearson.

6

Managers as Insiders or Outsiders to Public Organizations

Publicness Fit, Leadership, and Organizational Performance

Oliver James, Ayako Nakamura, and Nicolai Petrovsky

6.1 Introduction

Public management research pays particular attention to features of publicness and their outcomes. This focus is absent from conceptualizations of management as generic (Boyne 2002; Boyne et al. 2011a; 2011b; Corley and Gioia 2011; Hill 2005; O'Toole and Meier 2003; Petrovsky 2010; Rainey and Chun 2005). In the generic management literature, a large body of research has examined the fit between people and their work environments, along with the outcomes for those individuals and the organizations for which they work (Edwards et al. 2006; Ekehammer 1974; Kristof-Brown et al. 2005; Parsons 1909; Pervin 1968). Within this broad topic, a strand of research has found that the fit between top managers' backgrounds and their current organizations can matter for management practices and outcomes. The public management literature adds the insight that publicness is an important aspect of fit. In this chapter, we develop this linkage between the two literatures, review the state of current theory and evidence, and draw out the implications for future research.

We start by setting out the concept of managerial publicness fit for senior managers of organizations. Section 6.2 defines insiderness/outsiderness on the publicness dimensions of public ownership, funding, and regulation. The degree of fit has implications for how management operates and affects organizational outcomes, particularly performance in terms of meeting its goals. In Section 6.3, we systematically review the state of research on publicness "insider/outsider" fit. However, because such work is currently limited, we take a broad approach and seek to incorporate insights from the more general literature on the effects of managerial background. Section 6.4 explores data from UK central government with regard to the performance of managers with different levels of match on publicness dimensions between themselves and the agencies they run. Our data exploration suggests that

Oliver James, Ayako Nakamura, and Nicolai Petrovsky, *Managers as Insiders or Outsiders to Public Organizations: Publicness Fit, Leadership, and Organizational Performance* In: *Managing for Public Service Performance: How People and Values Make a Difference.* Edited by: Peter Leisink, Lotte B. Andersen, Gene A. Brewer, Christian B. Jacobsen, Eva Knies, and Wouter Vandenabeele, Oxford University Press (2021). © Oliver James, Ayako Nakamura, and Nicolai Petrovsky.
DOI: 10.1093/oso/9780192893420.003.0006

organizations headed by outsiders perform no better or even slightly worse than those headed by insiders in this context do. The chapter concludes with an agenda for extending research on public managerial fit informed by the literature review and the state of current evidence.

6.2 Publicness of Organizations and the Insiderness/ Outsiderness of Managers

New managerial leaders' background and the fit with the organizations where they acquire leadership roles are commonly discussed in studies of generic management, with empirical evidence often coming from research on private businesses. Managerial fit and career patterns are considered on many dimensions, especially the sector of activity, geographical location, processes handled, and type of organization (Biemann and Wolf 2009; Booth et al. 2016; Hamori and Kakarika 2009). Managers' experiences affect their skills, ways of thinking, and the forms of tacit and explicit knowledge that they bring to their jobs. These experiences are a key part of research on the "upper echelons" of management, alongside other factors including managers' values and personalities (Hambrick and Mason 1984).

In public management research, the public or private background of leaders, along with the implications for performance of organizations, has increasingly been studied at different levels of government, from local to national (Boyne and Meier 2009; Boyne et al. 2011a; 2011b; Corley and Gioia 2011; Hill 2005; Jas and Skelcher 2005; O'Toole and Meier 2003; Petrovsky 2010). A recent strand of this research has focused on the characteristics of public organizations and the career background of senior managers in terms of "publicness" fit (Petrovsky et al. 2015; 2017).

Many organizations have some aspect of "publicness" (Bozeman 2004). However, three dimensions capture the key differences between public and private organizations that are most commonly found in the literature (Andrews et al. 2011; Boyne 2002; Hood et al. 1999; see also Chapter 4). These are: (1) public ownership; (2) public funding of the organization; and (3) public control, or regulation, of the organization. In principle, the degree of each dimension can be assessed independently of each other, and they can be aggregated using weights for each to determine an overall degree of publicness. Each dimension also allows a binary simplification to create a distinction between "insiders" and "outsiders" for that aspect of the organization.

The first dimension, public ownership, assesses whether the organization is collectively owned by a political community, such as a nation-state or a municipality. Typically, this implies reporting to political overseers, at a minimum through their representation on a board of directors. For this dimension, "insiders" are classified as managers who have experience of reporting in an organization to political overseers, while "outsiders" are those who do not have these experiences. Clearly, privately owned organizations are examples of bodies that are not public, but there are hybrid public–private organizations. As an extension of this concept, further delimitations within the public sector are possible to assess intra-public sector insiderness and outsiderness by experience of different accountability systems. For example, the level of government where the official experienced political reporting prior to becoming a CEO may matter since the accountability regime for officials in a national government reporting to ministers is very different from that found in local government.

The second dimension, the degree of public funding, is the extent to which the organizations are funded by public money, typically derived from taxpayers. In this context, if the organization sells products and obtains financing from markets, the level of publicness is lessened. Hence, if a manager moved from an organization which generated revenue by selling services (this includes public agencies operating on a fee basis) or products to an organization funded largely by taxpayers' money (or vice versa), the manager is classified as an "outsider" on this dimension.

The third dimension is public control or regulation, the extent to which an organization is subject to elected officials or their agents exercising public authority to constrain policies and practices. This is often based on the monitoring of specific rules or standards as part of the "regulation of government" (Hood et al. 1999; 2000; James 2000). In many systems subject to new public management (NPM) reforms, public regulators such as oversight departments, inspectors, and audit/standards bodies have been established to oversee public organizations. On this basis, if a manager comes from an organization not directly controlled by public regulators to an organization controlled by an oversight body, this manager is classified as an outsider of the organization to which they succeeded on this dimension.

In publicness fit theory, "an insider leader" by definition means that the degrees of publicness of previous experience match the degrees of publicness of the organization where the manager now serves. The concept of publicness fit is consistent with the broader tradition of research that focuses on the fit between individuals and the organizational environment in which they work (Edwards et al. 2006; Ekehammer 1974; Kristof-Brown et al. 2005; Parsons 1909; Pervin 1968). This research also helps show why publicness matters to management practices and organizational performance outcomes. A review of person–environment fit research (Kristof-Brown et al. 2005) notes three main elements in this body of work. First, the study of person–environment fit focuses on assessing the discrepancy between the characteristics of workers and their jobs or tasks at work. Existing studies in this area draw from Edwards (1991) to set out the two conceptualizations of the fit level between individual workers and their jobs. The first is a demands–abilities fit that assesses employees' knowledge and skills and whether these abilities are commensurate with what the job requires. The second is a needs–supplies fit that assesses the fit between what the job supplies and the employees' needs, desires, or preferences (Edwards 1991; Kristof 1996). In particular, the assessment of needs–supplies fit is related to several theories on whether fit and adjustment affect employees' well-being and satisfaction in workplaces (Caplan 1987; Porter 1961; 1962). In terms of publicness fit, publicness insiders on each dimension will have knowledge and skills from their previous work in similarly public organizations that will help them do their current job and will fit with the requirements and values of the public organization.

Second, research on person–organization fit further looks into the compatibility between people and entire organizations. The studies emphasizing this aspect hypothesize that individuals will be most successful in organizations that share their common personalities (Christiansen et al. 1997; Ryan and Schmitt 1996; Tom 1971). The congruence between individual and organizational values has been a particular focus of study (Chatman 1989; O'Reilly et al. 1991). In publicness fit, individuals who have previously worked in similarly public organizations on the three dimensions will have had experience of working in environments with similar demands, making them compatible with the organization in which they currently work.

Third, the research focused on person–group fit looks into the interpersonal compatibility between individuals and their work groups (Judge and Ferris 1992; Kristof 1996; Werbel and Gilliland 1999). Relatedly, a focus on supervisor–subordinate fit emphasizes the importance of a matching level between supervisors and subordinates in assessing the person–environment fit level of subordinate workers since the supervisors' personalities often represent the overall characteristics of the work environment. This includes the congruence of the values shared between leaders and followers (Krishnan 2002), the similarities between supervisor and subordinate personalities (Schaubroeck and Lam 2002), and the congruence between the goals shared between manager and employees (Witt 1998). In publicness fit, managerial leaders with experience of public organizations will have worked in groups with similar characteristics previously, making them more familiar with the pressures and opportunities of working in such groups and of supervising employees in such environments.

Publicness fit incorporates insights from some elements of the person–environment fit literature more than others. First, the background experience of a manager in a public or private organization affects the fit between managerial characteristics and the task at hand in managing the organization. Second, the fit between personality and organization is less central to publicness fit because the focus is on the role of the previous experience rather than innate characteristics of the manager that are part of the person–environment theory, except in so far as these are altered by previous managerial experience. On the third dimension, the previous experience affects skills and behavior that affect the compatibility between the manager, the organization, and the other employees of the organization, including those whom they supervise. This could be in terms of congruence of values or goals in so far as these are shaped by experience, and also how these factors influence the managers' ability to operate in the broader public environment of which the organization forms a part. A key insight of the perspective is that, in general, a higher fit on publicness leads to better performance of the organization. The main exception to this situation is where an organization is performing poorly such that a new perspective, reflected in different experiences of an incoming "outsider" manager, is beneficial for

Table 6.1 Relationship between conceptualizations of person–environment fit and the theory of publicness fit

	High publicness fit	Low publicness fit
Demands–abilities fit	• Familiarity in dealing with political overseers • Familiarity with governmental budget cycles and restrictions • Ability to demonstrate accountability on multiple dimensions	• Lack of connections among, or finesse in dealing with, political overseers • Familiar only with funding through the market • Experience in demonstrating accountability to shareholders
Supplies–needs fit	• Acceptance and endorsement of restrictions on managerial decisions by political environment • Being comfortable with a lack of influence over funding of organization • Seeing organizational performance as inherently multidimensional	• Desire to shape overall direction of an organization • Desire to expand into new markets • Focused view of organizational performance as shareholder value

performance because it brings about a new direction for management (Petrovsky 2010; Petrovsky et al. 2015).

The relationship between the person–environment fit literature and publicness fit theory is set out in Table 6.1, looking at the case of an organization that is publicly owned, receives its funding through public appropriations, and is closely overseen by the political executive.

6.3 Empirical Evidence on Publicness Fit: Systematic Literature Review

The theoretical argument about publicness fit implies that unless the organization already performs poorly, it is beneficial to appoint a manager with a degree of fit (an "insider") on publicness dimensions as that will limit the inevitable disruption associated with the succession. We undertook a systematic literature review to identify research on public and private management that provides evidence about the effects of managerial publicness fit between leaders and their organizations. To do this, we searched for research specifically using the "publicness fit" framework of three dimensions. Unfortunately, there is relatively little systematic empirical research on whether the sectoral origin of government agency chief executives affects organizational outcomes. The major exception is Lewis (2007). He found that previous broad public managerial experience in and of itself did not influence the performance of federal agency heads. Rather, having previous experience in the same agency of which they became head as well as the length of time serving as agency heads were positively associated with performance. These two variables explain the on average higher performance of career civil servants as agency heads compared to outside appointees.

We supplemented this evidence with research on the fit between managers and their organizations based on their previous experience on dimensions of management fit in general. This enables us to include relevant insights for publicness fit from theory and evidence about the role of managerial fit in general. The review identified research on concepts and theories, about the extent and trends in insider/outsider hiring, and effects on organizational outcomes, especially performance, as well as outcomes for individual managers.

We included research on both the public and private business sectors in the Organisation for Economic Co-operation and Development (OECD) member states and affiliates.[1] We excluded studies on other countries to enhance comparability. The search used the ISI Web of Science, the electronic database for social sciences articles. We used search terms that are common in the study of career patterns of CEOs and senior managers. The full title search[2] used the following keywords: "CEOs" [CEO*] AND "career" [career*], "managers" [manag*] AND "career patterns" [career pat*], and "managers" [manag*], and "career mobility" [career mob*].

Using these criteria, we identified 128 articles. A subset of the forty-eight most relevant in discussing fit of managers and their organizations was identified by reading the abstract, supplemented by reading the full text when the abstract was insufficiently informative of content. We include a full set of the articles identified in an online appendix.[3] The methods used by the studies are summarized in Table 6.2. An existing systematic literature review in this field (Vinkenburg and Weber 2012) analyzed thirty-three studies of career patterns of CEOs and senior managers in the private sector. According to their classification, four of those studies focused on career patterns based on population or labor force panel data, five of those analyzed were based on the panel data of alumni from educational institutions, ten studies focused on career patterns of members of professional associations (i.e. accountants and lawyers), and eleven studies focused on single organization or intra-organizational career patterns based on employees' survey data. Our literature review shows the similar tendencies in the use of research methods. Among the forty-eight studies we reviewed, fifteen studies analyzed the career patterns of CEOs in relation to their performance, and the other thirty-three studies analyzed the career patterns of senior–mid-rank managers. Additionally, within the forty-eight studies, thirty studies analyzed the career patterns of CEOs and managers across multiple industries, and fifteen studies focused on those in single industries.

---

[1] The OECD has member states, candidates for membership, key partners (Brazil, China, India, Indonesia, and South Africa), and members of regional initiatives.

[2] The ISI title search picks up the sources that include keywords in titles. In the parentheses, the symbol * is a special function key of ISI for the purpose of searching for any words entailing the term. For example, [manag*] searches any words including "manag" such as "managers," "management," and "managing."

[3] The appendix is available at www.oup.co.uk/companion/managingforpublicservice.

Table 6.2 Research method of forty-eight selected articles

Type of study	Method	Number
Qualitative	Analysis of interview data or reports	6
Quantitative	Analysis of survey data, administrative data	39
Hybrid qualitative/quantitative	Mixed methods	2
Other	Systematic literature review	1

Quantitative methods and data analysis are dominant in the literature. Table 6.2 shows that of the total forty-eight studies reviewed, thirty-nine studies are based on the quantitative analysis using individual workers' career development data. The use of surveys is also common. Within the thirty-nine studies, fifteen studies collected the data by original surveys. The sample size of those studies varied depending on the type of research. For surveys and other quantitative studies, the sample sizes varied between approximately 100 and 4,000 in each sample, while the qualitative studies are mostly small N studies ranging between 3–30 cases. For the study of CEOs, most studies collected data from widely recognized business magazines (e.g. *Forbes, The Economist,* and *Fortune*) because the CEOs are highly profiled figures. Meanwhile, the studies focused on senior managers tended to collect data by national labor force surveys or by means of conducting original surveys. In order to identify the career patterns of CEOs and senior managers, various regression models were typically applied by quantitative studies, with recent studies applying optimal matching analysis to identify the job mobility of CEOs (Biemann and Wolf 2009; Koch et al. 2017; Vinkenburg and Weber 2012).

Existing studies holistically analyzing career patterns and job mobility of top managers are limited. Only seven articles conducted systematic research identifying CEOs' career patterns and managerial fit of those CEOs to the organizations, although there was conceptual work and research focused on the analysis of individual cases (Biemann and Wolf 2009; Booth et al. 2016; Boyer and Ortiz-Molina 2008; Crossland et al. 2014; Hamori and Kakarika 2009; Koch et al. 2017; Wu 2004). If we include case studies of senior and general managers, eleven articles focused on the job mobility of managers in relation to insiderness/outsiderness. Sammarra et al. (2013) compared the inter-organizational career mobility of senior managers and highly skilled professionals such as lawyers and accountants in multiple industries. In terms of the career patterns of these professionals, Coen and Vannoni (2016) analyzed the career patterns of managers who engage in EU regulatory matters across twenty-six countries. Donnelly (2009) analyzed the career mobility of knowledge workers (i.e. IT consultants) within the IT industry in the US and the UK. Some studies focused on the career patterns of senior managers in specific industries, including the hotel industry (Kim et al. 2009; Okumus et al. 2016), and city managers of large cities in the US (Watson and Hassett 2004. Additionally, there are several studies focused on the career patterns of female managers in multiple industries (Burke 2000; Burke and McKeen 1993; Durbin and Tomlinson 2010; Voss and Speere 2014).

In studies of career patterns of managers and professionals, a common finding is that the highly mobile career that seamlessly moves positions across inter-organizations or intra-organizations is positively evaluated for individuals and organizational performance (Arthur and Rousseau 2001; Donnelly 2009; Sammarra et al. 2013). It is considered that high job mobility provides workers with more personal choice and freedom to get better opportunities throughout their careers. However, in spite of the generally positive conclusions from broad-based studies, the existing studies focused on particular cases suggest that inter-organizational moves at top management levels are still limited, providing evidence that lack of fit with previous experience places constraints on mobility.

Koch et al. (2017) analyzed the job mobility of the Fortune 100 CEOs and reported that 38 percent of the CEOs are "insiders" who spent their entire careers in single companies, and 62 percent of the CEOs had never worked in more than one industry. According to Koch et al. (2017), the organizational preferences in appointing insider CEOs are concerned with the size of companies and the required management skills for the CEOs in big firms. In the global firms, required management skills for the CEOs are not transferable even in the same industry since the size of business is significantly large. For example, if the board of directors look for the CEOs of a global corporation, such as Walmart, most external candidates would have experience in the retail industry; however, they would not have the skills to manage the organizational and institutional complexity of a company with over $400 billion in sales, which is not a comparable scale to other retailing companies. In this situation, it is more practical for the board to appoint the CEO from insiders.

The role of firm-specific fit is emphasized in some studies. Sammarra et al. (2013) report that in order to assess the managerial fit of the newly appointed CEOs, the type of required knowledge and skills should be considered by individual organizations. Often, the management skills and knowledge of senior rank managers, including CEOs, relate to knowledge about people in the firm, specific organizational procedures, organizational culture, company history, and business and products specificity. Those are not forms of transferable knowledge across organizations but essential for running large corporations.

There is considerable evidence that from the perspective of personal career success, a close fit with previous experience is often beneficial. Hamori and Kakarika (2009) analyzed the CEOs affiliated with 100 large corporations and found that CEOs who largely rely on firm-specific knowledge inside the single organization progress their careers more rapidly than outsiders who have knowledge about general human capital. They concluded that external job experiences prior to gaining the current CEO positions negatively correlate to their career success measured by increased salaries. Similarly, Sammarra et al. (2013) compare the level of success brought by the inter-organizational moves of senior managers and professionals measured by the salaries those workers gained. According to them, as far as the success assessed by salary, frequent inter-organizational moves are not paid for individual workers since the pay scales of the majority of business organizations still tend to expect workers to climb up ladders to managerial positions inside single organizations. In this way, frequent inter-organizational mobility does not promote personal career success.

Some studies show specific managerial conditions where organizations prefer outsider CEOs to insiders. Wu (2004) analyzed the influence of public scrutiny on the companies' directorship. The study assessed the impact of inspection reports by the California Public Employees' Retirement System (CalPERS), the largest pension fund in the US, on the US corporations listed by Forbes 500 companies. CalPERS publicly criticizes poor governance of individual companies in their reports, and corporations tend to respond by changing their governance strategy. Wu (2004) concluded that organizations are more likely to dismiss the CEOs who were in post at the time of the report or decrease the number of inside directors from the boards. Although those departing insiders are less likely to take up future directorships, and the relationship between performance and CEO dismissal becomes tighter after companies are named by CalPERS, it is considered that appointing an external CEO after the report is a good decision for the organization to show the improvement on corporate governance. Similarly, Boyer and Ortiz-Molina (2008) analyzed the patterns of succession of CEOs in US business firms across multiple industries between 1993 and 2002. From the 1,123 sampled cases of new CEO appointments, the board of directors is more likely to appoint the insider candidate to the position of CEO if the candidate's managerial ownership stake is high. In other words, if the ownership stakes of the insider candidates are low, the likelihood of appointing an external candidate as CEO increases.

Industry differences affect the importance of the managerial fit of external hires. Several studies find that certain industries demand workers to have longer engagement in a single industry, with senior managers often rising up through the ranks inside single organizations. This is especially evident in manufacturing and engineering and the hospitality industries (Kim et al. 2009; Koch et al. 2017; Okumus et al. 2016; Vinkenberg and Weber 2012). Also, Goodall (2009) provides evidence that "scholar leaders" of universities, i.e. university presidents or vice chancellors with more research expertise, are associated with better research performance for the organization as a whole. Looking at a different aspect of the performance of universities, Rutherford (2017) finds that student outcomes tend to be better when university presidents have high, but not too high, degrees of fit between their current and prior positions. Overall, technical attainment and acquired expert knowledge of leaders have been found in other contexts to predict organizational performance (Goodall et al. 2011). On the contrary, inter-organizational moves of managers are rather common and more acceptable in other industries such as the financial and IT industries. In these industries, the skills and knowledge required for management positions are often more transferable; hence, the job mobility of senior managers tends to be higher, and the insider/outsider distinction does not severely affect performance.

The insider/outsider distinctions for working in different kinds of companies or across sectors diminish in importance for professional workers such as lawyers, legal advisors, and accountants (Coen and Vannoni 2016; Donnelly 2009). For example, EU affairs managers specializing in EU regulatory matters of companies' businesses tend to move seamlessly between multiple organizations since the knowledge and skills are transferable across multiple corporations (Coen and Vannoni 2016). In this type of job, corporations often seek the candidates who have experience in various regulatory matters; hence, the organizations rather prefer external candidates who have external knowledge and experiences. Thus, depending on the type of industry and required professional skills, organizational preferences also differ, and in some situations, outsider managers could fit the organizations better.

6.4 Empirical Research on Publicness Fit: Evidence from UK Central Government Executive Agencies

The limited existing evidence directly on publicness fit and its consequences suggests the need for more research. We illustrate the potential for such research and some indicative findings for the role of publicness fit in the context of UK central government executive agencies. This research setting provides an opportunity to consider insiders and outsiders in charge of the same organization, in contrast to contexts where insiders or outsiders tend to be in charge of different types of bodies (e.g. as in Lewis's 2007 study of US federal agencies. Specifically, we look at all British central government executive agencies. Northern Ireland agencies are excluded as they operate under different arrangements. Our data begins in 1989, when this type of agency first came into operation, and extends into 2012. Our method here is exploratory analysis of the data without the aim of identifying causal relationships. Specifically, we tabulate transitions between agency heads and the performance levels associated with them.

Executive agencies are a specific class of organization responsible for the implementation of the executive functions of government. They operate with managerial discretion and are semi-detached from central government departments that supervise them (James 2003). Their personnel currently make up over 50 percent of the British civil service. The organizational form emerged in 1988 in response to a review of the civil service, which sought to separate policy from implementation and create a more business-like, managerialist approach to the delivery of government services (James 2001; Jenkins et al. 1988). The tasks of executive agencies range from research to regulation, internal government services, and frontline service delivery. Examples include driver licensing, issuing passports, controlling borders, maritime safety, logistics support to the armed forces, delivery of social security benefits, and the procurement of government services. From 1988, these tasks, traditionally performed directly by government departments, were gradually hived off into the executive agencies. Each executive agency operates under a specific performance framework with accountability to the relevant government minister in the agency's parent department. This is different from bodies such as "quangos" (quasi-autonomous non-governmental organizations), also known as "non-departmental public bodies," which have more formal independence from ministers and report to other stakeholders, such as independent boards (Flinders 2009; Hood and Lodge 2006; Horton and Jones 1996; James 2001; 2003).

Each agency is headed by a chief executive who enjoys considerable managerial freedom within the aims and responsibilities set out in the agency's Framework Document (there is one for each agency. While ministers are ultimately accountable for the agency's functions, chief executives are personally accountable to ministers for operational performance against published targets. Chief executives are typically employed on three-year or five-year fixed-term contracts with the possibility of extension subject to performance. The selection process is usually through fair and open competition, with the search process headed by the agency's parent government department and the appointment approved by a panel including Civil Service Commissioners. Generally, either insiders or outsiders to the agency, the civil service, or indeed the public sector may be recruited through this process.

A major thrust of the executive agency reform itself was to encourage more outsiders with diverse management experience in different contexts to apply for senior public sector management positions. Consequently, chief executive appointments in executive agencies come from a variety of backgrounds. Below, we provide findings from research on how insider versus outsider differences between chief executives are associated with performance outcomes.

We compare public sector insiders (whose previous appointment was also in the public sector) to public sector outsiders (whose previous appointment was in the private sector, in most cases in for-profit businesses. Differences in performance can be identified whenever one chief executive is succeeded by another, i.e. whenever there is a transition. There are four types of transitions in this example:

1. insider → outsider
2. outsider → insider
3. insider → insider
4. outsider → outsider

The data is rich in that all four types of transitions occur, although the third category of insider-to-insider is the most frequent.

We look at performance outcomes as the percentage of ministerial targets met, ranging from 0–100 percent. This is an important measure of the extent to which an agency delivers on the political priorities set for it by their overseers, with the targets being set and reported on publicly each year. Data for the first performance variable was gathered from the annual "Next Steps Reviews" and from agency annual reports, which are official House of Commons Command Papers published online as part of the House of Commons Parliamentary Papers and are also available from the British Library or directly from agencies. Data on chief executive tenure was taken from executive agencies' annual reports, which provide exact start and finish dates of agency chief executives' employment contracts. Information on chief executive career history was extracted from the *Whitehall Companion*, a published source that documents key information on the UK Home Civil Service (England, Scotland, and Wales. We omit interim chief executives from our analysis not only because of missing data but because most are in post only for one year, and so it is not possible to attribute annual performance target changes to individuals in post for such a short period of time. Where there were other entries missing, we contacted individual chief executives (or former chief executives) personally to obtain the required information, using either LinkedIn or other web sources to make contact. Additional searches were made of Who's Who; Who's Who in Scotland; Nexis UK (an online database of media stories); official government department and agency websites; and in the case of former agencies, the UK Government Web Archive.

As the descriptive statistics of transitions between executive agency chief executives indicate in Table 6.3, changes in performance tend to be incremental, even from insiders to outsiders or vice versa. Specifically, in most cases, a performance change of less than 5 percentage points has little substantive meaning as agencies tended to have an average of twenty targets in a year, and many had fewer. However, there is some evidence suggestive of outsiders generally not performing as well as insiders. In particular, there is some indication that the entry of public sector outsiders brings about some disruption (cf. the first row of Table 6.3 showing lower achievement of targets), but the substantive magnitude is not large. In contrast, when there is a move from an outsider to an insider, there is a small improvement in performance against targets.

As noted in Section 6.2, there may be situations where the disruption brought by a change from an insider as agency head to an outsider is outweighed by the fresh

Table 6.3 Descriptive statistics on British executive agency chief executive transitions, 1989–2012

Type of transition and number of occurrences	Mean percentage point change in target achievement after transition
Public sector insider → public sector outsider: 39 transitions	−2.9
Public sector outsider → public sector insider: 26 transitions	+3.3
Public sector insider → public sector insider: 239 transitions	+0.8
Public sector outsider → public sector outsider: 11 transitions	+1.0

strategies and tactics they bring. In our data, there are two cases of a substantial performance improvement following an insider-to-outsider succession. They are the Central Office of Information (reporting to the Cabinet Office) in the 1990s and the Hydrographic Office (reporting to the Department of Defence) in the 2000s. In both cases, insiders to these agencies were followed by managers directly recruited from the private sector through open competitions. In both cases, the average target achievement rate of the agency head increased by at least 25 percentage points. These two cases may be the exception that proves the broader rule.

6.5 Conclusion

There are a number of directions for research suggested by our review. Focusing on publicness fit is an important part of an account of the role of managerial fit and its relationship with the performance of public organizations, but it is only one of the relevant components. Therefore, we suggest that research focuses directly on such a broader conceptualization of managerial fit, including publicness, and assessing its implications for outcomes, including organizational performance. The classic person–environment fit literature supports our emphasis on the importance of the multidimensional background experiences of managers to assess the match between managers and the organizations where they newly acquire their managerial roles. The literature also suggests that the fit between managers and organizations should be distinguished from that between other workers and their work environment since the managerial fit often creates—or alters—organizational environment and culture, which affects overall performance as a consequence.

The state of theory and empirical patterns facilitate the development of a broader conceptualization of managerial insiderness or outsiderness. This incorporates the three major dimensions of publicness fit according to public ownership, public regulation, and public funding. However, the systematic review also finds the importance of insiderness/outsiderness on several other important aspects. The two main additional dimensions identified are the function that an organization serves (industry/service area fit)—for example, whether it is focused on financial services or information technology—and the personal and resource networks in which the organization is embedded. These dimensions cut across publicness, for example, networks in science policy communities often cut across public/private ownership or funding boundaries.

The recognition of publicness embedded as one form of management fit suggests the potential to combine these dimensions to look at multiple types of fit/lack of fit and how different kinds of fit moderate each other's effects. Empirically, such an approach will deepen the operationalization of managerial fit in the public settings where we already have some evidence. This particularly includes the contexts of the US, the UK, EU member states, and a few other countries, notably South Korea. In these cases, research has considered aspects of public careers in some depth but has not developed highly multidimensional measures of fit, tending instead to focus on one or two aspects of fit at a time.

There is also a need to extend the existing evidence about managerial fit, including publicness fit, to other institutional contexts beyond the most commonly researched jurisdictions. The review reveals gaps in the currently available research, suggesting benefits especially for contexts with complex or blurred public/private sector boundaries. In these ways, insider/outsider status differences and their implications for organizational performance should be further developed as a topic.

As this volume shows, there are many ingredients to an effective management of public services. In this chapter, we focused on the background senior managers bring with them and how it affects their work. In a nutshell, managers with a relatively high level of fit will, in most cases, be more effective in running a public service. Prior experience in handling the political complexities of a public service, limited influence on funding, and responding to demands for high performance along multiple dimensions are very valuable skills for a public manager. This prior experience brings with it a repertoire of feasible actions and other largely tacit knowledge that cannot be acquired quickly. The importance of a relatively high level of fit also extends to the technical aspects of the service area, for instance, education or public health.

The chapter provides one facet of the answer to this volume's central research question of how public management meaningfully contributes to public service performance. We highlight how a better fit between managers' experience and the demands of the public service they are leading results in higher performance. These insights are primarily derived from a systematic review of relevant academic literature, which we complement with an exploratory analysis of publicness fit using data we collected on British executive agencies. We further build on the implications of these findings by suggesting the merits of a broader conceptualization of managerial fit than is currently used in the public management literature.

Acknowledgments

All authors made an equal contribution to this chapter. This work contains research funded by the UK ESRC Project "Chief Executive Succession and the Performance of Central Government Agencies" (RES-062-23-2471).

References

Andrews, R., G. Boyne, and R. Walker. 2011. "Dimensions of Publicness and Organizational Performance: A Review of the Evidence." *Journal of Public Administration Research and Theory 21* (3i): pp. 301–19.

Arthur, M. B., and D. M. Rousseau. 2001. *The Boundaryless Career: A New Employment Principle for a New Organizational Era*. Oxford: Oxford University Press.

Biemann, T., and J. Wolf. 2009. "Career Patterns of Top Management Team Members in Five Countries: An Optimal Matching Analysis." *The International Journal of Human Resource Management 20* (5): pp. 975–91.

Booth, T., A. L. Murray, M. Overduin, M. Matthews, and A. Furnham. 2016. "Distinguishing CEOs from Top Level Management: A Profile Analysis of Individual Differences, Career Paths and Demographics." *Journal of Business and Psychology 31* (2): pp. 205–16.

Boyer, M. M., and H. Ortiz-Molina. 2008. "Career Concerns of Top Executives, Managerial Ownership and CEO Succession." *Corporate Governance-an International Review 16* (3): pp. 178–93.

Boyne, G. 2002. "Public and Private Management: What's the Difference?" *Journal of Management Studies 39* (1): pp. 97–122.

Boyne, G., O. James, P. John, and N. Petrovsky. 2011a. "Leadership Succession and Organizational Success: When Do New Chief Executives Make a Difference?" *Public Money and Management 31* (5): pp. 339–46.

Boyne, G., O. James, P. John, and N. Petrovsky. 2011b. "Top Management Turnover and Organizational Performance: A Test of a Contingency Model." *Public Administration Review 7* (4): pp. 572–81.

Boyne, G., and K. J. Meier. 2009. "Environmental Change, Human Resources and Organizational Turnaround." *Journal of Management Studies 46* (5): pp. 835–63.

Bozeman, B. 2004. *All Organizations Are Public: Comparing Public and Private Organizations*. Maryland: Beard Books.

Burke, R. J. 2000. "Career Priority Patterns among Managerial Women: A Study of Four Countries." *Psychological Reports 86* (3): pp. 1264–6.

Burke, R. J., and C. A. McKeen. 1993. "Career Priority Patterns among Managerial and Professional Women." *Applied Psychology 42* (4): pp. 341–52.

Caplan, R. D. 1987. "Person–Environment Fit Theory and Organizations: Commensurate Dimensions, Time Perspectives, and Mechanisms." *Journal of Vocational Behavior 31* (3): pp. 248–67.

Chatman, J. A. 1989. "Improving Interactional Organizational Research: A Model of Person–Organization Fit." *Academy of Management Review 14* (3): pp. 333–49.

Christiansen, N., P. Villanova, and S. Mikulay. 1997. "Political Influence Compatibility: Fitting the Person to the Climate." *Journal of Organizational Behavior 18* (6): pp. 709–30.

Coen, D., and M. Vannoni. 2016. "Sliding Doors in Brussels: A Career Path Analysis of EU Affairs Managers." *European Journal of Political Research 55* (4): pp. 811–26.

Corley, K. G., and D. A. Gioia. 2011. "Building Theory about Theory Building: What Constitutes a Theoretical Contribution?" *Academy of Management Review 36* (1): pp. 12–32.

Crossland, C., J. Zyung, N. J. Hiller, and D. C. Hambrick. 2014. "CEO Career Variety: Effects on Firm-Level Strategic and Social Novelty." *Academy of Management Journal* 57 (3): pp. 652–74.

Donnelly, R. 2009. "Career Behavior in the Knowledge Economy: Experiences and Perceptions of Career Mobility among Management and IT Consultants in the UK and the USA." *Journal of Vocational Behavior 75* (3): pp. 319–28.

Durbin, S., and J. Tomlinson. 2010. "Female Part-Time Managers: Networks and Career Mobility." *Work, Employment and Society 24* (4): pp. 621–40.

Edwards, J. R. 1991. "Person Job Fit: A Conceptual Integration, Literature Review, and Methodological Critique." In *International Review of Industrial and Organizational Psychology*, edited by C. Cooper and I. T. Robertson, Vol. 6, pp. 283–357. New York: Wiley.

Edwards, J. R., D. M. Cable, I. O. Williamson, L. S. Lambert, and A. J. Shipp. 2006. "The Phenomenology of Fit: Linking the Person and Environment to the Subjective Experience of Person–Environment Fit." *Journal of Applied Psychology 91* (4): pp. 802–27.

Ekehammer, B. 1974. "Interactionism in Personality from a Historical Perspective." *Psychological Bulletin 81* (12): pp. 1026–48.

Flinders, M. 2009. "The Politics of Patronage and Public Appointments: Shrinking Reach and Diluted Permeation." *Governance 22* (4): pp. 547–70.

Goodall, A. 2009. "Highly Cited Leaders and the Performance of Research Universities." *Research Policy 38* (7): pp. 1079–92.

Goodall, A. H., L. M. Kahn, and A. J. Oswald. 2011. "Why Do Leaders Matter? A Study of Expert Knowledge in a Superstar Setting." *Journal of Economic Behavior and Organization 77* (3): pp. 265–84.

Hambrick, D. C., and P. A. Mason. 1984. "Upper Echelons: The Organization as a Reflection of Its Top Managers." *Academy of Management Review 9* (2): pp. 193–206.

Hamori, M., and M. Kakarika. 2009. "External Labor Market Strategy and Career Success: CEO Careers in Europe and the United States." *Human Resource Management 48* (3): pp. 355–78.

Hill, G. C. 2005. "The Effects of Managerial Succession on Organizational Performance." *Journal of Public Administration Research and Theory 15* (4): pp. 585–97.

Hood, C., O. James, and C. Scott. 2000. "Regulation in Government: Has It Increased, Is It Increasing, Should It Be Diminished?" *Public Administration 78* (2): pp. 283–304.

Hood, C., and M. Lodge. 2006. *The Politics of Public Service Bargains.* Oxford: Oxford University Press.

Hood, C., C. Scott, O. James, G. Jones, and T. Travers. 1999. *Regulation Inside Government: Waste Watchers, Quality Police, and Sleaze-Busters.* Oxford: Oxford University Press.

Horton, S. and J. Jones 1996. "Who Are the New Public Managers? An Initial Analysis of 'Next Steps' Chief Executives and Their Managerial Roles." *Public Policy and Administration 11* (4): pp. 18–44.

James, O. 2000. "Regulation inside Government: Public Interest Justifications and Regulatory Failures." *Public Administration 78* (2): pp. 327–43.

James, O. 2001. "Business Models and the Transfer of Business-Like Central Government Agencies." *Governance 14* (2): pp. 233–52.

James, O. 2003. *The Executive Agency in Whitehall: Public Interest Versus Bureau-Shaping Perspectives*. Basingstoke: Palgrave.

Jas, P., and C. Skelcher. 2005. "Performance Decline and Turnaround in Public Organizations: A Theoretical and Empirical Analysis." *British Journal of Management 16* (3): pp. 195–210.

Jenkins, K., A. Jackson, K. Caines, and G. B. E. Unit. 1988. *Improving Management in Government: The Next Steps: Report to the Prime Minister*. London: HMSO. https://trove.nla.gov.au/version/22431483.

Judge, T. A., and G. R. Ferris. 1992. "The Elusive Criterion of Fit in Human Resources Staffing Decisions." *Human Resource Planning 15* (4): pp. 47–67.

Kim, S. S., H. Chun, and J. F. Patrick. 2009. "Career Path Profiles of General Managers of Korean Super Deluxe Hotels and Factors Influencing Their Career Development: Vocational Insights for HTM Students and Hotel Employees." *The Journal of Hospitality, Leisure, Sport and Tourism 8* (2): pp. 97–116.

Koch, M., B. Forgues, and V. Monties. 2017. "The Way to the Top: Career Patterns of Fortune 100 CEOs." *Human Resource Management 56* (2): pp. 267–85.

Krishnan, V. R. 2002. "Transformational Leadership and Value System Congruence." *International Journal of Value-Based Management 15*: pp. 13–33.

Kristof, A. L. 1996. "Person–Organization Fit: An Integrative Review of Its Conceptualizations, Measurement, and Implications." *Personnel Psychology 49* (1): pp. 1–49.

Kristof-Brown, A. L., R. D. Zimmerman, and E. C. Johnson. 2005. "Consequences of Individuals' Fit at Work: A Meta-Analysis of Person–Job, Person–Organization, Person–Group, and Person–Supervisor Fit." *Personnel Psychology 58* (2): pp. 281–342.

Lewis, D. 2007. "Testing Pendleton's Promise: Do Political Appointees Make Worse Bureaucrats?" *Journal of Politics 69* (4): pp. 1073–88.

Okumus, F., K. Karamustafa, M. Sariisik, S. Ulama, and O. Turkay. 2016. "Career Paths of Hotel General Managers in Turkey." *Asia Pacific Journal of Tourism Research 21* (11): pp. 1214–26.

O'Reilly, III, C. A., J. Chatman, and D. F. Caldwell. 1991. "People and Organizational Culture: A Profile Comparison Approach to Assessing Person–Organization Fit." *Academy of Management Journal 34* (3): pp. 487–516.

O'Toole, L. J., and K. J. Meier. 2003. "Plus ça Change: Public Management, Personnel Stability, and Organizational Performance." *Journal of Public Administration Research and Theory 13* (1): pp. 43–64.

Parsons, F. 1909. *Choosing a Vocation*. Boston: Houghton Mifflin Company.

Pervin, L., A. 1968. "Performance and Satisfaction as a Function of Individual–Environment Fit." *Psychological Bulletin* 69 (1): pp. 56–68.

Petrovsky, N. 2010. "The Role of Leadership." In *Public Service Improvement: Theories and Evidence*, edited by R. Ashworth, G. A. Boyne, and T. Entwistle, pp. 78–97. Oxford: Oxford University Press.

Petrovsky, N., O. James, and G. A. Boyne. 2015. "New Leaders' Managerial Background and the Performance of Public Organizations: The Theory of Publicness Fit." *Journal of Public Administration Research and Theory* 25 (1): pp. 217–36.

Petrovsky, N., O. James, A. Moseley, and G. A. Boyne. 2017. "What Explains Agency Heads' Length of Tenure? Testing Managerial Background, Performance, and Political Environment Effects." *Public Administration Review* 77 (4): pp. 591–602.

Porter, L. 1961. "A Study of Perceived Job Satisfactions in Bottom and Middle Management Jobs." *Journal of Applied Psychology* 45 (1): pp. 1–10.

Porter, L. 1962. "Job Attitudes in Management: I. Perceived Deficiencies in Need Fulfillment as a Function of Job Level." *Journal of Applied Psychology* 46 (1): pp. 375–84.

Rainey, H. G., and Y. H. Chun. 2005. "Public and Private Management Compared." In *The Oxford Handbook of Public Management*, edited by E. Ferlie, L. E. Lynn, Jr., and C. Pollitt, pp. 72–102. Oxford: Oxford University Press.

Rutherford, A. 2017. "The Role of Managerial Fit in Determining Organizational Performance: An Empirical Assessment of Presidents in U.S. Higher Education." *American Review of Public Administration* 47 (7): pp. 764–78.

Ryan, A. M., and M. J. Schmit. 1996. "An Assessment of Organizational Climate and P–E Fit: A Tool for Organizational Change." *International Journal of Organizational Analysis* 4 (1): pp. 75–95.

Sammarra, A., S. Profili, and L. Innocenti. 2013. "Do External Careers Pay Off for Both Managers and Professionals? The Effect of Inter-Organizational Mobility on Objective Career Success." *International Journal of Human Resource Management* 24 (13): pp. 2490–511.

Schaubroeck, J., and S. S. K. Lam. 2002. "How Similarity to Peers and Supervisor Influences Organizational Advancement in Different Cultures." *Academy of Management Journal* 45 (6): pp. 1120–36.

Tom, V. 1971. "The Role of Personality and Organizational Images in the Recruiting Process." *Organizational Behavior and Human Performance* 6: pp. 573–92.

Vinkenburg, C. J., and T. Weber. 2012. "Managerial Career Patterns: A Review of the Empirical Evidence." *Journal of Vocational Behavior* 80 (3): pp. 592–607.

Voss, K., and L. Speere. 2014. "Taking Chances and Making Changes: The Career Paths and Pitfalls of Pioneering Women in Newspaper Management." *Journalism & Mass Communication Quarterly* 91 (2): pp. 272–88.

Watson, D. J., and W. L. Hassett. 2004. "Career Paths of City Managers in America's Largest Council-Manager Cities." *Public Administration Review* 64 (2): pp. 192–9.

Werbel, J. D., and S. W. Gilliland. 1999. "Person–Environment Fit in the Selection Process." In *Research in Personnel and Human Resources Management*, edited by G. R. Ferris, Vol. 17, pp. 209–43. Greenwich, CT: JAI Press.

Witt, L. 1998. "Enhancing Goal Congruence: A Solution to Organizational Politics." *Journal of Applied Psychology 83* (4): pp. 666–74.

Wu, Y. L. 2004. "The Impact of Public Opinion on Board Structure Changes, Director Career Progression, and CEO Turnover: Evidence from CalPERS' Corporate Governance Program." *Journal of Corporate Finance 10* (1): pp. 199–227.

7

Antecedents of Managers' People Management

Using the AMO Model to Explain Differences in HRM Implementation and Leadership

Eva Knies, Sophie Op de Beeck, and Annie Hondeghem

7.1 Introduction

Over the past several years, we have seen a growing recognition of the notion that managers on different hierarchical levels can make a difference to performance (Purcell and Hutchinson 2007). Under the heading of people management, their role is considered to be twofold (Knies et al. 2020): On the one hand, managers are responsible for HRM implementation (Brewster et al. 2015), and, on the other, their leadership behavior has an impact on employees' attitudes and behaviors, and ultimately, on performance (Gilbert et al. 2011b). However, until now, the people management role of managers has mainly been studied in a private sector context. This raises the question as to what extent the people management role of public managers has been recognized and examined. This chapter therefore focuses on managers' role in people management within a public sector setting.

After a brief elaboration of what such a public sector role of people management actually entails, the bulk of this chapter discusses various antecedents of managers' people management, thereby answering the question why some managers' perform better than others. The main question guiding this contribution is: What are the antecedents (favoring and hindering factors) of public managers' HRM implementation and leadership behavior? In this chapter, we use the AMO model (Appelbaum et al. 2001; Boxall and Purcell 2008) as a conceptual framework to map and examine the antecedents of public managers' people management. This model has primarily been used to explain employees' behavior and performance, but some scholars have also applied it to managers' people management. We follow the latter stream of research.

In this chapter, we first discuss the general antecedents of managers' people management. Whenever possible, we contextualize these factors so that these reflect the typical characteristics of the public sector that stimulate or hinder managers'

Eva Knies, Sophie Op de Beeck, and Annie Hondeghem, *Antecedents of Managers' People Management: Using the AMO Model to Explain Differences in HRM Implementation and Leadership* In: *Managing for Public Service Performance: How People and Values Make a Difference.* Edited by: Peter Leisink, Lotte B. Andersen, Gene A. Brewer, Christian B. Jacobsen, Eva Knies, and Wouter Vandenabeele, Oxford University Press (2021). © Eva Knies, Sophie Op de Beeck, and Annie Hondeghem.
DOI: 10.1093/oso/9780192893420.003.0007

people management. Under the *ability* category of the AMO model, we specifically focus on managers' people management abilities and management development. Under the *motivation* category, we look at managers' willingness to take up people management responsibilities and their priorities. Finally, under the *opportunities* category, we focus on support from different organizational stakeholders (HR department, higher management, etc.) and (personnel) red tape.

7.2   Managers' People Management

Traditionally, the importance of managers in HRM has been recognized. In fact, the literature on managerial work shows a long-standing involvement of line managers in people management issues (Gilbert 2012). Nevertheless, in recent years, managers' involvement has become more formal and structured (Brewster et al. 2015; Larsen and Brewster 2003). There are some indications that managers, traditionally, played a more modest role in public sector people management compared to their private sector counterparts. In 1997, Poole and Jenkins pointed out that the main responsibility for HRM in the public sector is more likely to be vested in the HR department rather than in line management. In 2008, McGuire et al. pointed to the devolution of HR responsibilities to line managers in public organizations. Indeed, a recent empirical study by Brewster et al. (2015, 591) revealed that "there is no real difference in the likelihood of assigning responsibility to line managers across the public and private sectors." This might point to a converging effect where the public sector is increasingly mimicking the private sector. Various researchers have looked into managers' people management role and have aimed to shed light on what such a role actually entails and what the effectiveness of this so-called devolution is (Bainbridge 2015; Perry and Kulik 2008).

In this chapter, we define people management as managers' "implementation of HR practices and their leadership behavior in supporting employees they supervise at work" (Knies et al. 2020, 712). Following Purcell and Hutchinson (2007), we distinguish two components of people management: (1) the implementation of HR practices by managers; and (2) their leadership behavior. The concept of people management brings together different lines of research. The former component, which consists of the implementation of general HR practices and tailor-made arrangements, is rooted in the HRM literature, more specifically the literature on HRM devolution (Perry and Kulik 2008). The basic premise is that when studying employees' perceptions of HRM, it is not sufficient to look at the presence of practices, but managers' enactment has to be taken into account as well (Guest and Bos-Nehles 2013). The literatures on high-performance or high-commitment work practices (see also Chapter 9 of this volume) and on idiosyncratic deals are closely related to the implementation of HR practices. The latter component, leadership behavior, is focal in the leadership literature and is also widely studied from a public management perspective. Leadership behavior as part of the people management concept is understood as a manager demonstrating supportive behavior through specific acts that aim to help employees at work. We acknowledge that the leadership concept generally has a broader orientation, also including dimensions such as change-oriented or external leadership. However, these dimensions are not included in our understanding of people management. The leadership component of people management builds on notions of social exchange and perceived organizational support (POS) and perceived supervisor support (PSS) (Eisenberger et al. 1986). For a more elaborate discussion of people management, see Chapter 3 of this volume.

Until now, we have referred to managers in general when talking about the actors responsible for people management. By managers, we mean line managers who are responsible for the primary processes in the organization, i.e. managers outside the HRM function (Brewster et al. 2015, 578). We can make a distinction between top managers, on the one hand, and middle and frontline managers, on the other. Managers on all these hierarchical levels have people management responsibilities, although the nature of their responsibilities varies. Top or senior managers mainly have a responsibility for designing the organization's HRM policies and creating the conditions for effective implementation, while middle and frontline managers are primarily responsible for implementing people management (Wright and Nishii 2013). In practice, the division of responsibilities is highly dependent on the size of the organization: In larger organizations, managers on different hierarchical levels often have different responsibilities when it comes to people management, while in smaller organizations, such as schools in Belgium (Van Waeyenberg and Decramer 2018), top managers are responsible for both designing and implementing people management. In the literature, we witness a tendency for public management and public administration scholars to focus on top managers (e.g. Andrews and Boyne 2010; Forbes and Lynn 2005), while HRM scholars have taken an interest in middle and frontline managers (Purcell and Hutchinson 2007). In the remainder of this chapter, we will talk about middle and frontline managers when discussing people management unless stated otherwise because in many (larger) organizations, managers on this hierarchical level are primarily responsible for HRM implementation.

Although recent studies find little evidence for sector differences in managers' involvement in people management (Brewster et al. 2015), it appears that managers in the public sector have traditionally played a more modest role in people management compared to their private sector counterparts (Poole and Jenkins 1997). Possible explanations for this are bureaucratization, the size of the organization, and higher levels of union activity (Poole and Jenkins 1997). Also, public governance values, such as equality of treatment, might be challenged by the discretion of line managers in people management (Harris et al. 2002). In addition, Knies and Leisink (2014) rightly question how much discretionary room managers actually have for their people management tasks because public organizations are traditionally known for the limited room for managers due to detailed personnel systems and regulations (Boyne et al. 1999; Kessler et al. 2000; Truss 2008; 2009). These types of structural issues definitely impact the responsibilities that are assigned to line managers in the public sector in the first place. The rigidity of the regulatory context of public organizations therefore might result in managers signaling a lack of actual decision-making authority and financial power regarding their people management role (Cascón-Pereira et al. 2006; Op de Beeck 2016). In the remainder of this chapter, we will systematically address the antecedents of managers' people management activities using the AMO model and pay particular attention to public sector-specific antecedents.

7.3 The AMO Model

In this section, we introduce the AMO model (see Knies 2016, for a more elaborate overview), which serves as an analytical framework for examining relevant antecedents of people management. The AMO model is a generic framework with roots in industrial psychology. The rationale of the AMO model (Appelbaum et al. 2001) is that individuals perform well when they have the ability (A), motivation (M), and opportunities to perform (O). Employees are able to do their job if they possess the necessary knowledge and skills. They are willing to do their job if they feel adequately interested and incentivized. Employees have the opportunities to perform if their work structure and environment provide them with the necessary support and avenues for expression. Boxall and Purcell (2008, 173) summarize the reasoning behind the AMO framework by stating that "individual attributes have a huge impact but even the most able and motivated people cannot perform well if they lack 'the tools to finish the job' or work in an unsupportive social environment." We apply the AMO model as our theoretical lens in this chapter for several reasons. First, it is a generic model that can be applied to various contexts (including a public sector context). Second, it provides the basis for a systematic analysis of the antecedents that matter for managers' people management. Third, the model highlights the importance of both individual and contextual variables, which provides a rich understanding of the hindering and favoring factors explaining managers' people management.

Based on an overview study, Boselie et al. (2005) concluded that the AMO model is an often-used framework in HRM research. However, they also showed that the AMO model is often "presented as part of a general rationale for the study" but that "very few studies had derived an explicit set of propositions from a theory, and then tested these in the research design" (Boselie et al. 2005, 71). Since 2005, various empirical studies have been published testing the assumptions first outlined by Appelbaum et al. (2001). Most of these studies apply the model to employee performance (Marin-Garcia and Tomas 2016). Recently, scholars have also applied the AMO model to explain performance by managers, in particular, related to HRM–people management. Bos-Nehles et al. (2013) studied the effectiveness of line managers' HRM implementation in two private sector organizations and found that ability is the best predictor of effective implementation, followed by opportunity. Gilbert et al. (2015) conducted a similar study of effective HRM implementation in five organizations (three service, one industrial, and one non-profit) and also found support for the importance of line managers' abilities on effective HRM implementation. Van Waeyenberg and Decramer (2018) studied effective implementation as well, but they focused specifically on a "mini-bundle" of performance management practices. This study was conducted in a public sector context (education in Belgium). Van Waeyenberg and Decramer found overall support for the effect of all three AMO components on employees' satisfaction with the system. Another study that was conducted in a public sector context is that by Knies and Leisink (2014). Studying police and medical center middle managers, they found support for the effect of all three AMO factors. Moreover, this study helped to clarify how the AMO variables are interrelated. The results show that individual characteristics (i.e. ability and motivation) are directly related to managers' people management, whereas job characteristics (i.e. opportunity) have an indirect effect through motivation.

The studies highlighted here all explicitly refer to the AMO model and study all three elements (ability, motivation, and opportunity) in a comprehensive study. However, there are other studies that study only one or two relevant elements, often without direct reference to the AMO model. In Section 7.4, we draw from this pool of studies as well as discuss the main antecedents of people management in a public sector context. In each of the following sections, we will start by providing a rationale of why we selected particular antecedents and why these are relevant from a public sector perspective. Our aim is to provide a sector-specific understanding of the important antecedents that influence managers' people management activities. For each of the six antecedents discussed below, we report the results of relevant public sector studies. However, we do not claim to provide a comprehensive and systematic overview of all available empirical evidence.

7.4 Abilities: Managers' People Management Abilities and Management Development

In this section, we will discuss the first element of the AMO model: abilities. More specifically, we focus on managers' people management abilities and management development programs that are aimed at improving these abilities. These factors are particularly important in a public sector context because very often public managers are not selected or promoted based on their people management abilities. As a result of (the remnants of) the closed career system in many public organizations (Brewer 2005), it is often the best doctor or teacher who is appointed as manager, or the one who has the longest tenure (Hutchinson and Wood 1995). Because many public managers are not trained as managers, their abilities are a vital component influencing their people management activities, and so are the programs designed to develop their abilities (Bainbridge 2015).

7.4.1 People Management Abilities

Managers' people knowledge and skills are considered a key driving or constraining factor with regard to people management. Generally, a distinction is made between knowledge of formal policies and procedures, on the one hand, and soft skills to coach employees and deliver feedback aimed at goal attainment, on the other. That is, line managers should have insight into their organization's HR policy and (how to implement) the HR practices as they are intended. Depending on their actual responsibilities in HRM within an organization, managers will need sufficient knowledge of operational HR tasks in varying domains. Studying line managers in the Belgian federal government, Op de Beeck (2016; 2017) found that the HR domains with the highest manager involvement are follow-up and evaluation and the training and development of employees. She also found that the regulatory context of the federal government largely prevents line managers from playing a role in HR areas such as promotion, reward, and recruitment and selection. Whether their HR tasks are extensive or limited, managers will need skills and knowledge in line with the HR-related aspects of their managerial function (e.g. how to conduct an employee evaluation or identify training needs). In addition, several supporting leadership skills can be identified, such as managing change, motivating, communicating, interpersonal skills, team-building skills, and involving employees (McGovern et al. 1997; Thornhill and Saunders 1998).

All too often, however, managers lack the expertise necessary to tackle people management issues that are increasingly complex. A major issue here relates to the fact that line managers are often promoted because of their seniority or professional expertise in a certain field rather than because they have good people skills (Hutchinson and Wood 1995). This is especially valid in the public sector where the closed career system is still in place (Brewer 2005). As such, managers' actual leadership potential and people skills are rarely assessed within the public sector (Op de Beeck 2016). In fact, for many managers, people management issues are often not formally recognized as part of their job (Napier and Peterson 1984). As a result, managers are frequently left feeling underqualified or uncertain with regard to the people aspect of their managerial position (de Jong et al. 1999; Hutchinson and Wood 1995; Op de Beeck 2016). There is empirical evidence that line managers' lack of people management abilities has a negative impact on the performance they deliver regarding people management in general (Bos-Nehles et al. 2013; Gilbert et al. 2015) as well as in a public sector context (Knies and Leisink 2014; Van Waeyenberg and Decramer 2018).

7.4.2 Management Development

Given the skills issues we identified, Whittaker and Marchington (2003, 259) emphasize that more attention should be paid to how line managers are "recruited, inducted, appraised and rewarded, and trained up in the HR aspects of their jobs." As such, the proper people-oriented training at the right time may partly address the skills issue. Management development can provide a solution to managers feeling incompetent and also make them feel more confident in their people management role (Bach 2001; Gilbert 2012; Harris et al. 2002). McGurk (2009; 2010) has studied the effect of management and leadership development on organizational change and individual and organizational performance in several public service organizations (fire brigade, train-operating company, and adult social service). His findings highlight the relevance of a contextualized approach to management and leadership development. In one of the cases, McGurk (2009) showed that the design of the program is important for the outcome. In this case, the management development program was aimed at an effective implementation of HR policies. This top-down approach resulted in top-down change, but it did not stimulate bottom-up initiatives or innovation. McGurk (2010) reports similar results: Traditional management development programs lead to effective compliance with top-down determined objectives but have little or no impact on strategic change. On the other hand, a collective and emergent approach to leadership development had a significant impact on strategic change, although not always in the expected direction. A crucial factor in the effectiveness of management development is the transfer of knowledge into practice (McGurk 2009). Without such a transfer, investments in management development programs are a waste of money and time.

7.5 Motivation: Managers' Willingness to Take on People Management Responsibilities and Their Priorities

In this section, we will discuss the second element of the AMO model: motivation. More specifically, we focus on managers' willingness to take on people management responsibilities and their priorities. The first factor mainly has to do with individual managers' motivation to perform people management. The second factor also concerns the organizational context in which people management activities are incentivized or not. As such, the two factors are related. Both willingness to take on people management responsibilities and managers' priorities are particularly important in a public sector context because, as stated before, many public managers are former professionals who are not trained as managers. Many of them gain a management position later in their careers, and, according to Bainbridge (2015, 847), these new line managers "may be less than enthusiastic about their newly acquired people management responsibilities." Moreover, public managers are incentivized to focus on the attainment of short-term, operational goals instead of providing people management support to their employees (e.g. McGuire et al. 2008).

7.5.1 Willingness to Take on People Management Responsibilities

The success of people management will largely depend on the extent to which managers feel adequately willing, interested, and motivated to perform people management activities and to support their employees. In empirical research—mostly conducted in a private sector context—it is found that managers are often reluctant to accept their people management role (Bos-Nehles 2010), possibly because they do not recognize the value of people management (Thornhill and Saunders 1998). Overall, people management cannot be delivered effectively by managers who do not take people management seriously or who do not reflect a belief in HRM (Watson et al. 2007; Whittaker and Marchington 2003). In particular, people management depends on the extent to which managers are autonomously motivated (Bos-Nehles 2010; Op de Beeck et al. 2018; Vallerand and Ratelle 2004; Watson et al. 2007). Autonomous motivation stems from the person itself (intrinsic) and states that people engage in an activity because they find it inherently enjoyable and satisfying (Coursey and Vandenabeele 2012; Guay et al. 2000). In other words, managers who show a genuine interest in and a sense of ownership over their people management role are likely to be more successful in the enactment of people management. On the other hand, controlled motivation, where there is an obligation (extrinsic) to behave in a specific way (possibly linked to reward or sanction) (Coursey and Vandenabeele 2012), is expected to negatively affect people management (Perry et al. 2009; Vallerand and Ratelle 2004). Therefore, pushing people management upon managers will likely fail to deliver (Harris et al. 2002).

Several studies have provided support for the assumed effects of (intrinsic) motivation for people management on the delivery of people management activities in a public sector context (Knies and Leisink 2014; Op de Beeck et al. 2018; Van Waeyenberg and Decramer 2018). Also, Knies and Leisink (2014) have shown that managers' willingness to support the employees in their team is partly dependent on the level of discretionary room that managers perceive, which was an issue in the police and medical center units they studied. That is, if managers perceive that they can do no more than implement designed HR policies without paying attention to the local situation, this will limit their willingness to support their employees. This implies that the extent to which managers are willing to perform people management can be influenced by the organization.

7.5.2 Priorities/Capacity

In looking after their subordinates' well-being, one might expect managers to feel a natural responsibility in implementing people management. Nevertheless, a major drawback of people management is that managers often experience a lack of time to perform their people role and perceive people management as an increase in their workload (Bach 2001). This is because people management often conflicts with other daily duties. In dealing with these competing demands, long-term goals (such as investing in a relationship with your employees and supporting their development) often suffer under pressure from short-term, operational targets. As a result, managers' priorities often lie in meeting short-term, operational goals, while paying little attention to people management activities (Bos-Nehles 2010; McGuire et al. 2008; Watson et al. 2007; Whittaker and Marchington 2003). Altogether, managers may easily become "overloaded" by combining all of their leadership roles (e.g. steward, entrepreneur, professional, and coach) (Van Wart et al. 2012), which may lead them to be less successful in performing their people management role. Therefore, having the capacity to spend sufficient time on each of their respective roles will both help managers and benefit people management.

The fact that managers tend to focus on short-term goals and the activities leading to short-term goal attainment holds for both private and public sector contexts. However, public managers, compared to their private sector counterparts, might be even more incentivized to focus on the short term, at least in some parts of the public sector. This might have to do with a system for job rotation that is in place in many public (civil service) organizations. To overcome problems associated with the division of labor and the specialization of units, coordination is required. One of the instruments to stimulate coordination and prevent compartmentalization is job rotation for senior managers (Verhoest and Bouckaert 2005). For example, senior civil servants in the Netherlands are obliged to move to another department every 5–7 years. This incentivizes senior managers to focus on short-term results, and as a result, prioritize these short-term goals as well for the middle and frontline managers they supervise. As people management usually takes investment and results are only visible in the longer run, both top managers' willingness to stimulate people management activities and middle and frontline managers' willingness to perform people management activities are not stimulated by this system.

7.6 Opportunities: Support from Different Organizational Stakeholders and Red Tape

In this section, we will discuss the final element of the AMO model: opportunities. More specifically, we focus on the support that managers receive from different organizational stakeholders and red tape. While the abilities and motivation categories are mainly related to the individual characteristics of managers, the opportunities category primarily refers to the context in which the manager operates. Two characteristics of the context are relevant to highlight here as these distinguish private and public organizations: the degree of publicness (the degree to which they recognize various public values as an element of being part of the public sector) (Antonsen and Beck Jørgensen 1997), and related to this, the level of centralization of HR decision-making (Meyer and Hammerschmid 2010). Regarding the former, managers in high-publicness organizations are subject to more constraints than managers in low-publicness organizations. Regarding the latter, Meyer and Hammerschmid (2010) have shown that decision-making in central government across the EU is still highly centralized. Although the level of centralization varies across countries and across HR practices, this echoes the implication that public sector managers face more constraints.

7.6.1 Support for Managers' People Management

An important factor in assuring management's people management is the availability of support. Managers' interaction with different organizational stakeholders can contribute to the success of their people management activities. Following social and organizational support theory (e.g. Eisenberger et al. 1990; Shumaker and Brownell 1984), investing in support may help managers overcome the difficulties associated with their people management role. In this view, support is seen as a coping mechanism that may provide managers with the resources needed to resolve any problems they encounter in their people management (Cohen and Wills 1985; Vigoda-Gadot and Talmud 2010). In addition, the fact that support is generally characterized by some kind of exchange with the expectancy of reciprocity implies that an investment in support will result in favorable attitudes and behaviors on the receiver's end (Shumaker and Brownell 1984; Wayne et al. 1997). Managers may then reciprocate by returning the support they received from others through better performance in their people management or by providing support themselves (Tepper and Taylor 2003). Based on these insights, it is believed that managers' (confidence in their) people management activities is highly reliant on support.

Research attention regarding support of managers' people management has mainly been focused on HR professionals providing line managers with the necessary HR skills and the proper encouragement to perform their HR role (Gilbert et al. 2011a; Hutchinson and Wood 1995; Perry and Kulik 2008; Renwick 2003). Although HR professionals are probably the major source of support, this may be considered a rather narrow focus. Based on insights from social and organizational support theory, it is found that managers are able to rely on an entire support network in which various sources of support can complementarily contribute to managers' people management (Op de Beeck et al. 2017).

The main sources of support to be identified here are the organization in general, HR professionals, managers' supervisor, and their co-workers. First, support for managers from the organization is considered key in managers' efforts regarding people management (McGovern et al. 1997; Shore and Wayne 1993). The overall organizational climate and the direction upheld by top management may support managers through the encouragement and recognition of their people management role (Joiner 2007; Napier and Peterson 1984). We found no studies addressing public–private differences regarding the support for managers from their organization. Second, support from HR professionals seems crucial as they provide managers with the necessary expertise, encouragement, and advice (Bond and Wise 2003; Perry and Kulik 2008; Whittaker and Marchington 2003). In fact, it is believed that "without the support from HR, line managers are unable to acquire sufficient competences in people management skills to progress organizational effectiveness" (Bos-Nehles 2010, 109). In the public sector, however, the "accessibility" of the (central) HR department is often criticized as the bureaucratic nature and the size of government organizations may easily create a sense of distance between HR and the workplace (Op de Beeck 2016).

Third, the supportive treatment by managers' own supervisor is likely positively related to the performance in their people management role (Wayne et al. 1997). The supervisor may not only motivate managers but also controls and manages the immediate resources available to them (Bhanthumnavin 2003). Within the public sector in particular, where supervisors do not have a lot of resources to incentivize their subordinates compared to the private sector, the supervisor's contribution often lies in playing an exemplary role with regard to their own affinity with people management (Op de Beeck 2016). Fourth and finally, professional relationships with co-workers are found to be a vital source of support and motivation within an organizational setting (Paarlberg et al. 2008). Based on social comparison theory, co-workers at the same hierarchical level may motivate managers in their people management role through sharing their personal knowledge, expertise, and experiences and providing overall encouragement (Cohen and Wills 1985; Joiner 2007; Zhou and George 2001). As such, the encouragement of their peers may have a large impact on managers' people management (Op de Beeck et al. 2017). As for support for managers from the organization, we found no studies addressing public–private differences regarding the support from co-workers.

7.6.2 Red Tape

Managers in government organizations are, in particular, subjected to administrative constraints—including red tape—that may hinder their performance. Although not limited to the public sector, empirical research has shown that red tape is more prevalent in public organizations than in private sector organizations (e.g. Baldwin 1990; DeHart-Davis and Pandey 2005; Feeney and Rainey 2010). Often regarded as an effect of bureaucracy, red tape has, therefore, become an important variable in public administration research (Bozeman 1993; Feeney and Rainey 2010). An often adopted definition of red tape refers to "rules, regulations, and procedures that remain in force and entail a compliance burden for the organization but have no efficacy for the rules' functional object" (Bozeman 1993, 283). Employees experiencing (personnel) red tape are found to become dissatisfied, demotivated, and unproductive (Baldwin 1990; DeHart-Davis and Pandey 2005). At the same time, causality may also be reversed where managers' individual dispositions (e.g. work motivation) may affect their levels of perceived red tape (e.g. Scott and Pandey 2005).

In the context of HRM, Rainey et al. (1995) find that rules and laws concerning public personnel administration are the main sources of red tape (see also Van Loon et al. 2016). Therefore, personnel red tape is generally considered a distinct concept (e.g. Rainey et al. 1995). In fact, red tape is particularly perceived to be more prevalent in personnel (and finance) activities compared to other management domains (Coursey and Pandey 2007; Van Loon et al. 2016). An increasing responsibility in people management activities (i.e. HRM devolution) may thus indirectly cause managers to be confronted with red tape more often. Subsequently, managers' perceptions of (personnel) red tape are believed to decrease their motivation and their flexibility and autonomy in performing their tasks (Baldwin 1990). As a result, formal rules and regulations may sharply constrain (public) managers in performing their people management activities.

7.7 Conclusion

The aim of this chapter was to map and examine the antecedents of public managers' people management. As such, there has been a growing recognition of the role of managers in HRM implementation, on the one hand, and of the impact of managers' leadership behavior on employees' attitudes and performance, on the other, i.e. the two components of people management. This chapter reviewed evidence as to what extent managers' role of people management has been recognized and examined within a public sector setting, and which factors explain differences in people management performance between managers.

Although a recent study by Brewster et al. (2015) revealed that there are no public–private differences in the extent to which HRM responsibilities are devolved to the line managers, traditionally, managers in the public sector have played a more modest role in people management compared to their private sector counterparts (Poole and Jenkins 1997). The public sector setting confronts managers with all kinds of challenges that can generally be traced back to the rigidities of the regulatory context (e.g. detailed personnel systems) or conflicting values (e.g. equality of treatment versus managers' discretion in implementing people management activities to fit the needs of different workers). These types of structural issues limit the people management responsibilities that line managers in the public sector are assigned in the first place, but they also impede managers' discretionary room with regard to the people management tasks they do have. Furthermore, the closed career system in place in many public organizations has often led to employees being promoted to manager, based on seniority or professional expertise, resulting in managers feeling underqualified or uncertain with regard to the people aspect of their managerial position. Altogether, the public sector context not only determines the composition of managers' people management role, but also limits managers' discretionary room within that role, therefore affecting the way managers actually perform people management activities.

Using the AMO model as a framework, we addressed a broad range of antecedents of managers' people management activities, each of which affects their people management performance. The review shows that the AMO model generally holds within the public sector context. A number of factors are particularly prominent in the public sector. Consider, for example, red tape, where managers—particularly in public organizations—are subjected to administrative constraints that may decrease their motivation, flexibility, and autonomy, thus hindering their performance. Another example is the lack of investment in people management due to a lack of time and role overload.

The various antecedents of managers' people management activities also stress the importance of public organizations paying more attention to how public managers are selected and supported. For example, in selecting or promoting line managers, it is important to understand that the best candidate for a managerial position is not necessarily the one with the greatest technical expertise or with the most seniority. Instead, people-oriented competencies should be addressed. Furthermore, in training and development of managers, attention should be paid to people skills and leadership in line with the importance of the abilities element in the AMO model. Another example refers to the importance of the HR department providing support to managers in performing their people management activities and drawing their attention to other potential sources of support, such as co-workers. People management will benefit from public organizations adopting an HR approach directed at line managers in keeping with the broad array of job requirements—including the HR and leadership aspect—of a managerial position.

Several questions remain, highlighting that there is certainly room for additional research on public managers' people management. One of the relevant issues to examine further in a public sector context concerns the conflicting values that managers are confronted with when performing their people management activities, in particular, the potential trade-off between equality of treatment and managers' discretion in implementing people management activities to fit the needs of different workers. Do managers experience conflicting values, how do they manage these in practice, and how do these conflicting values play out for the people management support provided to employees?

Another relevant issue that is worth additional research is the regulatory and bureaucratic context that impacts public managers' people management. This context limits the support that managers receive from their HR department, the discretionary room managers perceive they have, and indirectly, their willingness to perform people management. It is relevant to study this issue in more detail and particularly address the question of why some public managers can deal with these constraints more effectively than others can. Finally, our understanding of people management in the public sector would benefit from a systematic investigation of the abilities that are needed for managers to perform their people management role effectively. How do sector-specific challenges shape the required skills and abilities for managers, and how can this information be used for recruitment and selection purposes? Additionally, further research may conduct a systematic comparison of people management and its antecedents in the public sector versus the private sector. Also, a comparison between different subsectors within the public sector may be conceivable.

In conclusion, this chapter aimed to enhance insight into the specific contribution of managers in bringing about effective people management. Elements such as a well-organized support system, considering the limitations of (personnel) red tape, the necessary people-oriented competencies, and genuine commitment on the part of managers were found to be key for managers performing people management activities. The public sector setting was found to pose additional challenges to managers' people management and should be taken into account in order to fully understand how managers can make a difference for performance.

References

Andrews, R., and G. A. Boyne. 2010. "Capacity, Leadership, and Organizational Performance: Testing the Black Box Model of Public Management." *Public Administration Review 70* (3): pp. 443–54.

Antonsen, M., and T. Beck Jørgensen. 1997. "The 'Publicness' of Public Organizations." *Public Administration 75* (2): pp. 337–57.

Appelbaum, E., T. Bailey, B. Berg, and A. L. Kalleberg. 2001. *Manufacturing Advantage: Why High-Performance Work Systems Pay Off.* Ithaca, NY: Cornell University Press.

Bach, S. 2001. "HR and New Approaches to Public Sector Management: Improving HRM Capacity." World Health Organization, Workshop on Global Health Workforce Strategy. Annecy, France, December 9–12, 2000.

Bainbridge, H. 2015. "Devolving People Management to the Line: How Different Rationales for Devolution Influence People Management Effectiveness." *Personnel Review 44* (6): pp. 847–65.

Baldwin, J. N. 1990. "Perceptions of Public Versus Private Sector Personnel and Informal Red Tape: Their Impact on Motivation." *The American Review of Public Administration 20* (7): pp. 7–28.

Bhanthumnavin, D. 2003. "Perceived Social Support from Supervisor and Group Members' Psychological and Situational Characteristics as Predictors of Subordinate Performance in Thai Work Units." *Human Resource Development Quarterly 14* (1): pp. 79–97.

Bond, S., and S. Wise. 2003. "Family Leave Policies and Devolution to the Line." *Personnel Review 32* (1): pp. 58–72.

Boselie, P., G. Dietz, and C. Boon. 2005. "Commonalities and Contradictions in HRM and Performance Research." *Human Resource Management Journal 15* (3): pp. 67–94.

Bos-Nehles, A. 2010. "The Line Makes the Difference: Line Managers as Effective HR Partners." Doctoral dissertation. Universiteit Twente, Enschede, the Netherlands.

Bos-Nehles, A. C., M. J. Van Riemsdijk, and J. K. Looise. 2013. "Employee Perceptions of Line Management Performance: Applying the AMO Theory to Explain the Effectiveness of Line Managers' HRM Implementation." *Human Resource Management 52* (6): pp. 861–77.

Boxall, P., and J. Purcell. 2008. *Strategy and Human Resource Management.* 2nd ed. Basingstoke: Palgrave Macmillan.

Boyne, G., M. Poole, and G. Jenkins. 1999. "Human Resource Management in the Public and Private Sectors: An Empirical Comparison." *Public Administration 77* (2): pp. 407–20.

Bozeman, B. 1993. "A Theory of Government 'Red Tape.'" *Journal of Public Administration Research and Theory 3* (3): pp. 273–303.

Brewer, G. A. 2005. "In the Eye of the Storm: Frontline Supervisors and Federal Agency Performance." *Journal of Public Administration Research and Theory 15* (4): pp. 505–27.

Brewster, C., M. Brookes, and P. Gollan. 2015. "The Institutional Antecedents of the Assignment of HRM Responsibilities to Line Managers." *Human Resource Management 54* (4): pp. 577–97.

Cascón-Pereira, R., M. Valverde, and G. Ryan. 2006. "Mapping out Devolution: An Exploration of the Realities of Devolution." *Journal of European Industrial Training 30* (2): pp. 129–51.

Cohen, S., and T. A. Wills. 1985. "Stress, Social Support, and the Buffering Hypothesis." *Psychological Bulletin 98* (2): pp. 310–57.

Coursey, D. H., and S. K. Pandey. 2007. "Content Domain, Measurement, and Validity of the Red Tape Concept. A Second-Order Confirmatory Factor Analysis." *The American Review of Public Administration 37* (3): pp. 342–61.

Coursey, D., and W. Vandenabeele. 2012. "Empirical Validation of the Relative Autonomy Index: A Self-Determination Perspective on Work Motivation in the Public Sector." Paper presented at the XVI Annual Conference of the International Research Society for Public Management (IRSPM), Rome, Italy, April 11–13, 2012.

DeHart-Davis, L., and S. K. Pandey. 2005. "Red Tape and Public Employees: Does Perceived Rule Dysfunction Alienate Managers?" *Journal of Public Administration Research and Theory 15* (1): pp. 133–48.

de Jong, J. A., F. J. Leenders, and J. G. L. Thijssen. 1999. "HRD Tasks of First-Level Managers." *Journal of Workplace Learning 11* (5): pp. 176–83.

Eisenberger, R., P. Fasolo, and V. Davis-LaMastro. 1990. "Perceived Organizational Support and Employee Diligence, Commitment, and Innovation." *Journal of Applied Psychology 75* (1): pp. 51–9.

Eisenberger, R., R. Huntington, S. Hutchison, and D. Sowa. 1986. "Perceived Organizational Support." *Journal of Applied Psychology 71* (3): pp. 500–7.

Feeney, M. K., and H. G. Rainey. 2010. "Personnel Flexibility and Red Tape in Public and Nonprofit Organizations: Distinctions Due to Institutional and Political Accountability." *Journal of Public Administration Research and Theory 20* (4): pp. 801–26.

Forbes, M., and L. E. Lynn. Jr. 2005. "How Does Public Management Affect Government Performance? Findings from International Research." *Journal of Public Administration Research and Theory 15* (4): pp. 559–84.

Gilbert, C. 2012. "HRM on the Line: Empirical Studies on the Prerequisites and Importance of Effective HRM Implementation." Doctoral dissertation, Faculty of Economics and Business, KU Leuven, Leuven, Belgium.

Gilbert, C., S. De Winne, and L. Sels. 2011a. "Antecedents of Front-Line Managers' Perceptions of HR Role Stressors." *Personnel Review 40* (5): pp. 549–69.

Gilbert, C., S. De Winne, and L. Sels. 2011b. "The Influence of Line Managers and HR Department on Employees' Affective Commitment." *The International Journal of Human Resource Management 22* (8): pp. 1618–37.

Gilbert, C., S. De Winne, and L. Sels. 2015. "Strong HRM Processes and Line Managers' Effective HRM Implementation: A Balanced View." *Human Resource Management Journal 25* (4): pp. 600–16.

Guay, F., R. J. Vallerand, and C. Blanchard. 2000. "On the Assessment of Situational Intrinsic and Extrinsic Motivation: The Situational Motivation Scale (SIMS)." *Motivation and Emotion 24* (3): pp. 175–213.

Guest, D. E., and A. C. Bos-Nehles. 2013. "HRM and Performance: The Role of Effective Implementation." In *HRM and Performance: Achievements and Challenges*, edited by D. E. Guest, J. Paauwe, and P. Wright, pp. 79–96. Chichester: Wiley Blackwell.

Harris, L., D. Doughty, and S. Kirk. 2002. "The Devolution of HR Responsibilities: Perspectives from the UK's Public Sector." *Journal of European Industrial Training 26* (5): pp. 218–29.

Hutchinson, S., and S. Wood. 1995. "The UK Experience." In *Personnel and the Line: Developing the New Relationship*, edited by S. Hutchinson and C. Brewster. Wimbledon: IPM.

Joiner, T. A. 2007. "Total Quality Management and Performance: The Role of Organization Support and Co-Worker Support." *International Journal of Quality & Reliability Management 24* (6): pp. 617–27.

Kessler, I., J. Purcell, and J. Coyle-Shapiro. 2000. "New Forms of Employment Relations in the Public Services: The Limits of Strategic Choice." *Industrial Relations Journal 31* (1): pp. 17–34.

Knies, E. 2016. "Entries on AMO Model." In *Encyclopedia of Human Resource Management*, edited by A. Wilkinson and S. Johnstone, pp. 12–13. Cheltenham: Edward Elgar.

Knies, E., and P. Leisink. 2014. "Leadership Behavior in Public Organizations: A Study of Supervisory Support by Police and Medical Center Middle Managers." *Review of Public Personnel Administration 34* (2): pp. 108–27.

Knies, E., P. Leisink, and R. Van de Schoot. 2020. "People Management: Developing and Testing a Measurement Scale." *The International Journal of Human Resource Management 31* (6): pp. 705–37.

Larsen, H., and C. Brewster. 2003. "Line Management Responsibility for HRM: What Is Happening in Europe?" *Employee Relations 25* (3): pp. 228–44.

Marin-Garcia, J. A., and J. M. Tomas. 2016. "Deconstructing AMO Framework: A Systematic Review." *Intangible Capital 12* (4): pp. 1040–87.

McGovern, P., L. Gratton, V. Hope-Hailey, P. Stiles, and C. Truss. 1997. "Human Resource Management on the Line?" *Human Resource Management Journal 7* (4): pp. 12–29.

McGuire, D., L. Stoner, and S. Mylona. 2008. "The Role of Line Managers as Human Resource Agents in Fostering Organizational Change in Public Services." *Journal of Change Management 8* (1): pp. 73–84.

McGurk, P. 2009. "Developing 'Middle Leaders' in the Public Services? The Realities of Management and Leadership Development for Public Managers." *International Journal of Public Sector Management 22* (6): pp. 464–77.

McGurk, P. 2010. "Outcomes of Management and Leadership Development." *Journal of Management Development 29* (5): pp. 457–70.

Meyer, R. E., and G. Hammerschmid. 2010. "The Degree of Decentralization and Individual Decision Making in Central Government Human Resource Management: A European Comparative Perspective." *Public Administration 88* (2): pp. 455–78.

Napier, N. K., and R. B. Peterson. 1984. "Putting Human Resource Management at the Line Manager Level." *Business Horizons 27* (1): pp. 72–82.

Op de Beeck, S. 2016. "HRM Responsibilities in the Public Sector: The Role of Line Managers." Doctoral dissertation, Faculty of Social Sciences, KU Leuven, Leuven, Belgium.

Op de Beeck, S. 2017. *Successful HRM Implementation in a Public Sector Setting: Why Line Managers Are the Vital Link.* Leuven: KU Leuven Public Governance Institute.

Op de Beeck, S., J. Wynen, and A. Hondeghem. 2017. "Effective HRM Implementation: Relying on Various Sources of Support." *International Journal of Public Administration 40* (2): pp. 192–204.

Op de Beeck, S., J. Wynen, and A. Hondeghem. 2018. "Explaining Effective HRM Implementation: A Middle Versus First-Line Management Perspective." *Public Personnel Management 47* (2): pp. 144–74.

Paarlberg, L. E., J. L. Perry, and A. Hondeghem. 2008. "From Theory to Practice: Strategies for Applying Public Service Motivation." In *Motivation in Public Management: The Call of Public Service,* edited by A. Hondeghem and J. L. Perry, pp. 268–93. Oxford: Oxford University Press.

Perry, E. L., and C. T. Kulik. 2008. "The Devolution of HR to the Line: Implications for Perceptions of People Management Effectiveness." *The International Journal of Human Resource Management 19* (2): pp. 262–73.

Perry, J. L., T. A. Engbers, and S. Y. Jun. 2009. "Back to the Future? Performance-Related Pay, Empirical Research, and the Perils of Persistence." *Public Administration Review 69* (1): pp. 39–51.

Poole, M., and G. Jenkins. 1997. "Responsibilities for Human Resource Management Practices in the Modern Enterprise." *Personnel Review 26* (5): pp. 333–56.

Purcell, J., and S. Hutchinson. 2007. "Front-Line Managers as Agents in the HRM-Performance Causal Chain: Theory, Analysis and Evidence." *Human Resource Management Journal 17* (1): pp. 3–20.

Rainey, H. G., S. Pandey, and B. Bozeman. 1995. "Public and Private Managers' Perceptions of Red Tape." *Public Administration Review 55* (6): pp. 567–74.

Renwick, D. 2003. "Line Manager Involvement in HRM: An Inside View." *Employee Relations 25* (3): pp. 262–80.

Scott, P., and S. Pandey. 2005. "Red Tape and Public Service Motivation: Findings from a National Survey of Managers in State Health and Human Services Agencies." *Review of Public Personnel Administration 25* (2): pp. 155–80.

Shore, L., and S. Wayne. 1993. "Commitment and Employee Behavior: Comparison of Affective Commitment and Continuance Commitment with Perceived Organizational Support." *Journal of Applied Psychology 78* (5): pp. 774–80.

Shumaker, S. A., and A. Brownell. 1984. "Toward a Theory of Social Support: Closing Conceptual Gaps." *Journal of Social Issues 40* (4): pp. 11–36.

Tepper, B., and E. Taylor. 2003. "Relationships among Supervisors' and Subordinates' Procedural Justice Perceptions and Organizational Citizenship Behaviors." *Academy of Management Journal 46* (1): pp. 97–105.

Thornhill, A., and M. N. K. Saunders. 1998. "What if Line Managers Don't Realize They're Responsible for HR? Lessons from an Organization Experiencing Rapid Change." *Personnel Review 27* (6): pp. 460–76.

Truss, C. 2008. "Continuity and Change: The Role of the HR Function in the Modern Public Sector." *Public Administration 86* (4): pp. 1071–88.

Truss, C. 2009. "Changing HR Functional Forms in the UK Public Sector." *The International Journal of Human Resource Management 20* (4): pp. 717–37.

Vallerand, R. J., and C. F. Ratelle. 2004. "Intrinsic and Extrinsic Motivation: A Hierarchical Model." In *Handbook of Self-Determination Research*, edited by E. L. Deci and R. M. Ryan, pp. 37–63. Rochester, NY: University of Rochester Press.

Van Loon, N. M., P. Leisink, E. Knies, and G. A. Brewer. 2016. "Red Tape: Developing and Validating a New Job-Centered Measure." *Public Administration Review 76* (4): pp. 662–73.

Van Waeyenberg, T., and A. Decramer. 2018. "Line Managers' AMO to Manage Employees' Performance: The Route to Effective and Satisfying Performance Management." *The International Journal of Human Resource Management 29* (22): pp. 1–22.

Van Wart, M., A. Hondeghem, G. Bouckaert, and S. Ruebens. 2012. "Administrative Leadership in the Context of Governance." Paper presented at the XVI Annual Conference of the International Research Society for Public Management (IRSPM). Rome, Italy, April 11–13, 2012.

Verhoest, K., and G. Bouckaert. 2005. "Machinery of Government and Policy Capacity: The Effects of Specialization and Coordination." In *Challenges to State Policy Capacity*, edited by M. Painter and J. Pierre, pp. 92–111. Basingstoke: Palgrave Macmillan.

Vigoda-Gadot, E., and I. Talmud. 2010. "Organizational Politics and Job Outcomes: The Moderating Effect of Trust and Social Support." *Journal of Applied Social Psychology 40* (11): pp. 2829–61.

Watson, S., G. A. Maxwell, and L. Farquharson. 2007. "Line Managers' Views on Adopting Human Resource Roles: The Case of Hilton (UK) Hotels." *Employee Relations 29* (1): pp. 30–49.

Wayne, S. J., L. M. Shore, and R. C. Liden. 1997. "Perceived Organizational Support and Leader–Member Exchange: A Social Exchange Perspective." *Academy of Management Journal 40* (1): pp. 82–111.

Whittaker, S., and M. Marchington. 2003. "Devolving HR Responsibility to the Line: Threat, Opportunity or Partnership?" *Employee Relations 25* (3): pp. 245–61.

Wright, P., and L. H. Nishii. 2013. "Strategic HRM and Organizational Behaviour: Integrating Multiple Levels of Analysis." In *HRM and Performance: Achievements and Challenges*, edited by J. Paauwe, D. Guest, and P. Wright, pp. 97–110. Chichester: Wiley.

Zhou, J., and J. M. George. 2001. "When Job Dissatisfaction Leads to Creativity: Encouraging the Expression of Voice." *The Academy of Management Journal 44* (4): pp. 682–96.

8

How Can Public Managers Use Performance Management for Improvement Without Demotivating Employees?

Poul A. Nielsen and Caroline H. Grøn

8.1 Introduction

The development of increasingly sophisticated performance measurement systems comprises one of the most important structural changes in government in recent decades (Moynihan 2008). Performance management reforms have been introduced across different countries and types of organizations with the dual aim of improving both government performance and accountability (Jakobsen et al. 2018). Accordingly, the availability and dissemination of performance information have placed new demands on public managers to engage with the data and use it to inform various management decisions.

Existing research has predominantly focused on the study of particular performance management reforms, as well as on why and for what purposes public managers use performance information (Moynihan and Pandey 2010; Van Dooren 2008). In a recent meta-analysis, Gerrish (2016) finds negligible effects of performance management, suggesting that public managers have struggled to deliver on the promises of performance management. Less attention has been paid to how performance management reform affects the relations between public managers and their subordinates, even as studies document how performance systems have created widespread resistance among public sector employees (e.g. Pihl-Thingvad 2016). If performance systems are implemented in ways that demotivate employees, it is difficult to see how performance management can succeed in improving public service performance. Particularly important in this regard, public managers have been charged with transmitting to their employees the purposes, meaning, and usefulness of performance systems that have often been designed by actors external to the individual public organization (Döring et al. 2015; Grøn 2018).

Poul A. Nielsen and Caroline H. Grøn, *How Can Public Managers Use Performance Management for Improvement Without Demotivating Employees?* In: *Managing for Public Service Performance: How People and Values Make a Difference.* Edited by: Peter Leisink, Lotte B. Andersen, Gene A. Brewer, Christian B. Jacobsen, Eva Knies, and Wouter Vandenabeele, Oxford University Press (2021). © Poul A. Nielsen and Caroline H. Grøn. DOI: 10.1093/oso/9780192893420.003.0008

In this chapter, we review research on public sector performance management with emphasis on the role of public managers in implementing performance management. We focus on existing work about how managers can use performance information for organizational learning and decision-making, and we incorporate related literatures to discuss how managers can avoid the adverse motivational effects of performance systems and instead use them to bolster employee engagement. For instance, a considerable body of work has examined various attempts at gaming performance measurement systems (e.g. Bevan and Hood 2006). Similarly, recent research building on self-determination theory and motivation crowding theory has shown the importance of whether performance measurement is perceived as being supportive and meaningful or controlling and signaling distrust (Grøn 2018; Masal and Vogel 2016; Mikkelsen et al. 2017). Affecting how employees perceive performance measurement is by no means easy, and performance measurement systems can be designed in ways that make it difficult for public managers to avoid demotivating effects. Yet in many cases, public managers have some leeway in terms of how they choose to implement performance management systems (e.g. Grøn 2018; Masal and Vogel 2016). Overall, we argue that performance management practices can be more useful, motivating, and ultimately create value if:

- Managers are given increased procedural autonomy that enables them to respond to performance information by engineering performance-oriented changes.
- Performance information is used actively to generate organizational learning based on meaningful comparisons and interpretations. The numbers do not speak for themselves but need to be interpreted and potentially benchmarked in meaningful ways.
- The link between performance and rewards is considered carefully to avoid gaming and other unintended consequences, both at the organizational level and at the individual level.
- Managers are aware that performance management should be implemented to support professional development to avoid negative motivational effects and gaming.
- Managers use performance management as a transformational tool for dialogue to ensure that performance information is used in the active management practices and to support a common vision for the organization.
- Managers use performance information to support employee autonomy and avoid documentation overload.

We first describe the concept and purposes of performance management and offer a review of some of the considerable challenges that have faced the implementation of performance management reforms. Based on this diagnosis, then we discuss in detail what public managers can do to better reap the benefits of performance management and make them more meaningful, focusing first on the broader organizational uses of performance information, and then on how managers can avoid the detrimental effects on employee motivation that are often seen in practice.

8.2 Performance Management: Definition, Purposes, and Problems

We understand performance management as a system that integrates goal-setting activities, performance measurement, and feedback of performance information into decision-making. The extent to which each element has to be present to talk about performance management is disputed, and a central empirical finding is that the dissemination of performance information to public managers (or to politicians and citizens) does not guarantee that it will be understood or accepted as valid information (Petersen et al. 2019) or subsequently be used in decision-making (Moynihan and Pandey 2010). Some authors have also included financial incentives at the organizational or individual level tied to performance indicators as a definitional characteristic (e.g. Jacobsen and Andersen 2014), but in many performance management systems, measured performance is not or is only vaguely linked to financial consequences. We therefore treat performance management more broadly as "a system that generates performance information through strategic planning and performance measurement routines and that connects this information to decision venues, where, ideally, the information influences a range of possible decisions" (Moynihan 2008, 5). This definition underlines that although performance information might not be used in public management, it remains the underlying rationale of performance management systems.

What constitutes information about performance will differ for different types of organizations and tasks, but it will generally be related to the outputs, outcomes, or responsiveness of public services (Boyne 2002). In public education, for instance, outputs could include the number of students and hours taught as well as the quality of teaching, whereas the outcomes are related to the impact on students (and potentially, on society more broadly) in terms of student learning or well-being, or more long-term indicators focused on future educational attainment, democratic participation, or earnings. Responsiveness concerns whether public services meet the needs and demands of users and citizens, often measured by satisfaction surveys. By contrast, we do not consider performance information to include information about inputs (such as funding or employee resources) or about the actions or means leading to outputs or outcomes—though these are often relevant to combine with performance information when trying to understand and explain variation in organizational performance. Certain elements of the process (how things are done) can also be relevant to include because process criteria related to democratic values such as transparency, probity, or equal treatment of citizens are important in their own right and often matter directly to the experiences of service users (Andersen et al. 2016;

Boyne 2002). For a more thorough introduction to the concept and dimensions of public service performance, we refer to Chapter 2 of this volume.

Performance information is published in a range of different formats, including in annual performance reports, rankings, or more elaborate benchmarking schemes. Yet performance information is generally characterized by being systematic, often in the sense of being continuously monitored, well-defined indicators of performance. Systematic performance measurement carried out at only one point in time would arguably still be performance information, although it might be less useful for decision-making purposes. Also worth noting is the distinction between subjective and objective performance criteria and measures. For instance, user satisfaction is inherently internal or subjective, and similarly, satisfaction surveys are subjective measures that reflect users' own perceptions. By contrast, standardized student test scores attempt to measure an objective dimension of performance, namely the learning and abilities of students, and can be based on objective standardized measures. Yet even if the grading process is fully automated, it will still be based on measurement instruments that require a qualitative assessment of question content and interpretation on the part of test developers, respondents/students, and those analyzing the data. Moreover, in tests that are more open-ended, large-scale data sets about student performance are based on graders forming a qualitative assessment when scoring students or organizations (e.g. Nielsen 2014b). The US federal Program Assessment Rating Tool (PART), for example, has relied on what are essentially subjective and qualitative assessments of agencies carried out by external Office of Management and Budget (OMB) auditors based on various statements and data sources (Heinrich 2012). Such qualitative assessments, if carried out systematically, would still qualify as performance information, whereas managers' or other actors' own and more vague impressions about performance would not.

Performance information can be used at the organizational level as indicated in the discussion above, but performance information can also concern individual performance and be used for pay for performance or other individual-level verbal or material rewards such as praise and feedback, promotions, or particularly interesting tasks (Ingraham 1993; Nielsen et al. 2019; Weibel et al. 2010).

8.2.1 Purposes of Performance Measurement and Management

The key emphasis of performance management is on performance improvement and a system of performance-based accountability, which, for instance, stands in contrast to models of rule-based accountability (Moynihan 2008). Through a cyclical process of goal-setting, performance measurement, and feedback of performance information into decision-making about organizational design, practices, and the next round of goal-setting, to name a few, performance management seeks to create a stronger focus on results and outcomes while reducing input and process controls that restrict actions aimed at performance improvement. Performance measurement is seen to create greater transparency, allowing political or top administrative officials to secure compliance by holding public managers accountable to official goals (Moynihan 2008). Goal-setting and performance measurement also provide clearer signals to public managers and employees about which goals to pursue, and how to prioritize between competing goals (Nielsen 2014b).

At the level of individual public managers, the provision of continuous and systematic feedback on performance offers several possible benefits. Perhaps most importantly, performance data facilitates organizational learning by helping managers and employees identify performance problems that require attention and directs their search for solutions (Moynihan and Landuyt 2009; Nielsen 2014a). The outcomes of such learning processes can involve changes to organizational structures or routines or a reallocation of budgetary resources within the organization. In a human resource perspective, data about performance and performance problems can also help direct the search for specific employee competences that are needed in the organization, which has implications for the recruitment, development, and allocation of human resources. According to goal-setting theory, providing explicit goals and feedback can have the additional benefit of motivating employees, at least if the goals do not conflict with the values or policy preferences of employees (Locke and Latham 1990). However, realizing these benefits depends on whether managers choose to make purposeful use of performance information in their decision-making (Moynihan and Pandey 2010).

Performance measurement can also serve other purposes and be aimed at other groups of information users, such as citizens and service users or elected political representatives. In this chapter, we focus primarily on the managerial uses of performance information and how these affect employee responses to performance management.

8.2.2 Well-Known Problems of Performance Management and Recent Research

Performance management systems have suffered from a number of problems and dysfunctional consequences that have, at least partly, undermined their ability to deliver on their promises. Van Dooren and Hoffmann (2018) argue that most of the expected positive effects of performance management reflect an unrealistic rational or modernist understanding of organizations that emphasizes progress through managerial control. This assumption has been challenged by developments in our understanding of what an organization is and how it works, as well as by empirical research on how performance management plays out in practice.

An important design issue is the failure to grant organizational autonomy in exchange for performance-based accountability (Moynihan 2008), one reason being the reluctance of political or administrative superiors to give up control. In turn, public managers are faced with accountability pressures for improved performance but with limited opportunities to engineer performance-oriented change. Related to this, a number of studies have shown that public managers often fail to use performance data in their decision-making, which undermines the learning potential of performance measurement. One of the identified antecedents of performance information use is the level of managerial authority or discretion, which again suggests that public managers are unlikely to realize the potential benefits of performance management if they are restricted in their ability to introduce organizational changes.

In a systematic review of the field, Kroll (2015) points to additional important drivers of managerial performance information use, among which goal clarity, measurement system maturity, and support capacity are perhaps the most intuitively important factors. Goal clarity concerns whether goals are clearly understood by various stakeholders. Measurement system maturity and support capacity concern the extent to which sufficient resources and support are available to conduct high-quality performance measurement, analyze data and compare it to other organizations, and make performance information readily available to information users. These appear to some extent to be factors which can be undertaken. Yet goal clarity can be difficult to achieve for more complex tasks, and the cross-sectional designs used in this body of work also make it difficult to tell whether measurement system maturity, for instance, is partly a function of the level of goal clarity and the complexity of tasks or conflict over goals. In other words, although some of these factors are design features, they might not work equally well in all organizational contexts. Kroll (2015) also points to other factors related to performance information use, including an innovative culture and setting up learning forums, both of which we will return to below.

Probably the best-known problems related to performance management concern the risks of gaming or cheating behaviors that lead to dysfunctional or perverse effects (e.g. see Bevan and Hood 2006; de Bruijn 2002). Gaming has sometimes been described as "hitting the target, but missing the point" (Bevan and Hood 2006). One general type refers to the pursuit of measured performance at the expense of unmeasured performance dimensions that are also considered important. Examples are many and include teaching-to-the-test behaviors whereby broader and untested skills and competences receive less attention. Some of these effects have been referred to as output distortion or unintended consequences. However, it is relevant to consider that some of these effects are both expected and intended, for instance, because of disagreement with bureaucratic agents over which goals to prioritize, leading political superiors to introduce performance indicators to ensure that their priorities are given adequate attention even if it occurs at the expense of unmeasured dimensions. For this reason, Kelman and Friedman (2009) instead use the more neutral term "effort substitution" to describe such behaviors. However, in other cases, it is obvious that gaming behaviors have been both unintended and have had clearly negative consequences. One example is when job councilors' focus on helping unemployed clients find a job is undermined by performance measures related to the number and timing of client interviews or activation efforts (Kelman and Friedman 2009).

Gaming behaviors are a rational response to incentives that are tied to performance indicators. Such incentives can include specific financial incentives operating at the organizational or individual level, both in terms of budgetary consequences and when public rankings affect organizations' ability to attract service users. Yet there can also be less clearly defined incentives related to loss of organizational reputation, increased oversight, risks of reorganization, or other real or imagined sanctions. This poses the general challenge that how public managers and employees respond to performance measurement depends not only on the actual incentives tied to performance indicators, but also on these actors' sometimes unrealistic perceptions and fears about what the consequences of poor performance might be.

Whereas gaming occurs within the rules of the game, cheating behaviors concern efforts to obtain better performance scores by illegal means, such as outright falsification of data, such as examples of teachers correcting students' tests in a US context (Jacob and Levitt 2003). When we think of gaming and cheating behaviors as rational responses to incentives, it is sometimes assumed that such behaviors result from self-interested motives, suggesting a need for better controls. However, research on prosocial motives of public sector employees—as discussed in Chapter 14—may shed a different light on such behaviors.

To the extent that negative performance scores have adverse organizational consequences because of reduced budgets and other such issues, they will often also have negative consequences for those in need of public services. The case of the Atlanta school teachers, who engaged in cheating by correcting students' test answers before external assessment, provides an interesting example (Aviv 2014). These teachers saw the positive differences their school made to the students and the otherwise troubled inner-city community but were also aware that low scores in the standardized testing system could result in significant budget cuts and school closure. As indicated by later interviews with the teachers involved, their cheating behavior, while clearly illegal, was motivated by a concern for their students and not by self-interest.

Such cheating behaviors are clearly at the extreme end of employee responses to performance measurement. More common responses are perceptions of performance measurement as signaling a lack of trust in the abilities and motives of public sector employees. According to motivation crowding theory, such perceptions are likely to result in less motivated employees (Frey and Jegen 2001). For instance, Andersen and Pallesen (2008) found that university researchers who found the defined performance standard of international publications controlling were demotivated by the economic incentives offered, even to a point where their productivity decreased. If public sector employees have no trust in the purposes and implementation of performance measurement schemes, it is difficult to see how performance management can succeed in creating more public value. This point is underlined by Pihl-Thingvad (2016) who illustrates how the implementation of a performance management system in Danish job centers led to a number of dysfunctional behaviors and loss of commitment among employees.

8.3 How Can Public Managers Use Performance Management for Organizational Learning and Improvement?

Having outlined the challenges that public organizations and managers face when working with performance management, we now turn to the discussion of how managers can work with performance management to avoid some of these negative effects and make performance management deliver on its promises. We first discuss how public managers can design and appropriate formal context around performance management and ensure that performance information is used for organizational decision-making and learning. In Section 8.3.1, we discuss how managers can implement performance management to avoid detrimental consequences to the motivation of employees and the relations between managers and employees.

8.3.1 Increase Procedural Autonomy to Ensure that Performance Information Can Be Used for Improvement

As previously mentioned, a central design recommendation is to grant greater procedural autonomy to public organizations and their managers in exchange for the performance goals and controls introduced by performance management. Without sufficient authority to create performance-oriented changes, it is difficult to see how public managers would be able to deliver on the promises of performance management. Ultimately, the goal of performance management is to operate as an overarching management system that integrates the rules and operations of different management subsystems—such as human resource management, financial management, capital management, or IT management—in pursuit of overall organizational goals (Moynihan and Ingraham 2004). These management subsystems can be described as the channels for exerting effective performance-oriented leadership. In other words, successful performance management requires the flexibility to respond strategically to performance information, for instance, by reallocating budgetary means or by selecting and retaining the specific human resources (and thereby bureaucratic expertise) that are necessary for a particular organization with its specific set of problems and circumstances.

In line with this, Nielsen (2014b), in a study of public education in Denmark, found that introducing performance management tools only succeeded in improving student performance when school principals possessed significant authority over the management of human resources. Which management subsystems are more important likely depends on the tasks of public organizations. In less human resource-intensive organizations, managerial authority over other subsystems could be more important. The study found that without sufficient managerial authority, the introduction of performance management tended to result in lower performance over time. Initiating elaborate goal-setting exercises and measuring and evaluating performance are costly activities, so without the ability to reap their benefits, public organizations may, in fact, be worse off by introducing performance management systems.

A seemingly obvious implication is that the introduction of performance management reforms should be accompanied by a simultaneous devolving of procedural authority to public managers, yet there are limits to the extent that this will happen. Most public organizations are subject to a variety of rules that, for instance, exist to promote democratic accountability and legitimacy or to empower citizens and ensure equal or responsive public service provision (Nielsen 2014b). Moreover, politicians and top administrative officials may be wary about giving away control, and electoral incentives can lead to political intervention in organizational affairs even when promises of autonomy have been made. Consequently, an alternative recommendation would be to be wary about introducing performance reforms if it is not feasible, for political or other reasons, to grant substantial procedural autonomy.

This discussion has stressed structural conditions concerning delegated autonomy. Yet for performance management to become an overarching and integrating management system, it is not only necessary that managers have formal decision authority but also that they use that authority to make performance-informed decisions across the different management subsystems. In larger organizations, this often requires coordination between the different structural units or departments that are primarily responsible for HR or IT functions, among others. In smaller organizations, or at lower hierarchical levels, the management subsystems will not necessarily be split between different units or even persons, in which case, public managers can more readily integrate them in pursuit of overall performance. This still requires managerial attention to the interplay between management subsystems, though, and a willingness to let performance data inform organizational learning and decision-making.

8.3.2 Use Performance Management to Facilitate Organizational Learning

A central challenge to the implementation of performance reforms has been the limited use of performance information in management decision-making (Moynihan and Pandey 2010). A considerable body of work has examined various individual, organizational, and environmental correlates of performance information use (Kroll 2015). Performance information can be used for multiple purposes, with Moynihan (2009) suggesting a distinction between purposeful, perverse, political, and passive uses. Here, we focus only on purposeful use, whereby performance data is used actively to inform decision-making about how to improve organizational functioning and performance. This can include various decisions such as resource allocation, personnel selection, or control, thereby linking back to the use of performance management as a means to integrate management subsystems.

A precondition for purposeful use of performance information is that credible and useful data is available and engaged with in a way that leads to organizational learning about how to improve (Van Dooren and Hoffmann 2018). What constitutes credible and useful data is an important question in its own right but also one about which we will not go into detail here. We do note, however, that apart from the technical issues involved in measurement, measures that were originally credible can sometimes be compromised by the performance system itself if the act of measuring leads actors to engage in gaming behaviors. Moreover, credibility is also a perceptional question in the sense that, for instance, employees' trust in those charged with implementing the performance system or whether the data presents a positive or a negative picture of specific employees can affect whether employees perceive the measures as credible (Grøn 2018; Petersen et al. 2019).

Concerning the interpretation of what the performance data shows, behavioral models of performance evaluation suggest that decision makers look for cues as to what constitutes acceptable performance levels and use those cues to construct performance standards or aspiration levels against which they can compare their own performance. Recent studies have shown that in public organizations, as in private businesses, organizational decision makers look to information about their organization's own past performance and to the performance of similar organizations to form standards for comparison, referred to as historical and social aspirations, respectively (e.g. Ma 2016; Nielsen 2014a). Using social comparisons of performance can sometimes be challenging, though, as social comparisons only make sense when comparable organizations are available and if organizational conditions and task difficulty are also comparable or can otherwise be explicitly accounted for. Similarly, comparisons to historical performance can be misleading if broader societal trends affecting all organizations are not accounted for, such as crime rates dropping because of improved economic conditions or standardized tests getting easier over time. To a naïve observer, improved numbers would suggest performance improvement, whereas positive trends might, in fact, conceal a decline in performance. To facilitate learning, and to avoid learning the wrong things, performance systems and the public managers using them need to be aware of these risks and attempt to overcome them. Benchmarking with otherwise similar units—or by statistically accounting for any differences—is an important way of seeking to overcome these challenges but also one that requires additional resources invested in analyzing performance data. For example, several countries publicize the performance rankings of public schools, and some of these also account statistically for differences in task difficulty. In a meta-analysis, Gerrish (2016) indeed finds that performance management systems appear to have a more positive impact on performance if they include some kind of benchmarking with other organizations.

Learning about organizational performance only establishes whether a performance problem exists, however, and not what the cause of that problem is. Sometimes statistical cross-organizational benchmarking can also help identify causes, but only among factors that have been described by standardized data and with the same methodological challenges that are faced by quantitative observational research. Often, this is beyond the capacity of any single organization, but collaborations among organizations or analyses conducted by a central government unit can be a means to overcome this. Comparison with one or two carefully chosen peer organizations is also possible and sometimes a more feasible way forward, though, again, it can only incorporate information that is available to those individuals engaged in the comparison. Therefore, regardless of whether benchmarking is used in the search for causes, intimate knowledge of one's own organization and its operation is critical, and in most cases, the search for causes will probably take place primarily or solely within the organization.

To facilitate learning from performance information, Moynihan and Landuyt (2009) therefore argue that public managers should create learning forums that include a variety of organizational members and facilitate open and purpose-driven dialogue about the content and causes of performance. To ensure that all relevant information is brought to bear, managers should encourage open discussion and dissent, thereby avoiding groupthink and defensive reactions arising from fear of negative consequences. Moynihan and Kroll (2016) similarly find that involvement in routine, data-driven review meetings, as well as the quality of those reviews, increases purposeful managerial use of performance information. An implication of this work is that learning from performance feedback is as much about creating a shared understanding of the purposes and benefits of performance management.

8.4   How Should Public Managers Use Performance Management in Relation to Their Employees?

We now turn to the discussion on what public managers should be aware of when using performance measures in relation to their employees. We structure this discussion around the three basic psychological needs as spelled out by self-determination theory: competence, relatedness, and autonomy (Gagné and Deci 2005; see also Chapters 4 and 14 in this volume).

8.4.1   Be Careful When Using Performance-Based Financial Incentives

As the literature on pay for performance makes clear, there are a number of arguments as to why it is difficult to use financial incentives to promote performance in the public sector (Weibel et al. 2010). For instance, studies have shown that pay for performance is difficult to use in organizations that are dependent on knowledge-sharing and teamwork (Burgess and Ratto 2003). In addition, the limited funds for financial rewards in the public sector can make pay for performance less efficient (Ingraham 1993; Perry et al. 2009). However, some studies have also found clearly positive effects on the performance outcomes of introducing financial incentives (e.g. Dee and Wyckoff 2015).

Motivation crowding theory states that extrinsic incentives can reduce intrinsic motivation and public service motivation among employees if these managerial interventions are perceived as controlling rather than supportive (Frey and Jegen 2001; Jacobsen et al. 2014). While incentives targeted at the organizational level are less likely to crowd out motivation (de Bruijn 2002; Weibel 2010), organizational-level incentives can be problematic among employees highly motivated by intrinsic or public service motivation (Weibel et al. 2010).

Research has illustrated how managerial implementation is essential in ensuring that managerial interventions are perceived as supportive rather than controlling, thereby avoiding potential crowding-out effects (Andersen and Pallesen 2008; Grøn 2018; Mikkelsen et al. 2017). Parts of the literature draw on self-determination theory (Gagné and Deci 2005), which argues that the perception of a managerial intervention as either supportive or controlling is based on an evaluation of whether an intervention is seen as supporting the three basic psychological needs for competence, autonomy, and relatedness. Many initiatives which middle managers are asked to implement come with some leeway in how they can be communicated to employees (Radaelli and Sitton-Kinet 2016). This is no less true for performance management initiatives, which can be seen as both promoting and hampering competence, autonomy, and relatedness. For example, a study by Grøn (2018) illustrates how a group of daycare workers interpreted a management by objectives system quite differently in terms of its contribution to their professional competences. Previous studies have also illustrated how groups of employees with similar educational and professional backgrounds can interpret initiatives very differently (Jacobsen et al. 2014). These results would suggest that whether financial incentives succeed in motivating employees depends to some degree on how managers implement and communicate about them. Having said that, large groups of public sector employees are highly skeptical about financial incentives. This may make it more difficult to avoid crowding-out effects when implementing financial incentives compared to other managerial interventions, including the introduction and use of performance measures for other purposes.

8.4.2 Implement Performance Management with a Focus on Professional Development

A key managerial task is to ensure that performance information is used to support the professional practice of employees (Grøn 2018). Recent research shows that instead of using financial incentives, public managers can use contingent verbal rewards such as praise and positive feedback to promote employee self-efficacy and intrinsic motivation and engagement because verbal rewards support the need for competence while creating fewer incentives for gaming and risks of crowding-out (Jacobsen and Andersen 2017; Nielsen et al. 2019). Andersen et al. (2018b) also show that employees' perceptions of governance initiatives are positively correlated with managers' use of contingent verbal rewards. Verbal rewards are primarily considered effective if they are contingent on a specific set of actions or delivered results by the employee. Here, performance information could be useful as a basis for praising actions taken by employees.

Following self-determination theory's focus on the need for competence, performance management systems should, therefore, be designed to promote learning and professional development among employees (de Bruijn 2002; Jakobsen et al. 2018; Weibel 2010). Building competences (abilities) is also an important part of the AMO framework, which supports much research in HRM (see Chapters 7 and 9).

8.4.3 Use Performance Management as a Transformational Tool for Dialogue

However, it is not enough that performance management does not reduce motivation among employees. For performance management to be worthwhile, performance data needs to be put to use in the everyday practices of public organizations. The literature on implementation has made it clear that this does not happen automatically (Sandfort and Moulton 2014). The same holds true for performance management (Moynihan 2008; Van Dooren 2008). Especially when studying areas of the public sector dominated by professionals, their ability to resist implementation is well known if they do not accept a managerial initiative (Brehm and Gates 2010). Previous research has shown that managerial support for performance management is important in putting performance information to use (Moynihan and Ingraham 2004), and studies have emphasized the extent to which information is used as a basis for dialogue (Moynihan and Landuyt 2009). Moynihan et al. (2012) argue that transformational leadership practices promote information use because transformational leadership promotes a developmental culture with a focus on performance as well as increased goal clarity. Their arguments are supported by the findings in a recent article by Andersen et al. (2018a), which illustrates that transformational leaders are better at promoting a common understanding of professional quality among their employees, which, in turn, is expected to make them more likely to strive toward organizational goals (Caillier 2014).

While the definition of transformational leadership diverges in the literature (see Chapter 5), recent studies in public administration have utilized the definition proposed by Jensen et al. (2018b, 8) who define transformational leadership as "behaviors that seek to develop, share, and sustain a vision with the intention to encourage employees to transcend their own self-interest and achieve organizational goals." Studies based on this definition have shown that transformational leadership is most effective when used in face-to-face dialogue with employees (Jensen et al. 2018a).

Nielsen and Jacobsen (2018) illustrate how performance information can be used by managers to generate support among employees for organizational change, especially in a context of low performance. Also in line with studies on change management (see Chapter 11), transformational leaders may be able to use performance data to justify and sustain their vision for the organization. Following Jensen et al. (2018a), this use of performance data would be most effective if used to promote dialogue among managers and employees on the relevance and implications of the data vis-à-vis the organizational vision, which could potentially increase goal clarity and employee motivation. Returning to the three basic psychological needs proposed by self-determination theory, we argue that by using performance information to support a shared vision for an organization, performance information might also help in supporting relatedness in the group.

8.4.4 Consider Whether Employee Autonomy Can Be Increased

Nielsen (2014b) shows that performance improvements from performance management are dependent on managerial autonomy. Similarly, Moynihan and Pandey (2010) find that flexibility as perceived by the manager correlates positively with performance information use. Self-determination theory would argue that the same effects should be expected among employees. The discussion of the use and non-use of performance information (e.g. Moynihan and Pandey 2010; Van Dooren 2008) illustrates that quite a lot of performance data is gathered without ever being used or is used in ways that are not obvious to those gathering the information. Rather than generating a sense of autonomy, the sheer amount of data collection may instead be perceived as documentation demands or red tape, which has been shown to entail negative motivational effects (Moynihan and Pandey 2007). The promise of performance management to replace input and procedural controls with output measures is far from always kept. Focusing on using performance management systems to increase employee autonomy might be a promising avenue to improve the use of performance management and potentially the performance of public organizations.

8.5 Conclusion: Making Sense of Performance Management

This chapter has outlined what performance management and its purposes are, as well as discussed some of the traditional problems associated with performance management. Following this, the main part of the chapter focused on how public managers can implement and use performance management systems in a way that mitigates these problems and has the potential to improve public service performance. In doing so, we pointed to six important lessons for managerial practice.

To sum up, ensuring managerial autonomy and meaningful data are important first steps, which can enable managers to foster both learning from and use of performance information. Managers have an indispensable role in making performance information meaningful to employees and ensuring that data is used to support a feeling of competence, a shared vision (relatedness), and autonomy. This does not imply that it is illegitimate to use performance management for accountability purposes, but the balance between control and learning is still not found in most contexts (Jakobsen et al. 2018).

These different purposes of performance management are not isolated from each other. In some instances, the achievement of one purpose reinforces another, for example, if performance-based accountability motivates managers to strive for performance improvement. However, different purposes can also be at odds with one another. For instance, some reward and punishment types of accountability systems have been found to increase gaming and cheating behaviors, which are often detrimental to organizational performance (Bevan and Hood 2006) and which undermine organizational learning from performance feedback (Moynihan and Landuyt 2009) or even inspire learning efforts aimed at how to better game the system (Aviv 2014).

We have included studies from a number of different cultural contexts in our discussion of the existing literature on performance management and the role of the manager in making it work. However, we need to remember that the use of performance information (Hammerschmid et al. 2013) as well as the way managers choose to lead vary greatly across cultural contexts, as illustrated by the GLOBE study (House et al. 2004). While we argue that the need for autonomy is relevant across cultural contexts, we may need to caution that the way autonomy is given to employees can vary between different cultural contexts just as the relative importance of different needs probably do. Departing from Hofstede and Hofstede's (2005) work on power distance, we would expect that when the power distance is low, a manager may enter into an extensive dialogue with employees on how data is to be interpreted, but when the power distance is higher, such a dialogue might prove difficult as this would put employees in a position where they potentially have to disagree with their manager. In these latter cultural contexts, a manager may be better served with letting employees have parts of the discussion without the manager. Similarly, we may expect that cultural contexts that are characterized by a higher degree of collectivism may place a greater value on relatedness compared to cultural contexts that are more individualized. These examples show the more general consideration that managers should take the local context into account when translating recommendations and findings into practice.

This chapter illustrates that questions of performance management have been widely debated but that we still have some way to go before we are able to design systems that balance the needs for learning and accountability. We also need more research on the role and responsibilities of the frontline managers in making performance management do good rather than bad in the public sector. Promising paths for research in this direction would seek to integrate our understanding of performance management with related research, for instance, about generic leadership strategies, what shapes employee perceptions and motivation, and organizational learning and behavioral decision-making.

References

Andersen, L. B., B. Bjørnholt, L. L. Bro, and C. Holm-Petersen. 2018a. "Achieving High Quality through Transformational Leadership: A Qualitative Multilevel Analysis of Transformational Leadership and Perceived Professional Quality." *Public Personnel Management 47* (1): pp. 51–72.

Andersen, L. B., A. Boesen, and L. H. Pedersen. 2016. "Performance in Public Organizations: Clarifying the Conceptual Space." *Public Administration Review 76* (6): pp. 852–62.

Andersen, L. B., S. Boye, and R. Laursen. 2018b. "Building Support? The Importance of Verbal Rewards for Employee Perceptions of Governance Initiatives." *International Public Management Journal 21* (1): pp. 1–32.

Andersen, L. B., and T. Pallesen. 2008. "'Not Just for the Money?' How Financial Incentives Affect the Number of Publications at Danish Research Institutions." *International Public Management Journal 11* (1): pp. 28–47.

Aviv, R. 2014. "Wrong Answer: In an Era of High-Stakes Testing, a Struggling School Made a Shocking Choice." *The New Yorker—Annals of Education*, July 21. https://www.newyorker.com/magazine/2014/07/21/wrong-answer.

Bevan, G., and C. Hood. 2006. "What's Measured Is What Matters: Targets and Gaming in the English Public Health Care System." *Public Administration 84* (3): pp. 517–38.

Boyne, G. A. 2002. "Concepts and Indicators of Local Authority Performance: An Evaluation of the Statutory Frameworks in England and Wales." *Public Money & Management 22* (2): pp. 17–24.

Brehm, J. O., and S. Gates. 2010. *Working, Shirking, and Sabotage: Bureaucratic Response to a Democratic Public*. Ann Arbor, MI: University of Michigan Press.

Burgess, S., and M. Ratto. 2003. "The Role of Incentives in the Public Sector: Issues and Evidence." *Oxford Review of Economic Policy 19* (2): pp. 285–300.

Caillier, J. G. 2014. "Toward a Better Understanding of the Relationship between Transformational Leadership, Public Service Motivation, Mission Valence, and Employee Performance." *Public Personnel Management 43* (2): pp. 218–39.

de Bruijn, H. 2002. *Managing Performance in the Public Sector*. London: Routledge.

Dee, T. S., and J. Wyckoff. 2015. "Incentives, Selection, and Teacher Performance: Evidence from IMPACT." *Journal of Policy Analysis and Management 34* (2): pp. 267–97.

Döring, H., J. Downe, and S. Martin. 2015. "Regulating Public Services: How Public Managers Respond to External Performance Assessment." *Public Administration Review* 75 (6): pp. 867–77.

Frey, B. S., and R. Jegen. 2001. "Motivation Crowding Theory." *Journal of Economic Survey* 15 (5): pp. 589–623.

Gagné, M., and E. L. Deci. 2005. "Self-Determination Theory and Work Motivation." *Journal of Organizational Behavior* 26 (4): pp. 331–62.

Gerrish, E. 2016. "The Impact of Performance Management on Performance in Public Organizations: A Meta-Analysis." *Public Administration Review* 76 (1): pp. 48–66.

Grøn, C. 2018. "Perceptions Unfolded: Managerial Implementation in Perception Formation." *International Journal of Public Sector Management* 31 (6): pp. 710–25.

Hammerschmid, G., S. Van de Walle, and V. Stimac. 2013. "Internal and External Use of Performance Information in Public Organizations: Results from an International Survey." *Public Money & Management* 33 (4): pp. 261–8.

Heinrich, C. J. 2012. "How Credible Is the Evidence, and Does It Matter? An Analysis of the Program Assessment Rating Tool." *Public Administration Review* 72 (1): pp. 123–34.

Hofstede, G., and G. J. Hofstede. 2005. *Cultures and Organizations: Software of the Mind.* 2nd ed. New York: McGraw-Hill.

House, R. J., P. J. Hanges, M. Javidan, P. W. Dorfman, and V. Gupta. 2004. *Culture, Leadership, and Organizations: The GLOBE Study of 62 Societies.* Thousand Oaks, CA: Sage.

Ingraham, P. W. 1993. "Of Pigs in Pokes and Policy Diffusion: Another Look at Pay-for-Performance." *Public Administration Review* 53 (4): pp. 348–56.

Jacob, B., and S. D. Levitt. 2003. "Rotten Apples: An Investigation of the Prevalence and Predictors of Teacher Cheating." *Quarterly Journal of Economics* 117 (3): pp. 843–77.

Jacobsen, C. B., and L. B. Andersen. 2014. "Performance Management in the Public Sector: Does It Decrease or Increase Innovation and Performance?" *International Journal of Public Administration* 37 (14): pp. 1011–23.

Jacobsen, C. B., and L. B. Andersen. 2017. "Leading Public Service Organizations: How to Obtain Employees with High Self-Efficacy." *Public Management Review* 19 (2): pp. 253–73.

Jacobsen, C. B., J. Hvitved, and L. B. Andersen. 2014. "Command and Motivation: How the Perception of External Interventions Relates to Intrinsic Motivation and Public Service Motivation." *Public Administration* 92 (4): pp. 790–806.

Jakobsen, M. L., M. Baekgaard, D. P. Moynihan, and N. Van Loon. 2018. "Making Sense of Performance Regimes: Rebalancing External Accountability and Internal Learning." *Perspectives on Public Management and Governance* 1 (2): pp. 127–41.

Jensen, U. T., L. B. Andersen, L. L. Bro, A. Bøllingtoft, T. L. Mundbjerg Eriksen, A.-L. Holten, C. B. Jacobsen, J. Ladenburg, P. A. Nielsen, H. H. Salomonsen, N. Westergård-Nielsen, and A. Würtz. 2018b. "Conceptualizing and Measuring Transformational and Transactional Leadership." *Administration & Society* 51 (1): pp. 3–33.

Jensen, U. T., H. H. Salomonsen, and D. P. Moynihan. 2018a. "Communicating the Vision: How Face-to-Face Dialogue Facilitates Transformational Leadership." *Public Administration Review 78* (3): pp. 350–61.

Kelman, S., and J. N. Friedman. 2009. "Performance Improvement and Performance Dysfunction: An Empirical Examination of Distortionary Impacts of the Emergency Room Wait-Time Target in the English National Health Service." *Journal of Public Administration Research and Theory 19* (4): pp. 917–46.

Kroll, A. 2015. "Drivers of Performance Information Use: Systematic Literature Review and Directions for Future Research." *Public Performance & Management Review 38* (3): pp. 459–86.

Locke, E. A., and G. P. Latham. 1990. *A Theory of Goal Setting and Task Performance.* Englewood Cliffs, NJ: Prentice-Hall, Inc.

Ma, L. 2016. "Performance Feedback, Government Goal-Setting and Aspiration Level Adaptation: Evidence from Chinese Provinces." *Public Administration 94* (2): pp. 452–71.

Masal, D., and R. Vogel. 2016. "Leadership, Use of Performance Information, and Job Satisfaction: Evidence from Police Services." *International Public Management Journal 19* (2): pp. 208–34.

Mikkelsen, M. F., C. B. Jacobsen, and L. B. Andersen. 2017. "Managing Employee Motivation: Exploring the Connections between Managers' Enforcement Actions, Employee Perceptions, and Employee Intrinsic Motivation." *International Public Management Journal 20* (2): pp. 183–205.

Moynihan, D. P. 2008. *The Dynamics of Performance Management: Constructing Information and Reform.* Washington, DC: Georgetown University Press.

Moynihan, D. P. 2009. "Through a Glass, Darkly. Understanding the Effects of Performance Regimes." *Public Performance & Management Review 32* (4): pp. 592–603.

Moynihan, D. P., and P. W. Ingraham. 2004. "Integrative Leadership in the Public Sector: A Model of Performance-Information Use." *Administration & Society 36* (4): pp. 427–53.

Moynihan, D. P., and A. Kroll. 2016. "Performance Management Routines that Work? An Early Assessment of the GPRA Modernization Act." *Public Administration Review 76* (2): pp. 314–23.

Moynihan, D. P., and N. Landuyt. 2009. "How Do Public Organizations Learn? Bridging Structural and Cultural Divides." *Public Administration Review 69* (6): pp. 1097–105.

Moynihan, D. P., and S. K. Pandey. 2007. "The Role of Organizations in Fostering Public Service Motivation." *Public Administration Review 67* (1): pp. 40–53.

Moynihan, D. P., and S. K. Pandey. 2010. "The Big Question for Performance Management: Why Do Managers Use Performance Information?" *Journal of Public Administration Research and Theory 20* (4): pp. 849–66.

Moynihan, D. P., S. K. Pandey, and B. E. Wright. 2012. "Setting the Table: How Transformational Leadership Fosters Performance Information Use." *Journal of Public Administration Research and Theory 22* (1): pp. 143–64.

Nielsen, P. A. 2014a. "Learning from Performance Feedback: Performance Information, Aspiration Levels and Managerial Priorities." *Public Administration 92* (1): pp. 142–60.

Nielsen, P. A. 2014b. "Performance Management, Managerial Authority, and Public Service Performance." *Journal of Public Administration Research and Theory 25* (2): pp. 431–58.

Nielsen, P. A., S. Boye, A. L. Holten, C. B. Jacobsen, and L. B. Andersen. 2019. "Are Transformational and Transactional Types of Leadership Compatible? A Two-Wave Study of Employee Motivation." *Public Administration 97* (2): pp. 413–28.

Nielsen, P. A., and C. B. Jacobsen. 2018. "Zone of Acceptance under Performance Measurement: Does Performance Information Affect Employee Acceptance of Management Authority?" *Public Administration Review 78* (5): pp. 684–93.

Perry, J. L., T. A. Engbers, and S. Y. Jun. 2009. "Back to the Future? Performance-Related Pay, Empirical Research, and the Perils of Persistence." *Public Administration Review 69* (1): pp. 39–51.

Petersen, N. B. G., T. V. Laumann, and M. Jakobsen. 2019. "Acceptance or Disapproval: Performance Information in the Eyes of Public Frontline Employees." *Journal of Public Administration Research and Theory 29* (1): pp. 101–17.

Pihl-Thingvad, S. 2016. "The Inner Workings of Performance Management in Danish Job Centers: Rational Decisions or Cowboy Solutions?" *Public Performance & Management Review 40* (1): pp. 48–70.

Radaelli, G., and L. Sitton-Kent. 2016. "Middle Managers and the Translation of New Ideas in Organizations: A Review of Micro-Practices and Contingencies." *International Journal of Management Reviews 18* (3): pp. 211–23.

Sandfort, J., and S. Moulton. 2014. *Effective Implementation in Practice: Integrating Public Policy and Management.* San Francisco, CA: Jossey-Bass.

Van Dooren, W. 2008. "Nothing New under the Sun? Change and Continuity in Twentieth Century Performance Movements." In *Performance Information in the Public Sector: How It Is Used*, edited by S. Van de Walle and W. Van Dooren, pp. 11–23. Houndsmills: Palgrave Macmillan.

Van Dooren, W., and C. Hoffmann. 2018. "Performance Management in Europe: An Idea Whose Time Has Come and Gone?" In *The Palgrave Handbook of Public Administration and Management in Europe*, edited by E. Ongaro and S. Van Thiel, pp. 207–25. Houndsmills: Palgrave Macmillan.

Weibel, A. 2010. "Managerial Objectives of Formal Control: High Motivation Control Mechanisms." In *Organizational Control*, edited by S. B. Sitkin, L. B. Cardinal, and K. M. Bijlsma-Frankema, pp. 434–62. Cambridge: Cambridge University Press.

Weibel, A., K. Rost, and M. Osterloh. 2010. "Pay for Performance in the Public Sector: Benefits and (Hidden) Costs." *Journal of Public Administration Research and Theory 20* (2): pp. 389–412.

9

Linking HRM Systems with Public Sector Employees' Performance

The Way Forward

Julian Seymour Gould-Williams and Ahmed Mohammed Sayed Mostafa

9.1 Introduction

For almost thirty years, scholars have researched the relationship between human resource management (HRM) and organizational performance in the belief that people hold the key to competitive advantage. Much of the early research in the field of HRM was concerned with the extent of "fit" between HRM and organizational strategies (e.g. see Miles and Snow 1984; Schuler and Jackson 1987; Storey and Sisson 1993). HR practices were measured at the organizational level (HR policy), with firm performance often considered in terms of financial returns or profits. As such, employees' reactions to HR practices were largely ignored (Huselid 1995). So while there was growing evidence that HR policy decisions made by senior managers at the firm level were linked with superior performance, key questions remained unanswered. For instance, *why* are HR practices linked with superior performance? *What* are the process mechanisms explaining this relationship? Are there conditions under which HR practices are more or less effective? Sometime later, scholars began to address these issues by seeking employees' perceptions of HR practices (Guest 1998). It was at this point that public sector scholars entered the debate, seeking employees' views on how their perceptions of HR practices affected their attitudes and behaviors toward work (Gould-Williams 2003).

Despite a considerable expansion of cumulative research investigating the HRM–performance relationship across the private, public, and not-for-profit sectors, surprisingly few studies were theory-driven (Boselie et al. 2005). It is the aim of this chapter to begin to address this issue by taking a closer look at the contributions made by public sector scholars toward our understanding of the relationship between HR practices and performance. So far, the literature has noted three dominant approaches to managing people: "high performance," "high commitment," and

Julian Seymour Gould-Williams and Ahmed Mohammed Sayed Mostafa, *Linking HRM Systems with Public Sector Employees' Performance: The Way Forward* In: *Managing for Public Service Performance: How People and Values Make a Difference.* Edited by: Peter Leisink, Lotte B. Andersen, Gene A. Brewer, Christian B. Jacobsen, Eva Knies, and Wouter Vandenabeele, Oxford University Press (2021). © Julian Seymour Gould-Williams and Ahmed Mohammed Sayed Mostafa.
DOI: 10.1093/oso/9780192893420.003.0009

"high involvement" (Boxall and Macky 2009). Our review notes the related theoretical underpinnings for each of the three dominant approaches. On this basis, we develop research propositions in which we predict the anticipated relationships between the three distinct approaches to HRM and public service outcomes. Thereafter, we turn to the public sector studies and consider whether the content of the HR systems is consistent with their associated theoretical underpinnings. As our review will focus on strategic HR "systems" (Boselie et al. 2005, 73), the early public sector HRM research will not be included in our analysis as it took a non-systems perspective based on discrete, individual HR practices. We conclude by noting potential avenues for future research in public organizations based on advances made in private sector organizations.

9.2 Theoretical Approaches for Assessing the HRM–Performance Relationship

HRM scholars have long assumed that managers will have an overarching philosophy or approach to managing people (Boxall and Macky 2009; Lepak et al. 2004). In the main, these philosophies can be classified as "soft" or "hard" approaches to people management (Storey 1992). "Hard" HRM is based on high-control, low-trust approaches to people management as advocated by the Tayloristic management school. In contrast, the "soft" or high-trust, low-control approaches are consistent with humanistic, high-commitment approaches to people management (Storey 1992). These dominant perspectives are not mutually exclusive in that some managers within the same organization may adopt a high-trust approach, whereas others may not. Also, individual managers may adopt a high-trust approach when dealing with "core" workers and a low-trust approach when dealing with "peripheral" workers (Hauff et al. 2014; Lepak and Snell 1999; Marescaux et al. 2012). Although we acknowledge these different scenarios, our review will assume that organizations adopt a consistent philosophical approach to HRM based on high- or low-trust philosophies.

The hard and soft approaches to HRM are reflected in the labels used to describe systems of HR practices: "high performance," "high commitment," or "high involvement." Although scholars have used these labels interchangeably or as synonyms (Wood 1999), we believe the labels should be treated as distinct as they identify the *primary intent* of the HR system, be it "performance," "commitment," or "involvement" (Boxall and Macky 2009). For instance, we associate high-performance systems with high-control/low-trust philosophies, as their primary focus is on improving performance metrics. In contrast, we associate high-commitment and high-involvement systems with low-control/high-trust philosophies as they emphasize employee well-being, mutuality, and social exchanges (Collins and Smith 2006). Nevertheless, we accept the labels can be confusing because of "assumptions about the etymology of the name – whether these practices have already been identified as associated empirically with [these outcomes] as many assume and some assert, or whether it is just a name" (Cappelli and Neumark 2001, 738). Thus, our approach diverges from those who use the "high performance" label as an umbrella term for *many* different approaches to the practice of HR management (e.g. see Kalleberg et al. 2006, 296, who associate "high-involvement," "high-commitment," and many other forms of management approaches with "high-performance" systems).

Before we elaborate on these different HR systems and their affiliated theories, we will first discuss the importance of employees' responses to investments in HR systems. As their personal experiences of HR practices may vary from one employee to another, the effects of HR systems on work-related attitudes and behaviors may differ. Importantly, attribution theory will help answer questions of "why" employees respond in a particular way to HR systems.

9.2.1 Attribution Theory

Although attribution theories have been in use for some considerable time (e.g. see Heider 1958; Kelley 1967; Weiner 1985), it is only recently that HRM scholars have begun to investigate their role in explaining the links between HR practices and performance. The recent interest in this field of research was stimulated by two key articles, namely Bowen and Ostroff's (2004) theory on HR systems' strength, and Nishii et al.'s (2008) HR attributions theory. These two attribution theories are complementary in that Bowen and Ostroff (2004) focus on the "strength" of the signals sent to employees by HR systems, whereas Nishii et al. (2008) focus on the motives employees attribute to managers' investments in HR systems.

9.2.2 Bowen and Ostroff's HR Systems' Strength

Bowen and Ostroff (2004) assert that systems of HR practice send signals to employees about the types of behaviors managers expect, value, and reward. They propose that the collective response of employees to systems of HR practices affects the organization's HR climate and employees' work-related attitudes and behaviors. If individual HR practices within a system are consistent with each other, the resultant "signal" is likely to be strong. In contrast, if the HR practices within a system are misaligned and inconsistent, then employees are likely to experience difficulty interpreting the signal, and hence, the signal will be "weak." "Strong" HR systems are more likely to drive employees' behaviors as intended by managers. For instance, if managers are desirous of improving joint group working, a strong HR system is likely to do the following: (1) select individuals on the basis of group-fit; (2) train group members to work flexibly and supportively of each other; (3) reward employees for combined group performance; and (4) provide opportunities for group members to communicate with each other. In contrast, in the same context, a "weak" HR system may include: (1) group member selection based on individual achievements;

(2) training focused on specialized tasks; (3) rewards based on individual performance; and (4) functional-based communication. Where the HR system is perceived to send a weak signal, employees are unlikely to understand which behaviors are being encouraged. Hence, Bowen and Ostroff's (2004) thesis is that strong HR systems are desirable and have a greater impact on employees' work-related attitudes and behaviors.

9.2.3   Nishii et al.'s Employee Attributions Theory

While Bowen and Ostroff (2004) focus on signals sent by HR systems, Nishii et al. (2008) adopt a different perspective, focusing instead on the motives employees attribute to managers' investments in HR systems. These attributions occur independently of the content or strength of the HR system. According to Nishii et al. (2008), employees attribute high- or low-trust motives to management investments in systems of HR practices based on their past dealings with them. Nishii et al. (2008) propose that employees' attributions impact their responses to HR systems. The same HR system can, therefore, impact employees in very different ways depending on which motives employees attribute to managers' investments (e.g. see Van de Voorde and Beijer 2015). To illustrate, consider two different motives managers may have for investing in an HR system consisting of performance appraisal, training programs, and reward systems. Employees may believe that managers have invested in this HR system because they want to do the following: (1) closely monitor their performance; (2) ensure they have the skills needed to get the most out of them; and (3) pay them for what they have achieved in line with their employment contract. Alternatively, employees may believe that managers have made such investments so they can: (1) discuss their experiences at work and develop areas of interest and expertise; (2) recommend specific training and development portfolios to address any skill gaps that are identified; and (3) thank them for their contributions toward organizational achievements and discuss meaningful ways their contributions could be recognized and rewarded. It is proposed that employees' responses to the same HR system will be influenced by their personal attributions as to *why* managers have invested in them. In the case of our illustration, employees could believe that managers want to get the most out of them or that managers care about them and their well-being (Nishii et al. 2008).

The two attribution theories above have different implications for HR system design. Whereas Bowen and Ostroff's (2004) HR systems' strength theory focuses directly on the content of HR systems, Nishii et al.'s (2008) does not. Instead, Niishii et al. (2008) propose that it is the inferred motives employees attribute to managers for investments in HR systems that are of principal concern. On this basis, the following section will now focus on different types of HR systems. We will refer to the content of each HR system using descriptive labels commonly used by HRM scholars, namely "high performance," "high commitment," and "high involvement."

9.3 High-Performance HR Systems

High-performance systems of HR practices are designed to achieve improved organizational performance through the collective responses of employees. The popular theoretical lens used to explain the effects of high-performance HR practices on employee outcomes is the ability, motivation, and opportunity (AMO) framework (Appelbaum et al. 2000; Boselie et al. 2005; see also Chapter 7). AMO theory proposes that HR systems provide employees with the ability (A) and motivation (M) to want to perform, and thereafter create opportunities (O) to perform to their full potential. In this way, systems of high-performance HR practices will: (1) equip employees with the skills and abilities needed to undertake their roles; (2) motivate employees to exert discretionary effort on behalf of the organization through incentivized reward and remuneration packages; and (3) create opportunities for employees to demonstrate their high skill levels and motivation through job design. This perspective takes a resource-based view of employees in which they are considered key organizational resources who become valuable, rare, inimitable, and non-substitutable (Barney 1991). These characteristics are regarded as essential to the achievement of sustained superior performance as they are difficult to replicate by competitors. As noted by Messersmith et al. (2011, 1106), this perspective is predicated on the notion that organizational-level resources are heterogeneous and that the differences in combinations of resources over time lead to sustainable competitive advantage.

Of course, in the majority of instances, public sector organizations tend not to have competitive advantage as their core performance outcome (see Chapter 2 where public sector performance is discussed in more detail). If we adopt the original interpretation of performance as used by Appelbaum et al. (2000), then performance would refer to profits and increased productivity. In this way, high-performance HR systems are likely to signal that employees are another organizational resource alongside IT systems, machinery, and equipment and a means to improve performance output. If so, employees are likely to perceive that the organization is primarily interested in their *resource* capability rather than their *human* capacity, and they are used as a means to an end—to improve organizational performance (Barney and Wright 1998).

As the AMO model makes no reference to potential negative employee experiences from the implementation of HR practices, it is possible that workers may achieve ambitious performance outcomes while simultaneously experiencing work overload, anxiety, stress, and burnout (Van de Voorde and Beijer 2015). We are not alone in raising this concern as there is growing skepticism among HRM scholars (Wall and Wood 2005; Wood 1999) that high-performance models are increasingly associated with work overload, work–life imbalance, stress, and anxiety (empirical evidence corroborating these concerns is presented by Jensen et al. 2013). In fact, there is evidence demonstrating that high-performance workplace cultures are increasingly leading to burnout as highly skilled employees seek to achieve increasingly challenging and ambitious performance targets (Ehrnrooth and Bjorkman 2012).

As such, we propose that high-performance HR systems are likely to lead to increased performance but at a potential "hidden" cost to employees. Further, although high-performance systems may equip employees with essential skills to deliver public services, it is questionable if this approach is consistent with promoting public service motivation (PSM) and delivering public value across the workforce. These outcomes are primarily driven by HR practices that promote autonomous forms of motivation, such as those emphasizing meaning and values (as we discuss later in this chapter). Instead, high-performance HR practices, such as payment contingent on performance, goal-setting, and performance measurement, are more likely to promote controlled extrinsic forms of motivation (Deci and Ryan 2000). In other words, high-performance HR systems are likely to signal that employees are treated as "resources." In turn, employees are likely to adopt a mechanistic, target-driven approach to delivering vital public services. Of course, this approach may be suited to some public services such as those where performance outcomes are easily measurable (e.g. refuse disposal services and car parking fines), but it is less so when public employees provide services directly to service users (e.g. community health, teaching, and social services). Under the latter conditions, high-performance HR practices are likely to be simultaneously associated with higher employee productivity along with work-related stress and anxiety. Therefore, we propose the following:

Proposition 1: Strong "high-performance" HR systems are more likely to result in both enhanced in-role performance and work-related stress when compared with "high-commitment" and "high-involvement" HR systems, especially when public employees deliver public services directly to service users.

9.4 High-Commitment HR Systems

High-commitment HR systems should signal loyalty, trust, mutuality, well-being, and job security. These trademarks emphasize the human, relational qualities of strategic HRM. Thus, instead of employees simply being viewed as a means to achieve improved performance outcomes, systems of high-commitment HR practices seek to generate an affective response to the organization through mutually beneficial exchanges between the organization and the employee. Strong high-commitment HR systems seek to address employees' developmental and emotional needs and signal that the organization cares for them and values their personal contributions. Within public sector organizations, systems of high-commitment HR practices should clearly signal that organizational successes are *not* achieved at a cost to employees as mutually beneficial outcomes should be achieved. In other words, we anticipate that high-commitment HR systems will be viewed as "socially acceptable" approaches to people management as employees are treated "holistically and equitably" (Kalleberg et al. 2006, 274).

Social exchange theory is often used as the theoretical lens explaining the outcomes of high-commitment HR systems. Social exchanges are typified by "actions that are contingent on the rewarding reactions of others, which over time provide for mutually and rewarding transactions and relationships" (Cropanzano and Mitchell 2005, 890). Social exchanges differ from economic exchanges as the latter are based on pre-specified contractual arrangements, such as rates of pay, working hours, and holiday entitlements. Relationships based on economic exchanges are discrete and financially oriented with no explicit expectation for performance to go beyond the terms of the contract (Shore et al. 2006). Economic exchanges are likely to typify high-performance HR systems. In contrast, social exchanges are based on non-specified transactions in which both parties in the exchange relationship benefit from mutually beneficial interchanges. Normative rules of reciprocity (Gouldner 1960) govern the extent to which the recipient (the employee) feels obligated to respond in a positive way to the donor's (the organization) initial offering. Such offerings may include payment of an employee's request to undertake a program of further study for their personal development, or the discretionary provision of time off work to care for an elderly relative or child. The normative response to receiving a desired and valued offering is for the recipient to reciprocate in kind at some future time. Under such conditions, employees' affective response to the organization will be in the form of increased organizational commitment and discretionary behaviors, such as defending the organization or assisting new starters (Kehoe and Wright 2013).

As social exchange relationships occur between the organization (or their managerial representatives) and the individual employee, it is important to assess how systems of high-commitment HR practices are experienced by the individual employee. While we accept that employees will be affected by the way the organization treats others within the workforce (e.g. during downsizing programs), on the basis of social exchange relationships, we propose that it is important to determine whether the high-commitment system is experienced by the responding employee rather than the workforce as a whole. For instance, employees may witness others within their team or work group being offered desired perquisites or flexible working programs, but if they are personally unable to benefit from these rewards, they are not part of the social exchange relationship. Similarly, if employees do not perceive organizational responses to their reciprocating actions to be fair, they are likely to feel an imbalance in the exchange as the high-commitment HR system fails to deliver. It is likely they will then expect additional offerings from the organization before engaging in discretionary behaviors.

Theoretically, we predict that "strong" systems of high-commitment HR practices will be associated with higher levels of affective commitment to the organization, PSM, public value, and discretionary effort or organizational citizenship behaviors (OCBs) as employees strive to reciprocate organizational investments in their personal development and well-being. In other words, the reciprocal nature of the exchange should result in beneficial outcomes for both the organization (PSM, public value, and OCBs) and the employees (personal development, growth, and improved well-being). Nevertheless, based on private sector experiences, we acknowledge that "mutuality *may be* somewhat unbalanced... as managers appear to gain more [than employees]" (Guest and Peccei 2001, 231; emphasis added). We therefore propose:

Proposition 2: Strong "high-commitment" HR systems will produce "mutually" beneficial exchanges with employee well-being considered alongside the achievement of superior performance. Public sector employees are more likely to reciprocate organizational investments in them by enhanced PSM, the delivery of public value, and the display of extra-role behaviors in comparison with high-performance systems.

9.5 High-Involvement HR Systems

The description "high involvement" signals the *raison d'être* of these HR systems, namely to transfer decision-making from managers to employees. Unlike the labels "high performance" and "high commitment," high-involvement HR systems do not focus on intended outcomes of HR practices but the processes through which hoped-for outcomes may be achieved. As with high-commitment systems, the high-involvement system contrasts with Tayloristic, high-control, low-trust approaches as it decentralizes control and gives employees the capacity to self-manage and engage in problem-solving activities (Lawler 1986). In fact, high-involvement approaches are often used in conjunction with high-commitment HR systems (e.g. see Lepak and Snell 1999). However, theoretically, we propose that high-involvement HR practices differ from high-commitment practices as they are not premised on notions of mutuality. Nevertheless, strong high-involvement systems are likely to lead to performance outcomes that are advantageous to both employees and organizations as high-involvement contexts are likely to satisfy employees' basic psychological needs. In other words, high-involvement systems are likely to provide the kind of environment in which employees' psychological needs for autonomy, competence, and relatedness will be satisfied as proposed by self-determination theory (SDT) (Andrews 2016; Jacobsen et al. 2014; see Chapter 4).

As a theory of work motivation, SDT is premised on the observation that "to be self-determining means to experience a sense of choice in initiating and regulating one's own actions," hence, we attribute SDT to high-involvement HR systems (Deci et al. 1989, 580). SDT is based on the assumption that all individuals have an inherent desire to develop and grow until they reach their full potential. Accordingly, individuals develop to their full potential only if they are able to satisfy their basic psychological needs (the need for autonomy, relatedness, and competence), which are regarded as "innate, essential, and universal" (Ryan and Deci 2000, 74). The need for *autonomy* refers to individuals exercising control over their own actions and behaviors, or engaging in actions of their own volition rather than in response to external forces. The need for *competence* involves feeling effective or having mastery over one's work and having an effect on one's outcomes. The need for *relatedness* is associated with having a sense of belonging and being connected to others and of being important to other persons (Kovjanic et al. 2012). When employees' basic psychological needs are satisfied, they are more likely to work because they want to rather than because they have to.

Unlike other theories of motivation, SDT differentiates between the quality (self-determined versus controlled) and quantity (levels) of motivation, rather than quantity only (the assumption that higher or more motivation alone is related to superior performance). In this way, the more the work environment is able to satisfy employees' psychological needs, the more likely the resultant work motivation will be of better quality and quantity; thus, employees will be more persistent and endure in their tasks. However, even though the three psychological needs may have universal relevance to individual growth, the extent to which employees are able to fulfill them will vary depending on their work environments. We propose that strong systems of high-involvement HR practices will create suitable work environments for autonomous forms of motivation to thrive.

SDT proposes that the fulfillment of psychological needs will lead to higher levels of autonomous motivation—employees' motivation to work is generated from within themselves and is self-determined. SDT differentiates between autonomous (i.e. high quality) and controlled forms (i.e. low quality) of motivation. There are two types of autonomous motivation: (1) intrinsic motivation, where individuals find enjoyment and experience pleasure from engaging in the work task; and (2) identified motivation, where individuals identify with their work, realizing its value and importance. These forms of autonomous motivation are energized from within the person. They do not require external pressures or forces such as close supervision, peer pressure, financial rewards, or recognition to engage with the task.

In contrast, controlled forms of motivation are non-self-determining and tend to be external to the employee in that the motivation to engage in a task is external to the task itself. For instance, externally controlled forms of motivation include pay for performance or discretionary rewards (employees have to work to achieve the pay award) and "saving face" or maintaining self-image (employees work in order not to embarrass themselves or because they are expected to undertake the task). Internal forms of controlled motivation may include avoidance of guilt (employees engage in the task because they do not want to live with the consequences of not engaging). "Avoiding guilt" is an internal pressure in which the employee questions the consequences of not engaging to be worse than engaging in the work task. As the employee feels they "have to" engage, this internal process is non-self-determined and thus controlled. If any of these controlled influences (externally or internally imposed) are removed, it is likely that the employee will cease engaging with the task. In this way, controlled motivation is regarded as "poor" or of "lesser quality" than autonomous motivation.

According to SDT, the higher quality motivation will lead to positive work-related outcomes (such as job satisfaction and discretionary effort) and employee well-being (Gagné and Deci 2005). Hence, the central tenet of SDT is that if organizational contexts fulfill employees' needs, employees' behaviors will be self-determined, thus enhancing their well-being and work performance (Deci and Ryan 2000). In this way, we propose that high-involvement HR systems will be associated with higher levels of job satisfaction, a greater willingness to exert discretionary effort, and employee well-being. As with high-commitment HR systems, theoretically, organizational performance will not be achieved at a cost to employee well-being. Due to the psychologically rewarding and nourishing environment promoted by high-involvement HR practices, we anticipate that high-involvement HR systems are likely to promote PSM, public value, and discretionary effort, along with employee well-being, as employees are more likely to internalize the importance of public service work and be more autonomously motivated.

Proposition 3: Strong "high-involvement" HR systems will fulfill employees' basic psychological needs for autonomy, relatedness, and competence. In so doing, public sector employees will experience higher levels of job satisfaction, be motivated to serve the public, and display discretionary effort without undermining their well-being.

9.6 Public Sector Studies of HR Systems

Our summary review of public sector studies includes those that have examined the relationship between HR systems and employee outcomes, as summarized in Table 9.1. As mentioned earlier, we do not claim that this is an exhaustive list of studies in that we have not included studies investigating the effects of *individual* rather than *collective* systems of HR practices. Further, our selection of studies serves to illustrate the kinds of approaches adopted by public management scholars. To date, we report fifteen studies based on the experiences of public sector employees working in health services, local government, transportation, and education. Eighty percent of studies referred to an underlying theory to explain the relationship between HR systems and employee outcomes. Just over half of these studies refer directly to either "hard" (AMO theory) or "soft" (social exchange theory) approaches. We also classify theories that include references to employee well-being and stress avoidance as "soft" (e.g. affective events and job demands–resources theory) and those that give no consideration to employee well-being as "hard" (e.g. attraction–selection–attrition; resource-based theory).

To assess whether the HR practices identified in systems are likely to send strong signals to employees, we evaluated whether the majority of HR practices in the

Table 9.1 Summary of empirical public sector studies on the link between HRM practices and employee outcomes in last 10 years

Author(s)	HRM practice	Theory used	Mechanism	Context	Findings
Conway and Monks (2008)	Career and performance development, autonomy, communication, training, staffing and reward, teamwork, and job security	N/A	N/A	Irish health service (central administration division, community care sector of one regional hospital)	Satisfaction with HRM practices was related to affective commitment to change, work–life balance, industrial relations climate, and psychological contract
Boselie (2010)	HPWPs that enhance Abilities: skills training, general training, personal development, coaching, and task variety; HPWPs that enhance Motivation: high wages, fair pay, and pay for performance; HPWPs that enhance Opportunities to participate: employee influence, involvement in decision-making, and job autonomy	AMO theory	N/A	Health sector (one Dutch general hospital)	HPWPs that enhance Abilities are positively related to employee commitment, and HPWPs that enhance Opportunity to participate are positively related to OCB. HPWPs that enhance Motivation are not related to affective commitment and OCB
Messersmith et al. (2011)	Recruitment and selection, training and development, communication, job security, teamwork, information sharing, rewards, promotion, career management, performance appraisal, flexible work arrangements, and family-friendly policies	Social exchange theory	Job satisfaction	Local government	Job satisfaction, organizational commitment, and psychological empowerment partially mediated the HPWS–OCB relationship

(Continued)

Table 9.1 Continued

Author(s)	HRM practice	Theory used	Mechanism	Context	Findings
Jensen et al. (2013)	Moderated-mediation model: Anxiety and role overload mediate the relationship between the interaction of HPWS utilization and control perceptions on turnover intentions	Job demands–control theory	N/A	Local government	Anxiety and role overload partially mediated the relationship between the interaction of HPWS and job control on turnover intentions
Cho and Poister (2013)	Autonomy, compensation, communication, performance appraisal, career development, and training	Social exchange theory	N/A	Transportation	Perceptions of HRM practices are associated with trust in public organizations (i.e. trust in department leadership, trust in one's leadership team, and trust in one's supervisor)
Kooij et al. (2013)	Maintenance HR practices: formal performance appraisal, career advice, as much information as needed to do the job, and a chance to give ideas for improvement Developmental HR practices: formal training to improve operational skills, formal training to develop knowledge and skills for future jobs, a challenging job, and a job that makes full use of training, knowledge, and skills	AMO theory; social exchange theory; signaling theories; and selection, optimization, and compensation theory	Age—as moderator not mediator	N/A (three organizations in the UK public sector)	The associations of development HR practices with commitment, satisfaction, and organizational fairness weakened; and the associations of maintenance HR practices with commitment, satisfaction, and organizational fairness strengthened

Author(s)	HRM practice	Theory used	Mechanism	Context	Findings
Melnik et al. (2013)	HRM unit, total quality management, workplace training, appraisal interviews, organized events, job-alternating systems, profit sharing or other incentives, and information sharing	N/A	N/A	Services sector	HRM practices bundle or system is strongly and positively associated with workers' overall workplace satisfaction
Takeuchi and Takeuchi (2013)	Staffing and recruitment, a fair performance appraisal system, comprehensive training and development, and competitive compensation	N/A	P–O fit	Healthcare	P–O fit partially mediated the relationship between HPHRP and commitment in Japan
Shen et al. (2014)	Selective staffing, extensive training, internal mobility, employment security, job description, results-oriented appraisal, incentive rewards, and participation	Resource-based view	Quality of working life	Education sector (schools)	Quality of working life partially mediated the relationship between HPWSs and public schools, teachers' in-role performance, and extra-role behavior
Mostafa and Gould-Williams (2014)	Selection and training and development, job security, promotion and performance-related pay, autonomy, and communication	Attraction–Selection–Attrition (ASA) framework and AMO theory	P–O fit	Health and higher education sectors	P–O fit partially mediated the relationship between HPHRP and both job satisfaction and OCBs
Gould-Williams et al. (2014)	Training and development, selection, job security, promotion, rewards, and involvement in decision-making	AMO theory and Perry's process theory	Civic duty	Local government	Civic duty partially mediated the relationship between HPHRP and both job satisfaction and commitment. However, it did not mediate the relationship between HPHRP and quit intentions.

(Continued)

Table 9.1 Continued

Author(s)	HRM practice	Theory used	Mechanism	Context	Findings
Mostafa et al. (2015)	Training and development, job security, autonomous work design, communication, and promotion	Social exchange theory and Perry's process theory	PSM	Health and higher education sector	PSM partially mediated the relationship between HPHRP and both affective commitment and OCBs
Mostafa (2016)	Training and development, job security, promotion, work autonomy, and communication	ASA framework	P–O fit	Health sector	P–O fit fully mediated the relationship between HPHRP and both job stress and quit intentions
Kilroy et al. (2017)	Empowerment, information sharing, rewards, and development practices.	Social learning	P–O fit	Health sector	P–O fit fully mediated the relationship between high-involvement HRM and burnout in Canada
Mostafa (2017)	Training, information sharing, teamwork, involvement in decision-making, communication, career management, promotion, and performance feedback and appraisal	Affective events theory	Positive affect	Local government	Positive affect fully mediated the relationships between HPHRP and both job satisfaction and OCBs in Welsh local government

system were consistent with each underlying theory. We define strong systems as those in which all but one HR practice is consistent with the chosen theory. It is possible that we have been overly generous with our inclusion criteria, but given that we are making judgments based on limited descriptions of HR contents, we believe this approach is reasonable. As such, we regard Shen et al.'s (2014) system of HR practices as a "strong" system even though it includes employment security when their underlying theory (resource-based theory) is based on hard HR systems. Similarly, we define Cho and Poister (2013), Messersmith et al. (2011), and Mostafa (2017) as "strong" systems even though they include performance appraisals, which are more likely to be associated with hard HR systems. Gould-Williams et al. (2014) was the only study to adopt an inconsistent approach between the content of their HR system and theory. For instance, their system of HR practices is likely to signal soft approaches to people management, but their research propositions are based on AMO theory. As Kooij et al. (2013) referred to several theories in their study, we are unable to assess whether their approach is consistent with their use of a soft HR system. Overall, it is pleasing to note evidence of consistency between HR systems and the underlying theories in public sector research.

Regarding the explanations of process mechanisms, we note that two-thirds of the studies identified mediation variables linking HR systems with employee outcomes. As Takeuchi and Takeuchi (2013) omitted to include a theoretical framework for their analysis, we excluded them from further analysis. We anticipate that affective commitment, PSM, quality of work life, and positive affect will be linked with soft HR systems, whereas person–organization (P–O) fit will be linked with hard HR systems. On this basis, we report two studies that included an "inconsistent" mediator (Kilroy et al. 2017; Shen et al. 2014), in that quality of work life was identified as the process through which a hard HR system is associated with teachers' performance, and P–O fit with soft, high-involvement HR practices.[1]

Finally, we consider whether soft HR systems are more likely to be associated with mutually beneficial outcomes in comparison with hard HR systems. We report that of the ten theory-based studies, a high proportion (two-thirds) reported outcomes that were consistent with their theoretical frameworks (e.g. "hard" approaches were associated with in-role performance and job satisfaction, whereas "soft" approaches were associated with trust, commitment, and OCBs). In this way, we can conclude that the studies conducted in public sector organizations are making good progress linking HR systems with appropriate theories and relevant performance outcomes. However, a significant gap exists in that only one study used high-involvement HR systems, and we did not identify any study that included the effects of employee attributions or HR system strength.

---

[1] We acknowledge Kilroy et al.'s (2017) findings that high-involvement HR systems increased P–O fit due to socialization activities (according to the authors' reasoning). However, we anticipate that this is a context-specific outcome as it is likely the healthcare workers already had a propensity to "fit" with the organizational values—hence, high-involvement HR practices further reinforced the degree of fit.

9.7 Managerial and Public Service Implications

We encourage managers to take a broader perspective than one in which high-performance outcomes are the primary focus. While all organizations want to achieve the best outcomes with the minimum of resources, doing so is likely to come at a cost to both staff well-being and public service delivery. We recommend that managers should strive to consider the implications of achieving improved performance on employee workload and work–life balance, which is consistent with the mutual benefit or social exchange approach. Similarly, *sustainable* employee performance is more likely to be achieved when managers consider the work context in which employees operate (see also Chapter 15). In this way, priority should be given to working relationships (are co-workers supportive?), competency in delivering public services (are employees equipped with the skills needed to undertake their tasks?), and autonomy (are employees empowered to make decisions without always having to rely on supervisory approval?). If managers' efforts are largely devoted to achieving a narrow range of performance outcomes, rather than more broadly considering the effects on employee well-being and work experience, then they may undermine the source through which these outcomes are achieved, namely the workforce.

Furthermore, it is worth remembering that employee responses to HR practices are likely to be influenced (to some extent at least) by employees' perceptions of why managers are adopting a particular approach. If, in the past, managers have had the best interests of employees in mind, this is likely to positively reinforce implementation. Alternatively, where managers have knowingly or unknowingly "deceived" workers, it is likely that employees will not trust new approaches adopted by management or will assume that managers are seeking ways to intensify their work. Under such circumstances, managers will need to be patient until trust is regained. As we mentioned in our review, public sector research in the field of attributions is very limited. On the basis of private sector experiences, it is likely to take some time before the benefits of adopting high-commitment or high-involvement approaches to managing people will be released, especially when managers face high levels of red tape and bureaucracy.

9.8 Conclusion

At the outset, we noted that the early studies based on private sector organizations support the notion that HRM is associated with firm-level performance. However, understanding why HR practices should have this effect remained limited. More recently, advances have been made across both sectors in our understanding of the process mechanisms linking HR practices and performance outcomes. However, the private sector has made further strides in understanding why HR practices affect employees' work-related attitudes and behaviors. This is due to their adoption of attribution theories which go beyond employees' experiences of and satisfaction with HR practices. They are now considering the motives employees attribute to managers when investments are made in HR systems, along with the signals or messages communicated via these systems. In this way, a more realistic approach to assessing the effects of HR systems is being adopted as the organizational context is taken into account. However, while Bowen and Ostroff's (2004) widely acclaimed article on HR system strength has, at the time of writing, 2,614 citations, the theory remains largely untested as originally intended (Hewett et al. 2018). Instead, scholars have used "system strength" to determine *individual* psychological climate assessments rather than *collective* views of the organization's climate (Sanders et al. 2008; Sanders and Yang 2016). In contrast, Nishii et al.'s (2008) employee attribution theory has been tested in seven private sector studies, but so far, not in a public sector study. As public managers are often constrained in their decision-making powers by political priorities and red tape, employees' attributions may have less effect on their work-related attitudes and behaviors (Nishii et al. 2008). Certainly, the public sector context will provide an interesting arena to assess whether the findings mirror those reported in private sector studies.

We note that a significant proportion of public sector studies referred to AMO theory (Boselie 2010; Gould-Williams et al. 2014; Kooij et al. 2013; Mostafa and Gould-Williams 2014), which, according to our theoretical discussion, may not be the most appropriate theory for public sector organizations. We accept, however, that under certain conditions, AMO may be appropriate as advocated elsewhere in this volume (e.g. see Chapter 7). Furthermore, the widespread use of AMO theory may simply reflect the influence of new public management (NPM). This was a time when public sector organizations were encouraged to imitate practices used by "successful" private sector organizations. Under these conditions, performance management came to the fore, emphasizing the importance of metrics, monitoring, performance feedback, target setting, and rewards contingent on performance (see Chapter 8). However, although there is no recent evidence suggesting that the public sector's traditional paternalistic approach to people management has remained intact following the NPM era, theoretically at least, we suggest that the high-commitment and high-involvement approaches should be seen as the way forward. Whereas high-commitment HR systems will strive to ensure employees experience the benefits of their loyal and dedicated service to the public, high-involvement HR systems are likely to provide the context in which autonomous forms of motivation will thrive. Again, the public sector context presents a paradox in that high levels of red tape and bureaucracy are likely to mitigate the desirable outcomes that could be achieved through high-involvement HR systems (see Chapter 12). Future research needs to assess the extent to which it is possible for public sector managers to overcome these barriers and create the kind of environment in which employees' basic psychological needs can be satisfied.

Our review has focused on studies that examined the effects of HR systems on proximal, employee work-related attitudes and behaviors. As far as we are aware, few studies have examined the collective effects of employee responses on organizational performance (for exceptions, see Messersmith et al. 2011; West et al. 2002). This area of research is particularly challenging for public sector scholars, given the range of performance outcomes associated with public organizations and the difficulty of linking employee behaviors to their achievement.

In conclusion, we hope that our review provides a clearer steer for those wanting to contribute to scholarship in the field of HRM and performance in the public sector. A fine foundation of insightful research findings has already been laid over the past ten years. We are confident that the next ten years will be similarly productive and insightful.

References

Andrews, C. 2016. "Integrating Public Service Motivation and Self-Determination Theory: A Framework." *International Journal of Public Sector Management 29* (3): pp. 238–54.

Appelbaum, E., T. Bailey, P. Berg, and A. Kalleberg. 2000. *Manufacturing Advantage: Why High Performance Work Systems Pay Off*. New York: Cornell University Press.

Barney, J. B. 1991. "Firm Resources and Sustained Competitive Advantage." *Journal of Management 17* (1): pp. 99–120.

Barney, J. B., and P. M. Wright. 1998. "On Becoming a Strategic Partner: The Role of Human Resources in Gaining Competitive Advantage." *Human Resource Management 37* (1): pp. 31–46.

Boselie, P. 2010. "High Performance Work Practices in the Health Care Sector: A Dutch Case Study." *International Journal of Manpower 31* (1): pp. 42–58.

Boselie, P., G. Dietz, and C. Boon. 2005. "Commonalities and Contradictions in HRM and Performance Research." *Human Resource Management Journal 15* (3): pp. 67–94.

Bowen, D. E., and C. Ostroff. 2004. "Understanding HRM–Firm Performance Linkages: The Role of the 'Strength' of the HRM System." *The Academy of Management Review 29* (2): pp. 203–21.

Boxall, P., and K. Macky. 2009. "Research and Theory on High-Performance Work Systems: Progressing the High-Involvement Stream." *Human Resource Management Journal 19* (1): pp. 3–23.

Cappelli, P., and D. Neumark. 2001. "Do 'High-Performance' Work Practices Improve Establishment-Level Outcomes?" *Industrial and Labor Relations Review 54* (4): pp. 737–75.

Cho, Y. J., and T. H. Poister. 2013. "Human Resource Management Practices and Trust in Public Organizations." *Public Management Review 15* (6): pp. 816–38.

Collins, C. J., and K. G. Smith. 2006. "Knowledge Exchange and Combination: The Role of Human Resource Practices in the Performance of High-Technology Firms." *Academy of Management Journal 49* (3): pp. 544–60.

Conway, E., and K. Monks. 2008. "HR Practices and Commitment to Change: An Employee-Level Analysis." *Human Resource Management Journal 18* (1): pp. 72–89.

Cropanzano, R., and M. Mitchell. 2005. "Social Exchange Theory: An Interdisciplinary Review." *Journal of Management 31* (6): pp. 874–900.

Deci, E. L., J. P. Connell, and R. M. Ryan. 1989. "Self-Determination in a Work Organization." *Journal of Applied Psychology 74* (4): pp. 580–90.

Deci, E. L., and R. M. Ryan. 2000. "The 'What' and 'Why' of Goal Pursuits: Human Needs and the Self-Determination of Behavior." *Psychological Inquiry 11* (4): pp. 227–68.

Ehrnrooth, M., and I. Bjorkman. 2012. "An Integrative HRM Process Theorization: Beyond Signalling Effects and Mutual Gains." *Journal of Management Studies 49* (6): pp. 1109–35.

Gagné, M., and E. Deci. 2005. "Self-Determination Theory and Work Motivation." *Journal of Vocational Behavior 26* (4): pp. 331–62.

Gould-Williams, J. S. 2003. "The Importance of HR Practices and Workplace Trust in Achieving Superior Performance: A Study of Public-Sector Organizations." *The International Journal of Human Resource Management 14* (1): pp. 28–54.

Gould-Williams, J. S., P. Bottomley, T. Redman, E. Snape, D. J. Bishop, T. Limpanitgul, and A. M. S. Mostafa. 2014. "Civic Duty and Employee Outcomes: Do High Commitment Human Resource Practices and Work Overload Matter?" *Public Administration 92* (4): pp. 937–53.

Gouldner, A. W. 1960. "The Norm of Reciprocity: A Preliminary Statement." *American Sociological Review 25* (2): pp. 161–78.

Guest, D. E. 1998. "Is the Psychological Contract Worth Taking Seriously?" *Journal of Organizational Behavior 19* (S1): pp. 649–64.

Guest, D. E., and R. Peccei. 2001. "Partnership at Work: Mutuality and the Balance of Advantage." *British Journal of Industrial Relations 39* (2): pp. 207–36.

Hauff, S., D. Alewell, and N. Hansen. 2014. "HRM Systems between Control and Commitment: Occurrence, Characteristics and Effects on HRM Outcomes and Firm Performance." *Human Resource Management Journal 24* (4): pp. 424–41.

Heider, F. 1958. *The Psychology of Interpersonal Relations.* Eastford, CT: Martino Publishing.

Hewett, R., A. Shantz, J. Mundy, and K. Alfes. 2018. "Attribution Theories in Human Resource Management Research: A Review and Research Agenda." *The International Journal of Human Resource Management 29* (1): pp. 87–126.

Huselid, M. A. 1995. "The Impact of Human Resource Management Practices on Turnover, Productivity and Corporate Financial Performance." *Academy of Management Journal 38* (3): pp. 635–72.

Jacobsen, C. B., J. Hvitved, and L. B. Andersen. 2014. "Command and Motivation: How the Perception of External Interventions Relates to Intrinsic Motivation and Public Service Motivation." *Public Administration 92* (4): pp. 790–806.

Jensen, J. M., P. C. Patel, and J. G. Messersmith. 2013. "High-Performance Work Systems and Job Control: Consequences for Anxiety, Role Overload, and Turnover Intentions." *Journal of Management 39* (6): pp. 1699–724.

Kalleberg, A. L., P. V. Marsden, J. Reynolds, and D. Knoke. 2006. "Beyond Profit? Sectoral Difference in High-Performance Work Practices." *Work and Occupations 33* (3): pp. 271–302.

Kehoe, R. R., and P. M. Wright. 2013. "The Impact of High-Performance Human Resource Practices on Employees' Attitudes and Behaviors." *Journal of Management 39* (2): pp. 366–91.

Kelley, H. H. 1967. "Attribution Theory in Social Psychology." In *Nebraska Symposium on Motivation*, edited by D. Levine, Vol. 15, pp. 192–238. Lincoln, NE: University of Nebraska Press.

Kilroy, S., P. C. Flood, J. Bosak, and D. Chênevert. 2017. "Perceptions of High-Involvement Work Practices, Person–Organization Fit, and Burnout: A Time-Lagged Study of Health Care Employees." *Human Resource Management 56* (5): pp. 821–35.

Kooij, T. A. M., D. Guest, M. Clinton, T. Knight, P. G. W. Jansen, and J. S. E. Dikkers. 2013. "How the Impact of HR Practices on Employee Well-Being and Performance Changes with Age." *Human Resource Management Journal 23* (1): pp. 18–35.

Kovjanic, S., S. C. Schuh, K. Jonas, N. Van Quaquebeke, and A. R. Van Dick. 2012. "How Do Transformational Leaders Foster Positive Employee Outcomes? A Self-Determination-Based Analysis of Employees' Needs as Mediating Links." *Journal of Organizational Behavior 33* (8): pp. 1031–52.

Lawler, E. E. 1986. *High-Involvement Management*. San Francisco, CA: Jossey-Bass.

Lepak, D. P., J. A. Marrone, and R. Takeuchi. 2004. "The Relativity of HR Systems: Conceptualising the Impact of Desired Employee Contributions and HR Philosophy." *International Journal of Technology Management 27* (6/7): pp. 639–55.

Lepak, D. P., and S. A. Snell. 1999. "The Human Resource Architecture: Toward a Theory of Human Capital Allocation and Development." *Academy of Management Review 24* (1): pp. 31–48.

Marescaux, E., S. De Winne, and L. Sels. 2012. "HR Practices and Affective Organisational Commitment: 'When' Does HR Differentiation Pay Off?" *Human Resource Management Journal 23* (4): pp. 329–45.

Melnik, E., F. Petrella, and N. Richez-Battesti. 2013. "Does the Professionalism of Management Practices in Nonprofits and For-Profits Affect Job Satisfaction?" *The International Journal of Human Resource Management 24* (6): pp. 1300–21.

Messersmith J. G., P. C. Patel, D. P. Lepak, and J. Gould-Williams. 2011. "Unlocking the Black Box: Exploring the Link between High-Performance Work Systems and Performance." *Journal of Applied Psychology 96* (6): pp. 1105–18.

Miles, R. E., and C. C. Snow. 1984. "Designing Strategic Human Resources Systems." *Organizational Dynamics 13* (1): pp. 36–52.

Mostafa, A. M. S. 2016. "High-Performance HR Practices, Work Stress and Quit Intentions in the Public Health Sector: Does Person–Organization Fit Matter?" *Public Management Review 18* (8): pp. 1218–37.

Mostafa, A. M. S. 2017. "High-Performance HR Practices, Positive Affect and Employee Outcomes." *Journal of Managerial Psychology 32* (2): pp. 163–76.

Mostafa, A. M. S., and J. S. Gould-Williams. 2014. "Testing the Mediation Effect of Person–Organization Fit on the Relationship between High Performance HR Practices and Employee Outcomes in the Egyptian Public Sector." *The International Journal of Human Resource Management 25* (2): pp. 276–92.

Mostafa, A. M. S., J. S. Gould-Williams, and P. Bottomley. 2015. "High-Performance Human Resource Practices and Employee Outcomes: The Mediating Role of Public Service Motivation." *Public Administration Review 75* (5): pp. 747–57.

Nishii, L. H., D. P. Lepak, and B. Schneider. 2008. "Employee Attributions of the 'Why' of HR Practices: Their Effects on Employee Attitudes and Behaviors, and Customer Satisfaction." *Personnel Psychology 61* (3): pp. 503–45.

Ryan, R. M., and E. L. Deci. 2000. "Self-Determination Theory and the Facilitation of Intrinsic Motivation, Social Development, and Well-Being." *The American Psychologist 55* (1): pp. 68–78.

Sanders, K., L. Dorenbosch, and R. de Reuver. 2008. "The Impact of Individual and Shared Employee Perceptions of HRM on Affective Commitment: Considering Climate Strength." *Personnel Review 37* (4): pp. 412–25.

Sanders, K., and H. Yang. 2016. "The HRM Process Approach: The Influence of Employees' Attribution to Explain the HRM–Performance Relationship." *Human Resource Management 55* (2): pp. 201–17.

Schuler, R. S., and S. E. Jackson. 1987. "Linking Competitive Strategies with Human Resource Management Practices." *Academy of Management Executive 1* (3): pp. 209–13.

Shen, J., J. Benson, and B. Huang. 2014. "High-Performance Work Systems and Teachers' Work Performance: The Mediating Role of Quality of Working Life." *Human Resource Management 53* (5): pp. 817–33.

Shore, L. M., L. E. Tetrick, P. Lynch, and K. Barksdale. 2006. "Social and Economic Exchange: Construct Development and Validation." *Journal of Applied Social Psychology 36* (4): pp. 837–67.

Storey, J. 1992. *Developments in the Management of Human Resources.* Oxford: Blackwell.

Storey, J., and K. Sisson. 1993. *Managing Human Resources and Industrial Relations.* Milton Keynes: Open University Press.

Takeuchi, N., and T. Takeuchi. 2013. "Committed to the Organization or the Job? Effects of Perceived HRM Practices on Employees' Behavioral Outcomes in the Japanese Healthcare Industry." *The International Journal of Human Resource Management 24* (11): pp. 2089–106.

Van de Voorde, K., and S. Beijer. 2015. "The Role of Employee HR Attributions in the Relationship between High-Performance Work Systems and Employee Outcomes." *Human Resource Management Journal 25* (1): pp. 62–78.

Wall, T. D., and S. J. Wood. 2005. "The Romance of Human Resource Management and Business Performance, and the Case for Big Science." *Human Relations 58* (4): pp. 429–62.

Weiner, B. 1985. "An Attributional Theory of Achievement Motivation and Emotion." *Psychological Review 92* (4): pp. 548–73.

West, M. A., C. Borrill, J. Dawson, J. Scully, M. Carter, S. Anelay, M. Patterson, and J. Waring. 2002. "The Link between the Management of Employees and Patient Mortality in Acute Hospitals." *The International Journal of Human Resource Management 13* (8): pp. 1299–310.

Wood, S. J. 1999. "Human Resource Management and Performance." *International Journal of Management Reviews 1* (4): pp. 367–413.

10
Managing a Diverse Workforce

Tanachia Ashikali, Sandra Groeneveld, and Adrian Ritz

10.1 Introduction

As a consequence of globalization, increased migration, and the labor market participation of minority groups, the workforce of many public organizations has become increasingly diverse. This creates opportunities for public organizations to improve their interactions with diverse citizens, and in doing so, improve bureaucratic outcomes for disadvantaged groups and gain legitimacy. Public organizations have a long history of developing and implementing equal opportunity and affirmative action policies in order to increase the representation of employees from disadvantaged groups and address inequalities in the labor market and society at large. As of the 1990s, in the wake of increasing managerialism in the public sector, the paradigm changed toward diversity management. From a diversity management perspective, diversity is primarily valued as an internal resource to inform work practices and policies with the aim of enhancing public organizations' overall performance (Groeneveld 2015; Groeneveld and Van de Walle 2010). This so-called business case argument for diversity leads organizations to develop and implement policies and programs that not only aim to increase the representation of employees with different backgrounds but also to realize their potential added value. Diversity, in that regard, generally refers to demographic characteristics such as race, ethnicity, and gender (Meier 2019; Riccucci and Van Ryzin 2017) but can also include less visible characteristics such as functional or educational background, learning behaviors, norms, and values.

The changing composition of the workforce impacts the ways that public organizations are to be led and managed (Selden and Selden 2001). In fact, workforce diversity may not only contribute to responsiveness, innovation, and effectiveness, but it may also induce team conflict and decrease group cohesion, which, in turn, may result in deteriorating organizational performance, as many studies have shown (Guillaume et al. 2017; Meeussen et al. 2014; Milliken and Martins 1996; Nishii and Mayer 2009; Pelled et al. 1999). These contradictory research findings indicate that the association between diversity and performance is not only complex but also needs specific managerial attention.

Tanachia Ashikali, Sandra Groeneveld, and Adrian Ritz, *Managing a Diverse Workforce* In: *Managing for Public Service Performance: How People and Values Make a Difference*. Edited by: Peter Leisink, Lotte B. Andersen, Gene A. Brewer, Christian B. Jacobsen, Eva Knies, and Wouter Vandenabeele, Oxford University Press (2021). © Tanachia Ashikali, Sandra Groeneveld, and Adrian Ritz. DOI: 10.1093/oso/9780192893420.003.0010

This chapter reviews the literature and focuses on conditions that may impact diversity outcomes and the underlying processes. In so doing, it will point to aspects of workforce diversity that may be the object of managerial intervention. The chapter proceeds as follows. In Section 10.2), the complexity of managing diversity is discussed, according to multiple and sometimes conflicting motives that underpin diversity policies and diversity management in organizations. This section concludes with the observation that both in academic debates and in practice, the focus has recently moved to inclusion as a pre-condition for effective diversity management. Therefore, in Section 10.3, recent studies on the inclusiveness of public organizations and its relation to diversity management are reviewed. In Section 10.4, we then explore the role of leadership in the management of diversity and inclusiveness. While so far under-researched in the literature on diversity management, we show how leadership may have an impact on the inclusiveness of diverse work groups. This chapter concludes with reflections on previously discussed subjects, resulting in a conceptual framework (Figure 10.1) for future research (Section 10.5).

10.2 Multiple Motives for Diversity

10.2.1 Diversity Paradigms and Conflicting Values

Diversity motives reflect an organization's rationale for increasing the diversity of the workforce or paying specific attention to diversity (Ely and Thomas 2001). The perspectives of diversity in public organizations are related to the overall discussion of public value and public values in public institutions (see Chapter 2). The motives underlying the different paradigms reflect the criteria to assess reasons for valuing diversity and follow the understanding of public values by Beck Jørgensen and Bozeman (2007). Two major paradigms can be distinguished (Dwertmann et al. 2016). On the one hand, the discrimination and fairness perspective mainly aims to prevent negative outcomes. It focuses on equal employment opportunity practices, fair treatment, the absence of discrimination in the employment process, and the elimination of social exclusion. On the other hand, the synergy perspective focuses on realizing the potential performance benefits of diversity. This perspective combines two other categories that Ely and Thomas (2001) specify as access and legitimacy and integration and learning.

The first part of a synergy perspective is an access and legitimacy perspective, and, according to the Beck Jørgensen and Bozeman framework, it includes values like responsiveness or balancing interests. In this perspective, the emphasis is on treating diversity as a resource to improve interaction with diverse clients and citizens, and increasing the organizations' legitimacy by doing so. According to representative bureaucracy theory, this motive allows bureaucrats to actively represent disadvantaged groups in society by shaping policies to compensate for inequalities that are persistent in society and not compensated for in political decision-making (Andrews and Ashworth 2015; Groeneveld and Van de Walle 2010). The second part of the synergy perspective is an integration and learning perspective. From this perspective, organizations view diversity as a resource to learn from and rethink ways of working in order to improve their effectiveness, creativity, and innovation. While the first discrimination and fairness motive is predominantly based on moral and social justice arguments, the access and legitimacy perspective also incorporates a business case argument for diversity, while the integration and learning perspective solely refers to a business case for diversity (Selden and Selden 2001).

The perspectives are not mutually exclusive, but they might include conflicting values and create tensions when simultaneously present, as is the case in most diversity policies and management, in particular in a public sector context (McDougall 1996). For instance, both the discrimination and fairness perspective and the synergy perspective are relevant for diversity management within the organization. What is considered to be effective diversity management is, therefore, dependent on the different perspectives and goals an organization has when implementing measures of diversity management. As different motives play a role in the diversity policies of most public organizations, various conflicts between policies, business strategy, HR policies, and diversity management measures can occur (Dwertmann et al. 2016; Ely and Thomas 2001; Selden 1997; Selden and Selden 2001). For instance, the discrimination and fairness perspective promotes affirmative action plans including quota and targets on the representation of minority groups, thus guiding HR recruitment, selection, and promotion. However, the integration and learning perspective does not enable itself through discrimination and fairness measures, and such actions may contradict the goals of the access and legitimacy perspective.

This is a dilemma since many public organizations will have multiple motives on which HR policies and practices are based. For instance, units close to citizens and client groups (e.g. police) are not eager to diversify their workforce and loosen a strong identity because of access and legitimacy gained through homogeneity rather than diversity. At the same time, certain stakeholders (e.g. politicians and interest groups) may be in favor of discrimination and fairness measures since specific client groups welcome more diversified frontline employees and thus call for heterogeneous workforces representing their background.

Furthermore, the integration and learning perspective values social identity as a resource for learning and innovation, whereas the discrimination and fairness one tends to devalue it because of potential unjust discrimination. Conflicts may also occur between measures of the access and legitimacy perspective and the two other approaches. The access and legitimacy perspective values diversity only as long as it serves the business case and might narrow down the recruitment and selection strategies of the discrimination and fairness approach to those positions in the organization where diversity is salient to the service delivered. Employees hired with the expectation of meeting criteria of diversity might realize that other internal job opportunities are closed to them and get demotivated. In addition, the external orientation of the access and legitimacy perspective may not focus enough on the incorporation of cultural competencies as pursued by the integration and learning perspective.

To prevent such conflicts, organizations need to incorporate diversity into strategic human resource management (SHRM) (Nishii et al. 2018). Combining SHRM and diversity management follows a resource-based view of SHRM and suggests that diversity provides an organization with valuable, rare, inimitable, and non-substitutable resources as a basis for competitive advantage (McMahan et al. 1998). Non-aligned diversity policies lessen such an advantage. Depending on the motives for diversity in play, SHRM may differ in its consequences for HR practices. For instance, under a discrimination and fairness perspective, public organizations implement diversity programs aimed at improving outcomes for employees of marginalized groups (Groeneveld and Verbeek 2012). HR will mainly focus on developing fair recruitment and selection practices without privileging any demographic groups over others by ensuring that selection processes are as anonymous as possible to ensure equal treatment of applicants.

However, driven by an access and legitimacy perspective, public organizations emphasize that units that interact with clients and citizens should reflect their (demographic) characteristics. This could as well translate to specific HR practices that focus on recruiting and selecting minority employees for specific positions within the organization. To avoid the downside of less-committed and low-performing employees who feel exploited and devalued (Ely and Thomas 2001; Selden and Selden 2001), SHRM needs to answer the question of which departments and sub-units the discrimination and fairness approach fits best, without interfering with business goals and the synergy perspective of diversity management. Thus, decisions in recruitment, selection, and promotion should depend on an assessment of both the most relevant diversity motives of the organization and future workforce characteristics in a specific sub-unit (Nishii et al. 2018).

10.2.2 Empirical Evidence on Diversity Paradigms and Policies

The implementation of the above-mentioned paradigms for managing workforce diversity leads to a variety of outcomes, such as increased representation, lower discrimination, or higher individual and organizational performance. Research and practice are both interested in getting evidence for the relationship between diversity, diversity management, and performance. However, a recent literature review shows that only 22 percent of the articles examined in public administration journals are investigating this relationship (Sabharwal et al. 2018). What is more, most of these studies are US based, leaving out studies performed in other (country) contexts.

Most research on diversity and diversity management is descriptive in nature, and public administration research has produced conflicting results at best when it comes to the relationship between diversity and performance, whereas the relationship between diversity management and work-related outcomes is heavily under-researched (Ashikali and Groeneveld 2015b; Groeneveld 2015; Sabharwal et al. 2018). Pitts (2009) shows with US federal data that perceived diversity management activities are positively related to self-reported job satisfaction and work group performance of racial minorities. Similarly, Ashikali and Groeneveld (2015a; 2015b) found a positive relation between diversity management and employees' affective commitment and organizational citizenship behavior. More importantly, the impact of diversity management on employees' outcomes did not vary between different sociodemographic groups (Ashikali and Groeneveld 2015a). Although these studies show a positive relation between diversity management and employee outcomes, it remains unclear what specific activities are being implemented. We therefore review research on the relation between the three perspectives and the performance outcomes achieved.

In regard to activities of the discrimination and fairness paradigm, research on affirmative action has been largely concerned with the desirability of policies and the extent to which it provides a just solution to the problem of minorities without an explicit examination of its impact (Kellough 2006). The empirical evidence shows positive findings in the context of private sector contractors and rather mixed results in the US federal service, not proving consistent improvement in the promotion, dismissal, or quit ratios across time due to diversity programs (Kellough 2006; Naff and Kellough 2003). However, affirmative action initiatives lead to higher minority admission in public education (Kellough 2006). In an evaluation of antidiscrimination measures of 708 private sector organizations from 1971 to 2002, Kalev et al. (2006) come to the conclusion that although inequality in attainment at work may be rooted in managerial bias and isolation of minorities, HR practices that assign organizational responsibility for change and structures that embed accountability, authority, and expertise (e.g. affirmative action plans and diversity task forces) are best for increasing the share of minorities. In a European context, Verbeek and Groeneveld (2012) found different results. Based on cross-sectional analysis, assigning responsibility for the implementation of diversity policies to a single person, committee, or task force was positively related to the representation of ethnic minorities. Preferential treatment and the use of targets were negatively related to their representation. However, in their analysis using a lagged dependent variable method, all three types of diversity policies were insignificant in relation to ethnic minorities' representation in the course of a year. These results suggest that the effectiveness of diversity policies might be contingent on contextual factors, due to which long-term effects remain uncertain.

In regard to the access and legitimacy perspective, empirical studies on representative bureaucracy give ample support for the claim that representation matters. For instance, positive findings are shown in regard to ethnic minority representation and its relationship to performance outcomes in an educational setting (Pitts 2005), ethnic minority representation and citizen perceptions of local authorities' performance depending on the strategic stance of an organization (Andrews et al. 2005), and gender and ethnic minority representation and effectiveness of firefighting organizations (Andrews et al. 2014).

Concerning the relationship between the integration and learning perspective of diversity management and the performance of public organizations, empirical research is scarce. However, in a longitudinal analysis, Groeneveld and Verbeek (2012) found that diversity management policies positively affect the representation of ethnic minority employees in the course of a year, in both public and private sector organizations, whereas equal opportunity and affirmative action policies do not. These results suggest that policies focused on managing diversity succeed in creating a work environment that prevents minority employees from leaving.

Furthermore, recent studies show the relevance of the integration and learning paradigm when comparing the effects of standard diversity management activities (e.g. mentoring programs and family-friendly policies) and inclusion practices on perceived work group performance. The studies indicate that the latter is important to create an environment where employees can influence work group decisions. In addition, the studies give evidence that the relationship between inclusion practices and organizational performance is strengthened by leaders who are committed to creating an environment wherein everyone's opinion matters (Ashikali and Groeneveld 2015b; Sabharwal 2014). Section 10.3 elaborates further on the concepts of diversity and inclusiveness.

10.3 Diversity, Inclusiveness, and Outcomes

10.3.1 Concepts and Theories on Diversity and Inclusiveness

Section 10.2 discussed several values that underpin diversity management in public organizations. Regardless of those values, but clearly linked to an integration and learning perspective, diversity management has recently been directed more and more toward enabling inclusiveness in both public and private sector organizations (Ashikali and Groeneveld 2015b; Mor Barak 1999; Mor Barak et al. 2016; Sabharwal 2014). Inclusiveness involves a work environment in which there is a shared openness to differences, valuing these and utilizing differences to inform work practices and decision-making processes (Nishii 2013). Since inclusiveness would contribute to their (active) representativeness and responsiveness, it is of particular relevance in public organizations. This development called for increased attention on understanding the antecedents and outcomes of inclusiveness, specifically so in a public sector context (Andrews and Ashworth 2015; Ashikali and Groeneveld 2015b; Ritz and Alfes 2018).

We follow the framework of Shore et al. that uses the optimal distinctiveness theory to conceptualize inclusion as "the degree to which an employee perceives that he or she is an esteemed member of the work group through experiencing treatment that satisfies his or her needs for belongingness and uniqueness" (Shore et al. 2011, 1265). According to the framework, individuals have two main needs they seek to satisfy. The first is an individual's need for similarities and identification with others in order to feel that they belong to the work group. This is based on a process of social identification in which people seek attachment to and acceptance into certain social groups. The second is an individual's need to be distinctive to others and have a certain uniqueness. The balance of these two needs at a high level would result in inclusion of all work group members. As the opposite of inclusion, there is a situation of exclusion when there is low belongingness and low value in uniqueness. An imbalance of both needs could further result in either assimilation when belongingness is high but with low value in uniqueness, or differentiation when there is high value in uniqueness but low belongingness.

Following up on the discussion in Section 10.2, diversity management could send contradictory signals regarding the valuing of uniqueness, on the one hand, and belongingness, on the other, when diversity policies and practices are misaligned. For instance, implementing anonymous recruitment processes might indicate that unique identities are not valued since managers in the recruitment need to ignore applicants' (demographical) differences. At the same time, managers need to acknowledge and value team members' differences in order to enhance work group inclusiveness.

Reaching a balance between belongingness and uniqueness at a high level of both is a complex issue. The extent to which such a balance is being realized in organizations is associated with two work group processes, social categorization and information elaboration, which are at the center of two distinct social-psychological perspectives on work group diversity. On the one hand, a social identity and categorization perspective posits that groups form subgroups that may exclude (perceived) distinct others, based on similarities and differences within and between groups (Van Knippenberg et al. 2004; Van Knippenberg and Van Ginkel 2010). Categorization could result in intergroup bias, causing in-group favoritism or prejudice if sub-groups feel their identity is under threat. As a result, more diverse work groups would experience more conflict and less cohesion and commitment, negatively impacting their functioning and effectiveness. Any perceived or objective differences between individuals and work group members might induce categorization processes which are dependent on the salience of particular categories within the work group and the extent to which diversity dimensions intersect (Homan et al. 2007; Van Knippenberg and Van Ginkel 2010).

An information elaboration and decision-making perspective, on the other hand, suggests that a diverse team has a broader range of perspectives, skills, and experiences. The use of these differences within the work group—for instance, by stimulating frequent meetings among staff and deliberation—results in more effective problem solving. Hence, based on this diversity advantage, diverse teams would outperform homogeneous teams. The two diversity processes interact, meaning that social categorization processes could prevent diverse work groups from achieving a productive level of elaboration that could be useful for a work group's performance. Section 10.3.2 discusses the relevant research findings.

10.3.2 Empirical Evidence on Team Diversity, Inclusiveness, and Outcomes

Research has, so far, shown inconclusive and mixed findings as to the link between team diversity and team outcomes, indicating that the above-mentioned work group processes are context-dependent (Bell et al. 2011; Horwitz and Horwitz 2007; Joshi and Roh 2009). Most of these studies were performed in a private sector context. For example, in a study on research development teams, Kearney and Gebert (2009) found non-significant effects of team age and educational diversity on the teams' collective identification and information elaboration. These findings suggest that team diversity does not self-evidently result in productive diversity processes. However, they also found that when transformational leadership was high rather than low, team diversity was positively related to the team's performance through the mediating role of team collective identification and information elaboration. Studying manufacturing teams, Mayo et al. (2016) found that racial and gender diversity both result in categorization saliency. Although positively related to categorization saliency, these diversity dimensions did not directly affect team performance. Only when team members rated their leaders as charismatic was the positive relation between diversity and categorization weaker. Moreover, when transformational leadership was high rather than low, high gender salience was positively related to team performance (Mayo et al. 2016). Both studies show that diversity processes are contingent on leadership behavior.

In a public sector context, a study showed that teams were engaged in higher degrees of information elaboration when the team had new hires. However, when the new hires were perceived to be socially distinct because of their different educational and functional backgrounds, the new team members were more likely to be viewed as less competent. The authors interpreted this finding as social categorization to be more prevalent in diverse teams (Andersen and Moynihan 2018).

Simply putting diverse individuals together will not automatically lead to the elaboration of relevant perspectives, but clear motivations, norms, and accountability structures are needed to encourage group members to challenge each other's perspectives and debate multiple solutions to problem solving (Dwertmann et al. 2016). The complexity of managing diversity stresses carefully considering how work practices are designed and managed, as well as how the HR system could support an organizational climate in which information elaboration can take place while categorization processes are minimized. Important in this respect is the perceived organizational support for both individuality and identification with organizational values and norms in order to foster inclusiveness and related positive outcomes.

Socialization of employees is one way that organizations through the implementation of formal or informal training programs and feedback from supervisors and peers could transform individual values and norms to fit those of the organization (Moyson et al. 2018). Organizational socialization is both important from an organizational and employee point of view (see Cooper-Thomas and Anderson 2006, for a review of the literature). Organizational socialization involves a process through which (new) employees change from outsider to the organization or work group into a well-integrated and effective insider. This process occurs whenever an individual crosses an organizational boundary, both external (between organizations) and internal (functional) (Cooper-Thomas and Anderson 2006; Van Maanen and Schein 1979). In this process, individuals develop skills, knowledge, abilities, attitudes, values, and relationships, as well as sense-making frameworks (Cooper-Thomas and Anderson 2006). As a result, (new) employees will perceive a better person–organization fit, thus feeling that they belong.

Previous studies indicate that diversity management contributes to a person–organization or person–group fit, resulting in greater employee commitment and less turnover (Ng and Burke 2005). Socialization could decrease the saliency of perceived differences between employees, thus minimizing social categorization processes within the work group or organization. Rather than individual identities, the organizational or work group identity becomes more salient when interacting with colleagues, which contributes to experiences of belongingness. Conversely, these same socialization processes might cause individuals to perceive their unique identities as undervalued since emphasis is placed on adapting to collective (organizational or group) norms and values. This causes minority groups in an organization to adhere to the same values and practices of dominant groups in the organization. The adherence to dominant norms, values, and practices prevents minority employees from adopting representative roles and making decisions that reflect their own values, thus affecting active representation (Moyson et al. 2018). Consequently, by only emphasizing and fostering belongingness, HRM may counteract the development of inclusiveness. There needs to be balanced attention to both belongingness and individual needs and values in public sector HRM strategies.

In sum, inclusiveness is reached when belongingness and uniqueness are balanced within the group. To do so requires well-aligned policies and practices. Furthermore, managing both categorization and information elaboration processes is important to achieve the desired team diversity outcomes. Previous studies have shown the indispensable role of leadership in attenuating both negative and supportive diversity outcomes (Kearney and Gebert 2009; Mayo et al. 2016). Section 10.4 elaborates further on the role of leadership and its connection with managing diversity and fostering inclusion.

10.4 The Role of Leadership

Previous research has suggested that well-intended HR practices do not always result in intended outcomes and might even result in adverse effects. As discussed in Chapter 3, this is related to people management that involves both (line) managers implementing HR practices and their leadership in supporting employees.

Leadership in particular is a possible conditional factor in fostering inclusion (Ashikali and Groeneveld 2015b; Guillaume et al. 2017). Accordingly, diversity management research has called for more and more attention on shifting the focus from formal policies to actual practices of the supervisor in order to reach diversity management's intended outcomes as described previously (Ashikali 2018; Pitts and Wise 2010).

Furthermore, leaders are important actors in shaping the organizational culture through their exemplary role behavior and communicating the value of diversity. Moreover, since inclusiveness develops in work groups as explained in Section 10.3.2, direct supervisors' leadership is crucial for attenuating negative and boosting positive diversity processes in order to realize inclusion (Ashikali et al. 2020; Randel et al. 2018; Shore et al. 2018). This section elaborates more specifically on how leadership is related to the management of diversity and the development of inclusiveness.

There is limited research available that studies leadership in relation to diversity and inclusiveness, specifically so in a public context. The few studies available indicate that transformational leadership supports diversity management and that it facilitates the inclusiveness of the organizational culture by doing so (Ashikali and Groeneveld 2015b). Transformational leadership is also shown to mitigate negative team diversity outcomes and boost positive team diversity outcomes (Chrobot-Mason et al. 2014; 2016; Kearney and Gebert 2009). Transformational leadership, for instance, is effective in developing a collective (team) identity, improving the team's cohesion, and communicating a vision on diversity. As a result, transformational leadership might minimize the potential negative effects of social categorization through the development of a collective identity. Transformational leadership also stimulates team members to use different and new perspectives on problem-solving, which, in turn, boosts a team's information elaboration and performance (Kearney and Gebert 2009).

However, an aspect that has not yet been fully discovered is how leaders themselves view diversity and diversity management, and how this in turn affects inclusiveness (Buengler et al. 2018). Previous research among teams of a retail organization has shown that leaders themselves could have a categorization tendency impacting on team diversity processes and outcomes. Greer et al. (2012) found that for ethnically diverse teams, high visionary leadership in combination with a high categorization tendency were negatively related to team communication and team financial performance. Ashikali et al. (2020), in a study of forty-five teams in the Dutch public sector, revealed that a leader's perception affected the positive impact of transformational leadership on their team's work processes and engagement. The findings indicated that transformational leadership only affected information elaboration (a cognitive process) through supporting team cohesion (an affective process) when the leader perceived their team to be demographically diverse. This indicates that leaders who perceive their team as demographically diverse use transformational leadership to emphasize the team's cohesion in order to stimulate cognitive processes (Ashikali et al. 2020). This shows some evidence of transformational leadership emphasizing the groups' cohesion in order to facilitate group functioning.

Transformational leadership can potentially place a greater emphasis on belonging-ness at the expense of uniqueness. Randel et al. (2018) argue that through transforming individual identities into a shared group identity, transformational leadership socializes team members to integrate the group's identity to their own, resulting in less oppor-tunity for individuation. It is therefore necessary to explore leadership that facilitates both belongingness and uniqueness in a balanced way. Inclusive leadership is argued to contribute to inclusiveness through stimulating the exchange, discussion, and utilization of different perspectives, ideas, and skills, as well as facilitating the full participation of all team members (Ashikali et al. 2020; Randel et al. 2018). Ashikali et al. (2020), for instance, have found that inclusive leadership positively moderates the effect of ethnic–cultural team diversity on an inclusive climate. While greater team diversity is related to a lower inclusive climate, high inclusive leadership miti-gates this negative effect.

What the studies above have in common is that they emphasize the crucial role of leadership as discussed in Chapters 3 and 5. These studies provide promising insights for public managers in order to manage diversity and support inclusiveness. Yet it remains a difficult task in which a balance has to be found between enhancing cohesiveness within a work group, on the one hand, and supporting individual dis-tinctiveness, on the other.

10.5 Conclusion

This section reflects on the previously discussed subjects and integrates perspectives from research on diversity, diversity management, and representative bureaucracy. A conceptual framework is shown in Figure 10.1 that explicates the association between concepts at different levels of analysis.

The two major diversity paradigms—a discrimination and fairness perspective and a synergy perspective—can be connected to different public values, more specif-ically to equity and social justice, on the one hand, and organizational effectiveness and responsiveness, on the other. While it is highly relevant to take the underlying values into account for the assessment of the effectiveness of diversity management policies and practices, research on how diversity motives are related to outcomes of diversity policies and practices is lacking to date. Since the paradigms result in dif-ferent practices and related outcomes, research that combines both perspectives is thus needed for a better comprehension of how diversity management relates to inclusiveness, employee outcomes, and subsequently, public service performance.

Furthermore, distinctive motives draw our attention to different levels of analy-sis (Dwertmann et al. 2016). Research studying the discrimination and fairness

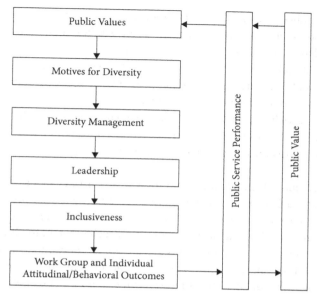

Figure 10.1 Conceptual framework linking managing diversity to public service performance

paradigm often looks at HR outcomes at the individual level. For instance, it is of interest to know how quotas and targets for minorities in the workforce change the job application behavior of individuals or how women are promoted to the management level of an organization. In contrast, the core of the synergistic perspective of access and legitimacy as well as integration and learning rests on interpersonal and team interaction. Leveraging distributed information associated with diversity is the underlying process of outcomes such as higher client satisfaction, organizational legitimacy, team creativity, or organizational innovation. Consequently, practices derived from a synergy paradigm would result in outcomes that are most apparent at the work group level.

The above-mentioned different levels of analysis have various implications for managerial intervention and leadership. Multiple motives result in conflicting practices with different goals that need to be studied while considering the conceptual distinctiveness of different perspectives and respective outcomes. Accordingly, diversity management may imply practices on an organizational level (fairness of recruitment and selection or equal opportunities), as well as group-level practices (such as training and development, team building, etc.). Different actors can be involved in the implementation of these practices, such as HR professionals, line managers/supervisors, and employees. As their behavior will impact whether and how those practices are implemented, as well as enhance the emergence of an inclusive work environment, they should be included as objects of analysis in research.

Although studied to a limited extent, some studies provide promising insights in leader behavior that fosters inclusiveness. These studies show that leadership is needed to balance work group cohesion and individual distinctiveness at the same time. Enhanced inclusiveness is positively related to work group outcomes such as team engagement and performance but also to employees' commitment and satisfaction. However, in the absence of leadership, team diversity could also result in less team cohesion as well as team conflict. Negative team outcomes could, in turn, deteriorate performance. Further research is needed to understand how leadership may contribute to inclusiveness and support the performance of diverse work groups by doing so.

On another note, in public administration research (and practice), diversity is most often approached from a representative bureaucracy framework. In so doing, demographic diversity characteristics are emphasized. However, diversity involves any attribute in which individuals may differ from each other, both visible (e.g. gender, age, and race/ethnicity) and less visible (functional, educational, and norms and values). Depending on the context, a particular dimension or combination of dimensions might be salient, impacting team processes and outcomes. This issue is yet underdeveloped within public management studies. Future studies need to unravel how different diversity dimensions are related to inclusiveness and how this would impact performance.

The aspects above are represented in the conceptual framework in Figure 10.1 that integrates multiple concepts at different levels of analysis for studying the management of a diverse workforce, as discussed in this chapter. A feedback loop is included to show a linkage between public service performance and public value as an outcome of diversity and inclusiveness, on the one hand, and, on the other, public service performance and public value as an important driver for workforce diversity.

References

Andersen, S. C., and D. P. Moynihan. 2018. "How Do Socially Distinctive Newcomers Fare? Evidence from a Field Experiment." *Public Administration Review 78* (6): pp. 874–82.

Andrews, R., and R. Ashworth. 2015. "Representation and Inclusion in Public Organizations: Evidence from the UK Civil Service." *Public Administration Review 75* (2): pp. 279–88.

Andrews, R., G. A. Boyne, K. J. Meier, L. J. O'Toole, and R. M. Walker. 2005. "Representative Bureaucracy, Organizational Strategy, and Public Service Performance. An Empirical Analysis of English Local Government." *International Journal of Public Sector Management 15* (4): pp. 489–504.

Andrews, R., R. Ashworth, and K. J. Meier. 2014. "Representative Bureaucracy and Fire Service Performance." *International Journal of Public Sector Management 17* (1): pp. 1–24.

Ashikali, T. 2018. "Leadership and Inclusiveness in Public Organizations." Doctoral dissertation. Leiden University, Leiden, the Netherlands.

Ashikali, T., and S. Groeneveld. 2015a. "Diversity Management for All? An Empirical Analysis of Diversity Management Outcomes across Groups." *Personnel Review 44* (5): pp. 757–80.

Ashikali, T., and S. Groeneveld. 2015b. "Diversity Management in Public Organizations and Its Effect on Employees' Affective Commitment: The Role of Transformational Leadership and the Inclusiveness of the Organizational Culture." *Review of Public Personnel Administration 35* (2): pp. 146–68.

Ashikali, T., S. Groeneveld, and B. Kuipers. 2020. "The Role of Inclusive Leadership in Supporting an Inclusive Climate in Diverse Public Sector Teams." *Review of Public Personnel Administration.* Online first. https://doi.org/10.1177/0734371X19899722.

Beck Jørgensen, T., and B. Bozeman. 2007. "Public Values: An Inventory." *Administration & Society 39* (3): pp. 354–81.

Bell, S. T., A. J. Villado, M. A. Lukasik, L. Belau, and A. L. Briggs. 2011. "Getting Specific about Demographic Diversity Variable and Team Performance Relationships: A Meta-Analysis." *Journal of Management 37* (3): pp. 709–43.

Buengeler, C., H. Leroy, and K. De Stobbeleir. 2018. "How Leaders Shape the Impact of HR's Diversity Practices on Employee Inclusion." *Human Resource Management Review 28* (3): pp. 289–303.

Chrobot-Mason, D., A. Gerbasi, and K. L. Cullen-Lester. 2016. "Predicting Leadership Relationships: The Importance of Collective Identity." *The Leadership Quarterly 27* (2): pp. 298–311.

Chrobot-Mason, D., M. N. Ruderman, and L. H. Nishii. 2014. "Leadership in a Diverse Workplace." In *The Oxford Handbook of Leadership and Organizations*, edited by D. V. Day, pp. 683–708. Oxford: Oxford University Press.

Cooper-Thomas, H. D., and N. Anderson. 2006. "Organizational Socialization: A New Theoretical Model and Recommendations for Future Research and HRM Practices in Organizations." *Journal of Managerial Psychology 21* (5): pp. 492–516.

Dwertmann, D. J., L. H. Nishii, and D. Van Knippenberg. 2016. "Disentangling the Fairness & Discrimination and Synergy Perspectives on Diversity Climate: Moving the Field Forward." *Journal of Management 42* (5): pp. 1136–68.

Ely, R. J., and D. A. Thomas. 2001. "Cultural Diversity at Work: The Effects of Diversity Perspectives on Work Group Processes and Outcomes." *Administrative Sciences Quarterly 46* (2): pp. 229–73.

Greer, L., A. Homan, A. De Hoogh, and D. Den Hartog. 2012. "Tainted Visions: The Effect of Visionary Leader Behaviors and Leader Categorization Tendencies on the Financial Performance of Ethnically Diverse Teams." *Journal of Applied Psychology 97* (1): pp. 203–13.

Groeneveld, S. 2015. "Explaining Diversity Management Outcomes: What Can Be Learned from Quantitative Survey Research?" In *The Oxford Handbook of Diversity in Organizations*, edited by R. Bendl, I. Bleijenbergh, E. Henttonen, and A. Mills, pp. 281–97. Oxford: Oxford University Press.

Groeneveld, S., and S. Van de Walle. 2010. "A Contingency Approach to Representative Bureaucracy: Power, Equal Opportunities and Diversity." *International Review of Administrative Sciences 76* (2): pp. 239–58.

Groeneveld, S., and S. Verbeek. 2012. "Diversity Policies in Public and Private Sector Organizations: An Empirical Comparison of Incidence and Effectiveness." *Review of Public Personnel Administration 32* (4): pp. 353–81.

Guillaume, Y. R. F., J. F. Dawson, L. Otaye-Ebede, S. A. Woods, and M. A. West. 2017. "Harnessing Demographic Differences in Organizations: What Moderates the Effects of Workplace Diversity?" *Journal of Organizational Behavior 38* (2): pp. 276–303.

Homan, A. C., D. Van Knippenberg, G. A. Van Kleef, and C. K. De Dreu. 2007. "Interacting Dimensions of Diversity: Cross-Categorization and the Functioning of Diverse Work Groups." *Group Dynamics: Theory, Research, and Practice 11* (2): pp. 79–94.

Horwitz, S. K., and I. B. Horwitz. 2007. "The Effects of Team Diversity on Team Outcomes: A Meta-Analytic Review of Team Demography." *Journal of Management 33* (6): pp. 987–1015.

Joshi, A., and H. Roh. 2009. "The Role of Context in Work Team Diversity Research: A Meta-Analytic Review." *Academy of Management Journal 52* (3): pp. 599–627.

Kalev, A., F. Dobbin, and E. Kelly. 2006. "Best Practices or Best Guesses? Assessing the Efficacy of Corporate Affirmative Action and Diversity Policies." *American Sociological Review 71* (4): pp. 589–617.

Kearney, E., and D. Gebert. 2009. "Managing Diversity and Enhancing Team Outcomes: The Promise of Transformational Leadership." *Journal of Applied Psychology 94* (1): pp. 77–89.

Kellough, J. E. 2006. *Understanding Affirmative Action. Politics, Discrimination, and the Search for Justice.* Washington, DC: Georgetown University Press.

Mayo, M., D. Van Knippenberg, L. Guillen, and S. Firfiray. 2016. "Team Diversity and Categorization Salience: Capturing Diversity-Blind, Intergroup-Biased, and Multicultural Perceptions." *Organizational Research Methods 19* (3): pp. 433–74.

McDougall, M. 1996. "Equal Opportunities Versus Managing Diversity: Another Challenge for Public Sector Management?" *International Journal of Public Sector Management 9* (5–6): pp. 62–72.

McMahan, G. C., M. P. Bell, and M. Virick. 1998. "Strategic Human Resource Management: Employee Involvement, Diversity, and International Issues." *Human Resource Management Review 8* (3): pp. 193–214.

Meeussen, L., S. Otten, and K. Phalet. 2014. "Managing Diversity: How Leaders' Multiculturalism and Colorblindness Affect Work Group Functioning." *Group Processes & Intergroup Relations 17* (5): pp. 629–44.

Meier, K. J. 2019. "Theoretical Frontiers in Representative Bureaucracy: New Directions for Research." *Perspectives on Public Management and Governance 2* (1): pp. 39–56.

Milliken, F. J., and L. L. Martins. 1996. "Searching for Common Threads: Understanding the Multiple Effects of Diversity in Organizational Groups." *Academy of Management Review 21* (2): pp. 402–33.

Mor Barak, M. E. 1999. "Beyond Affirmative Action: Toward a Model of Diversity and Organizational Inclusion." *Administration in Social Work 23* (3–4): pp. 47–68.

Mor Barak, M. E., E. L. Lizano, A. Kim, L. Duan, M. K. Rhee, H. Y. Hsiao, and K. C. Brimhall. 2016. "The Promise of Diversity Management for Climate of Inclusion: A State-of-the-Art Review and Meta-Analysis." *Human Service Organizations: Management, Leadership & Governance 40* (4): pp. 305–33.

Moyson, S., N. Raaphorst, S. Groeneveld, and S. Van de Walle. 2018. "Organizational Socialization in Public Administration Research: A Systematic Review and Directions for Future Research." *The American Review of Public Administration 48* (6): pp. 610–27.

Naff, K. C., and J. E. Kellough. 2003. "Ensuring Employment Equity: Are Federal Diversity Programs Making a Difference?" *International Journal of Public Administration 26* (12): pp. 1307–36.

Ng, E. S., and R. J. Burke. 2005. "Person–Organization Fit and the War for Talent: Does Diversity Management Make a Difference?" *The International Journal of Human Resource Management 16* (7): pp. 1195–210.

Nishii, L. H. 2013. "The Benefits of Climate for Inclusion for Gender-Diverse Groups." *Academy of Management Journal 56* (6): pp. 1754–74.

Nishii, L. H., J. Khattab, M. Shemla, and R. M. Paluch. 2018. "A Multi-Level Process Model for Understanding Diversity Practice Effectiveness." *Academy of Management Annals 12* (1): pp. 37–82.

Nishii, L. H., and D. M. Mayer. 2009. "Do Inclusive Leaders Help to Reduce Turnover in Diverse Groups? The Moderating Role of Leader–Member Exchange in the Diversity to Turnover Relationship." *Journal of Applied Psychology 94* (6): pp. 1412–26.

Pelled, L. H., K. M. Eisenhardt, and K. R. Xin. 1999. "Exploring the Black Box: An Analysis of Work Group Diversity, Conflict, and Performance." *Administrative Science Quarterly 44* (1): pp. 1–28.

Pitts, D. W. 2005. "Diversity, Representation, and Performance: Evidence about Race and Ethnicity in Public Organizations." *Journal of Public Administration Research and Theory 15* (4): pp. 615–31.

Pitts, D. W. 2009. "Diversity Management, Job Satisfaction, and Performance: Evidence from US Federal Agencies." *Public Administration Review 69* (2): pp. 328–38.

Pitts, D. W., and R. L. Wise. 2010. "Workforce Diversity in the New Millennium: Prospects for Research." *Review of Public Personnel Administration 30* (1): pp. 44–69.

Randel, A. E., B. M. Galvin, L. M. Shore, K. H. Ehrhart, B. G. Chung, M. A. Dean, and U. Kedharnath. 2018. "Inclusive Leadership: Realizing Positive Outcomes through Belongingness and Being Valued for Uniqueness." *Human Resource Management Review 28* (2): pp. 190–203.

Riccucci, N. M., and G. G. Van Ryzin. 2017. "Representative Bureaucracy: A Lever to Enhance Social Equity, Coproduction, and Democracy." *Public Administration Review 77* (1): pp. 21–30.

Ritz, A., and K. Alfes. 2018. "Multicultural Public Administration: Effects of Language Diversity and Dissimilarity on Public Employees' Attachment to Employment." *Public Administration 96* (1): pp. 84–113.

Sabharwal, M. 2014. "Is Diversity Management Sufficient? Organizational Inclusion to Further Performance." *Public Personnel Management 43* (2): pp. 197–217.

Sabharwal, M., H. Levine, and M. D'Agostino. 2018. "A Conceptual Content Analysis of 75 Years of Diversity Research in Public Administration." *Review of Public Personnel Administration 38* (2): pp. 248–67.

Selden, S. C. 1997. *The Promise of Representative Bureaucracy. Diversity and Responsiveness in a Government Agency.* Armonk, NY: ME Sharpe.

Selden, S. C., and F. Selden. 2001. "Rethinking Diversity in Public Organizations for the 21st Century: Moving toward a Multicultural Model." *Administration & Society 33* (3): pp. 303–29.

Shore, L. M., J. N. Cleveland, and D. Sanchez. 2018. "Inclusive Workplaces: A Review and Model." *Human Resource Management Review 28* (2): pp. 176–89.

Shore, L. M., A. E. Randel, B. G. Chung, M. A. Dean, K. Holcombe Ehrhart, and G. Singh. 2011. "Inclusion and Diversity in Work Groups: A Review and Model for Future Research." *Journal of Management 37* (4): pp. 1262–89.

Van Knippenberg, D., C. K. De Dreu, and A. C. Homan. 2004. "Work Group Diversity and Group Performance: An Integrative Model and Research Agenda." *Journal of Applied Psychology 89* (6): pp. 1008–22.

Van Knippenberg, D., and W. P. Van Ginkel. 2010. "The Categorization-Elaboration Model of Work Group Diversity: Wielding the Double-Edged Sword." In *The Psychology of Social and Cultural Diversity*, edited by R. Crisp, pp. 257–80. Chichester: Wiley Blackwell.

Van Maanen, J., and E. H. Schein. 1979. "Toward a Theory of Organizational Socialization." In *Research in Organizational Behavior*, edited by B. M. Staw, pp. 209–64. Greenwich, CT: JAI Press.

Verbeek, S., and S. Groeneveld. 2012. "Do 'Hard' Diversity Policies Increase Ethnic Minority Representation? An Assessment of Their (In)Effectiveness Using Administrative Data." *Personnel Review 41* (5): pp. 647–64.

11

Leading Change in a Complex Public Sector Environment

Anne Mette Kjeldsen and Joris Van der Voet

11.1 Introduction

Organizational change in the public sector is widespread, which is related to at least three issues. First, the multidimensional nature of public performance makes public organizations a natural target for reform initiatives. Public organizations must balance between values such as effectiveness, efficiency, legality, transparency, responsiveness, and flexibility (Hood 1991). Since these values are often at odds with each other, public organizations are subject to a permanent sub-optimality of performance, resulting in "pendulum swings" of administrative reform (Van de Walle 2016). A second issue is that public organizations are inert in the sense that they cannot match the pace of dynamism in the external environment with organizational adaptation (Hannan and Freeman 1984). Public organizations are bureaucracies, which "with their reporting structures too rigid to adapt to faster-paced change, have to be unfrozen to be improved" (Weick and Quinn 1999, 381). As a consequence, they are easily "out of fit" in the sense that there is limited congruence between their structures, systems, and processes and the demands of external stakeholders, citizens, and political principals. Third, decision makers such as politicians and senior public managers have an instrumental view of public organizations. There is generally a great belief that the structures, processes, systems, and ideologies of public organizations can be shaped and modified through leadership (Brunsson and Olsen 1993).

The mix of these ingredients means that public organizations are in a perpetual state of intentional, episodic, organizational changes, and successful organizational change greatly depends on leadership. As is argued by Greenwood and Hinings (1996), organizations are subject to institutional forces that favor stability over change. Leadership is concerned with formulating an alternative organizational archetype by communicating such a change to employees in order to ensure that the organizational change translates into commitment and changed behavior of employees. Yet only a few scholarly contributions within the public administration and public leadership literatures deal systematically with leadership in different public organization change processes (e.g. Kuipers et al. 2014; Van der Voet 2014; Vann 2004).

Anne Mette Kjeldsen and Joris Van der Voet, *Leading Change in a Complex Public Sector Environment* In: *Managing for Public Service Performance: How People and Values Make a Difference.* Edited by: Peter Leisink, Lotte B. Andersen, Gene A. Brewer, Christian B. Jacobsen, Eva Knies, and Wouter Vandenabeele, Oxford University Press (2021). © Anne Mette Kjeldsen and Joris Van der Voet. DOI: 10.1093/oso/9780192893420.003.0011

The aim of this chapter is to summarize and analyze research regarding leadership of organizational change in public sector organizations. We analyze the (intra-) organizational level and are thus concerned with administrative rather than political leadership. Leadership does not occur in a vacuum but is contingent on the process of change and the characteristics of the organizational context in which it takes place. We therefore structure our chapter according to the distinction between leadership in planned and emergent processes of change (Kuipers et al. 2014). We outline the conceptual foundations and empirical research findings concerning change leadership in both types of change processes while at the same time discussing their complementary status. Moreover, in accordance with different governance paradigms (cf. Chapters 1 and 2), we discuss how the characteristics of the public sector organizational environment and structures influence the occurrence and effectiveness of change leadership. Finally, we provide a concluding discussion of leading change in public sector organizations and outline an agenda for future research.

11.2 Setting the Stage: Organizational Change and Leadership

Organizational change is a catch-all term in the sense that it can encompass a wide range of phenomena. Just like a river is both a thing and a process of flowing water, organizations can be said to be constantly evolving, growing, learning, and thereby changing. What organizational change *is* exactly thus depends on the perspective. Most theories of organizations emphasize a perspective on organizations as things (Tsoukas and Chia 2002). Politicians, managers, employees, and citizens tend to refer to "things" or "entities" when they talk about organizations. In such a perspective, change is something out of the ordinary that happens to the organization in a certain period. In discussing organizational change and its leadership in this chapter, we take this dominant view of organizational change as an "episode" rather than a continuous occurrence (Weick and Quinn 1999).

Viewing organizational change as an episode does not fully resolve conceptual questions about its nature since organizational changes can still take on many different forms and patterns. Organizational changes can be classified in terms of their order, scope, and pace (e.g. Dunphy and Stace 1988; Greenwood and Hinings 1996). The order of change refers to the parts of the organization that are affected by the change, with first order referring to departments within an organization, second order referring to organization-wide changes, and the third order referring to changes that affect the entire sector or system in which the organization is embedded (Kuipers et al. 2014). The scope of change refers to the degree in which the organization is different after a change is implemented, and the pace of change refers to whether a change is completed quickly or slowly. Although the scope and pace of change can be conceptually separated, many authors integrate them in two competing theses (e.g. Dunphy and Stace 1988; Plowman et al. 2007).

Organizational change is also characterized by the means used to bring about change. This is what is commonly referred to as the process of change, in which change leadership is an important aspect (Kuipers et al. 2014). Despite an abundance of change process typologies, these usually distinguish between directive top-down processes of change driven by managers versus participatory bottom-up processes of change driven by employees. In this chapter, we refer to these broad approaches by means of the terms *planned* and *emergent* change (cf. Van der Voet et al. 2016).

Planned organizational change processes are aimed at realizing a predefined objective. The direction of the change is top-down in the sense that the organization's senior management initiates the change and defines the objectives (By 2005). Planned organizational changes are often comprehensive in the sense that they encompass the entire organization and tend to focus on "hard" aspects of the organization, such as strategy, structures, and systems. An emergent change process, in contrast, is more open-ended in the sense that no strict, detailed objectives of change are formulated (By 2005). Instead, a general direction of change is set—often by senior management—but lower-level managers and employees are enabled to elaborate and contribute to the objectives of change. Thus, employees are not merely passive recipients of change but have a more active role. Rather than aspects of the formal organization, emergent change processes often aim to improve learning, collaboration, and trust in the organization.

The view that leadership is a key driver of organizational change is widespread (Kuipers et al. 2014), and both approaches of planned and emergent change emphasize the important role of change agents as part of the change process but in different ways. In Sections 11.3 and 11.4, we expand on theory and research regarding the role of leadership in planned and emergent processes of organizational change.

11.3 Leadership in Planned Processes of Change: Transformational Leadership

For public organizations, we see that organizational changes often take the form of planned organizational changes. Such planned changes can, for instance, concern turnarounds due to poor performance, strategic reorientations due to the changing demands of clients or political supervisors, policy reforms that have been imposed at the national level, or reorganizations and downsizing as a result of austerity and financial decline. Leadership is generally seen as a central component of planned organizational change.

The literature on the leadership of planned organizational change portrays a leader-centric, "heroic" approach of leadership (Stewart and Kringas 2003). Accounts of leadership typically describe the efforts of a single top-level manager or a small guiding coalition in an "I came, I saw, I implemented" type of fashion. Nadler and Tushman (1990) separate three clusters of leadership activities in organizational change: (1) charismatic (envisioning, energizing, and enabling); (2) instrumental (structuring, controlling, and rewarding); and (3) institutional (making sure changes stick). Envisioning in particular has been deemed important: "radical change cannot be nakedly prescribed, but it is better accomplished by appeals to normative 'visions'" (Greenwood and Hinings 1996, 1038). This visionary emphasis is strongly present in the two main strands of literature that inform the actual behavior of leaders in planned organizational change.

The first strand is commonly referred to as "change leadership" and is rooted in the literature on organizational change (Herold et al. 2008). Partly, this literature is aimed at practitioners and consists of recommendations about the types of behavior in which leaders should engage in order to "successfully" implement organizational change. Recommendations are, for instance, to "communicate a sense of urgency," to "provide resources," and to "formulate a vision" (e.g. Kotter 1996). Such "factors" (Fernandez and Rainey 2006), "steps" (Kotter 1996), or "commandments" (Kanter et al. 1992) for successful change are intuitive, but from a research perspective, one limitation is that they are largely based on anecdotal evidence and the personal experiences of the authors, rather than systematic empirical investigation. Another limitation is that the recommended behavior seems to be based exclusively on successful examples. The same behaviors may also be present in unsuccessful cases of organizational change. This raises questions regarding the internal validity of this particular type of change leadership recommendations. Herold et al. (2008) have developed a quantitative measurement instrument that measures the degree to which a leader engages in change leadership behaviors. Research using this measurement scale has shown that the perceived change leadership behavior of public managers is positively related to employees' affective commitment to change (Herold et al. 2008; Van der Voet 2016).

The second strand of leadership literature that informs the behavior of leaders in planned organizational change is transformational leadership theory (see also Chapter 5). Transformational leadership is leadership behavior with the purpose of "transforming" or "elevating" the interests of followers from the individual level to the collective level. Although the theory originally emphasized multiple dimensions of behavior, more recent conceptions of the theory emphasize the visionary aspect of transformational leadership (Jacobsen and Andersen 2015; Van Knippenberg and Sitkin 2013). Transformational leaders thus contribute to the implementation of planned organizational change "by defining the need for change, creating new visions, [and] mobilizing commitment to these visions" (Den Hartog et al. 1997, 20). Using a range of measurement instruments, research has indicated that transformational leadership behavior is positively related to employees' constructive reactions to change.

In a study of the public school system in Israel, Oreg and Berson (2011) collected data about the transformational leadership behaviors of school principals and the resistance to a school reform among teachers. The study provides insights into the effect of transformational leadership behavior during organizational change as the results indicate that transformational leadership reduces resistance to change. Moreover,

Van der Voet et al. (2016) conducted a quantitative study in a local government agency in order to examine the relationship between the transformational leadership behaviors of direct supervisors and the affective commitment to change of employees. The study indicates that perceptions of transformational leadership and commitment to change are positively correlated. However, this relationship appears to be mediated by two characteristics of the change process: (1) the quality of change-related communication; and (2) employee participation in change. This result suggests that the relationship between the leadership behavior of direct supervisors and the commitment to change should be understood as an indirect relationship: Transformational leaders disseminate higher quality communication about the purpose and implementation of organizational change and stimulate employees to actively contribute to the implementation of organizational change, thereby creating commitment to change.

Although the change leadership and transformational leadership literatures have distinct origins, the actual behaviors that are prescribed by the approaches are highly similar. Interestingly, some studies have simultaneously examined change leadership and transformational leadership behaviors (Herold et al. 2008; Van der Voet 2016). These studies not only indicate that change leadership and transformational leadership are highly correlated but also that they jointly affect employees' responses to change. Herold et al. (2008) find that both leadership styles can replace each other in the sense that transformational leadership has stronger effects when change leadership is absent, whereas Van der Voet (2016) finds that change leadership has stronger effects in combination with transformational leadership behaviors.

11.4   Leadership in Emergent Processes of Change: Distributed Leadership

In contrast to planned processes of change taking place as smaller or larger reforms in all organizations, there are also many ongoing and less top-down initiated changes. These include the more incremental and emergent changes or adjustments that oftentimes, but not always, follow planned reforms. As mentioned, this emergent approach to change is a more devolved and bottom-up way to implement change (Beer and Nohria 2000; By 2005), which is typically characterized by another leadership focus than the "heroic" leadership approach we see in planned change implementations. Specifically, decentralized leadership often accompanies emergent change processes since more evolving and fluent leadership constellations are needed to fit the emergent nature of the changes (Van der Voet et al. 2014). Among other types of bottom-up and collective leadership approaches, such decentralized leadership has been labeled "distributed leadership."

The appeal of distributed leadership has recently gained momentum in the leadership field, and the term has been widely used to capture all forms of bottom-up and shared leadership activities (Bolden 2011; Harris et al. 2007). One of the most cited definitions of distributed leadership is proposed by Spillane et al. (2004). They emphasize that it describes leadership constellations where the leadership function is "stretched over the work of a number of individuals where the leadership task is accomplished through the interaction of multiple leaders" (Harris and Spillane 2008, 32). This implies that the social context of organizations is a vital part of the leadership activity, and distributed leadership is thus essentially an organizational-level variable. Furthermore, it underscores that distributed leadership is occupied with leadership as a collective process that involves the distribution of leadership authority and agency to many individuals within the organization in order to implement change and for the organization to achieve its goals (Yukl 2002).

This is well in line with Gronn's (2000) emphasis on distributed leadership as a form of concerted action, which constitutes the additional dynamic that occurs when people work together or that is the product of conjoint agency (Harris et al. 2007, 339). In this sense, distributed leadership has been promoted as a "leader-plus" phenomenon that highlights the additional resources which already exist in organizations in the form of organization members' abilities and willingness to engage in leadership whenever needed (Spillane et al. 2004). These organization members are not the formal leaders, but they are rank-and-file employees, who, in a given situation, see the need for leadership and have the competences, knowledge, and autonomy to carry out required leadership tasks. In addition to traditional delegation of leadership, such spontaneous leadership initiatives from employees are crucial for implementation success when changes are emergent and actions and responsibilities are not (or cannot be) planned beforehand.

Recent years have provided an increasing number of studies that link distributed leadership to various organizational outcomes and organizational change (for general literature overviews, see Bennet et al. 2003; Bolden 2011; Harris 2008; Tian et al. 2016). Many of these studies are situated in the education and (health) care sectors. Harris et al.'s (2007) literature review specifically targets the link between distributed leadership and organizational change. They highlight a number of education studies showing the positive contribution of distributed leadership to change implementation and school improvement (e.g. Harris and Chapman 2002; Leithwood et al. 2007; Møller et al. 2005). In a study of teacher leadership in England, Harris and Muijs (2004), for instance, found that the degree of teacher involvement in decision-making was positively associated with student motivation and self-efficacy. This positive contribution of distributed leadership is argued (and shown) to be due to the development of professional learning communities and leadership capacity building at all levels of the organization. These HRM practices serve as important mediators which help ensure that human potential within the organization is released to make the school improve and develop (Harris et al. 2007, 340). Distribution of leadership tasks within the schools makes the teachers more committed and motivated; it enhances social trust, collaboration, and professional learning, which ultimately prove to have an effect on various student outcomes and contribute to making the organization more flexible and adaptive. These are important properties of emergent change processes.

In addition, we see an increasing number of studies of distributed leadership and change in the healthcare sector (e.g. Buchanan et al. 2007; Fitzgerald et al. 2013; Jakobsen et al. 2016), in social care (e.g. White et al. 2014), and in a wider array of public sector departments and agencies. In a qualitative comparative study of two Dutch public sector units within the same department—one with a planned approach to change and the other with an emergent approach to change—Van der Voet et al. (2014, 184) show that the participation of employees in leading the changes was much more extensive in the emergent change process. On the other hand, leadership in the organization undergoing a planned change process was much more "traditional" and top-down oriented with a priori formulated objectives of change, with managers serving as role models, and with participation from the employees only at a late stage of the process. A recent study of hospital mergers in Denmark found similar results (Jonasson et al. 2018). Here, the more emergent change processes following the merger were characterized by extensive employee participation and distributed leadership practices, contrary to the overall political and top-down organized hospital merger process. Employees with different skills and resources pooled their expertise and resources to induce and manage change across newly merged units and units that now had to cooperate more closely than before. Hence, the merger resulted in widened distributed leadership practices at the local hospital level. Yet a pattern of restricted distributed leadership was also observed in some local units, characterized by very scarce resources and high employee turnover. In these latter instances, the formal leadership hierarchy had to step in.

11.5 Complementary or Contradictory Leadership Practices?

As is evident from the two preceding sections, leader-centric leadership is most pronounced in processes of planned organizational change, whereas distributed models of leadership are more often used in emergent processes of change. It may thus appear that transformational and distributed models of leadership are rivalrous rather than complementary. Nonetheless, based on existing research, we argue that transformational and distributed leadership are complementary and that the occurrence of distributed leadership is dependent on formal leaders' transformational leadership.

First, while the prior discussion separated ideal types of planned and emergent change processes, most real-world organizational changes reflect elements of both. Moreover, the characteristics of change processes may fluctuate over time. Some organizational changes start out as local experimentations but later shift to top-down planned change. As an example, Van der Voet et al. (2015) describe an open-ended, developmental change process in a local government agency that took on a pronounced top-down directive nature over time due to severe budget cuts and political pressure to improve performance. Other organizational changes, such as the case in the Danish hospital study by Jonasson et al. (2018), may be initiated as top-down changes but are later followed by a period of emergent adaptation. It is therefore important that organizations display the right leadership balance, which necessitates the simultaneous application of distributed and transformational models of change leadership.

A second reason why transformational and distributed leadership are complementary is that the occurrence of collective leadership constellations is dependent on a conscious delegation of leadership authority, especially in public sector organizations. While the professional nature of the workforce and the complexity of the environment invite or even require a distribution of leadership, as further discussed in Section 11.6, an organic distribution of leadership responsibilities is ultimately hampered by the primacy of politics and bureaucratic organizational structures. With public organizations' structures and strict job descriptions, formal leadership in most instances needs to be actively delegated to lower hierarchical levels before distributed leadership emerges and is institutionalized. Günzel-Jensen et al. (2018) and Van der Voet et al. (2014) thus suggest that formal leadership, for instance, transformational leadership behavior by senior managers, is a requirement for distributed leadership to flourish.

However, when delegating leadership and providing room for employees to take on leadership tasks, the more critical side of the literature on shared and distributed leadership warns us that there are different patterns of distribution, and not all of these are productive in contributing to change implementation (Harris et al. 2007; Harris 2008). Findings from a study by Leithwood et al. (2007) suggest that both planful and spontaneous alignment patterns of distributed leadership practices have potential for positive short-term organizational change.[1] However, planful alignment is more likely to also contribute to long-term organizational productivity given that here the configuration of leadership tasks is a more institutionalized practice (cf. also Gronn 2000). By contrast, the opposite situation of misalignment in the distribution of leadership tasks and goal conflict is likely to result in an unproductive and damaging rejection of influence by others and competition between units. This is important knowledge when exerting leadership in the ongoing change processes with change after change after change, which we see in many public sector organizations. Studies in the literature on transformational leadership also highlight the importance of low goal conflict within the organization if successful outcomes of this leadership approach are to be achieved (e.g. Krogsgaard et al. 2014). This is crucial in a public sector setting with multiple stakeholders and high goal ambiguity. In

---

[1] Alignment entails within-organization agreement about which leadership functions or practices are best carried out by which source, at which organizational level, and according to which values and norms. The difference between planned and spontaneous alignment, respectively, refers to whether the distribution and delegation of leadership tasks have been given careful consideration by organization members (including both formal management and rank-and-file employees) and planned accordingly, or whether alignment is more spontaneous, where leadership tasks are taken care of through tacit and intuitive processes, eventually resulting in agreement.

sum, for transformational and distributed leadership to be complementary in bringing about public sector organizational changes, awareness of the aligned enactment of leadership responsibilities is thus vital.

11.6 Context of Change: Environmental–Structural Influences on Leadership of Change

Leadership activities must fit not only the process of change in which they are embedded but also the wider contextual characteristics of the organization, specifically the context of public sector organizations. Context refers to both the external and internal environment of the organization, which may create certain opportunities and constraints on leadership behavior (Boyne 2002; Kuipers et al. 2014; O'Toole and Meier 2014). In accordance with different governance paradigms (cf. Chapters 1 and 2), we analyze and discuss the influence of general characteristics of the public organizational context in exerting leadership in different change processes in order to achieve organizational goals.

11.6.1 The Bureaucratic Structure of Public Organizations and the Primacy of Politics

Public sector organizations are, first and foremost, characterized by being bureaucracies that are hierarchically structured and led by politicians who ultimately define goals and allocate resources (cf. the bureaucratic governance paradigm in Chapter 2). This implies a high degree of formalization and centralization of organizational activities. Moreover, external accountability to democratically elected political bodies is a key source of legitimacy (Rainey 2009). A bureaucratic organizational structure is, therefore, expected to lead to a top-down-oriented planned approach to change to ensure transparency in accountability relations and alignment of change implementation with organizational goals. However, Van der Voet (2014) shows that both planned and emergent change processes can be effective strategies when implementing change in public organization departments perceived as highly bureaucratic. One of the challenges and critiques of the applicability of more collective leadership approaches in a public sector context is, however, to make formal (political) leaders acknowledge the need for informal leaders, to delegate responsibility, and to preserve accountability and goal congruence when doing so (Currie and Lockett 2011; Woods et al. 2004). It is thus important to note that emergent change processes with (oftentimes) extensive employee participation and more collective leadership constellations by no means imply that hierarchical structures and vertical leadership are no longer required—rather, the opposite holds (Leithwood et al. 2007; Van der Voet et al. 2014).

In line with our discussion of the complementary nature of the two leadership approaches, recent studies have shown that bottom-up distributed leadership can exist alongside formal leadership enacted through, for instance, transformational or transactional leadership styles (Günzel-Jensen et al. 2018; Van der Voet et al. 2014). The latter is important in order to allocate resources, set the goals, take care of personnel management, and monitor achievements/give feedback when running the organization and implementing organizational changes. While collective leadership constellations create an organization in constant movement because many actors take part in organizational decision-making, traditional (political) leadership and bureaucratic organizational structures are part of the public sector organizational DNA and vital for their effectiveness in ensuring goal achievement in the public interest as well as democratic accountability.

11.6.2 Public Service Professionals

Another key characteristic of public sector organizations emphasized by the professional rule governance paradigm (cf. Chapter 2), which constitutes an important internal environment condition for the effectiveness of leadership (O'Toole and Meier 2014), is that these organizations are largely staffed by professionals (Mosher 1982). Professionals are individuals belonging to occupations with specialized, theoretical knowledge (usually obtained through higher education) and firm intra-occupational norms for acceptable behavior within their field of expertise (Andersen 2005; Freidson 2001; Roberts and Dietrich 1999). This implies that they have high autonomy in performing their discretionary tasks and mostly base their decisions on expertise and commitment to the public interest rather than relying on hierarchy and furthering personal economic gain.

The level of professionalization among employees in the organization and the esteem accorded to these professions affect how managers can and should lead in order to have an impact on organizational outcomes, including change objectives (O'Toole and Meier 2017, 18). The consensus of the public management literature is that professionalization requires collegial management styles and decentralization of decision-making to the lowest level possible. This speaks in favor of bottom-up and distributed leadership approaches in public sector organizations staffed with many professionals as they have the required expertise in complex tasks to reach desired outcomes in change processes. At the same time, however, professionalization also implies an escalation of the level of necessary management skills (O'Toole and Meier 2017, 18). The formal leaders of public service organizations such as hospitals, schools, daycare, police, and defense organizations with a highly professionalized staff are typically expected to have skills and education levels on a par with the professions they manage. This is likely to make change leadership and transformational leadership directed toward successful change implementation that is easier to exert as the managers will "speak the language of the professionals" and be able to communicate the changes in accordance with professional norms for acceptable behavior.

The importance of emphasizing the norms and values that are valued by a particular profession has recently been empirically demonstrated by Andersen and Jakobsen (2017). In a survey-experimental study among teachers in Denmark and the United States, the authors frame change-related communication in such a way that the professional values of teachers are emphasized over other considerations, such as the schools' budget or the preferences of parents. They find that framing organizational change according to the norms and values of the professional group can increase their support for organizational changes.

However, empirical evidence also tells a different story regarding the influence of having organizations staffed with professionals for successful change implementation. Multiple studies connect the prevalence of professionals in public service organizations with higher skepticism and resistance to implement changes (e.g. Berlin 1969; Kumar et al. 2007; Schilling et al. 2012). Employees generally resist changes because they expect them to have unwanted outcomes (Kuipers et al. 2014, 10), and the reasons for professionals' resistance to change may (at least) be threefold. First, they perceive the change to limit their professional autonomy and to be at odds with professional norms for appropriate behavior based on expertise. Second, the content and expected outcome of the change are not perceived to contribute to the public interest as it is perceived and defined by the professionals. Third, the change may represent a clash between traditional bureaucratic governance paradigms and the implementation of private business tools, such as those favored by the new public management governance paradigm (Vann 2004).

In a survey-based study of the implementation of two different performance-increasing policies in the change process of planned hospital mergers—an austerity type of reform aimed at cost containment and a strategic service improvement reform—Jakobsen et al. (2017) show that such reforms trigger very different reactions among professionals. When seeking to implement austerity reform policies rather than service-oriented change policies, political leaders and top hospital managers confront more "saboteurs"—i.e. professionals who are highly public service-motivated and efficacious and who participate in distributed leadership tasks while being very critical of the change at the same time. These results point to important implications of the different content of changes and illustrate the difficulty of leadership approaches with high employee participation when "unpopular" reforms are on the agenda. These results are in line with other change management studies identifying a gap between managers and health professionals as a central reason for implementation failures in healthcare (Denis et al. 1999; Kitchener 2002). The literature highlights distributed leadership as a beneficial leadership approach in overcoming such gaps and obstacles in organizational change implementations as it increases professionals' opportunities to become engaged stakeholders (Fitzgerald et al. 2013; McGivern et al. 2015).

11.6.3 Environmental Complexity and Complexity in Tasks

Finally, but no less important, public sector organizations are also characterized by a high degree of environmental complexity and task complexity (O'Toole and Meier 2014; Rainey 2009) in accordance with the new public governance paradigm (cf. Chapter 2). Regarding the external complexity, public organizations are very open systems, implying that many environmental forces influence their performance. Managers, as part of their responsibilities, need to monitor this and sometimes seek to tap its aspects for organizational purposes or for buffering (O'Toole and Meier 2017, 10). Complexity refers to the homogeneity/heterogeneity and concentration/dispersion of the interests of the many different public organization stakeholders that have an interest in organizational activities and in how they perform and develop. Besides, most public sector organizations are subject to influence from organizational networks, corporatist structures involving interest organizations, unions and NGOs, public–private partnerships, and more. This all adds to environmental complexity when seeking to implement organizational changes, which requires more managerial effort to be devoted to managing outwards.

Very few studies have specifically addressed the implications of the complexity of the public sector organizational environment for successful change implementation and performance in public organizations. Directly linking different patterns of change processes with the environmental complexity, Van der Voet et al.'s (2015) case study of a merger of three government departments shows that a high degree of environmental complexity forces public organizations to implement a planned, top-down approach to change. However, at the same time, the effectiveness of this approach is also limited by this complexity as typical change leadership (outlined in Section 11.2) needs to be supplemented with externally oriented leadership activities. A planned change process with top-down leadership may, on the one hand, be better equipped to resolve conflicts and take the interests of all stakeholders into account as this can be worked with in the very beginning of the change process. As such, a study by Currie et al. (2011) has shown that in the establishment and consolidation of public service reform characterized by a regulatory regime with high levels of external accountability, the opportunities for distributed leadership were limited. On the other hand, more pluralist and collective leadership approaches in emergent change processes may also provide important additions, given that the complexity implies absence of straightforward and consensually supported goals (Robertson and Seneviratne 1995). In a change process with more emergent characteristics, conflicts can thus be resolved on the go more easily, and due to the flexibility in this set-up, emergent change processes with bottom-up leadership are better suited to handle complexities in the environment.

Bottom-up leadership becomes even more important when internal task complexity is high. Public sector organizations' service delivery tasks are generally considered very complex to perform, both on the input and output side (Currie and Lockett 2011). Successful student learning in schools, citizen well-being in social care, and patient treatments in hospitals require collaboration between many actors, and important decisions for organizational outcomes are taken all the time at multiple levels of the organization. Many leadership tasks in such organizations will thus inevitably be carried out by non-formal leaders because the complexity and coordination efforts involved in performing the tasks demand it. This is also why it has been argued that a distributed leadership approach is particularly suitable in a public sector context (Currie and Lockett 2011; Harris 2008; Jakobsen et al. 2016). In fact, it has been claimed that the complexity of change implementation in public service tasks calls for distributed leadership, and thus, to a large extent, it already takes place in some form in all public sector organizations (Currie and Lockett 2011; Harris 2008). In line with the above-mentioned insights regarding the external complexity of public sector organizations, planned processes of change with an embedded "heroic" leadership may, however, also be a means to focus and prioritize on behalf of frontline employees and thereby try to reduce the task complexity. However, a strictly vertical approach may not suffice in conditions of environmental complexity, and more distributed leadership constellations are likely required to address this complexity.

11.7 Conclusion

Our analysis of theory and research about leadership in organizational change has shown that the role of leadership is strongly contingent on the process of organizational change. In processes of planned organizational change, we mostly observe leader-centric leadership behavior, whereas distributed leadership more often accompanies emergent processes of change. Yet in a public sector context with many ongoing changes and complex tasks, which require flexible and autonomous day-to-day leadership, while attention simultaneously needs to be paid to the bureaucratic structure of delegation and extensive accountability relations, we have argued that these two leadership approaches are often complementary rather than contradictory. Formal hierarchical leadership is necessary to formulate change goals and coordinate and distribute resources, whereas aligned distributed leadership makes the changes come alive and ensures ownership at all organizational levels. Although this chapter has discussed transformational and distributed leadership approaches as separated forms of leadership, the relationship overlaps, and combinations between these two types of leadership during organizational change are an important avenue for future research. How may transformational leadership behaviors of formal managers contribute to the distribution of leadership in public organizations? And to what extent is it possible for public managers to balance both leadership practices at the same time? From a theoretical point of view, the objective of transformational leadership is to make employees perform above and beyond the task at hand and contribute to collective rather than personal goals, and this may give rise to distributed leadership behavior. The work by Günzel-Jensen et al. (2018) provides initial evidence for such a conditional role of formal leadership. Future research should address this relationship in more detail. In addition, future research can also focus on the interaction effect of transformational and distributed leadership in order to examine the extent to which they jointly affect the implementation of organizational change.

Our discussion of transformational and distributed leadership of organizational change also reveals that these literatures have different emphases. Research on leadership in planned organizational change has mostly addressed the behavior of change leaders with the question: "What is leading change?" The result has largely been a relatively narrow focus on the visionary and charismatic behaviors associated with change leadership, while behaviors such as planning, structuring, controlling, rewarding, and institutionalizing change have been relatively overlooked. Rather than behavior, the literature on collective leadership approaches has mostly emphasized the social interactions and distribution of leadership and thus addresses the question: "Who is leading change?" However, it provides less insight into what these leadership agents are actually doing. Research on transformational and distributed change leadership that addresses both the "what" and "who" questions can meaningfully advance the literature. For instance, it could examine to what extent the transformational aspects of change leadership can be distributed across a larger group of individuals. Such research can uncover how a wide range of change leadership behaviors, from envisioning and planning to communicating and institutionalizing change, should be distributed between formal and informal leadership actors.

Given the prevalence of organizational change in the public sector, opportunities to study change leadership are widely available. We believe that large-scale, third-order reforms provide a particularly good setting. Such reforms—for instance, the nationwide implementation of education, healthcare, or social welfare policies—provide researchers with relatively "clean" comparisons within a large group of relatively homogeneous organizations. In such a setting, it is thus possible to study local variations in leadership, as well as its effects on outcome variables, such as employee support for change, client satisfaction, and organizational performance. Since the implementation of large-scale reforms often takes a long period of time, it also provides opportunities for longitudinal research. An example of such a study is the one by Winter and Skov (2018) about an ongoing school reform. This project longitudinally observes the leadership behaviors of school principals in a large number of Danish schools. In doing so, it can determine how variations in leadership behavior, both between different schools and within the same schools over time, affect teachers' support for change, the implementation of the reform's objectives, and ultimately, the performance of pupils. We welcome more such studies because they can explain the processes and mechanisms through which leadership contributes to the implementation of organizational change, as well as how different HRM practices, learning, and experiences in a change implementation process at one stage affect change implementation at later stages.

References

Andersen, L. B. 2005. *Offentligt ansattes strategier.* Aarhus, Denmark: Politica.

Andersen, S. C., and M. Jakobsen. 2017. "Policy Positions of Bureaucrats at the Front Lines: Are They Susceptible to Strategic Communication?" *Public Administration Review 77* (1): pp. 57–66.

Beer, M., and N. Nohria. 2000. *Breaking the Code of Change.* Boston, MA: Harvard Business School Press.

Bennett, N., C. Wise, P. A. Woods, and J. A. Harvey. 2003. "Distributed Leadership: A Review of Literature." Research paper, National College for School Leadership. http://oro.open.ac.uk/8534/1/bennett-distributed-leadership-full.pdf.

Berlin, I. N. 1969. "Resistance to Change in Mental Health Professionals." *American Journal of Orthopsychiatry 39* (1): pp. 109–15.

Bolden, R. 2011. "Distributed Leadership in Organizations: A Review of Theory and Research." *International Journal of Management Reviews 13* (3): pp. 251–69.

Boyne, G. A. 2002. "Public and Private Management: What's the Difference?" *Journal of Management Studies 39* (1): pp. 97–122.

Brunsson, N., and J. P. Olsen. 1993. *The Reforming Organization.* London: Routledge.

Buchanan, D. A., R. Addicott, L. Fitzgerald, E. Ferlie, and J. I. Baeza. 2007. "Nobody in Charge: Distributed Change Agency in Healthcare." *Human Relations 60* (7): pp. 1065–90.

By, R. T. 2005. "Organisational Change Management: A Critical Review." *Journal of Change Management 5* (4): pp. 369–80.

Currie, G., S. Grubnic, and R. Hodges. 2011. "Leadership in Public Services Networks: Antecedents, Process and Outcome." *Public Administration 89* (2): pp. 242–64.

Currie, G., and A. Lockett. 2011. "Distributing Leadership in Health and Social Care: Concertive, Conjoint or Collective?" *International Journal of Management Reviews 13* (3): pp. 286–300.

Den Hartog, D. N., J. J. Van Muijen, and P. L. Koopman. 1997. "Transactional Versus Transformational Leadership: An Analysis of the MLQ." *Journal of Occupational and Organizational Psychology 70* (1): pp. 19–34.

Denis, J.-L., L. Lamoth, and A. Langley. 1999. "The Struggle to Implement Teaching-Hospital Mergers." *Canadian Public Administration 42* (3): pp. 285–311.

Dunphy, D. C., and D. A. Stace. 1988. "Transformational and Coercive Strategies for Planned Organizational Change: Beyond the OD Model." *Organization Studies 9* (3): pp. 17–34.

Fernandez, S., and H. G. Rainey. 2006. "Managing Successful Organizational Change in the Public Sector." *Public Administration Review 66* (2): pp. 168–76.

Fitzgerald, L., E. Ferlie, G. McGivern, and D. Buchanan. 2013. "Distributed Leadership Patterns and Service Improvement: Evidence and Argument from English Healthcare." *The Leadership Quarterly 24* (1): pp. 227–39.

Freidson, E. 2001. *Professionalism: The Third Logic.* Chicago: University of Chicago Press.

Greenwood, R., and C. R. Hinings. 1996. "Understanding Radical Organizational Change: Bringing Together the Old and New Institutionalism." *The Academy of Management Review 21* (4): pp. 1022–54.

Gronn, P. 2000. "Distributed Properties: A New Architecture for Leadership." *Educational Management & Administration 28* (3): pp. 317–38.

Günzel-Jensen, F., A. K. Jain, and A. M. Kjeldsen. 2018. "Distributed Leadership in Health Care: The Role of Formal Leadership Styles and Organizational Efficacy." *Leadership 14* (1): pp. 110–33.

Hannan, M. T., and J. Freeman. 1984. "Structural Inertia and Organizational Change." *American Sociological Review 49* (2): pp. 149–64.

Harris, A. 2008. "Distributed Leadership: According to the Evidence." *Journal of Educational Administration 46* (2): pp. 172–88.

Harris, A., and C. Chapman. 2002. "Leadership in Schools Facing Challenging Circumstances." *Management in Education 16* (1): pp. 10–3.

Harris, A., K. Leithwood, C. Day, P. Sammons, and D. Hopkins. 2007. "Distributed Leadership and Organizational Change: Reviewing the Evidence." *Journal of Educational Change 8* (4): pp. 337–47.

Harris, A., and D. Muijs. 2004. *Improving Schools through Teacher Leadership*. London: McGraw-Hill Education.

Harris, A., and J. Spillane. 2008. "Distributed Leadership through the Looking Glass." *Management in Education 22* (1): pp. 31–4.

Herold, D. M., D. B. Fedor, S. Caldwell, and Y. Liu. 2008. "The Effects of Change and Transformational Leadership on Employees' Commitment to Change: A Multilevel Study." *Journal of Applied Psychology 93* (2): pp. 346–57.

Hood, C. 1991. "A Public Management for All Seasons?" *Public Administration 69* (1): pp. 3–19.

Jacobsen, C. B., and L. B. Andersen. 2015. "Is Leadership in the Eye of the Beholder? A Study of Intended and Perceived Leadership Practices and Organizational Performance." *Public Administration Review 75* (6): pp. 829–41.

Jakobsen, M. L. F., A. M. Kjeldsen, and T. Pallesen. 2016. "Distributed Leadership: A Hidden Organizational Resource or Cost?" Paper presented at the 2016 Public Management Research Conference (PMRC), organized by the Department of Political Science, Aarhus University, Aarhus, Denmark, June 22–24, 2016.

Jakobsen, M. L. F., A. M. Kjeldsen, and T. Pallesen. 2017. "Loyal Agents or Saboteurs? Performance-Increasing Policies and Public Service Motivation among Hospital Workers in Denmark." In *Comparative Public Management: Why National, Environmental, and Organizational Context Matters*, edited by K. J. Meier, A. Rutherford, and C. Avellaneda, pp. 130–53. Washington, DC: Georgetown University Press.

Jonasson, C., A. M. Kjeldsen, and M. S. Ovesen. 2018. "Dynamics of Distributed Leadership during a Hospital Merger." *Journal of Health Organization and Management 32* (5): pp. 691–707.

Kanter R. M., B. A. Stein, and T. D. Jick. 1992. *The Challenge of Organizational Change*. New York: The Free Press.

Kitchener, M. 2002. "Mobilizing the Logic of Managerialism in Professional Fields: The Case of Academic Health Centre Mergers." *Organization Studies 23* (3): pp. 391–420.

Kotter, J. P. 1996. *Leading Change*. Boston, MA: Harvard Business School Press.

Krogsgaard, J. A., P. Thomsen, and L. B. Andersen. 2014. "Only If We Agree? How Value Conflicts Moderate the Relationship between Transformational Leadership and Public Service Motivation." *International Journal of Public Administration 37* (12): pp. 895–907.

Kuipers, B. S., M. Higgs, W. Kickert, L. Tummers, J. Grandia, and J. Van der Voet. 2014. "The Management of Change in Public Organizations: A Literature Review." *Public Administration 92* (1): pp. 1–20.

Kumar, S., S. Kant, and T. L. Amburgey. 2007. "Public Agencies and Collaborative Management Approaches: Examining Resistance among Administrative Professionals." *Administration & Society 39* (5): pp. 569–610.

Leithwood, K., B. Mascall, T. Strauss, R. Sacks, N. Memon, and A. Yashkina. 2007. "Distributing Leadership to Make Schools Smarter: Taking the Ego out of the System." *Leadership and Policy in Schools 6* (1): pp. 37–67.

McGivern, G., G. Currie, E. Ferlie, L. Fitzgerald, and J. Waring. 2015. "Hybrid Manager–Professionals' Identity Work: The Maintenance and Hybridization of Medical Professionalism in Managerial Contexts." *Public Administration 93* (2): pp. 412–32.

Møller, J., A. Eggen, O. L. Fuglestad, G. Langfeldt, A.-M. Presthus, S. Skrøvset, E. Stjernstrøm, and G. Vedøy. 2005. "Successful School Leadership: The Norwegian Case." *Journal of Educational Administration 43* (6): pp. 584–94.

Mosher, F. C. 1982. *Democracy and the Public Service*. Oxford: Oxford University Press.

Nadler, D., and M. L. Tushman. 1990. "Beyond the Charismatic Leader: Leadership and Organizational Change." *California Management Review 32* (2): pp. 77–9.

Oreg, S., and Y. Berson. 2011. "Leadership and Employees' Reactions to Change: The Role of Leaders' Personal Attributes and Transformational Leadership Style." *Personnel Psychology 64* (3): pp. 627–59.

O'Toole, L. J., and K. J. Meier. 2014. "Public Management, Context, and Performance: In Quest of a More General Theory." *Journal of Public Administration Research and Theory 25* (1): pp. 237–56.

O'Toole, L. J., and K. J. Meier. 2017. "Introduction: Comparative Public Management: A Framework for Analysis." In *Comparative Public Management: Why National, Environmental, and Organizational Context Matters*, edited by K. J. Meier, A. Rutherford, and C. Avellaneda, pp. 1–26. Washington, DC: Georgetown University Press.

Plowman, D. A., L. T. Baker, T. E. Beck, M. Kulkarni, S. T. Solansky, and D. V. Travis. 2007. "Radical Change Accidentally: The Emergence and Amplification of Small Change." *Academy of Management Journal 50* (3): pp. 515–43.

Rainey, H. G. 2009. *Understanding and Managing Public Organizations*. 4th ed. San Francisco, CA: Jossey-Bass.

Roberts, J., and M. Dietrich. 1999. "Conceptualizing Professionalism: Why Economics Needs Sociology." *American Journal of Economics and Sociology 58* (4): pp. 977–98.

Robertson, P. J., and S. J. Seneviratne. 1995. "Outcomes of Planned Organizational Change in the Public Sector: A Meta-Analytic Comparison to the Private Sector." *Public Administration Review 55* (6): pp. 547–58.

Schilling, A., A. Werr, S. Gand, and J.-C. Sardas. 2012. "Understanding Professionals' Reactions to Strategic Change: The Role of Threatened Professional Identities." *The Service Industries Journal 32* (8): pp. 1229–45.

Spillane, J., R. Halverson, and J. Diamond. 2004. "Towards a Theory of Leadership Practice: A Distributed Perspective." *Journal of Curriculum Studies 36* (1): pp. 3–34.

Stewart, J., and P. Kringas. 2003. "Change Management–Strategy and Values in Six Agencies from the Australian Public Service." *Public Administration Review 63* (6): pp. 675–88.

Tian, M., M. Risku, and K. Collin. 2016. "A Meta-Analysis of Distributed Leadership from 2002 to 2013: Theory Development, Empirical Evidence and Future Research Focus." *Educational Management Administration & Leadership 44* (1): pp. 146–64.

Tsoukas, H., and R. Chia. 2002. "On Organizational Becoming: Rethinking Organizational Change." *Organization Science 13* (5): pp. 567–82.

Van de Walle, S. 2016. "Reforming Organizational Structures." In *Theory and Practice of Public Sector Reform*, edited by S. Van de Walle and S. Groeneveld, pp. 131–43. London: Routledge.

Van der Voet, J. 2014. "The Effectiveness and Specificity of Change Management in a Public Organization: Transformational Leadership and a Bureaucratic Organizational Structure." *European Management Journal 32* (3): pp. 373–82.

Van der Voet, J. 2016. "Change Leadership and Public Sector Organizational Change: Examining the Interactions of Transformational Leadership Style and Red Tape." *The American Review of Public Administration 46* (6): pp. 660–82.

Van der Voet, J., S. Groeneveld, and B. Kuipers. 2014. "Talking the Talk or Walking the Walk? The Leadership of Planned and Emergent Change in a Public Organization." *Journal of Change Management 14* (2): pp. 171–91.

Van der Voet, J., B. Kuipers, and S. Groeneveld. 2015. "Held Back and Pushed Forward: Leading Change in a Complex Public Sector Environment." *Journal of Organizational Change Management 28* (2): pp. 290–300.

Van der Voet, J., B. Kuipers, and S. Groeneveld. 2016. "Implementing Change in Public Organizations: The Relationship between Leadership and Affective Commitment to Change in a Public Sector Context." *Public Management Review 18* (6): pp. 842–65.

Van Knippenberg, D., and S. B. Sitkin. 2013. "A Critical Assessment of Charismatic–Transformational Leadership Research: Back to the Drawing Board?" *Academy of Management Annals 7* (1): pp. 1–60.

Vann, J. L. 2004. "Resistance to Change and the Language of Public Organizations: A Look at 'Clashing Grammars' in Large-Scale Information Technology Projects." *Public Organization Review 4* (1): pp. 47–73.

Weick, K. E., and R. E. Quinn. 1999. "Organizational Change and Development." *Annual Review of Psychology 50* (1): pp. 361–86.

White, L., G. Currie, and A. Lockett. 2014. "The Enactment of Plural Leadership in a Health and Social Care Network: The Influence of Institutional Context." *The Leadership Quarterly 25* (4): pp. 730–45.

Winter, S. and P. R. Skov. 2018. "The Effects of Change Management." Paper presented at the 2018 Public Management Research Conference (PMRC), organized by the National University of Singapore, Bukit Timah, Singapore, May 31–June 2, 2018.

Woods, P. A., N. Bennett, J. A. Harvey, and C. Wise. 2004. "Variabilities and Dualities in Distributed Leadership Findings from a Systematic Literature Review." *Educational Management Administration & Leadership 32* (4): pp. 339–57.

Yukl, G. 2002. *Leadership in Organisations*. Englewood Cliffs, NJ: Prentice Hall.

PART III

PUBLIC MANAGEMENT, JOB PERFORMANCE, AND EMPLOYEE OUTCOMES

12

Public Sector Employee Well-Being

Examining Its Determinants Using the JD–R and P–E Fit Models

Bram Steijn and David Giauque

12.1 Introduction

Within the organizational sciences, employee well-being is arguably one of the most frequently studied subjects (Boxall et al. 2016; Judge and Klinger 2007). Studying employee well-being is not only considered worthwhile from an employee perspective, it is also believed to be an important determinant of organizational performance (Alfes et al. 2012; Van de Voorde et al. 2012). In this respect, the happy–productive worker hypothesis, which states "happy employees exhibit higher levels of job-related performance behaviors than do unhappy employees" (Cropanzano and Wright 2001, 182), is widely acknowledged (Zelenski et al. 2008). One can thus argue that managing for public performance also implies managing public sector employee well-being.

Apart from being an important topic in the academic HRM literature, well-being is increasingly a concern for organizations. Public and private organizations are confronted with huge "well-being issues" with respect to their employees as, since the 1980s, organizations have implemented new management practices and tools to improve their external adaptation and their internal functioning. Furthermore, "doing more with less" has become the new managerial mantra, leading organizations to develop and implement detailed performance targets in order to achieve results in terms of efficiency and effectiveness. These managerial practices and tools shape the work environment and result in positive but also negative effects on employees. Numerous empirical studies demonstrate that stress, burnout, and hardship at work are clearly increasing (Demerouti et al. 2001; Hsieh 2012). Managing these "well-being issues and challenges" is of great importance, and this requires knowledge of how to deal with this issue, which is one of the objectives of this chapter.

In this chapter, we focus on employee well-being within the public sector, and especially on its main determinants, using two theoretical models: the job demands–resources (JD–R) model and the person–environment (P–E) fit model. These are not the only models that have been deployed in empirical studies but are often seen in the literature as the main theoretical frameworks for studying well-being issues in

Bram Steijn and David Giauque, *Public Sector Employee Well-Being: Examining Its Determinants Using the JD–R and P–E Fit Models* In: *Managing for Public Service Performance: How People and Values Make a Difference.* Edited by: Peter Leisink, Lotte B. Andersen, Gene A. Brewer, Christian B. Jacobsen, Eva Knies, and Wouter Vandenabeele, Oxford University Press (2021). © Bram Steijn and David Giauque. DOI: 10.1093/oso/9780192893420.003.0012 organizations. Further, these models are relevant here as they clarify how individual, job, and organizational characteristics have a (positive or negative) effect on employee well-being. Although these models are general and have not been specifically developed for the public sector, we will show that they can easily be applied in a public sector context. In this respect, as Chapter 1 argued, one has to give attention to public sector characteristics and deal with the question: "How does a public sector context affect employee well-being?" In the same vein, we will also shed light on the current discussion regarding well-being and public service motivation (PSM). As is also explained in Chapter 14 of this volume, PSM is an important topic in the public administration (PA) literature. In terms of well-being, some studies argue that PSM can be an individual resource that helps in fighting stress and other negative outcomes, while others have identified negative consequences of PSM.

Before continuing, we should make clear that this chapter has its limitations. First, the literature on employee well-being—even when only considering public administration literature—is vast, and we are not able to deal with every single study or even every aspect. It is also not our aim to produce a full systematic review. Our objective is more modest, namely to show the relevance of the JD–R and P–E fit frameworks when studying public sector employee well-being. Second, we will not discuss the relationship between well-being and performance. In this respect, we just note that the happy–productive worker hypothesis is contested (Cropanzano and Wright 2001) and that not all studies have found a relationship between well-being and performance (Taylor 2018). Moreover, as we will discuss in Section 12.2, employee well-being is a multidimensional concept (Grant et al. 2007). Noting two competing perspectives on the relationship between well-being and organizational performance, Van de Voorde et al. (2012) showed that for some dimensions of employee well-being, a "mutual gains" perspective holds (i.e. well-being is congruent with organizational performance), but for other dimensions, "conflicting outcomes" are visible (i.e. employee well-being is at odds with organizational performance). Although we do not deny the importance of this issue, we do not address it in this chapter (see Chapter 9). The final limitation has to do with possible differences between public and private sector employees with respect to aspects of employee well-being. Some studies have suggested that public sector employees score lower on several dimensions of well-being than private sector employees do (Goulet and Frank 2002; Lyons et al. 2006) and that this might be related to specific characteristics of public sector organizations (Rainey 2009). Although this is a relevant observation, we limit ourselves to investigating determinants of well-being *within* the public sector and do not make comparisons with other sectors.

The outline of the chapter is as follows. Section 12.2 sets the stage and outlines the three main ingredients that will be discussed: the concept of employee well-being plus the two theoretical frameworks (the JD–R and P–E fit models). This is followed by Section 12.3 that discusses studies using the JD–R model in a public sector context, followed by a similar discussion of studies using a P–E fit framework

(Section 12.4). Finally, in Section 12.5, we draw conclusions and propose some possible directions for future research.

12.2 Employee Well-Being, JD–R, and P–E fit

12.2.1 Employee Well-Being

Drawing on the work of Warr (1987), Grant et al. (2007, 52) define well-being as "the overall quality of an employee's experience and functioning at work." Various concepts are included within this overarching concept such as job satisfaction, organizational commitment, engagement, burnout, absence due to sickness, and organizational support. As such, the concept is multidimensional (Grant et al. 2007; Van de Voorde et al. 2012), and several authors have tried to identify distinct dimensions. Some have made a distinction between hedonic and eudaemonic well-being (Ryan and Deci 2001). Hedonic well-being equates well-being to the attainment of pleasure or the avoidance of pain (using concepts such as happiness and satisfaction). Eudaemonic well-being focuses on the importance of "living a complete life, or the realization of valued human potentials" (Ryan et al. 2008) using concepts such as mastery and personal growth, as well as engagement. Self-determination theory—which, with respect to well-being, stresses the importance of fulfillment in the areas of relatedness, competence, and autonomy—is one relevant theory in this respect (see also Chapter 4).

This distinction between hedonic and eudaemonic well-being relates to only one aspect of employee well-being, namely psychological well-being. Psychological well-being focuses on the subjective experiences of individuals, while Grant et al. (2007, 53) discern two other dimensions of employee well-being: physical and social well-being. Physical well-being is related to both objective and subjective aspects of bodily health and includes work-related illnesses, stress, and sick leave. Social well-being (or "relations") focuses on the interactions that occur between employees (Grant et al. 2007), including interaction with their supervisors or leaders. This dimension includes variables such as social support, leader–membership exchange (LMX), and trust.

In our description of existing public sector research, we will refer to these three psychological, physical, and social dimensions of well-being. The JD–R and P–E fit models look for factors related to employees' well-being, such as engagement, and adopt a positive view of work. Further, both models include the three well-being dimensions identified earlier (psychological, physical, and social). As such, these perspectives might, therefore, bring relevant results for practitioners who seek to develop a healthy organizational environment, rather than merely identifying aspects that are detrimental to employees' well-being. Another important point is whether there are aspects of well-being that are specific to public sector workers. An obvious candidate for such a variable is public service motivation (PSM), especially if one sees it as a eudaemonic concept. Enhancing PSM could contribute to a higher degree of self-realization, and in this way, it could contribute to enhanced employee well-being. We limit ourselves to discussing PSM as a concept that affects employee well-being within the JD–R and P–E fit frameworks. In other words, PSM will be discussed as a possible determinant of well-being and not as an aspect of it.

12.2.2 The JD–R Model

The focus in this chapter is on how individual and organizational determinants affect public sector employees' well-being. A popular model to explain how and why specific job and organizational characteristics affect employee well-being is the JD–R model developed by, among others, Bakker, Schaufeli, and Demerouti (Bakker and Demerouti 2007; Demerouti et al. 2001). This model is a heuristic model that specifies how employee well-being may be affected by two specific sets of working conditions:

> A central assumption in the JD-R model is that work characteristics may evoke two psychologically different processes. In the first process, demanding aspects of work (i.e., work overload and complaining customers) lead to constant psychological overtaxing and in the long run to exhaustion...In the second process proposed by the JD-R model, a lack of job resources precludes actual goal accomplishment, which causes failure and frustration.   (Bakker et al. 2008, 311)

In other words, job demands are factors that cost energy to deal with, such as high work pressure, complexity, and role ambiguity (Bakker 2015). Job resources are factors that help individuals to deal with these demands, such as support and autonomy (Bakker and Demerouti 2007). The JD–R theory proposes that job demands and job resources interact in shaping the work experiences and well-being of employees. In essence, job resources help in dealing with job demands. In principle, there is an unlimited number of variables that one could include under the headings of "demands" and "resources," and the choice depends on the specific research question or research context. This makes the model flexible (Bakker et al. 2014). Further, the model also includes personal resources (such as personality characteristics) alongside job resources.

The model describes two distinct pathways linking job demands and resources to employee well-being: a health impairment process and a motivational process (Bakker et al. 2014). Job demands are, if not matched by adequate resources, important predictors of health problems (such as burnout or repetitive strain injuries) because they deplete energy. Job resources, in contrast, are important determinants of motivation and engagement and contribute to the fulfillment of basic psychological, physical, and social needs (Bakker et al. 2014). More recently, the literature has made a further distinction between hindrance and challenging job demands, which can have different effects (Tadić et al. 2015). According to Tadić et al. (2015, 703), "challenge demands can trigger positive emotions and cognitions and increase work engagement and performance, whereas hindrance demands trigger negative emotions and cognitions and seem to undermine work engagement and performance."

12.2.3 The P–E Fit Model

Kristof-Brown et al. (2005) observe that the idea that there should be a "congruence" or "fit" between what individuals want and what they get from their work and/or organization has a long history in management science. The overarching concept that describes this has been called the "person–environment (P–E) fit" and is defined by Kristof-Brown et al. (2005, 281) as "the compatibility between an individual and [their] work environment that occurs when their characteristics are well matched." Several distinctions can be made within this overarching concept. First, a complementary fit (individuals add something that was missing in the environment) should be discerned from a supplementary fit (individuals and the environment have similar characteristics). Second, a distinction can be made between a demand–abilities fit (individual skills are met by environmental demands) and a needs–supplies fit (environmental supplies meet individual needs) (Edwards and Rothbard 1999). Finally, it is important to distinguish between four critical domains of fit: person–organization (P–O), person–job (P–J), person–group (P–G), and person–supervisor (P–S) (Kristof-Brown et al. 2005). This chapter focuses on the first two fit domains. Nevertheless, one should note that other fit domains, such as the P–G fit, have also been identified as important antecedents of job satisfaction and stress in a public sector context (Giauque et al. 2014). It is also relevant to note that in their study, Edwards and Billsberry (2010) showed that the P–E fit is a multidimensional concept and that different dimensions of the P–E fit separately influence work outcomes (commitment, job satisfaction, and intention to leave).

The P–E fit framework is—like the JD–R model—a well-accepted model within the organizational sciences, especially within organizational psychology. There, the attraction–selection–attrition (ASA) model (Schneider et al. 1995) is often used to explain why people feel attracted to organizations (e.g. because they believe they "fit" within the organization), why they are selected (because the organization believes they fit), and why they stay or leave (maybe because they are disappointed in the degree of fit). Implicitly, this model assumes that P–E fit is related to employee well-being, especially with respect to the attrition component. Put simply, fit leads to well-being. Indeed, when joining an organization, employees expect to find themselves in a healthy work climate, one that fits with their expectations. Thus, they will compare their work environment with their expectations (their values, a specific vision of missions, tasks, and so on), which will result in either a perceived fit or misfit. This perception could be based on different fit domains such as organization fit or job fit. Explicitly, many studies have linked P–E fit and well-being. For instance,

Verquer et al. (2003) conducted a meta-review that identified relationships between P–O fit and job satisfaction, organizational commitment, and turnover intention. Later studies have also related the P–O fit to engagement (Memon et al. 2014) and health (Merecz and Andysz 2012). Similar findings have also been reported concerning P–J fit and employee well-being (Boon et al. 2011; Park et al. 2011).

Perhaps surprisingly, the fit concept was seldom used in PA research until the early 2000s (Steijn 2008). Vigoda and Cohen (2003, 195) considered this unfortunate since "the environment of non-profit organizations is unique and highly distinguished from ordinary for-profit companies." However, as we will see, much has changed since then, with more recent PA studies having embraced the P–E fit perspective, especially with respect to the relevance of PSM as an important motivational lever within public organizations (Van Loon et al. 2017).

12.3 The JD–R Model and Public Sector Research

Although the JD–R model is one of the most significant models used in organizational sciences to explain well-being, it is not often referred to in the PA literature. An early 2020 literature search (using the keywords "job demands" and "job resources" plus "public sector" or "public administration") generated only twenty empirical studies within core PA journals (*JPART*, *Public Administration*, *Public Administration Review*, and *Public Management Review*) that have explicitly used the JD–R model between 2001–2019. Only four of these were published before 2015. However, many more articles dealing with public sector employees have been published outside the PA field, mostly in journals linked to organizational behavior (including the *Journal of Organizational Behavior* and the *International Journal of Stress Management*). We first give a brief overview of the main findings from the latter studies.

Many studies published outside the PA field have taken place in non-profit or public service organizations such as schools, home care organizations, and hospitals. A typical study is by Bakker et al. (2003) within the Dutch home care sector. This study explicitly tested the JD–R model and included seven job demands (workload, job content, problems with planning, physical demands, emotional demands, sexual harassment, and patient harassment) and six job resources (autonomy, social support, coaching by supervisor, possibilities for professional development, performance feedback, and financial rewards). Burnout was studied with respect to employee well-being. The study provided strong support for the relevance of the JD–R model in this public sector context. More specifically, it provided support for the health impairment pathway (when job demands are high) and the motivational pathway (when job resources are lacking), which results in "cynicism towards the job and reduced feelings of efficacy" (Bakker et al. 2003, 33). A later study by Xanthopoulou et al. (2007) in the same sector studied the buffering effect of job resources and found that these could indeed buffer the effect of job demands—especially with respect to the relationship between emotional demands/patient harassment and burnout. Another study by Bakker et al. (2005) tested the buffering effect of job resources in an institute for higher education. Again, the essence of the JD–R model was confirmed, and the results gave partial support for the hypothesis that a combination of high demands and low resources generates the highest levels of burnout. Similarly, a study of Spanish teachers by Lorente Prieto et al. (2008) illustrated the applicability of the JD–R model in public organizations. Unlike the previous studies, their study included not only burnout but also work engagement. It showed not only that work overload influenced burnout and engagement, but also that role conflict affected burnout and that role ambiguity had an effect on engagement. These effects of role conflict and role ambiguity are especially relevant from a public administration perspective.

A study by Van den Broeck et al. (2017) is significant because it tested the relevance of the JD–R model with respect to burnout and engagement across four different sectors (industry, healthcare, business services, and the public sector). It is one of the few studies that has applied the JD–R model to a core public sector, namely the civil service. The study looked at three job demands (workload, role conflict, and cognitive demands) and three job resources (social support, autonomy, and skill utilization). Interestingly, overall well-being (a combination of low burnout and high engagement) was highest in the healthcare sector. Burnout was highest in the public and the business services sectors. Work engagement was highest in the healthcare sector and at a lower level in the other sectors. An important finding is that their analysis found support for the JD–R model across all the sectors. As the authors stated, "each of the job demands and job resources were equally strongly related to burnout and work engagement across sectors" (Van den Broeck et al. 2017, 373). Notwithstanding the similar effect sizes, there were differences in the levels of job demands and job resources between sectors. In discussing the public sector, the authors noted that, on average, jobs seemed rather passive with both relatively low job demands and low job resources. The study therefore advised public sector managers to increase employees' challenges and invest in job resources (Van den Broeck et al. 2017, 374).

The studies discussed above did not explicitly study job demands and resources that are specific to public sector workers. For these, we need to turn to authors who have published in PA journals. In this respect, Hsieh (2012) studied emotional labor among public service workers and confirmed its potential effect on burnout. In line with the JD–R model, the study found that job resources (specifically job control, social support, and rewards) are able to mitigate this effect.

Recently, Borst et al. (2017) applied the JD–R framework in a public sector context (the Dutch local and central civil service). Based on their findings, they proposed three important adjustments to the original framework. First, they identified red tape as a potentially important hindrance demand on public sector employees. This fits with other studies that have identified red tape as a public sector-specific job demand (Giauque et al. 2013; Steijn and Van der Voet 2017). Second, building on a conceptual article by Bakker (2015), they identified PSM as an important personal resource that energizes public servants and thus, theoretically, should have a positive effect on engagement. This was confirmed in their study and resonates with other studies that have looked at PSM as a resource. However, Giauque et al. (2013) also studied PSM and found, in contrast to the hypothesis, that higher levels of PSM were related to higher levels of stress. This suggests that PSM does not always function as a resource and could have a "dark side" (see also Van Loon et al. 2015). Giauque et al. (2013, 73) suggested that employees with high PSM are also highly committed and "suffer from stress if they perceive an inability to reach their personal and organizational objectives due to organizational constraints or work environment burdens or pressures." Indeed, such a double-edged effect of PSM is also suggested by Borst et al. (2017) who found, alongside the positive effect on work engagement, that employees with higher PSM are also more inclined to turnover. Quratulain and Khan (2015) and Steijn and Van der Voet (2017) reported similar effects. These findings raise the question as to whether PSM also fuels feelings of incongruence between professionals' aspirations and their actual contributions to society (Quratulain and Khan 2015). This is an issue we will return to in Section 12.4 on the P–E fit.

Borst et al.'s (2017) third adjustment to the JD–R framework is that they make an explicit distinction between work-related job resources (teamwork, job content, and autonomy) and organization-related job resources (career development opportunities, supervisory support, and performance management). They argue that this distinction is important because "public servants are more motivated by work characteristics than by organization-related characteristics" (Borst et al. 2017, 5). Their findings supported this assertion, and they interpreted it as a sign that civil servants "become … most engaged by intrinsic factors including work-related resources" (Borst et al. 2017, 17). Interestingly, in their study, red tape has different relationships with work-related resources and with organizational-related resources. When red tape is high, work-related resources have a stronger effect on work engagement, but the effect of organizational-related resources is lower. Borst et al. (2017, 19) suggest that "it seems to be the case that organization-related resources in the public sector are automatically accompanied with more red tape which de facto lead to the evaporation of the positive effects of these resources on work engagement."

Overall, it can be concluded that the JD–R model is appropriate for explaining employee well-being in the public sector—although the number of studies that have done so for the core public sector (e.g. the civil service) is limited. In general, the model can be used to study the effects of public sector employees' job demands and job resources. In particular, the literature suggests that certain public sector demands (red tape) and resources (PSM) should be included in public sector research. That being said, further investigation is needed to assess and better distinguish the mechanisms and conditions that explain the contradictory effects of PSM identified in the literature: When is it a resource with positive effects, and when does it have unexpected negative effects (dark sides)? It should also be noted that JD–R studies have only addressed employees' psychological and physical well-being and not considered social well-being as an outcome variable. To date, JD–R studies often treat social well-being (e.g. supervisor or social support) as a resource and not as a dimension of well-being (Dunseath et al. 1995; Giauque et al. 2016; Johnson 1986).

12.4 The P–E fit Model and Public Sector Research

Before the early 2000s, few studies had adopted a P–E fit perspective within PA research. A notable exception is a study by Boxx et al. (1991) which showed that value congruence—"the fit between professed organizational values and the values deemed appropriate by employees" (Boxx et al. 1991, 195)—is an important predictor of satisfaction, commitment, and cohesion. As such, this early study showed a relationship between P–O fit (value congruence) and psychological well-being. More recently, many studies have taken a similar perspective and have used a P–O fit perspective to look at how individual needs (the values looked for by employees) are met by the organization.

Several studies have used the P–E fit perspective to study well-being. Indeed, numerous studies have found empirical evidence that this fit is positively associated with job attitudes (job satisfaction, subjective career success, and intention to remain) and job behaviors such as citizenship behavior (Christensen and Wright 2011; Kristof-Brown et al. 2005). Others have explicitly looked at employee well-being, with Vigoda-Gadot and Meiri (2008) demonstrating a relationship between new public management (NPM) values and employee well-being (e.g. satisfaction and commitment). Employees who were positive about their organization's core NPM values (responsiveness, transparency, innovativeness, and achievement) expressed greater job satisfaction and commitment. Liu et al. (2010), who used a more traditional way of measuring the P–O fit of public sector employees, also reported a positive effect of P–O fit on job satisfaction.

In using NPM values as espoused organizational values, Vigoda-Gadot and Meiri (2008) are among the few who have not used PSM as part of a public sector P–O fit perspective. Vandenabeele (2007, 552), in his development of an institutional theory of PSM, was one of the first to do so and stated: "In terms of PSM, this means that civil servants will only demonstrate public service behavior to the extent that their organization embraces public service values as a principle." Bright (2008) showed that P–O fit mediated the relationships between PSM and both job satisfaction and turnover intention. His study not only showed that value congruence (in terms of PSM and organizational values) is important for employee well-being but also that PSM and P–O fit are distinct and have separate effects. Gould-Williams et al. (2015) also looked at P–O fit as a mediator between PSM and several outcome variables, including work-related stress. Similar to Bright, they found that P–O fit acted as a mediator: PSM was positively related to P–O fit, and through P–O fit, it was negatively related to work-related stress. Similar findings are also reported by Kim (2012) who studied job satisfaction and commitment.

In a conceptual article, Ryu (2017) warned against equating PSM with the P–E fit framework. One of his arguments was that PSM studies only use a needs–fulfillment fit perspective and were thus unable to "explain why individuals with high PSM prefer working for a specific organization over other organizations" (Ryu 2017, 363). Although a valid observation, not all PSM researchers would probably agree with this assessment. Steijn (2008) introduced the concept of PSM fit to argue that the effect of PSM on outcome variables depends on employees being able "to use" their PSM. In support, he found a relationship between the degree of PSM fit and job satisfaction. This argument fits within the P–E fit framework and could also partly explain why people prefer one organization to another. Possibly, employees perceive a greater ability to put their PSM values into practice in one public organization than in another.

Accepting the concept of PSM fit also implies that there could be a misfit. Steijn (2008) suggested that the increase of NPM-like values within the public sector could increase this misfit if these values are at odds with the values held by the employees. This suggests that the effect of PSM on employee well-being is not always positive and could be negative under certain conditions. For instance, Van Loon et al. (2015) showed that the relationship between PSM and well-being is dependent on institutional logics. More specifically, the effect of PSM on well-being is related to the societal impact potential (SIP) through the job and organization type. According to their study, PSM is linked to higher burnout and lower job satisfaction in people-changing organizations when SIP is high. However, in people-processing organizations, it is a low SIP that leads to higher burnout and lower job satisfaction. In the first scenario, employees sacrifice themselves too much for society, while in the second, they are dissatisfied because they cannot contribute sufficiently. In other words, PSM can have a "dark side."

We referred to this "dark side" earlier when we noted that PSM could also fuel feelings of incongruence between professionals' aspirations and their actual contributions to society as observed by Quratulain and Khan (2015). They empirically concluded that "PSM exacerbates the adverse effects of red tape on negative employee attitudes and behaviors and that these effects are transmitted through the mechanism of resigned satisfaction" Quratulain and Khan (2015), 324). This view is supported by Steijn and Van der Voet (2017), who came to a similar conclusion about the relationship between PSM (or in their case, prosocial motivation) and red tape, noting that red tape acts as a hindrance stressor that thwarts the realization of prosocial aspirations. PSM's "dark side" is clearly a work in progress. Schott and Ritz (2018) identified only nine articles dealing with the unexpected negative consequences of PSM during the 1990–2016 period. They reported that PSM had been found to be related to stress, resigned satisfaction, lower physical well-being, involuntary or long-term absenteeism, and even to presentism. They also concluded that the empirical results were mixed and generally inconclusive. Schott and Ritz tried to explain the mechanisms through which such negative consequences occur. They argued that a complementary P–E misfit might lead to negative attitudes, thereby highlighting the importance of the P–E fit perspective when attempting to explain work outcomes. They invoked various theories (identity theory, psychological contract theory, and the ASA model) to explain how a P–E misfit has negative consequences, and "why highly public-service motivated individuals experience negative attitudes if they feel that their jobs do not allow them to contribute to society" (Schott and Ritz 2018, 33).

Overall, it seems fair to conclude that the P–E fit framework has earned its place within public sector research. As in traditional organizational studies, "fit" is able to explain employee well-being. The general view is that higher fit translates into increased employee well-being. Nevertheless, it should be noted that the number of PA studies that have studied employee well-being from this perspective is rather limited. In fact, only certain elements (job satisfaction, commitment, and work-related stress) have been studied in relation to well-being. There are virtually no PA studies addressing eudaemonic well-being (e.g. engagement) or more general aspects of health. Further, there are only a few studies on social well-being. Moreover, most studies have investigated only one dimension of P–E fit and mainly P–O fit. This is regrettable since some studies have shown that other fit dimensions are worth studying in relation to work outcomes (Edwards and Billsberry 2010; Giauque et al. 2013).

12.5 Conclusion

A number of conclusions can be drawn. First, well-being is an important topic for organizations and further research is required to fully understand its antecedents and consequences in a public sector context. In this respect, the two models most commonly deployed to investigate well-being (the JD–R and P–E fit models) give valuable insights, but so far, these models have not been sufficiently exploited in the PA literature. For example, only a limited number of employee well-being outcomes have been studied. Although some concepts (such as organizational commitment and job satisfaction) have been extensively studied, others need further investigation, including eudaemonic well-being concepts (such as engagement) and more "negative" concepts, such as burnout, resignation, and absenteeism. Referring to the three-way distinction made earlier between psychological, physical, and social well-being, it should also be noted that very few PA studies have addressed social well-being using either the JD–R or the P–E fit perspective.

Second, it would be useful to investigate differences in employees' well-being between sectors (public, private, and non-profit) and within subsectors of the public sector. The study by Van den Broeck et al. (2017) is an important starting point for this. However, their study included only a limited number of demands and resources, and it is not certain that their conclusion that the JD–R model is equally relevant for the various sectors will hold if other demands or resources are included. Indeed, some occupations, or jobs, could be more susceptible than others to emotional demands or job strains. For instance, the literature on street-level bureaucracies suggests that frontline workers have more difficult working conditions, which could lead to negative work outcomes (Brodkin 2012; Destler 2017). Further, as we have seen, red tape has already been identified as a significant hindrance demand that may well be specific to a public sector context. Further research is needed, especially with respect to issues as to whether recent public management reforms have increased red tape, which types of employees are most affected by it, and what resources employees have to deal with it. Further, the observation by Borst et al. (2017) that the positive effects of organizational resources are thwarted by red tape in a public sector context deserves further study. Although red tape appears to be a job demand that is particularly relevant for public administration studies, other potential demands also deserve further study. In this respect, role conflict and role ambiguity are relevant since public sector workers are potentially more prone to these phenomena. Although some studies have addressed emotional labor (Rayner and Espinoza 2015), the effect of emotional labor on well-being and the possible mitigating effect of job resources also warrant further study in a public sector context.

Third, PSM is clearly an important concept when studying well-being in a public sector context. It fits well within both the P–E fit perspective and the JD–R model. In terms of the former, employees with high PSM are attracted to public organizations as the values espoused by public organizations match their needs, and through a P–O fit mechanism, PSM enhances employee well-being. Nevertheless, further investigations are needed because, as Bright (2008) showed, P–O fit values are distinct from PSM values, and it would be valuable to test this "non-congruence" hypothesis. With respect to the JD–R model, PSM has been explicitly identified by Bakker (2015) as an important personal resource for public sector workers. Indeed, the PSM literature has extensively demonstrated that it may lead to positive outcomes. However, there is some empirical evidence that PSM is also related to negative outcomes when employees are confronted by certain organizational constraints (such as red tape). Currently, it is unclear whether this issue is specific to public organizations or also exists in private and non-profit organizations. In this respect, it is likely that recent public management reforms have influenced employees' well-being. Recent literature has reported that the frequency and impact of change influence employee behaviors, that organizational support and resources may enhance positive attitudes toward change, and that reforms are not always seen as negative by public employees (Akhtar et al. 2016; Giauque 2015; Greasley et al. 2009). These and other studies demonstrate the value of continuing the study on the links between reforms and well-being.

A final important avenue for further research concerns the relationship between the P–E fit perspective and the JD–R model. This topic arose in the discussion on the possible dark side of PSM. On the one hand, employees with high PSM are attracted to public organizations (which fits with the P–O fit perspective), but on the other, the JD–R model would suggest that specific demands (red tape) thwart the fulfillment of employees' PSM. Further, some resources (such as leader or social support) could also affect this relationship between demands and needs fulfillment. The question of how job demands and resources could affect the various fits seems an interesting subject for further study.

To conclude, this discussion suggests some relevant practical considerations. We have seen that there are many ways in which managers can positively influence employee well-being. The P–E fit perspective illustrates the importance of aligning the employees' and the organization's values (Gould-Williams et al. 2015) as this will have a positive effect on employee well-being. The JD–R model provided additional insight into the importance of balancing job demands and job resources. When it comes to well-being, other research has highlighted the importance of resources, such as trust (Alfes et al. 2012), perceived organizational support (Eisenberger et al. 1990), social support (Johnson 1986), work–life balance (Worrall and Cooper 2007), and public service values (Andersen et al. 2013). Also relevant is the observation by Van den Broeck et al. (2017) that many public sector jobs appear to be passive and would benefit from an increase in employees' challenges and an investment in job resources. Borst et al. (2017) concur by showing that increasing work resources (such as autonomy and social support) will be more effective in enhancing well-being than investing in organizational resources, albeit only when red tape is high. Thus, investing in organizational resources is worthwhile provided that managers are able to reduce red tape.

Well-being is also influenced by job and organizational characteristics (Van Loon et al. 2015). Consequently, practices and tools aimed at enhancing public employees' well-being need to be adapted to the specifics of the organization's main mission (people-changing or people-processing organizations) or to the specificities of the job (street-level or back-office jobs). Without doubt, practitioners can benefit from the considerable empirical evidence when addressing well-being and occupational health issues in their organization.

References

Akhtar, M. N., M. Bal, and L. Long. 2016. "Exit, Voice, Loyalty, and Neglect Reactions to Frequency of Change, and Impact of Change: A Sensemaking Perspective through the Lens of Psychological Contract." *Employee Relations* 38 (4): pp. 536–62.

Alfes, K., A. Shantz, and C. Truss. 2012. "The Link between Perceived HRM Practices, Performance and Well-Being: The Moderating Effect of Trust in the Employer." *Human Resource Management Journal* 22 (4): pp. 409–27.

Andersen, L. B., T. Beck Jørgensen, A. M. Kjeldsen, L. H. Pedersen, and K. Vrangbæk. 2013. "Public Values and Public Service Motivation: Conceptual and Empirical Relationships." *The American Review of Public Administration* 43 (3): pp. 292–311.

Bakker, A. B. 2015. "A Job Demands–Resources Approach to Public Service Motivation." *Public Administration Review* 75 (5): pp. 723–32.

Bakker, A. B., and E. Demerouti. 2007. "The Job Demands–Resources Model: State of the Art." *Journal of Managerial Psychology* 22 (3): pp. 309–28.

Bakker, A. B., E. Demerouti, and M. C. Euwema. 2005. "Job Resources Buffer the Impact of Job Demands on Burnout." *Journal of Occupational Health Psychology 10* (2): pp. 170–80.

Bakker, A. B., E. Demerouti, and A. I. Sanz-Vergel. 2014. "Burnout and Work Engagement: The JD–R Approach." *Annual Review of Organizational Psychology and Organizational Behavior 1* (1): pp. 389–411.

Bakker, A. B., E. Demerouti, T. W. Taris, W. B. Schaufeli, and P. J. Schreurs. 2003. "A Multigroup Analysis of the Job Demands–Resources Model in Four Home Care Organizations." *International Journal of Stress Management 10* (1): pp. 16–38.

Bakker, A. B., H. Van Emmerik, and P. Van Riet. 2008. "How Job Demands, Resources, and Burnout Predict Objective Performance: A Constructive Replication." *Anxiety, Stress and Coping 21* (3): pp. 309–24.

Boon, C., D. N. Den Hartog, P. Boselie, and J. Paauwe. 2011. "The Relationship between Perceptions of HR Practices and Employee Outcomes: Examining the Role of Person–Organisation and Person–Job Fit." *The International Journal of Human Resource Management 22* (1): pp. 138–62.

Borst, R. T., P. M. Kruyen, and C. J. Lako. 2017. "Exploring the Job Demands–Resources Model of Work Engagement in Government: Bringing in a Psychological Perspective." *Review of Public Personnel Administration 39* (3): pp. 372–97.

Boxall, P., J. P. Guthrie, and J. Paauwe. 2016. "Editorial Introduction: Progressing our Understanding of the Mediating Variables Linking HRM, Employee Well-Being and Organisational Performance." *Human Resource Management Journal 26* (2): pp. 103–11.

Boxx, W. R., R. Y. Odom, and M. G. Dunn. 1991. "Organizational Values and Value Congruency and Their Impact on Satisfaction, Commitment, and Cohesion: An Empirical Examination within the Public Sector." *Public Personnel Management 20* (2): pp. 195–205.

Bright, L. 2008. "Does Public Service Motivation Really Make a Difference on Job Satisfaction and Turnover Intentions of Public Employees?" *The American Review of Public Administration 38* (2): pp. 149–66.

Brodkin, E. Z. 2012. "Reflections on Street-Level Bureaucracy: Past, Present, and Future." *Public Administration Review 72* (6): pp. 940–9.

Christensen, R. K., and B. E. Wright. 2011. "The Effects of Public Service Motivation on Job Choice Decisions: Disentangling the Contributions of Person–Organization Fit and Person–Job Fit." *Journal of Public Administration Research and Theory 21* (4): pp. 723–43.

Cropanzano, R., and T. A. Wright. 2001. "When a 'Happy' Worker Is Really a 'Productive' Worker: A Review and Further Refinement of the Happy–Productive Worker Thesis." *Consulting Psychology Journal: Practice and Research 53* (3): pp. 182–99.

Demerouti, E., A. B. Bakker, F. Nachreiner, and W. B. Schaufeli. 2001. "The Job Demands–Resources Model of Burnout." *Journal of Applied Psychology 86* (3): pp. 499–512.

Destler, K. N. 2017. "A Matter of Trust: Street Level Bureaucrats, Organizational Climate and Performance Management Reform." *Journal of Public Administration Research and Theory 27* (3): pp. 517–34.

Dunseath, J., T. A. Beehr, and D. W. King. 1995. "Job Stress–Social Support Buffering Effects across Gender, Education and Occupational Groups in a Municipal Workforce." *Review of Public Personnel Administration 15* (1): pp. 60–83.

Edwards, J. A., and J. Billsberry. 2010. "Testing a Multidimensional Theory of Person–Environment Fit." *Journal of Managerial Issues 22* (4): pp. 476–93.

Edwards, J. R., and N. P. Rothbard. 1999. "Work and Family Stress and Well-Being: An Examination of Person–Environment Fit in the Work and Family Domains." *Organizational Behavior and Human Decision Processes 77* (2): pp. 85–129.

Eisenberger, R., P. Fasolo, and V. Davis-LaMastro. 1990. "Perceived Organizational Support and Employee Diligence, Commitment, and Innovation." *Journal of Applied Psychology 75* (1): pp. 51–9.

Giauque, D. 2015. "Attitudes toward Organizational Change among Public Middle Managers." *Public Personnel Management 44* (1): pp. 70–98.

Giauque, D., S. Anderfuhren-Biget, and F. Varone. 2013. "Stress Perception in Public Organisations: Expanding the Job Demands–Job Resources Model by Including Public Service Motivation." *Review of Public Personnel Administration 33* (1): pp. 58–83.

Giauque, D., S. Anderfuhren-Biget, and F. Varone. 2016. "Stress and Turnover Intents in International Organizations: Social Support and Work–Life Balance as Resources." *The International Journal of Human Resource Management 30* (5): pp. 879–901.

Giauque, D., F. Resenterra, and M. Siggen. 2014. "Antecedents of Job Satisfaction, Organizational Commitment and Stress in a Public Hospital: A P–E Fit Perspective." *Public Organization Review 14* (2): pp. 201–28.

Gould-Williams, J. S., A. M. S. Mostafa, and P. Bottomley. 2015. "Public Service Motivation and Employee Outcomes in the Egyptian Public Sector: Testing the Mediating Effect of Person–Organization Fit." *Journal of Public Administration Research and Theory 25* (2): pp. 597–622.

Goulet, L. R., and M. L. Frank. 2002. "Organizational Commitment across Three Sectors: Public, Non-Profit, and For-Profit." *Public Personnel Management 31* (2): pp. 201–10.

Grant, A. M., M. K. Christianson, and R. H. Price. 2007. "Happiness, Health, or Relationships? Managerial Practices and Employee Well-Being Tradeoffs." *The Academy of Management Perspectives 21* (3): pp. 51–63.

Greasley, K., P. Watson, and S. Patel. 2009. "The Impact of Organisational Change on Public Sector Employees Implementing the UK Government's 'Back to Work' Programme." *Employee Relations 31* (4): pp. 382–97.

Hsieh, C.-W. 2012. "Burnout among Public Service Workers: The Role of Emotional Labor Requirements and Job Resources." *Review of Public Personnel Administration 34* (4): pp. 379–402.

Johnson, J. V. 1986. "The Impact of Workplace Social Support, Job Demands and Work Control upon Cardiovascular Disease in Sweden." Unpublished doctoral dissertation. Johns Hopkins University, Baltimore, MD.

Judge, T. A., and R. Klinger. 2007. "Job Satisfaction: Subjective Well-Being at Work." In *The Science of Subjective Well-Being*, edited by M. Eid and R. J. Larsen, pp. 393–413. New York: Guilford Press.

Kim, S. 2012. "Does Person–Organization Fit Matter in the Public-Sector? Testing the Mediating Effect of Person-Organization Fit in the Relationship between Public Service Motivation and Work Attitudes." *Public Administration Review 72* (6): pp. 830–40.

Kristof-Brown, A. L., R. D. Zimmerman, and E. C. Johnson. 2005. "Consequences of Individuals' Fit at Work: A Meta-Analysis of Person-Job, Person–Organization, Person–Group, and Person–Supervisor Fit." *Personnel Psychology 58* (2): pp. 281–342.

Liu, B., J. Liu, and J. Hu. 2010. "Person–Organization Fit, Job Satisfaction, and Turnover Intention: An Empirical Study in the Chinese Public Sector." *Social Behavior and Personality: An International Journal 38* (5): pp. 615–25.

Lorente Prieto, L., M. Salanova Soria, I. Martínez Martínez, and W. Schaufeli. 2008. "Extension of the Job Demands–Resources Model in the Prediction of Burnout and Engagement among Teachers over Time." *Psicothema 20* (3): 354–60.

Lyons, S. T., L. E. Duxbury, and C. A. Higgins. 2006. "A Comparison of the Values and Commitment of Private Sector, Public Sector, and Parapublic Sector Employees." *Public Administration Review 66* (4): pp. 605–18.

Memon, M., R. Salleh., M. Baharom, and H. Harun. 2014. "Person–Organization Fit and Turnover Intention: The Mediating Role of Engagement." *Global Business and Management Research: An International Journal 6* (3): pp. 205–9.

Merecz, D., and A. Andysz. 2012. "Relationship between Person–Organization Fit and Objective and Subjective Health Status (Person–Organization Fit and Health)." *International Journal of Occupational Medicine and Environmental Health 25* (2): pp. 166–77.

Park, H. I., M. J. Monnot, A. C. Jacob, and S. H. Wagner. 2011. "Moderators of the Relationship between Person–Job Fit and Subjective Well-Being among Asian Employees." *International Journal of Stress Management 18* (1): pp. 67–87.

Quratulain, S., and A. K. Khan. 2015. "Red Tape, Resigned Satisfaction, Public Service Motivation, and Negative Employee Attitudes and Behaviors: Testing a Model of Moderated Mediation." *Review of Public Personnel Administration 35* (4): pp. 307–32.

Rainey, H. G. 2009. *Understanding and Managing Public Organizations.* 4th ed. San Francisco, CA: Jossey-Bass.

Rayner, J., and D. E. Espinoza. 2015. "Emotional Labour under Public Management Reform: An Exploratory Study of School Teachers in England." *The International Journal of Human Resource Management 27* (19): pp. 2254–74.

Ryan, R. M., and E. L. Deci. 2001. "On Happiness and Human Potentials: A Review of Research on Hedonic and Eudaimonic Well-Being." *Annual Review of Psychology 52* (1): pp. 141–66.

Ryan, R. M., V. Huta, and E. Deci. 2008. "Living Well: A Self-Determination Theory Perspective on Eudaimonia." *Journal of Happiness Studies 9* (1): pp. 139–70.

Ryu, G. 2017. "Rethinking Public Service Motivation from the Perspective of Person–Environment Fit: Complementary or Supplementary Relationship?" *Review of Public Personnel Administration 37* (3): pp. 351–68.

Schneider, B., H. W. Goldstein, and D. B. Smith. 1995. "The ASA Framework: An Update." *Personnel Psychology 48* (4): pp. 747–73.

Schott, C., and A. Ritz. 2018. "The Dark Sides of Public Service Motivation: A Multi-Level Theoretical Framework." *Perspectives on Public Management and Governance 1* (1): pp. 29–42.

Steijn, B. 2008. "Person–Environment Fit and Public Service Motivation." *International Public Management Journal 11* (1): pp. 13–27.

Steijn, B., and J. Van der Voet. 2017. "Relational Job Characteristics and Job Satisfaction of Public Sector Employees: When Prosocial Motivation and Red Tape Collide." *Public Administration 97* (1): 64–80.

Tadić, M., A. B. Bakker, and W. G. M. Oerlemans. 2015. "Challenge Versus Hindrance Job Demands and Well-Being: A Diary Study on the Moderating Role of Job Resources." *Journal of Occupational and Organizational Psychology 88* (4): pp. 702–25.

Taylor, J. 2018. "Working Extra Hours in the Australian Public Service: Organizational Drivers and Consequences." *Review of Public Personnel Administration 38* (2): pp. 193–217.

Vandenabeele, W. 2007. "Toward a Public Administration Theory of Public Service Motivation: An Institutional Approach." *Public Management Review 9* (4): pp. 545–56.

Van den Broeck, A., T. Vander Elst, E. Baillien, M. Sercu, M. Schouteden, H. De Witte, and L. Godderis. 2017. "Job Demands, Job Resources, Burnout, Work Engagement, and Their Relationships: An Analysis across Sectors." *Journal of Occupational and Environmental Medicine 59* (4): pp. 369–76.

Van de Voorde, K., J. Paauwe, and M. Van Veldhoven. 2012. "Employee Well-Being and the HRM–Organizational Performance Relationship: A Review of Quantitative Studies." *International Journal of Management Reviews 14* (4): pp. 391–407.

Van Loon, N. M., W. Vandenabeele, and P. Leisink. 2015. "On the Bright and Dark Side of Public Service Motivation: The Relationship between PSM and Employee Wellbeing." *Public Money & Management 35* (5): pp. 349–56.

Van Loon, N. M., W. Vandenabeele, and P. Leisink. 2017. "Clarifying the Relationship between Public Service Motivation and In-Role and Extra-Role Behaviors: The Relative Contributions of Person–Job and Person–Organization Fit." *The American Review of Public Administration 47* (6): pp. 699–713.

Verquer, M. L., T. A. Beehr, and S. H. Wagner. 2003. "A Meta-Analysis of Relations between Person–Organization Fit and Work Attitudes." *Journal of Vocational Behavior 63* (3): pp. 473–89.

Vigoda, E., and A. Cohen. 2003. "Work Congruence and Excellence in Human Resource Management: Empirical Evidence from the Israeli Nonprofit Sector." *Review of Public Personnel Administration 23* (3): pp. 192–216.

Vigoda-Gadot, E., and S. Meiri. 2008. "New Public Management Values and Person–Organization Fit: A Socio-Psychological Approach and Empirical Examination among Public Sector Personnel." *Public Administration 86* (1): pp. 111–31.

Warr, P. 1987. *Work, Unemployment, and Mental Health.* Oxford: Clarendon Press.

Worrall, L., and C. L. Cooper. 2007. "Managers' Work–Life Balance and Health: The Case of UK Managers." *European Journal of International Management 1* (1–2): pp. 129–45.

Xanthopoulou, D., A. B. Bakker, E. Demerouti, and W. B. Schaufeli. 2007. "The Role of Personal Resources in the Job Demands–Resources Model." *International Journal of Stress Management 14* (2): pp. 121–41.

Zelenski, J. M., S. A. Murphy, and D. A. Jenkins. 2008. "The Happy–Productive Worker Thesis Revisited." *Journal of Happiness Studies 9* (4): pp. 521–37.

13

Value Conflicts in Public Organizations

Implications and Remedies

Ulrich T. Jensen, Carina Schott, and Trui Steen

13.1 Introduction: Values and Value Conflicts

The public sector is characterized by a plurality of values. Elected officials seek to advance the interests of their constituencies, unions and interest groups represent their members' preferences, service users voice their individual demands and desires, and service professionals orient themselves toward the norms and ethics of their profession. Taking inventory, Beck Jørgensen and Bozeman (2007) identify no less than seventy-two different public values. This is important for two reasons.

First, a value is a "conception, explicit or implicit, distinctive of an individual or characteristic of a group, of the desirable which influences the selection from available modes, means, and ends of action" (Kluckhohn 1951, 395). In other words, values can be seen as informing and guiding behavior in public organizations. Values as drivers of behavior are also central in what March and Olsen (2011) call "the logic of appropriateness." From this perspective, individual behavior and decision-making are shaped by institutions, which are assumed to play a key role in defining appropriate norms and values (see also Chapter 4). Yet, at the same time, Rutgers and Steen (2016) point out that there is not always a direct causal relation between values and behavior: Some values will result in (immediate) action, and others will not. If an individual holds certain values as internalized standards for judgment and guidelines for action, we still cannot directly conclude from this what behavior that individual will show.

Second, different values can be conflicting. We define value conflicts as confrontations between two or more values that cannot be realized at the same time as they have conflicting implications for behavior. Stimulated by the rise of managerialism (Frederickson 2005), economic individualism (Bozeman 2007), and privatization (De Bruijn and Dicke 2006), public organizations and their employees are increasingly challenged to balance "classic" public values, such as integrity, neutrality, and legality. on the one hand, with values usually associated with the private sector, such as efficiency, innovation, and effectiveness, on the other (Schott et al. 2015). Values might conflict, not only when these classic public values stand in tension with more

Ulrich T. Jensen, Carina Schott, and Trui Steen, *Value Conflicts in Public Organizations: Implications and Remedies* In: *Managing for Public Service Performance: How People and Values Make a Difference.* Edited by: Peter Leisink, Lotte B. Andersen, Gene A. Brewer, Christian B. Jacobsen, Eva Knies, and Wouter Vandenabeele, Oxford University Press (2021).
© Ulrich T. Jensen, Carina Schott, and Trui Steen. DOI: 10.1093/oso/9780192893420.003.0013

economic values but also within these clusters of values where tensions can exist (Hood 1991). Working in the specific context of government therefore inevitably entails a need to engage in behavior and make decisions in the face of dilemmas (De Graaf et al. 2016). This highlights the need to understand: (1) how values—and value conflicts—influence the attitudes and performance of public service professionals in various contexts (O'Toole and Meier 2015); (2) how employees attempt to resolve and deal with tensions between conflicting values; and (3) how leaders of public organizations can support their employees in reaching this aim and ensure a shared cognition among all organizational members through organizational socialization tactics.

Value conflicts can arise at both the individual and organizational level. At an individual level, public service professionals can face competing values in interactions with others, including service users, citizens, co-producers, co-workers, or public managers.[1] For instance, they may face value conflicts between responding to client preferences and norms embedded in professional codes of conduct (e.g. see Jensen and Andersen 2015). Value conflicts resulting from interactions with others have also been researched in the literature on co-production. Co-production provides opportunities to advance a sense of community between service professionals and users since it brings the professional in close contact with the public, the latter not only as clients receiving services but as citizens who have an interest in public services and actively participate in their provision. This involves not only "accountability and responsibility on the part of the professions. It also calls for active participation and public concern on the part of citizens whom the professions serve" (Sullivan 2005, 5). However, since the interests of the individual and the collective do not always coincide—as shown, for instance, by Brandsen and Helderman (2012) in their study of co-production in the area of housing—collaboration with citizens might add to rather than resolve some of the value conflicts experienced by professionals.

Conflicting values can also manifest at the organizational level. Mission statements represent organizational prioritizations of desirable end-states to be achieved for the collective. In public contexts, organizational missions are often framed in terms of both "classic" public values and more economic values (Schott et al. 2015). While multiple values may all be legitimate end-states for the members of the organization to pursue, multiple values risk undermining the extent to which expressions of image-based words, such as in organizational visions, foster a shared representation of an ultimate goal for the collective (Carton et al. 2014). Value conflicts at an organizational level are closely related to the challenge of goal ambiguity, which can be considered a defining characteristic of public sector organizations (Rainey 2009). As noted by Pandey and Wright (2006), goal ambiguity is an inevitable outcome of policy conflict and complexity caused by the lack of traditional market information prevalent in the public sphere.

---

[1] In addition, individuals can experience intra-organizational value conflicts arising from conflicting roles or identities (e.g. Schott et al. 2015). However, this chapter focuses on value conflicts in the interactions with others.

In this chapter, we outline theoretical perspectives on value conflicts in public organizations. To do so, we review empirical studies from public administration and related fields to illustrate the implications of value conflicts for professionals' attitudes, behavior, and performance. Second, we draw on recent studies on identity theory, leadership, and organizational socialization to discuss how individuals and management can deal with value conflicts arising in public organizations. Before concluding with the key insights of existing research on value conflicts, we outline a series of important but unanswered questions about the implications and remedies of value conflicts in public organizations.

13.2 Implications of Value Conflicts

13.2.1 Implications for Employee Attitudes

The notion of conflicting values has been studied using a variety of labels and terminologies inside and outside of public administration research. Common to these perspectives is an interest in how the compatibility, congruence, match, or fit between the values of individual professionals and those of their surrounding environment influence their attitudes to their job, work, and organization more broadly. Subsumed under the umbrella concept of "person–environment fit" (Kristof-Brown et al. 2005; see Chapter 12 in this volume), an array of empirical studies have, for example, demonstrated the positive implications of a fit between the values held by individuals and those embraced and promoted by their organization, and the negative consequences of situations in which values are not aligned. In their study of Egyptian public sector employees, for example, Gould-Williams et al. (2015) found negative correlations between perceived value congruence and self-reported job stress and intentions to quit the job. Relatedly, Kim (2012) reported stronger organizational commitment and higher job satisfaction among Korean civil servants with high levels of value fit. These findings align well with observations outside public organization contexts, with meta-analyses in industrial and organizational psychology linking value congruence to lower intentions to quit, higher job satisfaction, and organizational commitment (Verquer et al. 2003). Central to these findings is the argument that individuals ascribe inherent importance to their work and to organizational outcomes when these fall within the realm of what the individuals perceive as desirable end-states.

The flipside of these findings and this argument is that individuals in situations of value conflict experience a disconnect between end-states promoted by their organization and end-states deemed desirable by the individuals themselves. Recent work on the "darker" sides of public service motivation offers illustrative examples of the implications of person–environment misfits. In these studies, it is argued that strong identification with public service values can become a source of frustration if the job or organization does not allow the individual service professional to pursue such values, for instance, by doing good for user groups or advancing a broader collective interest (Steen and Rutgers 2011; Van Loon et al. 2015). Schott and Ritz (2018) went a step further and tried to explain the underlying mechanism of this relationship by combining public service motivation research with insights from identity theory. Central to identity theory is the idea that people constantly try to verify who they are by engaging in behavior that is consistent with their identity standard (Burke and Stets 2009). However, despite extra efforts, if individuals who are highly public service-motivated are prevented from engaging in this type of behavior due to a person–environment misfit, they are likely to become over-engaged and experience negative feelings in the long term (Schott and Ritz 2018). Consistent with this line of reasoning, public service motivation—which is otherwise perceived as a motivational resource in public organizations—has been linked to higher stress, feelings of resignation, burnout, and indirectly to sickness absenteeism (Giauque et al. 2012; 2013; Gould-Williams et al. 2015; Jensen et al. 2019; Van Loon et al. 2015; see also Chapter 12).

It is true that the majority of existing evidence from public management research and related fields such as organizational psychology and management rests on cross-sectional observational studies vulnerable to endogeneity concerns. However, they appear to speak with a fairly unified voice: Individuals experiencing incompatibility between values held by the individual service professional and those promoted by the organization are more likely to report negative attitudes, such as feelings of stress and quit intentions, and are less likely to report positive attitudes toward their job and organization, such as satisfaction with one's job and commitment to one's organization. Before we explore how individuals and managers can attempt to reconcile value conflicts in order to promote positive attitudes among public sector personnel, we first turn to the implications of value conflicts for professional behavior and performance.

13.2.2 Implications for Professional Behavior and Performance

Professionals' behavior and decision-making directly influence citizens and society more broadly, and it is therefore critical to survey not only professionals' attitudes but also their actual behaviors and performance. Performance is one of the key concepts in the public management literature (Andersen et al. 2016; see Chapter 2). Very broadly defined, the concept of performance can be viewed as actual achievements of an organization relative to its intended achievements, such as the attainment of goals, values, and objectives (Jung 2011, 195). Because of the ambiguity surrounding the goals of many public organizations and the fact that there is no "common scale" for ranking the importance and legitimacy of different values (Van der Wal et al. 2011), the question of what it means to perform well in the public sector is difficult to answer in situations where values are conflicting.

Fortunately, values are not always conflicting. Oftentimes, public service professionals face multiple values that are complementary in terms of service outcomes. Innovative teaching methods, for example, stimulate both individual student learning and contribute to society in general. Unless elements of the new teaching methods violate the professional norms or principles of teaching, it seems straightforward that values of service quality, public interest, and innovation all foster the implementation of new and creative teaching methods. Yet professionals may also find themselves in situations of value conflict. When multiple values collide and no one value is more important or "legitimate" than other values, it is not immediately clear that one course of action is more appropriate than another.

Hence, if clear goals are absent and different values are clashing, it becomes hard to define what good performance actually means. In this section, we discuss studies on the behavior of public servants in situations of conflicting values and link them to the challenge of performing well in public sector organizations. An empirical cross-country survey among a specific group of employees—i.e. public sector executives in Europe—showed different priorities put forward when these public servants were presented with trade-offs such as a choice between quality and efficiency, equity and efficiency, or following rules and achieving results (Steen and Weske 2016). While the study revealed an overall tendency toward prioritizing hierarchical rather than market values, it also found large differences between respondents from different countries, suggesting that conceptions of what constitutes "good" performance depend on cultural norms and prescriptions. A preference for "traditional" public values was also found in an all-Dutch study among public managers (Van der Wal et al. 2008). In contrast to private sector managers, public sector managers consider "lawfulness" and "impartially" to be more important than "profitability" and "innovativeness." To our knowledge, no research addresses the question of whether similar value preferences can also be found among public servants without managing responsibilities.

Jensen and Andersen (2015) present one example of decision-making in the context of a social dilemma. Physicians can prescribe antibiotics whenever they will have the slightest chance of curing the patient of his or her illness. However, prescribing antibiotics also increases the likelihood of bacteria resistance, a state that eventually renders particular drugs ineffective for future treatment. Thus, responsiveness to the individual patient must be weighed against the public interest. The authors find that physicians who orient themselves strongly toward individual users prescribe more antibiotics while their public service-motivated peers prescribe fewer broad-spectrum antibiotics. This means that prosocial types of motivation (at least partly) determine which aspects of performance individual service professionals attempt to actualize.

In a study on the decision-making behavior of Dutch veterinary inspectors, Schott et al. (2018) draw on insights from identity theory and find that the concept of professional role identity—i.e. the way professionals view their professional role—is useful in order to uncover what drives public service professionals' decision-making in situations of conflicting values. Individuals who see safeguarding public health as a central aspect of their professional role were more likely to exclude any potential risk for public health than to make a decision that also included economic considerations. This means that identities which emerge out of the interaction with organizations and society also influence which aspects of performance public service professionals prioritize.

Following the line of research on person–organization fit referred to above, Jaspers and Steen's (2017) research on the co-production of public services focuses on professionals experiencing tensions between different values that they aspire to actualize, as well as the value (in)congruence between public professionals and citizens, the latter being both the users and co-producers of the public services delivered. Their research shows that professionals adjust their behavior when they experience conflicts between the values they pursue through the co-production initiative and the concerns of citizens/co-producers. For example, in a project aimed at de-isolating elderly persons, professionals saw effectiveness, reciprocity, and the creation of social capital as ingrained values to pursue. Yet professionals also experienced that citizens/co-producers valued their individual freedom highly, namely the choice of when, how, and how much to co-produce. In order to attain the engagement of the co-producers, the public servants sought strategies that took into account this individual freedom. At the same time, the professionals' willingness to bias in favor of co-producers' individual freedom is limited as they found values such as effectiveness and reciprocity to be more dominant and in need of guarding. Jaspers and Steen (2017) further find that the type of coping strategies applied by professionals to deal with these value tensions impact the extent to which public value is being (co-)created or destroyed, for example as they bias in favor of some values.

In line with previous notions that employees only respond to policies that fall within their "zone of existing values" (Paarlberg and Perry 2007), the results of these different studies indicate that public service professionals' decision-making and behavior, at least to some extent, are guided by values to which they ascribe personal importance when faced with conflicts or competition between multiple legitimate values. These values help identify which aspect of performance service professionals seek to actualize in their jobs.

13.3 Dealing with Value Conflicts in Organizations

Value conflicts are important for behaviors and decision-making as discussed above, and this begs the question: How can value conflicts in organizations be dealt with? Answers to this question necessitate a focus both on individual professionals who are trying to navigate and adapt to their organizational environments, and on the organizations in which public managers seek to ensure congruence between the values of individual professionals and those of their organization.

13.3.1 Individual Professionals Dealing with Value Conflicts

For individual service professionals, value conflicts can arise out of a mismatch between values ascribed inherent and personal importance and values deemed desirable by their surrounding environment (resulting in value conflict at a personal level). Professionals' values can conflict with values embedded in organizational mission statements and promoted by the management of the organization or with values promoted by other stakeholders (e.g. by citizens or users in co-production efforts). In situations of a mismatch between personal and organizational values, professionals will redirect their energy and work effort toward end-states they believe are the most desirable to achieve. This is apparent in research on public service motivation where individual providers of public services have been shown to pursue conceptions of what they believe it means to do good for other people and society (e.g. Andersen and Serritzlew 2012). However, if the meaning of "doing good" differs between professionals and management, there is little reason to expect that all employee inputs will be directed toward attainment of the organizational mission. In other words, motivated employees can be a double-edged sword (Gailmard 2010; Maesschalck et al. 2008; Steen and Rutgers 2011). In situations of conflicting values, public service professionals can be expected to redirect their effort and energy toward goals not necessarily embedded in the organizational mission (Jensen 2018). This can be negative for public organizations because dealing with value conflict by redirecting efforts can result in inconsistent treatment of similar cases and rule bending or even rule breaking. Alternatively, employees can also deal with value conflicts by reducing their levels of motivation. Giauque et al. (2012, 188) argue that when employees' expectations are incompatible with the working environment, they cope passively by reducing "their personal expectations in order to reach a new equilibrium in their employment relationship."

The impact of various types of coping strategies on the way public service professionals experience work-related tensions has been the focus of Schott et al.'s (2016) research on public professionalism. The authors found that employees who are primarily guided by organizational norms and who are able to integrate organizational and professional norms and values experience conflicting work forces as less stressful than individuals who are strongly oriented toward professional principles and individuals who combine but have not managed to integrate both types of work forces. This means that individuals who face conflicting values might benefit most from training and courses that stimulate the development of so-called organizing and connective capacities and the ability to be reflective (Noordegraaf 2016).

However, we know from identity theory that individuals possess many different identities, which together form an individual's self (Stets and Burke 2000). Next to having a professional and organizational identity, someone can, for example, be a friend, a parent, somebody's child, and/or a member of a team or organizational unit. This means that conflicts are not restricted to clashing organizational and professional logics but may also be caused by conflicting logics and values associated with other identities. Experiences of conflict can be solved by the principle of identity salience, which addresses which identity a person will play out in a situation when behavior associated with more than one identity may be appropriate (Stryker 1968). In a study on nurses, Piliavin et al. (2002) describe the case of reporting healthcare errors and the identity conflicts associated with this deed. From an occupational point of view, "reporting errors" is essential as this is closely related to a key value of nursing: integrity. As a team member, however, reporting misconduct is seen as something negative as it potentially jeopardizes relationships with co-workers. How will a nurse behave in such a situation where different internal values are conflicting? The idea of an identity salience offers a line of explanation. The relative levels of an individual's qualitative and quantitative commitment to different role identities determine which role identity is more salient, and consequently, more likely to be played out in situations of conflicting values (Stets and Burke 2000).

13.3.2 Leadership and Socialization as a Way to Deal with Value Conflicts in Organizations

Reconciling value conflicts is also a critical leadership task. Given that value conflicts risk imposing agency loss on public organizations, a central concern for public managers should be with questions of how dynamic professionals' values are and how such values can come to be more aligned with the values of the organization. In the leadership literature, several concepts focus on the importance of values. Ethical leadership, for example, focuses on leaders as role models and individuals who demonstrate normatively appropriate behaviors and treat others with consideration and respect (Hassan et al. 2014, 334). This concept does not specify, however, how values are conveyed in organizations nor how managers appeal to the emotions and beliefs of their employees. These dynamics are captured in theories of charismatic and transformational leadership (e.g. Day and Antonakis 2012; Hoffman et al. 2011; see also Chapter 5). Transformational leaders, it is argued, "can increase value congruence by articulating, sharing, and sustaining attention to a vision that emphasizes collectivist norms such as social responsibility, service, and altruism, and infuse day-to day work tasks with meaning and purpose, such as contributing to others and society" (Jensen 2018, 48–9). The assumptions of this argument are thus that: (1) service professionals' values are dynamic and can—at least to some extent—be altered over time; and (2) visions emphasizing social responsibility and service can stimulate or amplify some internalization process whereby individuals come to ascribe personal importance to organizational values.

Despite the appealing logic of the argument, few studies have been able to test it empirically. First, to assess whether service professionals' values change over time, researchers need repeated measures of the same individuals. Second, researchers ideally can identify exogenous variation in leadership to help isolate the effects of leadership behaviors on value congruence. In a recent study, Jensen et al. (2018) offer some evidence of the temporal dynamics of value congruence and the role of transformational leadership behaviors. Using data over a period of one year, the authors show that employees became more attracted to the mission of their organization when their manager was perceived to increase his or her use of transformational leadership behaviors. This finding was amplified in conjunction with managers' use of face-to-face dialogue as a tool for communicating the vision to organizational members.

Using experimental variation in leadership, the few existing studies offer more mixed evidence on the effect of transformational leadership behaviors. In an experiment with 194 students, Jung and Avolio (2000) found an indirect effect of a transformational leadership manipulation via increased value congruence on students' performance in a brainstorming exercise. However, in a more recent study on actual workplace tasks and public sector workers, Jensen (2018) found only partial support for the effectiveness of transformational leadership behaviors. In a field experimental leadership training program, service professionals of managers exposed to the transformational leadership condition reported higher value congruence as compared to service professionals of managers receiving no training, but only when service professionals initially had a vivid understanding of the prosocial impact of their work (Jensen 2018, 53–4). While transformational leadership behaviors thus seem to hold some potential for managers to reconcile potential value conflicts, more research is needed to disentangle the various managerial practices that might help public sector managers promote the values embedded in the organizational mission and their alignment with professionals' values and higher performance among public sector personnel.

In addition to public leadership studies, research on organizational socialization provides insights into how managers attempt to ensure a shared cognition among organizational members. Organizational socialization refers to "the process through which individuals acquire the knowledge, skills, attitudes, and behaviors required to adapt to their job and to the organization they work in" (Wanberg 2012, 17). For example, research by Van Kleef (2016) on inspectors working for food safety services shows that through consciously structuring the socialization processes of its employees, the management of the food safety services tries to influence inspectors' attitudes and behavior, especially when they are confronted with stressful situations and value dilemmas. Knowledge gained through training or information received from more experienced colleagues—for example, feedback and supervisory support—can stimulate both successful coping behavior as well as behavior that is seen as appropriate and consistent from an organizational point of view. Socialization research, however, also outlines limits to leaders' ability to socialize professionals in the organization. Next to formal or "institutionalized socialization" practices such as training programs, internships, or mentorships (Kaufman 1960; Oberfield 2014), informal socialization practices take place that "are spontaneous in nature and uncontrolled by the organization's management" (Van Kleef et al. 2019, 82), such as day-to-day contact with colleagues and work-floor experiences. Such informal socialization can even take place outside the organization, for instance, in contact with clients, creating the risk of employees being "captured" by their clients' interests (cf. Kaufman 1960) and acting against organizational interests in situations of value conflicts.

13.4 Unanswered Questions about Value Conflicts in Public Organizations

Our review of (empirical) studies on value conflicts, the implications of these conflicts for professionals' attitudes and performance, and studies related to the question of how individuals and organizations deal with value conflicts arising in public organizations has shown that important questions have been answered. However, our review also raises many new questions.

As mentioned in Section 13.1, a value is "a conception, explicit or implicit, distinctive of an individual or characteristic of a group, of the desirable which influences the selection from available modes, means, and ends of action" (Kluckhohn 1951, 395). It becomes clear from this definition that values are not necessarily explicit. Rather, people can hold and act in accordance with values without being fully conscious of them (Beck Jørgensen 2006). This adds an additional layer of complexity to the discussion of value conflicts, the implications hereof, and the question of how these conflicts can be resolved. For example, questions such as "are implicit value conflicts also associated with negative attitudes and experiences?" and "how can implicit conflicts be identified in the first place?" provide interesting avenues for future research.

Another interesting line of future research relates to the changeability of values. Panel research has shown that values seem to be fairly stable predispositions, which remain stable during a lifetime (e.g. Huesmann et al. 1984; Sears and Funk 1999). This raises the question of how much individuals' values can be expected to change in order to reach, for example, more compatibility between personal and organizational values.

We would also like to raise the question whether some degree of heterogeneity might be a good thing. Based on insights from the attraction–selection–attrition model (ASA) and research on diversity, Schott and Ritz (2018) argue that not only person–environment incongruence but also person–environment congruence can lead to negative outcomes, such as problems related to less critical attitudes and the phenomenon of "groupthink." Put differently, experiences of conflicting values may stimulate employees to uphold critical attitudes and to engage in a frequent dialogue, thereby increasing the possibility of detecting wrongs and initiating change. A critical note on the benefits of high levels of homogeneity and the idea of "fit" between personal and organizational values has also been offered by Van Loon et al. (2015). After finding that in certain organizations—i.e. organizations that offer the opportunity to become very involved with clients—highly motivated employees go over the edge of their abilities, the authors raise the question of whether something like an "overfit" exists.

Next to this, it can be questioned whether organizational values should always be leading as there is no guarantee that they prioritize a healthy and productive work environment. This opens up space for more normative discussions pertaining to the emergence and consequences of value misfits in public organizations. If one accepts that officials elected in fair and democratic elections hold the ultimate power to define what is desirable to achieve for a given collective, and that such values and objectives are loyally and accurately represented by the management of agencies and service organizations, misfits can be seen as a democratic problem. For empirical research, however, this does not mean that we should always expect value incongruence to result in negative attitudes and outcomes among the people who staff those organizations. The ethics of dissent highlighted in other venues of research (e.g. O'Leary 2005) are therefore one area that could help nuance our understanding of the emergence and consequences of value conflicts in public organizations.

13.5 Conclusion

Studying values, and value conflicts more specifically, stands at the core of public administration research. Research provides insights into the values that public service professionals appraise, which value conflicts they experience, and how they cope with such conflicts. Likewise, research discusses how public organizations deal with value tensions experienced by professionals and how, through leadership and socialization tactics, they seek to align professionals' behavior to organizational norms. Only to a lesser extent, however, does research lead to empirical understandings of the impact hereof on the individual, organizational, and societal level, and it is our hope that this chapter can help spur more research into these critical issues.

References

Andersen, L. B., A. Boesen, and L. H. Pedersen. 2016. "Performance in Public Organizations: Clarifying the Conceptual Space." *Public Administration Review* 76 (6): pp. 852–62.

Andersen, L. B., and S. Serritzlew. 2012. "Does Public Service Motivation Affect the Behavior of Professionals?" *International Journal of Public Administration* 35 (1): pp. 19–29.

Beck Jørgensen, T. 2006. "Public Values, Their Nature, Stability and Change: The Case of Denmark." *Public Administration Quarterly* 30 (3/4): pp. 365–98.

Beck Jørgensen, T., and B. Bozeman. 2007. "Public Values: An Inventory." *Administration & Society* 39 (3): pp. 354–81.

Bozeman, B. 2007. *Public Values and Public Interest: Counterbalancing Economic Individualism.* Washington, DC: Georgetown University Press.

Brandsen, T., and J.-K. Helderman. 2012. "The Trade-Off between Capital and Community: The Condition for Successful Co-Production in Housing." *International Journal of Voluntary and Nonprofit Organizations 23* (4): pp. 1139–55.

Burke, P. J., and J. E. Stets. 2009. *Identity Theory.* Oxford: Oxford University Press.

Carton, A. M., C. Murphy, and J. R. Clark. 2014. "A (Blurry) Vision of the Future: How Leader Rhetoric about Ultimate Goals Influences Performance." *Academy of Management Journal 57* (6): pp. 1544–70.

Day, D. V., and J. Antonakis. 2012. *The Nature of Leadership.* 2nd ed. Thousand Oaks, CA: Sage Publications.

De Bruijn, H., and W. Dicke. 2006. "Strategies for Safeguarding Public Values in Liberalized Utility Sectors." *American Review of Public Administration 84* (3): pp. 717–35.

De Graaf, G., L. Huberts, and R. Smulders. 2016. "Coping with Public Value Conflicts." *Administration & Society 48* (9): pp. 1101–27.

Frederickson, H. G. 2005. "Public Ethics and the New Managerialism: An Axiomatic Theory." In *Ethics in Public Management*, edited by H. G. Frederickson and R. K. Ghere, pp. 165–83. Armonk, NY: M.E. Sharpe.

Gailmard, S. 2010. "Politics, Principal–Agent Problems, and Public Service Motivation." *International Public Management Journal 13* (1): pp. 35–45.

Giauque, D., S. Anderfuhren-Biget, and F. Varone. 2013. "Stress Perception in Public Organizations: Expanding the Job Demands–Job Resources Model by Including Public Service Motivation." *Review of Public Personnel Administration 33* (1): pp. 58–83.

Giauque, D., A. Ritz, F. Varone, and S. Anderfuhren-Biget. 2012. "Resigned but Satisfied: The Negative Impact of Public Service Motivation and Red Tape on Work Satisfaction." *Public Administration 90* (1): pp. 175–93.

Gould-Williams, J. S., A. M. S. Mostafa, and P. Bottomley. 2015. "Public Service Motivation and Employee Outcomes in the Egyptian Public Sector: Testing the Mediating Effect of Person–Organization Fit." *Journal of Public Administration Research and Theory 25* (2): pp. 597–622.

Hassan, S., B. E. Wright, and G. Yukl. 2014. "Does Ethical Leadership Matter in Government? Effects on Organizational Commitment, Absenteeism, and Willingness to Report Ethical Problems." *Public Administration Review 74* (3): pp. 333–43.

Hoffman, B. J., B. H. Bynum, R. F. Piccolo, and A. W. Sutton. 2011. "Person–Organization Value Congruence: How Transformational Leaders Influence Work Group Effectiveness." *Academy of Management Journal 54* (4): pp. 779–96.

Hood, C. 1991. "A Public Management for All Seasons." *Public Administration 69* (1): pp. 3–19.

Huesmann, L. R., L. D. Eron, M. M. Lefkowitz, and L. O. Walder. 1984. "Stability of Aggression over Time and Generations." *Developmental Psychology 20* (6): pp. 1120–34.

Jaspers, S., and T. Steen. 2017. "Balancing out Dilemmas between Public and Private Values in the Social Care Sector: Is Coproduction the Way to Go?" Paper presented at the 2017 Public Management Research Conference, American University, Washington, DC, June 8–10, 2017.

Jensen, U. T. 2018. "Does Perceived Societal Impact Moderate the Effect of Transformational Leadership on Value Congruence? Evidence from a Field Experiment." *Public Administration Review 78* (1): pp. 48–57.

Jensen, U. T., and L. B. Andersen. 2015. "Public Service Motivation, User Orientation, and Prescription Behaviour: Doing Good for Society or for the Individual User?" *Public Administration 93* (3): pp. 753–68.

Jensen, U. T., L. B. Andersen, and A.-L. Holten. 2019. "Explaining a Dark Side: Public Service Motivation, Presenteeism, and Absenteeism." *Review of Public Personnel Administration 39* (4): pp. 487–510.

Jensen, U. T., D. P. Moynihan, and H. H. Salomonsen. 2018. "Communicating the Vision: How Face-to-Face Dialogue Facilitates Transformational Leadership." *Public Administration Review 78* (3): pp. 350–61.

Jung, C. S. 2011. "Organizational Goal Ambiguity and Performance." *International Public Management Journal 14* (2): pp. 193–217.

Jung, D. I., and B. J. Avolio. 2000. "Opening the Black Box: An Experimental Investigation of the Mediating Effects of Trust and Value Congruence on Transformational and Transactional Leadership." *Journal of Organizational Behavior 21* (8): pp. 949–64.

Kaufman, H. 1960. *The Forest Ranger: A Study in Administrative Behavior*. Washington, DC: Johns Hopkins University Press.

Kim, S. 2012. "Does Person–Organization Fit Matter in the Public Sector? Testing the Mediating Effect of Person–Organization Fit in the Relationship between Public Service Motivation and Work Attitudes." *Public Administration Review 72* (6): pp. 830–40.

Kluckhohn, C. 1951. "Values and Value-Orientation in the Theory of Action: An Exploration in Definition and Classification." In *Toward a General Theory of Action*, edited by T. Parsons and E. Shills, pp. 388–433. New York: Harper and Row.

Kristof-Brown, A. L., R. D. Zimmerman, and E. C. Johnson. 2005. "Consequences of Individual's Fit at Work: A Meta-Analysis of Person–Job, Person–Organization, Person–Group, and Person–Supervisor Fit." *Personnel Psychology 58* (2): pp. 281–342.

Maesschalck, J., Z. Van der Wal, and L. Huberts. 2008. "Public Service Motivation and Ethical Conduct." In *Motivation in Public Management: The Call of Public Service*, edited by J. L. Perry and A. Hondeghem, pp. 157–76. Oxford: Oxford University Press.

March, J. G., and J. P. Olsen. 2011. "The Logic of Appropriateness." In *The Oxford Handbook of Political Science*, edited by R. E. Goodin, pp. 478–97. New York: Oxford University Press.

Noordegraaf, M. 2016. "Reconfiguring Professional Work: Changing Forms of Professionalism in Public Services." *Administration & Society 48* (7): pp. 783–810.

Oberfield, Z. W. 2014. *Becoming Bureaucrats: Socialization at the Front Lines of Government Service*. Philadelphia, PA: University of Pennsylvania Press.

O'Leary, R. 2005. *The Ethics of Dissent: Managing Guerilla Government*. Washington, DC: CQ Press.

O'Toole, L. J., and K. J. Meier. 2015. "Public Management, Context, and Performance: In Quest of a More General Theory." *Journal of Public Administration Research and Theory* 25 (1): pp. 237–56.

Paarlberg, L. E., and J. L. Perry. 2007. "Values Management: Aligning Employee Values and Organizational Goals." *The American Review of Public Administration 37* (4): pp. 387–408.

Pandey, S. K., and B. E. Wright. 2006. "Connecting the Dots in Public Management: Political Environment, Organizational Goal Ambiguity, and the Public Manager's Role Ambiguity." *Journal of Public Administration Research and Theory 16* (4): pp. 511–32.

Piliavin, J. A., J. A. Grube, and P. L. Callero. 2002. "Role as Resource for Action in Public Service." *Journal of Social Issues 58* (3): pp. 469–85.

Rainey, H. G. 2009. *Understanding and Managing Public Organizations.* San Francisco, CA: John Wiley & Sons, Inc.

Rutgers, M., and T. Steen. 2016. "The Miss Marple Enigma: Public Service Motivation as the Opportunity and Will to Commit Public Value." Paper presented at the Public Value Consortium, Arizona State University, Phoenix, Arizona, January 7–8, 2016.

Schott, C., and A. Ritz. 2018. "The Dark Sides of Public Service Motivation: A Multi-Level Theoretical Framework." *Perspectives on Public Management and Governance 1* (1): pp. 29–42.

Schott, C., D. D. Van Kleef, and M. Noordegraaf. 2016. "Confused Professionals? Capacity to Cope with Pressures on Professional Work." *Public Management Review 18* (4): pp. 583–610.

Schott, C., D. D. Van Kleef, and T. Steen. 2015. "What Does It Mean and Imply to Be Public Service Motivated?" *The American Review of Public Administration 45* (6): pp. 689–707.

Schott, C., D. D. Van Kleef, and T. Steen. 2018. "The Combined Impact of Professional Role Identity and Public Service Motivation on Decision-Making in Dilemma Situations." *International Review of Administrative Sciences 84* (1): pp. 21–41.

Sears, D., and C. L. Funk. 1999. "Evidence of the Long-Term Persistence of Adults' Political Predispositions." *Journal of Politics 61* (1): pp. 1–28.

Steen, T., and M. Rutgers. 2011. "The Double-Edged Sword: Public Service Motivation, the Oath of Office and the Backlash of an Instrumental Approach." *Public Management Review 13* (3): pp. 343–61.

Steen, T., and U. Weske. 2016. "Understanding Elites: Values, Attitudes, Motivations and Role Perceptions of Top Civil Sector Executives in Europe." In *Public Administration Reforms in Europe: The View from the Top,* edited by G. Hammerschmid, S. Van de Walle, R. Andrews, and P. Bezes, pp. 26–38. Cheltenham: Edward Edgar.

Stets, J. E., and P. J. Burke. 2000. "Identity Theory and Social Identity Theory." *Social Psychology Quarterly 63* (3): pp. 224–37.

Stryker, S. 1968. "Identity Salience and Role Performance." *Journal of Marriage and the Family 30* (4): pp. 558–64.

Sullivan, W. M. 2005. *Work and Integrity: The Crisis and Promise of Professionalism in America.* San Francisco, CA: Jossey-Bass.

Van der Wal, Z., G. De Graaf, and K. Lasthuizen. 2008. "What's Valued Most? Similarities and Differences between the Organizational Values of the Public and Private Sector." *Public Administration 86* (2): pp. 465–82.

Van der Wal, Z., G. De Graaf, and A. Lawton. 2011. "Competing Values in Public Management: Introduction to the Symposium Issue." *Public Management Review 13* (3): pp. 331–41.

Van Kleef, D. D. 2016. "Changing the Nature of the Beast: How Organizational Socialization Contributes to the Development of the Organizational Role Identity of Dutch Veterinary Inspectors." Doctoral dissertation, Leiden University, Leiden, the Netherlands.

Van Kleef, D. D., T. Steen, and C. Schott. 2019. "Informal Socialization in Public Organizations: Exploring the Impact of Informal Socialization on Enforcement Behaviour of Dutch Veterinary Inspectors." *Public Administration 97* (1): pp. 81–96.

Van Loon, N. M., W. Vandenabeele, and P. Leisink. 2015. "On the Bright and Dark Side of Public Service Motivation: The Relationship between PSM and Employee Wellbeing." *Public Money & Management 35* (5): pp. 349–56.

Verquer, M. L., T. A. Beehr, and S. H. Wagner. 2003. "A Meta-Analysis of the Relations between Person-Organization Fit and Work Attitudes." *Journal of Vocational Behavior 63* (3): pp. 473–89.

Wanberg, C. R. 2012. "Facilitating Organizational Socialization: An Introduction." In *The Oxford Handbook of Organizational Socialization*, edited by C. R. Wanberg, pp. 17–21. New York: Oxford University Press.

14
Public Service Motivation and Individual Job Performance

Adrian Ritz, Wouter Vandenabeele, and Dominik Vogel

14.1 Introduction

At the center of government, in public administration, the individual and their contribution to service for society are at the heart of the "public performance engine." At this micro-level of the organization, it is important to understand employees' motivation and the fit of an employee and their job as these factors contribute to service performance as well as to employee outcomes such as satisfaction, citizenship behaviors, or organizational commitment (Sayed et al. 2015).

There are several practical reasons for the relevance of motivation and specifically public service motivation (PSM) in public service performance. First, with an average of around 20 percent of total employment in the Organisation for Economic Co-operation and Development (OECD) countries, public employment plays a substantial role in the economies around the globe. It is inconceivable that an unmotivated and unqualified public workforce would substantially contribute to effective government functions, such as firefighting, policing, air traffic control, the judicial system, or tax administration. Second, international reforms of public human resource management (HRM) show a move from career-based HR systems toward position-based HR systems, with the decentralization of certain HR practices (e.g. performance-related pay and flexible working time) and increasing performance monitoring (Brewer and Kellough 2016; Van der Meer et al. 2015). Thus, the expectations within the psychological contract between public employer and employee are shifting away from offering job security for individuals' loyalty toward offering employability for individuals' motivation and performance (see also Chapter 15). Third, the majority of government organizations reflect typical service organizations that are HR-intensive. The HR costs can easily climb to more than 50 percent of the total expenses of a public organization. Thus, knowing how to incentivize and manage individuals' motivation to increase employee performance is highly relevant for public managers. Fourth, increased individual job performance through PSM may provide benefits for the organization as a whole (Brewer 2008).

Adrian Ritz, Wouter Vandenabeele, and Dominik Vogel, *Public Service Motivation and Individual Job Performance* In: *Managing for Public Service Performance: How People and Values Make a Difference.* Edited by: Peter Leisink, Lotte B. Andersen, Gene A. Brewer, Christian B. Jacobsen, Eva Knies, and Wouter Vandenabeele, Oxford University Press (2021).

Also, the effectiveness of extrinsic incentives in a public sector context is highly contested (Miller and Whitford 2007; Perry et al. 2009). Finally, demographic change increases labor market competition and makes it more and more difficult for public organizations to retain high-performing individuals through monetary rewards alone. Therefore, public employers need to develop HR strategies that facilitate the careful recruitment, promotion, and retention of high-performing individuals not driven primarily by extrinsic motives. It is assumed that PSM is a major element in the motivational structure of such individuals (Perry and Wise 1990).

Therefore, this chapter discusses the role of public employees' motivation and its relationship to individual performance. Individual performance is related to organizational performance, but the strength of this relationship is unclear because many other variables arguably have an impact (Brewer 2010). More specifically, we look into the relationship between individual motivation and performance by focusing on PSM, drawing on a stream of research developed over the last three decades stressing the service orientation of public employees' identity. We discuss the relevance of the topic and explain the most important questions that need to be addressed. Section 14.4 provides an overview of the existing empirical evidence concerning the relationship between PSM and individual performance. Section 14.5 offers reflections on meta-science as a specific set of methodological strategies for future research on the relationship between PSM and job performance. Finally, Section 14.6 summarizes the findings of the literature review and proposes some future research avenues.

14.2   Open Questions on the PSM–Job Performance Link

In their seminal article, Perry and Wise (1990) claimed that PSM is positively related to individual performance. A synthesis over the past thirty years of PSM research showed that the majority of empirical studies report a positive relationship between those two variables (Ritz and Petrovsky 2014; Ritz et al. 2016). Thus, most research assumes that PSM is highly relevant to the performance of individuals. Nevertheless, there remain many open questions on the PSM–performance link. First, and of particular interest, is the clarification of *direct and indirect links* between PSM and individual performance. Against the backdrop of institutional theory, the fit between employee and environment can act as a mediator or moderator (Bright 2007; Vandenabeele 2007; Van Loon 2015). However, when looking at this relationship from the theory of motivation, a direct link between PSM and individuals' performance can also be assumed (Grant 2008). Thus, the PSM–performance link is *context-dependent* (Vandenabeele et al. 2018; Van Loon et al. 2013). In certain contexts (e.g. task environment characterized by public values and organizations with public ownership and mission), the relationship might be stronger than in other contexts (e.g. private sector work without public purpose).

Second, we need to know more about the *types of individual performance* outcomes to which PSM relates. The heterogeneity across studies regarding the conceptualizations of performance is immense. Individual performance is measured for the most part in terms of some sort of job performance (e.g. supervisor ratings of individuals' job performance, self-assessed performance, subjective willingness to exert effort, number of publications, or number of certain tasks fulfilled). However, to date, it has not been possible to accumulate knowledge that would facilitate a better understanding of which dimensions or types of individual performance (e.g. in-role and extra-role performance and performance directed toward individuals or society) are linked primarily to PSM and which are not (Vandenabeele et al. 2018). That said, we need at least to differentiate between *subjective and objective measures* of individual performance (Brewer 2006; Ritz and Petrovsky 2014). Against the backdrop of the first question, we also need to differentiate between *contextualized and decontextualized measures* of performance.

Third, do we actually know *how strong the effect of PSM* on performance is? It is relevant for future research to know more about the relevance of PSM in explaining individual performance. This allows further investigation of how much variance of individual performance is explained by PSM when compared to other types of motivation and correlates, such as self-determined motivation, commitment, prosocial motivation, and job satisfaction (Breaugh et al. 2017; Ritz et al. 2020; Schott et al. 2019).

In the following sections, we will answer these questions by theoretically reflecting upon the PSM–performance relationship and by analyzing thirty-eight empirical studies which deal with this relationship.

14.3 Theoretical Reflections on the Link between PSM and Individual Performance

From a theoretical perspective, the relationship between PSM and individual performance follows two major theoretical approaches: (1) motivation theories; and (2) institutional theory and person–environment fit theory (see Chapters 4 and 12). Both offer well-grounded propositions on the underlying processes.

Most motivation theories show that different incentives have a distinct impact on employee motivation and performance. Whereas intrinsic motivation is based on rewards such as the activity itself, the source of extrinsic motivation is external rewards (e.g. money or threats) (Cameron and Pierce 2002). From the perspective of self-determination theory, extrinsic motivation can be increased in work situations by offering external rewards, resulting in more positive attitudinal and behavioral outcomes (Deci and Ryan 1985). PSM can be understood as a eudaemonic form of certain outcome-directed and future-directed employee motives based on identified goals that act upon external rewards and result in increased autonomous work motivation to perform (Ritz 2009) and as intrinsic motivation to a lesser extent (Vandenabeele and Breaugh forthcoming). However, this does not mean that only

PSM can activate individuals' performance. Extrinsic, enjoyment-based intrinsic, and prosocial intrinsic motivations complement one another where the behavioral motivation of individuals in a particular situation is concerned (Andersen et al. 2018; Neumann and Ritz 2015).

The institutional context and the objective, as well as the perceived fit between characteristics, such as demands, abilities, needs, supplies, values, and goals of an individual and the work environment, influence the PSM and performance relationship by defining structures and rules through norm and value-shaping communication and expectations that interact with individuals' attitudes and job performance (Perry 2000; Perry and Vandenabeele 2008; Van Loon 2015; see also Chapter 4). The fit can exist at various levels (e.g. environment, organization, and job) and results from recruitment and selection, as well as from socialization and adaptation over time (Kjeldsen and Jacobsen 2013). Thus, theory suggests that the higher the fit between an individual's PSM and the institutional environment, the higher the individual performance resulting from that motivation.

Both lines of theory need to be considered when developing a general framework within which to analyze the relationship between PSM and individual performance. Many different variables come into play, and context seems to be important. We begin our reflection with the following function:

Individual performance = f(individual characteristics, environmental characteristics)

This function is a substantial improvement compared to earlier formulations such as that of Maier (1958), who included motivation and individual ability but ignored context. Nevertheless, in our function, PSM serves as only one of the individual characteristics, next to general personality (Barrick and Mount 1991), other forms of motivation, and more importantly, cognitive and other skills (Antonakis 2004; Wright et al. 1995). Similarly, "environmental characteristics" is also a catchphrase for multiple characteristics, which may include resources provided by the environment (Rainey and Steinbauer 1999) but also characteristics at various institutional levels such as job, co-worker, or leadership attributes (Kristof-Brown et al. 2005).

However, the advantage of analyzing performance by means of a function with a set of broad variables is that variables can be controlled for or kept constant (*ceteris paribus*). This enables direct effects to be distinguished from indirect effects, where the former refers to effects stemming from individual characteristics and the latter to environmental conditions or interaction effects between the individual and a given environment.

With regard to PSM, the *direct effects* influencing performance for the most part derive from the regulation of motivation, as conceived in self-determination theory (SDT). As opposed to earlier motivational theories, such as motivator–hygiene theory (Herzberg 1966), the typology of motivations developed in SDT states that motivation can be on a continuum rather than a dichotomy (such as intrinsic vs. extrinsic types of motivation). Despite the observation that there are dichotomies—such as the distinction between intrinsic motivation and extrinsic motivation, or more importantly in SDT, the distinction between controlled or autonomous motivation— motivation is situated on a continuum depending on the degree present (Deci and Ryan 2004). The continuum ranges from amotivation (not being motivated to self-regulate one's behavior), through external regulation (obtaining a reward or avoiding a punishment), introjection (for reasons of guilt or honor), identification (regulation because it is an important element of one's identity), and integration (multiple identities which are aligned) to intrinsic motivation (doing something because you enjoy it). The stronger a motivation is internalized, the more it belongs to the core of oneself, with intrinsic motivation being the prime example of fully internalized motivation. This, in turn, influences outcomes in terms of strength and duration of the effects, for example, in terms of performance (Gagné and Deci 2005). Given that PSM is mostly a type of autonomous motivation—identified and to a lesser extent intrinsic (Vandenabeele and Breaugh forthcoming)—the outcomes are expected to be relatively long-lasting and stronger. However, in instances in which PSM is regulated along controlled lines—e.g. in terms of social desirability (Kim and Kim 2016)—the effect is expected to be less persistent and weaker.

Given our function stated earlier, these effects will largely depend on the environment, which will mitigate or strengthen the outcome of PSM on performance as the direct effects will be observed in a pure form only when all other factors are controlled for. Therefore, it is important to address the impact of the environment on this relationship. With regard to the *indirect effects* of PSM on performance, it is mainly institutional theory and person–environment fit theory that inform theoretical reflection on the relationship between PSM and performance.

With institutions being a "formal or informal, structural, societal or political phenomenon that transcends the individual level, that is based on more or less common values, has a certain degree of stability and influences behavior" (Peters 2000, 18), institutional theory comprises a broad array of possible guises, either at micro, meso, or macro levels of structured interactions. Micro-level institutions have a limited number of members who have substantial direct interaction to create an institutional identity, whereas meso- and macro-level institutions have less direct interaction (Vandenabeele et al. 2014). What they have in common is that they have a certain logic of appropriateness of behavior that makes sense within the boundaries of a given institution, making this behavior more likely to occur in that particular setting. According to Perry and Vandenabeele (2008), in an institutional approach to PSM, identity is an important variable. What researchers measure as PSM (Giauque et al. 2011; Kim et al. 2013; Perry 1996; Vandenabeele 2008) is mostly a set of self-descriptive statements which refer to an individual digestion of societal and public values. These provide a partial answer to the question, "Who am I?," making them very similar to what actually constitutes an identity—a generalized institutional identity that is based on public service values. In an institutional environment that emphasizes and rewards the values upon which this identity is grounded, these values and the associated identity will be the driving force behind performance.

This insight meshes well with findings based on person–environment fit theory (Kristof-Brown et al. 2005), which states that fit between the individual and their environment fosters motivation in this environment. The observation that there are various levels at which fit occurs only strengthens its ties with institutional theory, since a job, a set of structural relationships within a team or with a supervisor, or an organization as a whole—which represent the most commonly found types of person–environment fit—all represent different types of institutions. In particular, the (supplementary) fit based on the congruence of goals or values matches with the institutional perspective. The complementary fit perspective, in which an environment supplies what is needed by the individual or when an individual provides abilities demanded by the environment, matches less with this perspective (individual abilities do not refer to values). Only insofar as an identity provides what is needed by an organization (e.g. that it provides a pool of anticipatory members who already have a matching identity, and the institution does not, therefore, need to provide institutional training, such as a school hiring teachers) is a needs–supplies perspective useful for explaining the relationship between PSM and individual performance.

Analyzing the relationship described above from an institutional perspective means that what performance is also depends on the institutional context. Although there are general conceptions of what performance entails, be it role-based performance (in-role vs. extra-role performance), the value-component of performance is never far away. As mentioned earlier, Van Loon (2016) demonstrated that various types of performance are differently related to PSM depending on the type of organization. After all, the logic of appropriateness determines what is appropriate as performance and what is not. Teachers helping children with personal and non-education-related issues may or may not be considered as performance depending on what is institutionally appropriate. To the extent that performance is focused on providing public service and to the extent that this is apparent from how performance is conceptualized, the link between PSM and performance will be stronger.

For the purposes of this chapter, we will translate our performance function to make it case-specific in terms of PSM. Therefore,

Individual performance = f(individual characteristics, environmental characteristics)

would become

Individual public service performance = f(PSM, institutional characteristics)

In this function, the nature of the institution provides the context in which the process is enacted. Performance is contextualized to what is appropriate for a (specific) institution based on public service values. Similarly, PSM is a contextualized individual characteristic in two ways. First, it refers to the identity that is based on general values of public service. Next to this, it may possibly be an idiosyncratic operationalization of a general identity (Van Loon et al. 2013), distinguishing, for example, between the PSM of teachers versus policemen versus nurses or civil servants. All of these categories of public employees provide public service, but they have their own conception of what this actually entails. Depending on the degree of internalization of this PSM or the degree to which it is an autonomous part of their self-conception, there will or will not be a link with performance. Apart from the direct effect, the interaction with the institution, and the key values of the institution, the effect will be enhanced or decreased.

14.4   Empirical Evidence

In the next step, we review the empirical research on the relationship between PSM and individual performance to assess what is already known about the direct or indirect nature of the effect, the type of performance that is affected by PSM, and how strong the effect is. In doing so, we extend previous reviews by Ritz et al. (2016) as well as Ritz and Petrovsky (2014) and present an encompassing and systematic review of all relevant studies investigating the relationship, published from 1990 to 2017. We included thirty-eight studies on the effect of PSM on individual performance. The reviewed studies are listed in Table A14.1 (see online Appendix[1]). Table A14.1 also details what kind of performance the studies used, how they measured it, if a direct and/or indirect effect of PSM on performance was identified, and how pronounced the effect is.

14.4.1   Direct or Indirect Effect

In their 2016 review, Ritz et al. assessed twenty-six studies researching the relationship between PSM and individual performance. They concluded that only fifteen of the studies reviewed found a positive direct relationship, whereas eleven studies found mixed or no associations (Ritz et al. 2016). If we look at the overview in Table A14.1 (see online Appendix), we can draw a more positive conclusion. Of the thirty-eight reviewed studies, twenty-three find supporting evidence for a direct effect, nine find mixed effects, four studies did not find a significant effect, and no study reports a significant negative relationship. In the studies that find mixed evidence, either only a subset of the PSM dimensions is positively related to individual performance (Cheng 2015; Palma et al. 2017; Vandenabeele 2009) or PSM affects only some performance indicators (Alonso and Lewis 2001; Van Loon 2016). We nevertheless conclude that the empirical foundation for a direct effect of PSM on individual performance is convincing.

Furthermore, we are interested in establishing whether there are additional indirect effects or if direct effects even vanish if indirect effects are analyzed. Unfortunately,

---

[1] The online appendix is available at http://www.oup.co.uk/companion/managingforpublicservice.

a significant portion of the studies did not test for additional indirect effects. Nevertheless, eighteen studies did so, providing us with some insights on possible moderators and mediators.

First, we do not find evidence that a direct effect of PSM on individual performance disappears if studies test for mediating or moderating effects. The studies also testing indirect effects do not report more insignificant direct effects than the studies that test only for direct effects.

The most frequently tested indirect effect of PSM on individual performance is a moderating effect of transformational leadership. Four studies investigated whether a transformational leadership style of the supervisor strengthens the effect of PSM on individual performance. However, the results are inconclusive. Park and Rainey (2008) confirm that the effect of PSM on performance increases when employees have a transformational leader. Bellé (2014) confirms this in a field experiment. Caillier (2014), however, does not find a significant moderation effect in his study that is based on a convenience sample. In an even more contradictory finding, Bottomley et al. (2016) indicate that PSM reduces the positive effect of transformational leadership on organizational citizenship behavior (OCB).

Another common assumption in favor of an indirect effect of PSM on individual performance is the fit an employee perceives between themselves and their organization (person–organization fit, P–O fit) or their job (person–job fit, P–J fit). It is assumed that PSM has a stronger effect if employees see a fit with their organization and job (moderating effect), that a high level of PSM leads to a better fit with the organization and job, and that a better fit increases individual performance (mediation effect). As with transformational leadership, the empirical evidence is mixed. The two studies (Koumenta 2015; Leisink and Steijn 2009) considering P–O fit as a moderator of the PSM–performance relationship find evidence in favor of the effect. Meanwhile, the mediation analyses in four additional studies reveal mixed evidence. While Gould-Williams et al. (2015) find support for a partial mediation of P–O fit on OCB, Bright (2007), Jin et al. (2018), and Van Loon et al. (2017) find no evidence for a mediation effect of P–O fit on individual performance, extra-role performance, or OCB. However, Van Loon et al. (2017) find a mediating effect of P–J fit on extra-role performance. Two additional articles survey a related indirect effect. They assume that PSM increases organizational commitment, which, in turn, increases individual performance. Again, the evidence for such an indirect effect is mixed. Vandenabeele (2009) finds such an effect, but Jin et al. (2018) cannot confirm it.

In addition to these four indirect effects (transformational leadership, P–O fit, P–J fit, and organizational commitment), we found eight studies investigating additional indirect effects. However, each effect is investigated only once. The results are displayed in Table A14.1.

In summary, we conclude that while the evidence for a direct effect of PSM on individual performance is convincing, we do not see any clear evidence of indirect effects. None of the potential moderators or mediators were found to have an effect in multiple studies without being questioned by other studies.

14.4.2   Type of Performance

Most of the studies reviewed do not further specify what kind of performance they are interested in and leave it to the participants or their supervisors to define performance. There are, however, some exceptions. Park and Rainey (2007; 2008), for example, used the US Merit Principles Survey, which asks participants for a self-assessment of their productivity and quality of work. Quality was also a focus of the study by Levitats and Vigoda-Gadot (2017), who assessed performance using the SERVQUAL instrument. Van Loon (2016) explicitly tested whether PSM affects different types of performance differently. Assessing four types of performance (output, service outcome, responsiveness, and democratic outcome), she found that PSM positively affects all four performance types for "people-changing" organizations but only service outcome and democratic outcome in the case of "people-processing" organizations. This indicates that the effects of PSM depend on the type of performance analyzed and the institutional context. Furthermore, two experimental studies used specific aspects of performance to assess the direct effect of PSM on performance. In a laboratory experiment, Resh et al. (2018) used persistence as their performance measure of interest. They found that participants with high self-sacrifices are more persistent at a voluntarily repeated reaction time task than others. Pedersen (2015) found that PSM increases students' willingness to spend time on an additional survey and used this time expenditure willingness as a measure of performance.

In four additional studies, the authors focus more specifically on certain types of performance by distinguishing between in-role and extra-role performance. It can be assumed that in-role behavior is what most of the other studies measure when they ask participants about their overall performance. As Van Loon et al. (2017) point out, in-role performance refers to the activities that are required for a specific task. In-role performance is high when an employee meets the standards that are associated with their role (Williams and Anderson 1991). As previously pointed out by Katz (1964), for an organization to be successful, it is not sufficient if its members do only what is required in their specific role. To be successful, employees have to take on responsibility beyond their role, for example, by helping their colleagues or engaging in other activities that are beneficial to the organization. This is what is called extra-role behavior or extra-role performance. Overall, three of the four studies confirm a positive direct effect of PSM on extra-role performance (Caillier 2015; 2016; Van Loon et al. 2017), while one does not find any such effect (Wright et al. 2017).

Eight additional studies examined a construct that is strongly related to extra-role performance: organizational citizenship behavior (OCB). Like extra-role behavior, OCB captures behavior that is beneficial to the organization but not directly rewarded (Organ 2016). A substantial majority of seven studies found that PSM increases employees' OCB. Cun (2012) details this finding by analyzing the dimensions of PSM separately. Doing so, he finds support only for a positive effect of attraction to public policy-making and commitment to public interest, while the combined dimension of compassion and self-sacrifice is not related to OCB.

Overall, it is challenging to state whether PSM affects different types of performance in different ways. However, compared to specific performance measures, we see much more variance in the results when the studies do not further specify the kind of performance in which they are interested. While we found eleven studies with non-specific performance measures in favor of a direct effect on individual performance, there are also five studies with mixed results and five that did not find any direct effect. In contrast, the results of effects on extra-role performance and OCB are much clearer, with ten studies supporting a direct effect and only one with mixed results and one without any effect.

14.4.3   Measurement of Performance

The most common way to measure performance is to directly ask employees about their self-perception. Overall, twenty-eight of the thirty-eight studies summarized in Table A14.1 (see online Appendix) choose this approach. There are, however, two groups of studies that differ from this "standard approach." The first uses performance data from an external source. In this context, it is quite remarkable that both Schwarz et al. (2016) and Wright et al. (2017) are the only researchers conducting studies that ask supervisors to assess the performance of their subordinates and combine this performance measure with employees' own assessment of their PSM.[2] They conclude that PSM has a positive direct effect on performance as indicated by supervisor ratings.

Various Danish researchers have made another attempt to make performance measures more valid using external data. They use the register data of performance measures and combine them with employees' self-assessed PSM. Andersen and Serritzlew (2012) operationalize the performance of physiotherapists as the proportion of time they spent on difficult cases or types of treatment, but find only one of three tested direct effects of commitment to public interest on this performance measure to be significant. Andersen et al. (2014; 2015) and Lynggaard et al. (2018) focus on school teachers and draw on students' exam marks as a measure of teacher performance. Two studies (Andersen et al. 2014; 2015) find a positive direct effect of PSM on performance. Lynggaard et al. (2018), however, do not confirm such an effect. Instead, they argue that the effect of commitment to public interest on performance is contingent on teachers' work autonomy and user capacity.

With the increasing popularity of experimental designs in public administration (Grimmelikhuijsen et al. 2017), a stream of research has developed on performance effects of PSM that uses such an approach. We found five such studies. The first one

---

[2] The difficulties associated with the collection of such clustered data might explain its infrequent use (Vogel 2018).

to use experiments to assess the effect of PSM on individual performance was Bellé (2013; 2014). In his field experiments with nurses in Italian public hospitals, he observed participants' involvement in a developmental aid project in which they voluntarily assembled surgical kits for shipment to a former war zone. One study (Bellé 2013) used persistence, output, productivity, and vigilance concerning the assembly of surgical kits, and the other (Bellé 2014) only the output in the form of the number of assembled kits. The experiments confirm a positive effect of PSM on objective performance (Bellé 2013). Furthermore, PSM strengthens the positive effect of transformational leadership on performance (Bellé 2014). Resh et al. (2018) take a different approach. In a laboratory experiment, they used persistence as their performance measure of interest. They find that participants with high levels of self-sacrifice are more persistent at a voluntarily repeated reaction time task than others.

Finally, two articles can be added to our review of experimental approaches to the PSM–performance effect. Both use hypothetical scenarios. Bellé and Cantarelli (2015) asked Italian government employees about their current work effort, randomly assigned them to a vignette describing a task and a bonus the government pays for that task, and subsequently surveyed the participants on the effort they would invest into this task. The experimental manipulation was carried out by altering the amount of the bonus promised in the hypothetical scenario. Unfortunately, the study does not report the direct effect of PSM on work effort. However, it shows that the effect of the size of the bonus is not dependent on participants' PSM. Pedersen (2015) also designed a hypothetical scenario to test the performance effects of PSM. He asked students to fill in a survey assessing PSM, among other things. At the end of the survey, participants were asked how much time they would be willing to spend on another survey that would be conducted in the future. The reason they might be asked to participate again was varied between groups. Some got a PSM-related reason, some an extrinsic motivation-related reason, and some did not get a reason. Pedersen shows that those with a PSM reasoning are willing to spend significantly more time on an additional survey than others. He also shows that this effect is even stronger if participants have a high PSM.

14.4.4   Size of the Effect

So far, we have only discussed whether there is any effect of PSM on individual performance. We concluded that the evidence is generally in favor of such an effect. Additionally, we wanted to assess how much PSM contributes to individuals' performance. Therefore, we reviewed the literature with regard to the reported effect sizes and summarized the results in Table A14.1 (see online Appendix). As the reviewed studies use a variety of different statistical methods, we collected standardized effect sizes or calculated them from the reported statistics if no standardized effects were reported. Afterwards, we used common categorizations of effect sizes to give a verbal expression of the size of the effects. The categories are no effect, small effect, medium effect, and large effect. A small effect is equal to a correlation of Pearson's $r = 0.1–0.3$, a medium effect to $r = 0.3–0.5$, and a large effect to 0.5 and higher (Cohen 1988). The details of these categories are reported in Table A14.1.

Of the reviewed studies, six report effect sizes that have to be categorized as no effect. Five studies find a mix of no and small effects, fifteen studies find small effects, and one a mix of small and medium effects. Six studies find medium effects, and two additional studies find large effects. Considering that many studies test more than one effect, we can further differentiate. Of the seventy-one tested effects, twenty-three have to be categorized as no effect. Thirty-four additional effects can be categorized as small effects. Thirteen effects are of medium size, and three are large.

Overall, the direct effects of PSM on individual performance have to be considered as relatively small. This is, however, not particularly surprising as performance is a highly complex construct, and it cannot be assumed that a single factor will explain a large amount of the variance between employees.

14.4.5 Summary of Empirical Evidence

So what do we learn from the literature on the effect of PSM on individual performance? Keep in mind our theoretical function, which is:

individual institutional public service performance = f(PSM, institutional environmental characteristics)

If we simply count all the reviewed studies that support a positive effect of PSM, we can conclude that twenty-five studies are in favor of a direct or indirect effect, and six studies partially support it. Whereas thirty-six studies analyze a direct relationship, twenty-two studies confirm the positive link between PSM and individual performance. Only six studies do not find any direct effect.

Eighteen studies investigate the indirect link and include contextual effects. As PSM is a kind of generalized institutional identity that is based on public service values, an environment that emphasizes and rewards these values will interact with individuals' motives and drive performance. In our overview of empirical studies, a few moderators and mediators seem to be relevant: transformational leadership, person–organization fit, person–job fit, mission valence, public service orientation of the organization, type of organization (people-processing vs people-changing), work autonomy, emotional intelligence, and user capacity. Most of these concepts represent value-loaded phenomena and add some supportive evidence that the logic of appropriateness of behaviors guided by institutional values at the macro-level (e.g. mission valence), meso-level (e.g. organizational orientation), and micro-level (e.g. supervisor) drive individual performance. However, either these moderators have been tested only once or the evidence for their effect is inconclusive (transformational leadership, person–organization fit).

Against the backdrop of our second question about the type of performance measures, we ought not simply to treat all studies as equal evidence for the PSM–performance relationship but also take their rigor and design into account. The majority of empirical work on this subject is based on public employees' self-assessment of their performance. Although researchers have tried to improve the validity of such measures by asking about specific elements of performance, supervisor ratings, or performance compared to team members, subjective performance is problematic. Extensive psychological research shows that people are limited in their ability to assess their behavior correctly and often overestimate positive aspects, such as performance. Andersen et al. (2015) demonstrate that public employees overestimate their performance and that the effects of explanatory variables are much stronger when they come from the same data source (i.e. self-assessment). This is also the case for PSM. Therefore, we have to assume that studies using operationalizations of performance other than self-assessment provide a more accurate test of the PSM–performance relationship. We found nine such studies published over the last six years. They either use register data, such as students' exam marks, supervisor assessments, or objective measures in an experimental context (e.g. number of assembled surgical kits and persistence in reaction time task). Five of those studies find support for a positive direct effect of PSM on performance, while three do not confirm such an effect.[3] The body of evidence, therefore, seems to be slightly in favor of a PSM–performance effect. However, five to three is not a very convincing outcome.

Interestingly, of the studies using an objective measure of performance, especially those that use a limited assessment of PSM are the ones that do not confirm a positive effect of PSM on individual performance. Two of them (Andersen and Serritzlew 2012; Lynggaard et al. 2018) study only commitment to public interest and one (Wright et al. 2017) a combination of commitment to public interest and compassion. This brings us to the question of whether it is PSM in its full combination of four dimensions that has a positive effect on performance or whether specific dimensions drive this effect (see also Brewer 2010). The body of evidence we currently have does not allow for any conclusion on this question. We reviewed seventeen studies that used all four PSM dimensions. Twelve neglected attraction to public policy-making. Two studies used only two dimensions and five only a single dimension (mainly commitment to public interest). Only three studies tested the effects of the PSM dimensions separately. Even with the limited number of three studies separately analyzing the effect of the PSM dimension, all three come to different conclusions. Cheng (2015) found a positive effect of attraction to public policy-making and compassion. Cun (2012) only confirms the effect of attraction to public policy-making but finds an additional effect of commitment to public interest. Finally, Palma et al. (2017) report a positive effect of commitment to public interest and self-sacrifice. Hence, further research is required on the effects of the

---

[3] One study, (Bellé 2014), does not report the direct effect of PSM on performance.

respective PSM dimensions. This could also be carried out by reanalyzing the data of studies that have already been published.

However, it should be noted that the variety of PSM measures used to test whether PSM affects individual performance is quite staggering. We found twenty-five different measures of PSM in a set of thirty-seven studies. Only six item sets were used more than once. In four of those six cases, this can be observed because the same authors published multiple studies or multiple studies were based on the same dataset. Without an extensive assessment of the validity of all these different measures of PSM, it is difficult to conclude whether measurement issues play a role in the mixed evidence on the PSM–performance relationship. We assume that the variety of PSM measures reflects the length and therefore limitation of the two validated PSM measures (Kim et al. 2013; Perry 1996). As such, we strongly recommend the development of a comprehensive and validated measurement scale for PSM (Vandenabeele and Penning de Vries 2016).

To summarize, one can conclude that there is ample evidence for some positive relationship between PSM and performance. However, this is by no means a perfect relationship.

14.5 Methodological Strategies to Improve Future Research

Despite the substantial attention in terms of time, energy, and other resources that have been devoted to the study of the relationship between PSM and individual performance, the scientific evidence is not entirely convincing. Although our literature review shows that the majority of empirical findings point to a positive relationship, the relationship between the two core concepts has not been compellingly or undeniably demonstrated. To assess the causal value of our function, a number of strategies should be pursued. Below, we will elaborate on a few of the methodological approaches we think may contribute to better development of the causal analysis. Evidently, this is first and foremost oriented toward the field of PSM and performance. However, the strategies outlined below may also serve to facilitate improved causal analysis in other fields.

First, an important strategy is to fully appreciate the formulation as a performance function. Earlier, we stated that one advantage of this function is that parts of it can be investigated under the *ceteris paribus* assumption. However, this means that when carrying out this kind of research, one needs to live up to this assumption by actually controlling for all other things. Given that the majority of studies, in particular the earlier studies, rely on cross-sectional data, one should control for all other possible factors in order to assess an effect. This fictional requirement stamps all these studies with the label "plausible at best." To test for causality, the gold standard is the experimental design. This has recently also been advocated by scholars identifying "behavioral public administration" (Grimmelikhuijsen et al. 2017) as a strategy to further the field of public administration as a science. In such well-conducted experiments, everything apart from the treatment would be controlled for so that differences in outcomes can be attributed only to the treatment. Transposing this to our domain, this would require PSM to be manipulated randomly in order to keep other influences constant.

Despite some studies claiming to have manipulated PSM (Bellé 2013 and Christensen and Wright 2018 would be the prime examples of such a study) or to have reminded employees of their associated impact (Vogel and Willems 2020), one can readily question experiments' ability to actually manipulate PSM, given its multiple assumed antecedents (Perry 1997; Vandenabeele 2011) and its relative observed stability over time (Vogel and Kroll 2016). Moreover, not all settings lend themselves to experimental designs, ethically or for other reasons. In such cases, all other (observational) techniques that do not address the issue of endogeneity—due to common method bias or other causes—are useless for testing causality (Antonakis et al. 2010). Therefore, a valid non-experimental alternative would be a two-stage-least-squares (2SLS) approach, in which instrumental variables are iden- tified to correct for the endogeneity. Such an instrumental variable is not correlated to the dependent variable in the model but to the independent one.

When using the instrumental variable approach of 2SLS, these instrumental vari- ables are used to provide a proxy estimate of the independent variable that is not affected by endogeneity (as it is uncorrelated to the dependent variable). Any correl- ation between this proxy estimate and the dependent variables is, therefore, a "true" correlation. Combining this with the well-argued time order in which cause clearly precedes effect (e.g. by means of longitudinal data) changes the label on such studies from "plausible at best" to "likely causal."

However, one should also be aware of the phrase "well-conducted experiment" and extend it to "well-conducted research." Epidemiological work by Ioannidis (2005) states that in all likelihood, half of the studies conducted, if not more, are false due to the way in which science operates (the problem is that we do not know which half is false). This has been illustrated by the "replication project" (Open Science Collaboration 2015) in which only 37 percent of ninety-nine studies con- ducted were replicated. An experiment is therefore not a guarantee for true know- ledge. To account for this, we need meta-science strategies to counter this effect. The most common strategy would be meta-analysis, in which the results of multiple studies are combined to assess an actual relationship, mitigating possible outliers (Ringquist 2013). This would even facilitate the discovery of possible moderators that have not been included in the actual studies. The Achilles' heel of any such approach is, however, the number of studies available. Another strategy would be actual replication of studies by means of new data (Walker et al. 2018) collected in a different study, preferably multiple independent studies (the so-called Many Labs approach) (Klein et al. 2014). However, this would require a concerted effort by mul- tiple teams to devote their scarce resources to a project that would create limited individual exposure. In such an effort, rewards for participating researchers should be well designed in order to fit within the general institution of science.

A final strategy to increase the validity of the findings concerns the more fine-grained analysis in which the direct effect is explained by mediating mechanisms. This would, for example, be a causal chain in which PSM influences perceived person–environment fit, in turn influencing performance. Furthermore, regarding what was said earlier about the use of non-experimental data to test for causal effects, mediation has its own problems that are not solved by applying experimental approaches (Bullock et al. 2010). Just as independent variables should be manipulated, so should mediators. More importantly, however, when developing models with multiple mediators (e.g. when replacing person–environment fit with person–organization and person–job fit), it should be argued how manipulations would affect only one of the mediators. Bullock et al. (2010) put forward a number of solutions; however, given that the subtitle of the article is "Don't expect an easy answer," this complicates the research substantially.

14.6 Conclusion

The performance of public organizations is essential for the legitimacy of a state. However, as shown in Chapter 2 of this volume, public service performance is multifaceted and relates to various stakeholder perspectives on which public value has to be achieved and which public values should be prioritized. In this chapter, we focus on the motivation of individual employees as a contribution to individual public service performance, and therefore, we exclude many other factors contributing to the performance of public organizations, including non-directly performance-related variables, such as turnover and absenteeism. However, the equation we used for our literature review:

individual public service performance = f(PSM, institutional characteristics)

reflects how the link between individuals' motivation and individual performance is dependent on institutions. For instance, public values are one of the fundamental building blocks of public institutions, and thus, institutions matter in regard to the performance outcomes of public service-motivated individuals (see also Chapter 4). This is supported by the two theoretical lenses (motivation theory and institutional theory) we used to explain the underlying processes.

Our literature review reveals that the majority of empirical findings point to a positive relationship between public service motivation and individual performance. The evidence is based on research designs that analyze direct and indirect relationships using a variety of interacting variables, types of performance variables, and methodological strategies, such as surveys or experiments. However, the variety of study designs, data used, and performance types studied raise questions regarding the generalization of these findings. Nevertheless, the literature review sheds more light on one of the three fundamental claims about public service motivation raised by Perry and Wise in their seminal article in 1990.

First, we learn that the relationship is highly context-dependent. Person–organization fit, mission valence, and transformational leadership are relevant intervening variables. Value congruence between an organization, its supervisors, and the individual employee exemplifies how institutional characteristics filter down to organizational actors. Leadership behavior, which supports such a complementary fit between the organizational environment and the individual, further strengthens the performance outcomes of public service motivation. Future research needs to clarify whether complementary fit alone acts as a moderating variable or if public service motivation is also needed as a supply for the organization (supplementary fit).

In addition, research differentiating between various types of fit and different performance outcomes is scarce, and more knowledge is required in order better to understand the role played by context when it comes to explaining individual performance through public service motivation. For instance, more knowledge is needed about the influence of structural disaggregation, outsourcing, and agencification on the relationship between PSM and individual performance. This also includes the analysis of environmental fit measuring changes in institutional context over time, as well as institutional (publicness) differences between sectors, nations, policy fields, and organizations and the effects thereof on performance outcomes (see also Chapter 4). Empirical studies point to transformational leadership as a moderator; at the same time, we also find studies using public service motivation as a moderator of the leadership–performance link. Both perspectives can be theoretically explained. However, future research needs to further investigate what exactly context characterized by public service motivation means and what role it plays in an organizational environment. Furthermore, our knowledge is very limited concerning the specifications of non-public environments interacting with the public service motivation–performance relationship.

Second, when looking at the type of performance measures used in empirical research, our literature review leads us to conclude that institutional context matters. Differences were found in research analyzing the relationships between public service motivation and various performance measures in different contexts. Furthermore, we also find contradictory findings between studies investigating the same type of performance (e.g. extra-role behavior) in different contexts. However, with the exception of experimental studies and the study by Van Loon (2015), there is a lack of studies using contextualized measures of performance. Task performance in one policy field may differ from that in another when examining the concrete public values determining performance in a specific context. Thus, we encourage researchers to move away from using rather general HR survey measures to analyze performance effects of public service motivation. We suggest instead investing more time in the contextualization of performance variables.

Furthermore, while positive findings of experimental studies on the link between public service motivation and individual performance are very consistent, empirical studies using external sources of performance, such as supervisor ratings or registered data, show rather mixed results. Against the backdrop of supervisory ratings, which are a widespread element of public personnel policies linking performance with contingent pay, the underlying processes and impacts of such performance appraisals and their pay effects in relation to public service motivation need to be analyzed in more depth. Against the backdrop of a high variety of performance measures, we also need to question the relevance of the public service motivation–individual performance link because relationships of PSM with other non-directly performance-related variables, such as turnover and absenteeism could be of greater relevance when individual performance does not scale up to organizational performance. Thus, future research should also look at performance outcomes from a broader and more comparative perspective.

Third. and finally, we were interested in the strength of the relationship between public service motivation and individual performance. So far, we can conclude that the strength of correlations and effects measured is rather small. Giving due consideration to the fact that most models are not fully specified and empirical studies largely neglect correlates of public service motivation as explanatory variables, we can definitely conclude that individuals' performance depends to a larger extent on other factors (e.g. other types of motivations, personality characteristics, and cognitive and other skills), some of which may be more important than PSM.

Except for experimental studies, our knowledge is very limited when it comes to the relevance of public service motivation in comparison to other motivational and attitudinal variables predicting or relating to individual performance. For instance, job satisfaction is an antecedent of individual performance and is closely related to PSM (Homberg et al. 2015). However, from a content perspective, the two constructs are distinct and have different implications for leading employees in practice. Therefore, it is of great interest to find out which types of correlates (e.g. micro-level variables, such as controlled and self-determined motivation, meso-level variables, such as organizational commitment, or macro-level variables, such as societal value orientation) are more or less in competition with public service motivation and specific types of individual performance (see e.g. Breaugh et al. 2017).

Future research will need to unravel those relationships in order to better assess the role played by public service motivation. With an increase in experimental studies, it will be worth systematically comparing results from experimental studies to the results from the majority of non-experimental studies to gauge the distortion caused by model specification error in the latter set of studies.

References

Aloe, A. 2014. "An Empirical Investigation of Partial Effect Sizes in Meta-Analysis of Correlational Data." *The Journal of General Psychology 141* (1): pp. 47–64.

Alonso, P., and G. B. Lewis. 2001. "Public Service Motivation and Job Performance: Evidence from the Federal Sector." *American Review of Public Administration 31* (4): pp. 363–80.

Andersen, L. B., E. Heinesen, and L. H. Pedersen. 2014. "How Does Public Service Motivation among Teachers Affect Student Performance in Schools?" *Journal of Public Administration Research and Theory 24* (3): pp. 651–71.

Andersen, L. B., E. Heinesen, and L. H. Pedersen. 2015. "Individual Performance: From Common Source Bias to Institutionalized Assessment." *Journal of Public Administration Research and Theory 26* (1): 63–78.

Andersen, L. B., L. H. Pedersen, and O. H. Petersen. 2018. "Motivational Foundations of Public Service Provision: Towards a Theoretical Synthesis." *Perspectives on Public Management and Governance 1* (4): pp. 283–98.

Andersen, L. B., and S. Serritzlew. 2012. "Does Public Service Motivation Affect the Behavior of Professionals?" *International Journal of Public Administration 35* (1): pp. 19–29.

Antonakis, J. 2004. "Why 'Emotional Intelligence' Does Not Predict Leadership Effectiveness." *Organizational Analysis 12* (2): pp. 171–82.

Antonakis, J., S. Bendahan, P. Jacquart, and R. Lalive. 2010. "On Making Causal Claims: A Review and Recommendations." *Leadership Quarterly 21* (6): pp. 1086–120.

Barrick, M. R., and M. K. Mount. 1991. "The Big Five Personality Dimensions and Job Performance: A Meta-Analysis." *Personnel Psychology 44* (1): pp. 1–26.

Bellé, N. 2013. "Experimental Evidence on the Relationship between Public Service Motivation and Job Performance." *Public Administration Review 73* (1): pp. 143–53.

Bellé, N. 2014. "Leading to Make a Difference: A Field Experiment on the Performance Effects of Transformational Leadership, Perceived Social Impact, and Public Service Motivation." *Journal of Public Administration Research and Theory 24* (1): pp. 109–36.

Bellé, N., and P. Cantarelli. 2015. "Monetary Incentives, Motivation, and Job Effort in the Public Sector: An Experimental Study with Italian Government Executives." *Review of Public Personnel Administration 35* (2): pp. 99–123.

Bottomley, P., A. M. S. Mostafa, J. S. Gould-Williams, and F. León-Cázares. 2016. "The Impact of Transformational Leadership on Organizational Citizenship Behaviours: The Contingent Role of Public Service Motivation." *British Journal of Management 27* (2): pp. 390–405.

Breaugh, J., A. Ritz, and K. Alfes. 2017. "Work Motivation and Public Service Motivation: Disentangling Varieties of Motivation and Job Satisfaction." *Public Management Review 20* (10): pp. 1423–43.

Brewer, G. A. 2006. "All Measures of Performance Are Subjective: More Evidence on US Federal Agencies." In *Public Service Performance: Perspectives on Measurement and Management*, edited by G. A. Boyne, K. J. Meier, L. J. O'Toole, and R. M. Walker, pp. 35–54. Cambridge: Cambridge University Press.

Brewer, G. A. 2008. "Employee and Organizational Performance." In *Motivation in Public Management: The Call of Public Service*, edited by J. L. Perry and A. Hondeghem, pp. 136–56. New York: Oxford University Press.

Brewer, G. A. 2010. "Public Service Motivation and Performance." In *Public Management and Performance*, edited by R. M. Walker, G. A. Boyne, and G. A. Brewer, pp. 152–77. Cambridge: Cambridge University Press.

Brewer, G. A., and E. J. Kellough. 2016. "Administrative Values and Public Personnel Management: Reflections on Civil Service Reform." *Public Personnel Management 45* (2): pp. 171–89.

Bright, L. 2007. "Does Person–Organization Fit Mediate the Relationship between Public Service Motivation and the Job Performance of Public Employees?" *Review of Public Personnel Administration 27* (4): pp. 361–79.

Bullock, J. G., D. P. Green, and S. E. Ha. 2010. "Yes, but What's the Mechanism? (Don't Expect an Easy Answer)." *Journal of Personality and Social Psychology 98* (4): pp. 550–8.

Caillier, J. G. 2014. "Toward a Better Understanding of the Relationship between Transformational Leadership, Public Service Motivation, Mission Valence, and Employee Performance: A Preliminary Study." *Public Personnel Management 43* (2): pp. 218–39.

Caillier, J. G. 2015. "Towards a Better Understanding of Public Service Motivation and Mission Valence in Public Agencies." *Public Management Review 17* (9): pp. 1217–36.

Caillier, J. G. 2016. "Does Public Service Motivation Mediate the Relationship between Goal Clarity and Both Organizational Commitment and Extra-Role Behaviours?" *Public Management Review 18* (2): pp. 300–18.

Cameron, J., and D. W. Pierce. 2002. *Rewards and Intrinsic Motivation: Resolving the Controversy.* Westport, CT: Bergin & Garvey.

Cheng, K.-T. 2015. "Public Service Motivation and Job Performance in Public Utilities." *International Journal of Public Sector Management 28* (4/5): pp. 352–70.

Christensen, R. K., and B. E. Wright. 2018. "Public Service Motivation and Ethical Behavior: Evidence from Three Experiments." *Journal of Behavioral Public Administration 1* (1). https://doi.org/10.30636/jbpa.11.18.

Cohen, J. 1988. *Statistical Power Analysis for the Behavioral Sciences.* 2nd ed. Mahwah, NJ: Lawrence Erlbaum Associates.

Cun, X. 2012. "Public Service Motivation and Job Satisfaction, Organizational Citizenship Behavior: An Empirical Study Based on the Sample of Employees in Guangzhou Public Sectors." *Chinese Management Studies 6* (2): pp. 330–40.

Deci, E. L., and R. M. Ryan. 1985. *Intrinsic Motivation and Self-Determination in Human Behavior.* New York: Plenum Press.

Deci, E. L., and R. M. Ryan. 2004. *Handbook of Self-Determination Research.* Rochester, NY: University of Rochester Press.

Gagné, M., and E. L. Deci. 2005. "Self-Determination Theory and Work Motivation." *Journal of Organizational Behavior 26* (4): pp. 331–62.

Giauque, D., A. Ritz, F. Varone, S. Anderfuhren-Biget, and C. Waldner. 2011. "Putting Public Service Motivation into Context: A Balance between Universalism and Particularism." *International Review of Administrative Sciences 77* (2): pp. 227–53.

Gould-Williams, J. S., A. Mostafa, and P. Bottomley. 2015. "Public Service Motivation and Employee Outcomes in the Egyptian Public Sector: Testing the Mediating Effect of Person–Organization Fit." *Journal of Public Administration Research and Theory 25* (2): pp. 597–622.

Grant, A. M. 2008. "Does Intrinsic Motivation Fuel the Prosocial Fire? Motivational Synergy in Predicting Persistence, Performance, and Productivity." *Journal of Applied Psychology 93* (1): pp. 48–58.

Grimmelikhuijsen, S., S. Jilke, A. L. Olsen, and L. G. Tummers. 2017. "Behavioral Public Administration: Combining Insights from Public Administration and Psychology." *Public Administration Review 77* (1): pp. 45–56.

Herzberg, F. 1966. *Work and the Nature of Man*. Cleveland, OH: World Pub. Co.

Homberg, F., D. McCarthy, and V. Tabvuma. 2015. "A Meta-Analysis of the Relationship between Public Service Motivation and Job Satisfaction." *Public Administration Review 75* (5): pp. 711–22.

Ioannidis, J. P. A. 2005. "Why Most Published Research Findings Are False." *PLOS Medicine 2* (8): pp. e124.

Jin, M. H., B. McDonald, and J. Park. 2018. "Does Public Service Motivation Matter in Public Higher Education? Testing the Theories of Person–Organization Fit and Organizational Commitment through a Serial Multiple Mediation Model." *American Review of Public Administration 48* (1): pp. 82–97.

Katz, D. 1964. "The Motivational Basis of Organizational Behavior." *Behavioral Science 9* (2): pp. 131–46.

Kim, S. H., and S. Kim. 2016. "National Culture and Social Desirability Bias in Measuring Public Service Motivation." *Administration & Society 48* (4): pp. 444–76.

Kim, S., W. Vandenabeele, B. E. Wright, L. B. Andersen, F. P. Cerase, R. K. Christensen, C. Desmarais, M. Koumenta, P. Leisink, B. Liu, J. Palidauskaite, L. H. Pedersen, J. L. Perry, A. Ritz, J. Taylor, and P. de Vivo. 2013. "Investigating the Structure and Meaning of Public Service Motivation across Populations: Developing an International Instrument and Addressing Issues of Measurement Invariance." *Journal of Public Administration Research and Theory 23* (1): pp. 79–102.

Kjeldsen, A. M., and C. B. Jacobsen. 2013. "Public Service Motivation and Employment Sector: Attraction or Socialization?" *Journal of Public Administration Research and Theory 23* (4): pp. 899–926.

Klein, R. A., K. A. Ratliff, M. Vianello, R. B. Adams, Jr, Š. Bahník, M. J. Bernstein, K. Bocian, M. J. Brandt, B. Brooks, . . . and B. A. Nosek. 2014. "Investigating Variation in Replicability: A 'Many Labs' Replication Project." *Social Psychology 45* (3): pp. 142–52.

Koumenta, M. 2015. "Public Service Motivation and Organizational Citizenship." *Public Money & Management 35* (5): pp. 341–8.

Kristof-Brown, A. L., R. D. Zimmerman, and E. C. Johnson. 2005. "Consequences of Individuals' Fit at Work: A Meta-Analysis of Person–Job, Person–Organization, Person–Group, and Person–Supervisor Fit." *Personnel Psychology 58* (2): pp. 281–342.

Leisink, P., and B. Steijn. 2009. "Public Service Motivation and Job Performance of Public Sector Employees in the Netherlands." *International Review of Administrative Sciences 75* (1): pp. 35–52.

Levitats, Z., and E. Vigoda-Gadot. 2017. "Yours Emotionally: How Emotional Intelligence Infuses Public Service Motivation and Affects the Job Outcomes of Public Personnel." *Public Administration 95* (3): pp. 759–75.

Lynggaard, M., M. J. Pedersen, and L. B. Andersen. 2018. "Exploring the Context Dependency of the PSM–Performance Relationship." *Review of Public Personnel Administration 38* (3): pp. 332–54.

Maier, N. R. F. 1958. *Psychology in Industry*. Boston: Houghton Mifflin Co.

Miller, G. J., and A. B. Whitford. 2007. "The Principal's Moral Hazard: Constraints on the Use of Incentives in Hierarchy." *Journal of Public Administration Research and Theory* 17 (2): pp. 213–33.

Neumann, O., and A. Ritz. 2015. "Public Service Motivation and Rational Choice Modelling." *Public Money & Management* 35 (5): pp. 365–70.

Open Science Collaboration. 2015. "Estimating the Reproducibility of Psychological Science." *Science 349* (6251). DOI: 10.1126/science.aac4716.

Organ, D. W. 2016. "A Restatement of the Satisfaction–Performance Hypothesis." *Journal of Management 14* (4): pp. 547–57.

Palma, R., A. Hinna, and G. Mangia. 2017. "Improvement of Individual Performance in the Public Sector." *Evidence-Based HRM: A Global Forum for Empirical Scholarship* 5 (3): pp. 344–60.

Park, S. M., and H. G. Rainey. 2007. "Antecedents, Mediators, and Consequences of Affective, Normative, and Continuance Commitment: Empirical Tests of Commitment Effects in Federal Agencies." *Review of Public Personnel Administration* 27 (3): pp. 197–226.

Park, S. M., and H. G. Rainey. 2008. "Leadership and Public Service Motivation in U.S. Federal Agencies." *International Public Management Journal 11* (1): pp. 109–42.

Pedersen, M. J. 2015. "Activating the Forces of Public Service Motivation: Evidence from a Low-Intensity Randomized Survey Experiment." *Public Administration Review* 75 (5): pp. 734–46.

Perry, J. L. 1996. "Measuring Public Service Motivation: An Assessment of Construct Reliability and Validity." *Journal of Public Administration Research and Theory 6* (1): pp. 5–22.

Perry, J. L. 1997. "Antecedents of Public Service Motivation." *Journal of Public Administration Research and Theory 7* (2): pp. 181–97.

Perry, J. L. 2000. "Bringing Society In: Toward a Theory of Public-Service Motivation." *Journal of Public Administration Research and Theory 10* (2): pp. 471–88.

Perry, J. L., T. A. Engbers, and S. Y. Jun. 2009. "Back to the Future? Performance-Related Pay, Empirical Research, and the Perils of Persistence." *Public Administration Review* 69 (1): pp. 39–51.

Perry, J. L., and W. Vandenabeele. 2008. "Behavioral Dynamics: Institutions, Identities, and Self-Regulation." In *Motivation in Public Management: The Call of Public Service*, edited by J. L. Perry and A. Hondeghem, pp. 56–79. New York: Oxford University Press.

Perry, J. L., and L. R. Wise. 1990. "The Motivational Bases of Public Service." *Public Administration Review 50* (3): pp. 367–73.

Peters, G. B. 2000. *Institutional Theory in Political Science: The New Institutionalism*. London: Continuum.

Rainey, H. G., and P. Steinbauer. 1999. "Galloping Elephants: Developing Elements of a Theory of Effective Government Organizations." *Journal of Public Administration Research and Theory 9* (1): pp. 1–32.

Resh, W. G., J. D. Marvel, and B. Wen. 2018. "The Persistence of Prosocial Work Effort as a Function of Mission Match." *Public Administration Review 78* (1): pp. 116–25.

Ringquist, E. 2013. *Meta-Analysis for Public Management and Policy.* San Francisco, CA: Jossey-Bass.

Ritz, A. 2009. "Public Service Motivation and Organizational Performance in Swiss Federal Government." *International Review of Administrative Sciences 75* (1): pp. 53–78.

Ritz, A., G. A. Brewer, and O. Neumann. 2016. "Public Service Motivation: A Systematic Literature Review and Outlook." *Public Administration Review 76* (3): pp. 414–26.

Ritz, A., and N. Petrovsky. 2014. "Public Service Motivation and Performance: A Critical Perspective." *Evidence-Based HRM: A Global Forum for Empirical Scholarship 2* (1): pp. 57–79.

Ritz, A., C. Schott, C. Nitzl, and K. Alfes. 2020. "Public Service Motivation and Prosocial Motivation: Two Sides of the Same Coin?" *Public Management Review,* online first. https://doi.org/10.1080/14719037.2020.1740305.

Sayed, M. A. M., G.-W. J. Seymour, and B. Paul. 2015. "High-Performance Human Resource Practices and Employee Outcomes: The Mediating Role of Public Service Motivation." *Public Administration Review 75* (5): pp. 747–57.

Schott, C., O. Neumann, M. Baertschi, and A. Ritz. 2019. "Public Service Motivation, Prosocial Motivation and Altruism: Towards Disentanglement and Conceptual Clarity." *International Journal of Public Administration 42* (14): pp. 1200–11.

Schwarz, G., A. Newman, B. Cooper, and N. Eva. 2016. "Servant Leadership and Follower Job Performance: The Mediating Effect of Public Service Motivation." *Public Administration 94* (4): pp. 1025–41.

Vandenabeele, W. 2007. "Toward a Public Administration Theory of Public Service Motivation." *Public Management Review 9* (4): pp. 545–56.

Vandenabeele, W. 2008. "Development of a Public Service Motivation Measurement Scale: Corroborating and Extending Perry's Measurement Instrument." *International Public Management Journal 11* (1): pp. 143–67.

Vandenabeele, W. 2009. "The Mediating Effect of Job Satisfaction and Organizational Commitment on Self-Reported Performance: More Robust Evidence of the PSM–Performance Relationship." *International Review of Administrative Sciences 75* (1): pp. 11–34.

Vandenabeele, W. 2011. "Who Wants to Deliver Public Service? Do Institutional Antecedents of Public Service Motivation Provide an Answer?" *Review of Public Personnel Administration 31* (1): pp. 87–107.

Vandenabeele, W., and J. Breaugh. Forthcoming. "Further Integration of Public Service Motivation Theory and Self-Determination Theory: Concepts and Correlates." *International Public Management Journal.*

Vandenabeele, W., G. A. Brewer, and A. Ritz. 2014. "Past, Present, and Future of Public Service Motivation Research." *Public Administration 92* (4): pp. 779–89.

Vandenabeele, W., and J. Penning de Vries. 2016. "Validating a Global Measure of Public Service Motivation: Assessing Measurement Invariance." Paper presented at the 2016 Public Management Research Conference, Aarhus, Denmark, June 22–24, 2016.

Vandenabeele, W., A. Ritz, and O. Neumann. 2018. "Public Service Motivation: State of the Art and Conceptual Cleanup." In *The Palgrave Handbook of Public Administration and Management in Europe*, edited by E. Ongaro and S. Van Thiel, pp. 261–78. Basingstoke: Palgrave Macmillan.

Van der Meer, F. M., T. P. S. Steen, and A. Wille. 2015. "Civil Service Systems in Western Europe: A Comparative Analysis." In *Comparative Civil Service Systems in the 21st Century*, edited by F. M. Van der Meer, J. C. N. Raadschelders, and T. A. Toonen, pp. 38–56. 2nd ed. Basingstoke: Palgrave Macmillan.

Van Loon, N. M. 2015. "The Role of Public Service Motivation in Performance: Examining the Potentials and Pitfalls through an Institutional Approach." Doctoral dissertation, Utrecht University, Utrecht, the Netherlands.

Van Loon, N. M. 2016. "Is Public Service Motivation Related to Overall and Dimensional Work-Unit Performance as Indicated by Supervisors?" *International Public Management Journal 19* (1): pp. 78–110.

Van Loon, N. M., P. Leisink, and W. Vandenabeele. 2013. "Talking the Talk of Public Service Motivation: How Public Organization Logics Matter for Employees' Expressions of PSM." *International Journal of Public Administration 36* (14): pp. 1007–19.

Van Loon, N. M., W. Vandenabeele, and P. Leisink. 2017. "Clarifying the Relationship between Public Service Motivation and In-Role and Extra-Role Behaviors: The Relative Contributions of Person–Job and Person–Organization Fit." *American Review of Public Administration 47* (6): pp. 699–713.

Vogel, D. 2018. "Matching Survey Responses with Anonymity in Environments with Privacy Concerns." *International Journal of Public Sector Management 31* (7): pp. 742–54.

Vogel, D., and A. Kroll. 2016. "The Stability and Change of PSM-Related Values across Time: Testing Theoretical Expectations against Panel Data." *International Public Management Journal 19* (1): pp. 53–77.

Vogel, D., and J. Willems. 2020. "The Effects of Making Public Service Employees Aware of Their Prosocial and Societal Impact: A Microintervention." *Journal of Public Administration Research and Theory 30* (3), pp. 485–503. DOI: 10.1093/jopart/muz044.

Walker, R. M., G. A. Brewer, M. J. Lee, N. Petrovsky, and A. Van Witteloostuijn. 2018. "Best Practice Recommendations for Replicating Experiments in Public Administration." *Journal of Public Administration Research and Theory*, online first. https://doi.org/10.1093/jopart/muy047.

Williams, L. J., and S. E. Anderson. 1991. "Job Satisfaction and Organizational Commitment as Predictors of Organizational Citizenship and In-Role Behaviors." *Journal of Management 17* (3): pp. 601–17.

Wright, B. E., S. Hassan, and R. K. Christensen. 2017. "Job Choice and Performance: Revisiting Core Assumptions about Public Service Motivation." *International Public Management Journal 20* (1): pp. 108–31.

Wright, P. M., K. M. Kacmar, G. C. McMahan, and K. Deleeuw. 1995. "P= f (MXA): Cognitive Ability as a Moderator of the Relationship between Personality and Job Performance." *Journal of Management 21* (6): pp. 1129–39.

15
Managing Employees' Employability
Employer and Employee Perspectives

Jasmijn Van Harten and Brenda Vermeeren

15.1 Introduction

Employees' employability has mostly been viewed and hence studied as an issue for business organizations or as a general concern (e.g. Forrier and Sels 2003; Nauta et al. 2009; Van Dam 2004). Businesses are confronted with global changes that challenge their ability to compete and require them to have an employable workforce that has up-to-date skills and can be flexibly deployed. Only a few studies have examined the importance and features of employees' employability in public organizations (e.g. De Cuyper and De Witte 2011; Van Harten 2016). Nevertheless, there are specific reasons that make employees' employability an important issue for the public sector, and likewise, there exist an increasing number of examples of public sector organizations instigating employability policies.

Besides the general developments that initiate organizational changes (e.g. globalization, technological progress and innovation, and demographic trends), new public management (NPM) has come to play a central role in the public sector in recent decades, with values such as efficiency and effectiveness being emphasized (Boyne et al. 2006; Osborne and Gaebler 1992; Pollitt and Bouckaert 2004). Due to this business-oriented approach, strengthened by the economic crisis, many government organizations have adopted austerity measures and made changes to their organizational structures (Bozeman 2010; Pandey 2010; Raudla et al. 2013; see also Chapter 11). At the same time, civil servants face new public service demands coming from an increasingly demanding society. Taken together, these changes call for employable public sector workers, meaning that they need to adopt new roles and acquire new skills (OECD 2017c).

The relevance of investing in workers' employability in the public sector could, furthermore, be justified using the concept of public value and by seeing investments in employability as a retention strategy. Retaining employable workers enables organizations to meet fluctuating demands for new products and services (Nauta et al. 2009). Employability provides a means for employers to match labor supply with demand in a changing environment (Thijssen et al. 2008). For generations of

Jasmijn Van Harten and Brenda Vermeeren, *Managing Employees' Employability: Employer and Employee Perspectives* In: *Managing for Public Service Performance: How People and Values Make a Difference*. Edited by: Peter Leisink, Lotte B. Andersen, Gene A. Brewer, Christian B. Jacobsen, Eva Knies, and Wouter Vandenabeele, Oxford University Press (2021). © Jasmijn Van Harten and Brenda Vermeeren. DOI: 10.1093/oso/9780192893420.003.0015 employees, lifetime *employment* with the same employer was considered the norm. Today, lifetime *employability* is emphasized (Thijssen et al. 2008). In an environment which no longer readily offers long-term employment, a key goal for employees is to maintain and enhance their opportunities in the labor market—hence the term "employability" (Rothwell and Arnold 2007; Thijssen et al. 2008). In this respect, the HRM policies of public employers that enable their employees to strengthen their employability could be regarded as creating public value. It should be noted that the public sector labor market, specifically central government, has traditionally been different from that in the private sphere and that the dominant practice in many countries is still lifetime employment (Bordogna and Bach 2016). As a consequence, many public organizations in Western countries have more elderly workforces than seen in the private sector, which leads to employability issues specifically related to older workers.

In this chapter, based on important publications and recent research findings in the employability literature, we provide an overview of public sector workers' employability and particularly zoom in on research and examples from practice in public sector contexts. In Section 15.2, we outline perspectives on and definitions of employability in both research and practice. We then discuss findings from empirical research on employability outcomes, followed by an outline of the determinants of employability. We end this chapter with conclusions and propose future research and policy agendas.

15.2 Employability in Research and Practice

The concept of employability has been in the spotlight of empirical researchers since the late-1990s (Forrier and Sels 2003) when awareness grew that careers were becoming less stable and predictable and that individuals would need to adapt to constant changes in order to survive in the labor market (Van der Heijde and Van der Heijden 2006). Research attention continues to grow: Our Web of Science search for articles on employability published in the last decade yielded more than 400 articles, and while we found nineteen articles in 2008, we found sixty-one articles in 2017. The articles were spread over sixty-nine themes in Web of Science, with "education/educational research" and "psychology applied" being the largest themes with slightly over 100 articles in each. The theme "public administration" was ranked thirteenth with twelve articles. However, this does not imply that employability is little studied in the public sector as we also found some articles with the public sector as the research setting in the first two categories. Nevertheless, only a few studies have examined the importance and specific features of employees' employability in public organizations.

In essence, being employable means being able to survive or having reasonable job chances in the labor market (Forrier et al. 2015; Thijssen et al. 2008). However, research definitions and measurements of the concept are plentiful, making it a somewhat scattered field. Therefore, in Section 15.2.1, we first provide a generic overview of the employability notions that are used in research. We then discuss transnational and national policy discourses on employability and give attention to the public personnel policy field.

15.2.1 Employability in Research

In the last decade, employability has been increasingly studied from an individual perspective, meaning that employability is regarded as the individual's opportunities in the internal and/or external labor markets (Forrier et al. 2015). However, there are also literature streams that regard employability from societal and organizational perspectives. Within the societal perspective, employability is seen as the ability of different categories of the labor force to gain employment, and a country's employment rates are usually regarded as the indicator of employability (Thijssen et al. 2008). From an organizational perspective, employability concerns the ability to match labor supply and demand, often in a changing organizational environment. In this respect, employability is linked to an organization's functional flexibility (Thijssen et al. 2008). Investments in human capital or training are regarded as an indicator of the level of organizational employability. In this chapter, we predominantly (but not exclusively) make use of studies on the employability of individuals (usually employees) since these provide the most recent empirical insights based on an accessible range of employability concepts and measures.

There are quite a few differences in the way in which researchers conceptualize and measure the basic definition of workers' employability as an individual's likelihood or possibility of a job. Forrier et al. (2015) grouped these approaches into three categories. First, one group of researchers understand employability as an individual's range of abilities and attitudes (personal strengths) necessary to acquire a job. This is also referred to as movement capital (Forrier et al. 2009). Examples of employability variables in this category are employability competences (Van der Heijde and Van der Heijden 2006), up-to-date expertise (Van Harten et al. 2016), and a willingness to develop and change (Van Dam 2004). Second, employability is sometimes regarded as the individual's appraisal of available employment opportunities; in other words, their self-perceived job chances. Researchers may distinguish between internal and external job chances (e.g. Rothwell and Arnold 2007) or include an appraisal of chances of any job (quantitative appraisal) or a better job (qualitative appraisal) (e.g. De Cuyper and De Witte 2011). A third and less common notion of employability addresses the realization of personal strengths and job chances, which is most noticeable when transitioning between jobs (e.g. Raemdonck et al. 2012). It is often assumed that these different notions of employability are interrelated.

Movement capital allows and motivates individuals to increase their "employability radius" (Thijssen et al. 2008), making it likely that individuals' perceptions of their employment opportunities are also boosted. Based on the idea that perceptions drive behavior, these perceptions could consequently lead to individuals changing jobs (Forrier et al. 2015). Such job transitions could then feed back to movement

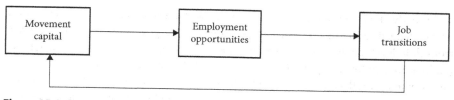

Figure 15.1 Dynamic chain of employability notions
Source: Based on Forrier et al. (2015).

capital by, for instance, increasing self-awareness and self-efficacy and acting as a strong signal of one's abilities (Nelissen et al. 2017). As such, a dynamic chain of employability is predicted (Forrier et al. 2009) as visualized in Figure 15.1. Various studies provide empirical evidence for the relationships although further research is needed (see Forrier et al. 2015).

The employability notions so far described involve general definitions that could be applied in a variety of organizational settings. We are unaware of any public sector-specific definitions for employability. General employability concepts are used and tested in public or semi-public organizations, such as schools (Veld et al. 2015), hospitals (Van Harten et al. 2016), and municipalities (Van Emmerik et al. 2012). Further, employability has been studied in a range of countries, such as Australia (Clarke 2008), Great Britain (Rothwell and Arnold 2007), the Scandinavian countries (Kirves et al. 2014), the Benelux countries (De Cuyper and De Witte 2011; Van Harten et al. 2016), and the US (Fugate and Kinikci 2008). Based on existing findings, employability is arguably relevant for employees in general (we elaborate further on this in Section 15.3), but comparative research across sectors and countries that would support this claim is largely lacking.

15.2.2 Employability Policy Discourses

Over the last decade, employability has increasingly become an issue of national and transnational concern. For example, China, when president of the G20 in 2016, introduced the topic of "innovation: decent work, enhanced employability, and adequate job opportunities (IDEA)" in the G20 Employment Working Group (OECD et al. 2016). Alongside demographic changes that have contributed to this growing interest in employability in Western countries (Clarke 2008), a recent joint publication by the OECD, the International Labour Organization (ILO), the World Bank, and the International Monetary Fund (IMF) (OECD et al. 2016) observed that developments, such as the speed and nature of globalization, technological changes, and changes in the organization of work, add to the necessity of paying attention to the employability of citizens. Although such trends involve different facets across G20 countries, generally speaking, they affect what kind of work needs to be done, by whom, where, and how it is carried out.

Similarly, the importance of the continuous skill development of citizens is widely acknowledged, and transnational organizations urge governments to move away from skill development policies that prepare for lifelong employment toward achieving lifetime employability (OECD et al. 2016). This focus on skill or human capital development is reflected in the employability discourse in many OECD countries such as the UK, which tries to stimulate employability through education and apprenticeships (OECD 2017b), and France, where employers play an important role in lifelong learning (OECD 2017a). In the Netherlands, explicitly the shared responsibility of employers and employees for enhancing employability (Stichting van de Arbeid 2013) is recognized, meaning that employees have to become more autonomous and resilient when it comes to their careers, while employers are expected to support rather than control their employees' development. According to a discourse analysis by Fejes (2010), there is a transnational consensus on the shared responsibility of the individual, state, and employer in policies concerning labor markets and lifelong learning. However, in countries such as the US where ideas about adaptability and flexibility have a key role in the debate, the individual is primarily held responsible for their own employability. Fejes (2010) particularly focused on the Swedish national discourse and found that the municipality and state, rather than the individual, are construed as being primarily responsible for employability, especially when it relates to public services such as healthcare where shortages of skilled workers are expected.

In short, employability is on the agenda of many OECD countries although they vary in how to enhance employability—to an extent because there are different notions as to which actors are responsible for enhancing employability. Although the OECD (2017a and 2017b) has found employability enhancement policies to be present in many countries, there is also critique of such policies. For example, Bowman et al. (2017) saw a "work-first" policy dominance in many OECD countries. They saw such policies as being primarily targeted at avoiding unemployment at all times, resulting in moving people into jobs as quickly as possible, and criticized this for its short-term focus that could lead to new skill imbalances in the near future.

Employability discourses focus on employability in general, and it is unclear whether there is a specific discourse on employability in the public sector that is different from the private sector. That is, employability appears as a general concern both in research and in practice. However, the OECD (2017c) recently published a report on the need to develop the employability of civil servants. Civil servants face new public service demands coming from an increasingly demanding society. They also have to deal with growing complexity in their work as, for instance, systems and tools of governance are increasingly digital and open. It is argued that to keep pace, civil servants should develop communicative and co-creating skills to engage with citizens and collaborative skills to work in networked organizations. These required changes are reflected in a plan by the UK government that aims to achieve a fully skilled and up-to-date civil service workforce by 2020 (see Box 15.1). Countries also increasingly acknowledge that demographic trends and constant technological

---

Box 15.1. The UK's Civil Service Workforce Plan, 2016–2020

In 2016, the UK government launched a workforce plan aiming to develop a civil service that is able to proactively adapt to the changing world of work. Part of the plan's strategy is to improve the commercial capability of the civil service and ensure that it becomes a world leader in terms of digital transformation. The UK government intends to achieve this by, in part, implementing a better recruitment and selection process that heavily focuses on the provision of apprenticeships (the aim is to deliver at least 30,000 civil service apprenticeships over the course of Parliament) and traineeships (e.g. the Civil Service Fast Stream that offers fifteen different programs).

Furthermore, although professional development programs already existed within the civil service, the government is aiming to develop clear career paths for core professions, with structured opportunities for learning and development that are linked to the career paths and with competencies and experience used to assess readiness for promotion. This is also intended to retain civil servants and show them that they can build a career within the civil service.

The National Audit Office (NAO) examined the UK government's approach to identifying and closing capability gaps in the civil service and concluded that the plans were not keeping pace with the growing challenges facing civil services. The initiatives outlined above were, for instance, considered as needing time to mature, and the NAO recommended government should develop a more sophisticated understanding of its capability needs within and across departments, for instance, by annual workforce planning and assessing the capability needs of significant projects before implementing solutions.

Sources: Cabinet Office and Civil Service 2016 and Morse 2017.

---

changes lead to a need to reallocate human resources across sectors, including healthcare, education, and social sectors (OECD 2017c). Public service workforces in Western countries age more rapidly than the rest of society. According to Truss (2013), this is linked to public sector employees tending to stay longer with their employers. An aging workforce in combination with a growing demand for labor, as is currently happening in healthcare organizations, presents challenges for public employers on how to attract and retain employable employees. In Section 15.4, we provide examples of employability investments made by public sector employers.

15.3 Employability Outcomes

The employability discourse regards employability as an important asset for individuals to survive in the labor market and argues that employable workers could also be valuable to organizations, since they are increasingly confronted with changing circumstances that impact on the nature and organization of work. Reflecting this, research has started to examine the outcomes of employability during the last decade. In this section, we outline research findings on employability outcomes from the perspectives of individual workers and their employers. As noted earlier, employability research has adopted a general perspective with little attention given to the specificity of the public sector context. Therefore, at the end of this section, we evaluate research on employability outcomes from a public sector perspective.

Research indicates that employability leads to employees' career success and better psychological well-being. Several studies have found that employable workers experience greater career success in terms of higher salaries and promotion opportunities when compared to less employable individuals (Kiong and Yin-Fah 2016; Van der Heijden et al. 2009). Further, employability decreases feelings of job insecurity (De Cuyper et al. 2012; McArdle et al. 2007). Researchers explain this finding by arguing that employable individuals feel in control of their careers and able to deal with challenges resulting from changes and uncertainty: They have the resources to deal with such circumstances. This results in them experiencing less stress and feeling better than less employable workers. In line with this reasoning, there are various studies, including longitudinal research, showing that employability positively affects well-being as, for instance, measured using variables such as general perceptions of well-being (Berntson and Marklund 2007), feelings of strain or burn-out (De Cuyper et al. 2012; Direnzo et al. 2015), and work–life balance satisfaction (Van Harten 2016). Other forms such as physical and social well-being (see Chapter 12) tend not to be linked to employability in research so far. Interestingly, studies generally theorize and empirically seek to demonstrate that employability has positive effects on well-being, while the possibility of negative well-being effects is rarely explored. The latter seem plausible since, for instance, stress reactions or decreased job satisfaction could develop when individuals experience pressure to constantly work on their employability, which could require individuals to invest significant amounts of their time that could then lead to a work–life imbalance. Even if, when regarded as an isolated concept, employability does not have negative well-being effects, there could be negative effects that depend on an employee's job and personal context.

Further, it has been shown that employability also has outcomes that are important from an organizational perspective. Employability has been found to impact on organizational commitment, turnover intentions, and job performance. De Cuyper and De Witte (2011) found that employees who perceive themselves as having employment opportunities within their organization (labeled as internal employability) are more committed to their organization. Only when they perceive *better* job chances elsewhere (external employability) do they become less committed to their employer. The latter finding has been corroborated by Philippaers et al. (2016). Dries et al. (2014) have shown that employees who find themselves employable in terms of, for instance, being flexible and adaptable do not have a greater intention to leave their organization than less employable workers. Furthermore, De Cuyper and

De Witte (2011) found a positive indirect effect of internal employability on job performance through increased commitment. The positive link between employability and performance has been demonstrated elsewhere. For instance, Camps and Torres (2011) showed that employability was positively related to individual task performance, and Stoffers et al. (2018) found a positive association with innovative work behavior. Van Harten (2016) found a positive relationship between the up-to-date expertise component of employability and job performance. It should be noted that the above-mentioned studies on the employability–performance link all use employees' self-perceptions of performance and do not use other performance measures or sources. There is also a study showing negative effects of external employability on self-rated job performance (Philippaers et al. 2016).

Overall, most of the research points to positive employability effects that benefit employers. This goes against the so-called employability management paradox that organizations face when investing in employability: Employers are afraid that as a result of increased employability, employees will start looking for another job and leave the organization (De Cuyper and De Witte 2011). In other words, organizations might make investments from which their competitors reap the benefits. Although the above research findings downplay this fear, there are instances in which increased turnover does occur. When employees perceive few promotion opportunities in their organization and/or perceive better jobs elsewhere, increased employability feelings boost turnover (Nelissen et al. 2017). Although a certain level of turnover maintains organizational flexibility, too much turnover could involve risks linked to organizational amnesia if vital knowledge disappears along with employees. This can result in decreased performance, less organizational learning, and increased vulnerability (Pollitt 2000).

Only a few studies have examined employability outcomes in a public or semi-public sector context. For instance, De Cuyper and De Witte (2011) looked at teachers in several schools in Belgium, while Camps and Torres (2011) researched the academic staff of universities in Costa Rica, and Van Harten (2016) studied hospital employees in the Netherlands. These studies all found positive effects of employability on self-rated performance measures, which suggests that employability also has merit for public service performance. However, this claim should be studied further by relating employability to other performance indicators, such as service quality or client satisfaction that are also relevant in a public sector setting (cf. Chapter 2). Further, theory and research are needed on the ways in which factors that are specific to the public sector are likely to impact the outcomes of employability. To date, employability studies that use data from multiple sectors have not investigated possible sectoral differences. At best, researchers have included such differences as control variables in their analyses while not reflecting on contextual or institutional factors that might explain employability outcomes. Insights from public administration research could provide input to investigate this idea. For example, based on research demonstrating the negative effects of red tape (e.g. DeHart-Davis and Pandey 2005), it can be hypothesized that red tape moderates the relationships between employability and its outcomes in a public sector context. Employees' experiences of red tape, which is more prevalent in public than in private sector organizations (cf. Chapter 12), could hinder performance effects or further stimulate the turnover of employable individuals who perceive better job chances elsewhere.

To summarize, research on employability outcomes indicates that employability is indeed a valuable asset—for both individuals and organizations. The extent to which employability also contributes to public service performance and how these effects are dependent on specific characteristics of the public sector need to be studied further.

15.4 Determinants of Employees' Employability

Knowing that employability has benefits, it is useful to gain knowledge of its determinants. A broad range of factors have been found to impact employability, and a recent review by Guilbert et al. (2016) reduced these to three groups of factors: (1) individual characteristics; (2) organizational strategies; and (3) governmental and educational factors.

The first group of determinants can be further divided into three groups (Guilbert et al. 2016): (1) sociodemographic attributes, e.g. age (Lu 2011); (2) interpersonal attributes, e.g. quality of social network (Cheung et al. 2018); and (3) psychological attributes, e.g. self-efficacy (Bargsted 2017). Although these factors are all somehow tied to the individual, their nature ranges from fairly static factors that cannot be easily changed (if at all), such as age, gender, and family situation, to factors that are more dynamic and that can be influenced, such as self-esteem and quality of one's social network. We note that recent studies especially provide empirical evidence for the impact of psychological attributes on employability. Wille et al. (2013) conducted a fifteen-year longitudinal study on perceived employability (referring to perceived job chances) and found that the Big Five traits had substantial effects, even after controlling for a number of demographic and career-related characteristics. Further, Nauta et al. (2010) showed that role breadth self-efficacy of employees in the healthcare and welfare sector significantly influences employees' employability orientation (similar to a readiness to develop and adapt), and Kim et al. (2015) showed that organization-based self-esteem is related to perceived employability.

In addition to these psychological attributes, the demographic attribute of age is increasingly studied, but research findings here are mixed. It has been shown that older people gain greater job security in their current job (internal employability) through an increase in experience/expertise but less easily find work elsewhere (external employability) (De Lange et al. 2006; Nauta et al. 2010). This is a particularly relevant finding for the public sector since public service workforces in Western countries tend to age more rapidly than the rest of society. We would argue that public service motivation (PSM) (see Chapter 14) could be another individual determinant of public sector employees' employability as, for instance, the motivation to deliver public service value might negatively influence employees' willingness to change work contexts and their perceptions of job opportunities outside their organization (i.e. it could influence at least two distinct employability variables). To the best of our knowledge, there are no studies examining the relationship between PSM and employability, indicating an area where further research is necessary to show whether and how the concepts are related.

The second group of determinants addresses organizational strategies aimed at stimulating employability. It is often argued that organizations have the responsibility to offer employees the support and facilities necessary to enhance their employability (Forrier and Sels 2003; Thijssen et al. 2008). Although it is recognized that employers are sometimes afraid of offering support to their employees to increase their employability in case they then start looking for another job and leave the organization (see Section 15.3), various studies indicate that a social exchange mechanism comes into play, resulting in employees having a strong intention to remain with their employer provided that they perceive internal employability or development opportunities (e.g. De Cuyper and De Witte 2011; Nauta et al. 2009). More specifically, Nauta et al. (2009) showed that the presence of a strong employability culture— defined as the standards, values, and behavioral patterns that are shared in an organization to encourage employees to focus on their personal development—stimulates employability while simultaneously decreasing turnover intentions. Further, HR policies and practices that reflect and accompany an employability culture are found to boost employability. For instance, formal training and job rotation programs stimulate employability (Fleischmann et al. 2015), employee participation in competency development initiatives is positively associated with workers' perceptions of employability (De Vos et al. 2011), and employees whose jobs provide more resources, such as autonomy and feedback, perceive more job opportunities and subsequently perceive greater employability (Van Emmerik et al. 2012). There are very few studies on how organizational strategies specifically impact on public sector workers' employability. It could be that public sector characteristics, such as an aging workforce and the salience of PSM, require employability policies and practices that are specific to the public sector, but research offers few clues. To provide an illustration of approaches, we present a specific employability policy in the Dutch national government in Box 15.2.

An important actor in the implementation and successful adaptation of HR policies, as also seen in Box 15.2, is the line manager (see Chapter 3). Similarly, employability research shows that it is vital that managers accept their role responsibilities in the implementation of employability practices (Van Dam 2004; Van der Heijden and Bakker 2011; Van Harten et al. 2016). More specifically, the degree to which managers identify with the employability goals as well as their awareness, willingness, and capability to perform their new role in supporting their employees' employability is important (Peters and Lam 2015).

The third group of employability determinants according to Guilbert et al. (2016) concerns governmental and educational policies. We expand this to include contextual

Box 15.2. The 3–5–7 model within the Dutch national government

The 3–5–7 model is an instrument aimed at stimulating the mobility and sustainable employability of civil servants within central government. It can be explained as follows:

- *0–3 years in a position*: Employees should focus on the full and qualitative performance of the tasks within the job description. In addition, employees engage in personal development for their further career opportunities.
- *3–5 years in a position*: Employees should be orientated toward their next career step. This means that employees should examine their wishes for their next workplace and what steps need to be taken to get there. This could already result in a new workplace.
- *5–7 years in a position*: If an employee has not yet taken a career step after five years, the employee and their manager should determine, as concretely as possible, what steps are needed to find a new position. In this period, customized agreements between employee and manager are made to realize the next career step, which the employee is to realize after seven years of working in the same job.

In this model, career steps can be horizontal or vertical and inside or outside the organization but usually remaining within government. This can mean a new job at another unit or even a different department/ministry.

This model was in use during the Balkenende IV Cabinet (2007–2010). There were some differences between departments in implementing this model. For instance, the Dutch Department of Health, Welfare, and Sport did not view the model as a compulsory framework in personnel management. Rather, they regarded it as a framework that employees could use when thinking about their career and personal development. With such an implementation, the success of the 3–5–7 model relied on cooperation between employees and managers. Here, the model had no legal consequences for employees with permanent employment, and participation was voluntary. However, the department introduced several practices that pressured employees to regularly think and discuss their mobility: (1) role models from the top management level started a conversation about their function retention time; and (2) the model was included in HR practices as a standard topic in the annual performance appraisal and as part of strategic HR planning.

Source: Ministry of the Interior and Kingdom Relations n.d.

conditions such as a country's macroeconomic situation. Although it is recognized that contextual conditions impact employability (Thijssen et al. 2008), there is less empirical evidence available than for the other two categories. McQuaid and Lindsay (2005), Duff et al. (2007), Lindsay and Mailand (2009), and Sing (2012) have all studied the measures taken by governments to achieve full employment, and they propose strategies designed to enhance the employability of different worker populations (e.g. the unemployed, youths in difficulty, minorities, and people with a disability). These might, for instance, involve adopting incentives or constraining measures to promote lifelong learning. However, significant differences exist between countries, making any attempt at generalization about these strategies and measures difficult (Guilbert et al. 2016). In addition, several studies on employability fail to give explicit attention to the public versus private contexts. In many studies, public and private employees are simply merged in the sample (e.g. De Battisti et al. 2016; Ngo et al. 2017; Pinto and Ramalheira 2017). A notable exception is De Grip et al. (2004), who argue that the employability of workers in a given sector or industry partly depends on the extent to which employees need to cope with developments (technological, demographic, economic, and organizational) in their particular sector. Their study, conducted in the Netherlands, showed that technological developments and demographic developments (workforce aging) clearly play an important role in the civil service, police, defense, and education services and that these sectors had some of the greatest needs for employability at the time of data collection.

In this section, we have provided a broad overview of the determinants of employability. What we know little about is how determinants on different levels (individual, organizational, and societal) relate to each other and influence each other in determining employees' employability (Van Harten et al. 2020). It is quite conceivable that the three levels complement each other. For example, it is plausible that an organization's employability policy works better when it takes account of important individual employee characteristics that influence employability. In addition, it is plausible that activities by an organization to increase its employees' employability are more effective, in the sense that employees are more inclined to develop and adapt when a country has a social safety net (such as with the flexicurity model in Denmark). Comparative research that examines the impact of factors across sectors is lacking, meaning that, for instance, we do not know whether contextual conditions have a greater impact on public or private sector workers' employability, or whether public sector employers provide more or different types of employability investments than private sector employers. On that note, it is worth mentioning that most studies that focus on individual level determinants are published in general management journals, while research on the impact of contextual conditions tends to appear in public sector journals (e.g. Kemp and Davidson 2010; Lindsay and Dutton 2012; Lindsay et al. 2008). This is not to suggest that contextual determinants are relevant only for public sector employers and workers, but clearly, further research attention is required.

15.5 Conclusion

This chapter has examined the issue of public sector workers' employability by analyzing research and examples taken from practice. We have demonstrated that both in research and in practice, the concept, including its determinants and outcomes, is predominantly treated in a generic, non-sector-specific way. A possible explanation for this generic approach is that the employability research field is still in its early days: It is only in the last decade that research attention has been growing significantly, and the field needs to further evolve. Furthermore, the field is dominated by researchers coming from educational sciences and psychology backgrounds who approach employability using an individual, micro-level perspective. This results in methodologically rigorous research but at the expense of attention to contextual (institutional) influences and differences.

To further develop the field, we believe that research would benefit from contextualization, which has also recently been called for by Forrier et al. (2018, 6) who argue that "employability is context dependent because it is shaped along common appraisals that are embedded in a specific space and time." We therefore call for comparative employability research across countries or sectors and for public sector- specific studies. One could perhaps have expected there to be more interest in public sector organizations or in public–private comparisons because semi-public and fully public organizations have been confronted with demographic developments, sometimes to an even greater extent than private organizations, and with public management reforms that urge greater employability. Further, since employee well-being is (or at least used to be) an important goal of public sector personnel policies, one would expect employability to be a key concern nowadays.

Although employability determinants have been extensively mapped, with considerable differences between the categories of determinants, and the evidence for employability outcomes is growing, there is no evidence on how public sector characteristics might influence or interfere with the identified relationships. For instance, in this chapter, we have hypothesized on the possibly hindering roles of red tape and PSM that require research. Further, since the evidence for the positive performance effects of employability is based solely on self-rated job performance, research is needed that examines the impact of employability on other types of performance indicators, such as service quality or client satisfaction. These indicators would provide meaningful operationalizations of public service performance (see also Chapter 2) and contribute to the contextualization of the employability concept.

Finally, when it comes to managing employability, we would argue that a fit between initiatives on the different levels (individual, organizational, and societal) is a prerequisite for achieving employability aims. This, among others, means that public sector employers need to consider the composition of the workforce and the characteristics and needs of their individual employees when developing employability policies and practices. For instance, noting that older workers usually rate their own employability lower when compared to their younger counterparts (e.g. Van Harten 2016), public organizations with a relatively large proportion of older workers could try to give an extra stimulus to their older workers' employability by providing them with training programs on how to best select and use skills and tasks that fit their abilities and interests (Truxillo et al. 2015). Furthermore, public sector organizations should pay attention to the specific labor market challenges facing civil services. For example, promoting external employability may not be desirable where there is a tight labor market, such as in education and care, as this could jeopardize the provision of these public services. Rather, it would seem more effective to invest in internal employability opportunities, such as the 3–5–7 model as employed by the Dutch government (see Box 15.2), and create resourceful and challenging jobs that match public employees' needs. However, as described in this chapter, more research is needed on the features of employability in a public sector setting that could ultimately lead to evidence-based and concrete interventions for managing the employability of public sector workers.

References

Bargsted, M. 2017. "Impact of Personal Competencies and Market Value of Type of Occupation over Objective Employability and Perceived Career Opportunities of Young Professionals." *Revista de Psicología del Trabajo y de las Organizaciones 33* (2): pp. 115–23.

Berntson, E., and S. Marklund. 2007. "The Relationship between Perceived Employability and Subsequent Health." *Work & Stress 21* (3): pp. 279–92.

Bordogna, L., and S. Bach. 2016. "Emerging from the Crisis: The Transformation of Public Service Employment Relations?" In *Public Service Management and Employment Relations in Europe*, edited by S. Bach and L. Bordogna, pp. 19–46. New York: Routledge.

Bowman, D., M. McGann, H. Kimberley, and S. Biggs. 2017. "'Rusty, Invisible and Threatening': Ageing, Capital and Employability." *Work, Employment and Society 31* (3): pp. 465–82.

Boyne, G. A., K. J. Meier, L. J. O'Toole, and R. Walker. 2006. *Public Service Performance: Perspectives on Measurement and Management*. Cambridge: Cambridge University Press.

Bozeman, B. 2010. "Hard Lessons from Hard Times: Reconsidering and Reorienting the 'Managing Decline' Literature." *Public Administration Review 70* (4): pp. 557–63.

Cabinet Office and Civil Service. 2016. "Civil Service Workforce Plan: 2016 to 2020." Policy paper. London: TSO. https://assets.publishing.service.gov.uk/government/uploads/system/uploads/attachment_data/file/536961/civil_service_workforce_strategy_final.pdf.

Camps, J., and F. Torres. 2011. "Contingent Reward Leader Behaviour: Where Does It Come From?" *Systems Research and Behavioral Science 28* (3): pp. 212–30.

Cheung, R., Q. Jin, and C. K. Cheung. 2018. "Perceived Employability of Nonlocal Chinese University Students in Hong Kong: The Impact of Acculturative and Vocational Variables." *Journal of Career Assessment 26* (1): pp. 137–53.

Clarke, M. 2008. "Understanding and Managing Employability in Changing Career Contexts." *Journal of European Industrial Training 32* (4): pp. 258–84.

De Battisti, F., S. Gilardi, C. Guglielmetti, and E. Siletti. 2016. "Perceived Employability and Reemployment: Do Job Search Strategies and Psychological Distress Matter?" *Journal of Occupational and Organizational Psychology 89* (4): pp. 813–33.

De Cuyper, N., and H. De Witte. 2011. "The Management Paradox: Self-Rated Employability and Organizational Commitment and Performance." *Personnel Review 40* (2): pp. 152–72.

De Cuyper, N., A. Mäkikangas, U. Kinnunen, S. Mauno, and H. D. Witte. 2012. "Cross-Lagged Associations between Perceived External Employability, Job Insecurity, and Exhaustion: Testing Gain and Loss Spirals According to the Conservation of Resources Theory." *Journal of Organizational Behavior 33* (6): pp. 770–88.

De Grip, A., J. Loo, and J. Sanders. 2004. "The Industry Employability Index: Taking Account of Supply and Demand Characteristics." *International Labour Review 143* (3): pp. 211–33.

DeHart-Davis, L., and S. K. Pandey. 2005. "Red Tape and Public Employees: Does Perceived Rule Dysfunction Alienate Managers?" *Journal of Public Administration Research and Theory 15* (1): pp. 133–48.

De Lange, A. H., T. W. Taris, P. Jansen, P. Smulders, I. Houtman, and M. Kompier. 2006. "Age as a Factor in the Relation between Work and Mental Health: Results from the Longitudinal TAS Survey." In *Occupational Health Psychology: European Perspectives on Research, Education and Practice*, edited by S. McIntyre and J. Houdmont, vol. 1: pp. 21–45. Maia, Portugal: ISMAI Publications.

De Vos, A., S. De Hauw, and B. I. Van der Heijden. 2011. "Competency Development and Career Success: The Mediating Role of Employability." *Journal of Vocational Behavior 79* (2): pp. 438–47.

Direnzo, M. S., J. H. Greenhaus, and C. H. Weer. 2015. "Relationship between Protean Career Orientation and Work–Life Balance: A Resource Perspective." *Journal of Organizational Behavior 36* (4): pp. 538–60.

Dries, N., A. Forrier, A. De Vos, and R. Pepermans. 2014. "Self-Perceived Employability, Organization-Rated Potential, and the Psychological Contract." *Journal of Managerial Psychology 29* (5): pp. 565–81.

Duff, A., J. Ferguson, and K. Gilmore. 2007. "Issues Concerning the Employment and Employability of Disabled People in UK Accounting Firms: An Analysis of the Views of Human Resource Managers as Employment Gatekeepers." *The British Accounting Review 39* (1): pp. 15–38.

Fejes, A. 2010. "Discourses on Employability: Constituting the Responsible Citizen." *Studies in Continuing Education 32* (2): pp. 89–102.

Fleischmann, M., F. Koster, and J. Schippers. 2015. "Nothing Ventured, Nothing Gained! How and under Which Conditions Employers Provide Employability-Enhancing

Practices to Their Older Workers." *The International Journal of Human Resource Management 26* (22): pp. 2908–25.

Forrier, A., N. De Cuyper, and J. Akkermans. 2018. "The Winner Takes it All, the Loser Has to Fall: Provoking the Agency Perspective in Employability Research." *Human Resource Management Journal 28* (4): pp. 511–23.

Forrier, A., and L. Sels. 2003. "The Concept Employability: A Complex Mosaic." *International Journal of Human Resources Development and Management 3* (2): pp. 102–24.

Forrier, A., L. Sels, and D. Stynen. 2009. "Career Mobility at the Intersection between Agent and Structure: A Conceptual Model." *Journal of Occupational and Organizational Psychology 82* (4): pp. 739–59.

Forrier, A., M. Verbruggen, and N. De Cuyper. 2015. "Integrating Different Notions of Employability in a Dynamic Chain: The Relationship between Job Transitions, Movement Capital and Perceived Employability." *Journal of Vocational Behavior 89*: pp. 56–64.

Fugate, M., and A. J. Kinicki. 2008. "A Dispositional Approach to Employability: Development of a Measure and Test of Implications for Employee Reactions to Organizational Change." *Journal of Occupational and Organizational Psychology 81* (3): pp. 503–27.

Guilbert, L., J. L. Bernaud, B. Gouvernet, and J. Rossier. 2016. "Employability: Review and Research Prospects." *International Journal for Educational and Vocational Guidance 16* (1): pp. 69–89.

Kemp, P. A., and J. Davidson. 2010. "Employability Trajectories among New Claimants of Incapacity Benefit." *Policy Studies 31* (2): pp. 203–21.

Kim, S., H. Kim, and J. Lee. 2015. "Employee Self-Concepts, Voluntary Learning Behavior, and Perceived Employability." *Journal of Managerial Psychology 30* (3): pp. 264–79.

Kiong, T. P., and B. C. Yin-Fah. 2016. "Exploring Factors towards Career Success in Malaysia." *International Business Management 10* (17): pp. 3936–43.

Kirves, K., U. Kinnunen, N. De Cuyper, and A. Mäkikangas. 2014. "Trajectories of Perceived Employability and Their Associations with Well-Being at Work." *Journal of Personnel Psychology 13* (1): pp. 46–57.

Lindsay, C., and M. Dutton. 2012. "Promoting Healthy Routes Back to Work? Boundary Spanning Health Professionals and Employability Programmes in Great Britain." *Social Policy & Administration 46* (5): pp. 509–25.

Lindsay, C., and M. Mailand. 2009. "Delivering Employability in a Vanguard 'Active' Welfare State: The Case of Greater Copenhagen in Denmark." *Environment and Planning C: Government and Policy 27* (6): pp. 1040–54.

Lindsay, C., R. W. McQuaid, and M. Dutton. 2008. "Inter-Agency Cooperation and New Approaches to Employability." *Social Policy & Administration 42* (7): pp. 715–32.

Lu, L. 2011. "Effects of Demographic Variables, Perceived Spousal Support, and Gender Role Attitudes on Taiwanese Women's Employability." *Journal of Career Development 38* (3): pp. 191–207.

McArdle, S., L. Waters, J. P. Briscoe, and D. T. T. Hall. 2007. "Employability during Unemployment: Adaptability, Career Identity and Human and Social Capital." *Journal of Vocational Behavior 71* (2): pp. 247–64.

McQuaid, R. W., and C. Lindsay. 2005. "The Concept of Employability." *Urban Studies 42* (2): pp. 197–219.

Ministry of the Interior and Kingdom Relations. n.d. "Het 3–5–7 Model." https://kennisopenbaarbestuur.nl/media/226168/het-3-5-7-model.pdf

Morse, A. 2017. "Capability in the Civil Service." Report. London: National Audit Office. https://www.nao.org.uk/report/capability-in-the-civil-service/.

Nauta, A., A. H. De Lange, and S. Görtz. 2010. "Lang zullen ze leven, werken en leren. Een schema voor het begrijpen en beïnvloeden van inzetbaarheid gedurende de levensloop." *Gedrag en Organisatie 23* (2): pp. 136–57.

Nauta, A., A. Van Vianen, B. Van der Heijden, K. Van Dam, and M. Willemsen. 2009. "Understanding the Factors that Promote Employability Orientation: The Impact of Employability Culture, Career Satisfaction, and Role Breadth Self-Efficacy." *Journal of Occupational and Organizational Psychology 82* (2): pp. 233–51.

Nelissen, J., A. Forrier, and M. Verbruggen. 2017. "Employee Development and Voluntary Turnover: Testing the Employability Paradox." *Human Resource Management Journal 27* (1): pp. 152–68.

Ngo, H. Y., H. Liu, and F. Cheung. 2017. "Perceived Employability of Hong Kong Employees: Its Antecedents, Moderator and Outcomes." *Personnel Review 46* (1): pp. 17–35.

OECD. 2017a. *Getting Skills Right: France.* Paris: OECD Publishing.

OECD. 2017b. *Getting Skills Right: United Kingdom.* Paris: OECD Publishing.

OECD. 2017c. *Skills for a High Performing Civil Service.* Paris: OECD Publishing.

Organisation for Economic Co-operation and Development (OECD), International Labour Organisation (ILO), World Bank (IBRD), and International Monetary Fund (IMF). 2016. *Enhancing Employability: Report Prepared for the G20 Employment Working Group.* Paris: OECD Publishing. http://www.oecd.org/g20/topics/employment-and-social-policy/Enhancing-Employability-G20-Report-2016.pdf.

Osborne, D., and T. Gaebler. 1992. *Reinventing Government: How the Entrepreneurial Spirit Is Transforming the Public Sector.* New York: Penguin.

Pandey, S. K. 2010. "Cutback Management and the Paradox of Publicness." *Public Administration Review 70* (4): pp. 564–71.

Peters, P., and W. Lam. 2015. "Can Employability Do the Trick? Revealing Paradoxical Tensions and Responses in the Process of Adopting Innovative Employability Enhancing Policies and Practices in Organizations." *German Journal of Human Resource Management 29* (3–4): pp. 235–58.

Philippaers, K., N. De Cuyper, A. Forrier, T. Vander Elst, and H. De Witte. 2016. "Perceived Employability in Relation to Job Performance: A Cross-Lagged Study Accounting for a Negative Path via Reduced Commitment." *Scandinavian Journal of Work and Organizational Psychology 1* (1): pp. 1–15.

Pinto, L. H., and D. C. Ramalheira. 2017. "Perceived Employability of Business Graduates: The Effect of Academic Performance and Extracurricular Activities." *Journal of Vocational Behavior 99*: pp. 165–78.

Pollitt, C. 2000. "Institutional Amnesia: A Paradox of the 'Information Age'?" *Prometheus 18* (1): pp. 5–16.

Pollitt, C., and G. Bouckaert. 2004. *Public Management Reform: A Comparative Analysis.* New York: Oxford University Press.

Raemdonck, I., H. Tillema, A. De Grip, M. Valcke, and M. Segers. 2012. "Does Self-Directedness in Learning and Careers Predict the Employability of Low-Qualified Employees?" *Vocations and Learning 5* (2): pp. 137–51.

Raudla, R., R. Savi, and T. Randma-Liiv. 2013. "Literature Review on Cutback Management." *COCOPS—(COordinating for COhesion in the Public Sector of the Future).* Research report. http://hdl.handle.net/1765/40927.

Rothwell, A., and J. Arnold. 2007. "Self-Perceived Employability: Development and Validation of a Scale." *Personnel Review 36* (1): pp. 23–41.

Sing, D. 2012. "Human Resource Challenges Confronting the Senior Management Service of the South African Public Service." *Public Personnel Management 41* (2): pp. 379–88.

Stichting van de Arbeid. 2013. *Prospects for a Socially Responsible and Enterprising Country: Emerging from the Crisis and Getting Back to Work on the Way to 2020.* Den Haag, the Netherlands: Stichting van de Arbeid.

Stoffers, J., A. Kleefstra, R. J. Loffeld, R. Gerards, M. Hendriks, and A. De Grip. 2018. "Sociale Innovatie Monitor Limburg 2018: "Werken aan Employability"." Maastricht: Zuyd Lectoraat Employability/Maastricht University ROA. Research report. https://www.zuyd.nl/~/media/Files/Onderzoek/Kenniskring%20Employability/Sociale%20Innovatie%20Monitor%20Limburg%202018_klein_220518.pdf.

Thijssen, J. G. L., B. I. J. M. Van der Heijden, and T. Rocco. 2008. "Toward the Employability–Link Model: Current Employment Transition to Future Employment Perspectives." *Human Resource Development Review 7* (2): pp. 165–83.

Truss, C. 2013. "The Distinctiveness of Human Resource Management in the Public Sector." In *Human Resource Management in the Public Sector*, edited by R. J. Burke, A. J. Noblet, and C. J. Cooper, pp. 17–36. Cheltenham: Edward Elgar Publishing.

Truxillo, D., D. Cadiz, and L. Hammer. 2015. "Supporting the Aging Workforce: A Review and Recommendations for Workplace Intervention Research." *Annual Review of Organizational Psychology and Organizational Behavior 2* (1): pp. 351–81.

Van Dam, K. 2004. "Antecedents and Consequences of Employability Orientation." *European Journal of Work and Organizational Psychology 13* (1): pp. 29–51.

Van der Heijde, C. M. V. D., and B. I. Van der Heijden. 2006. "A Competence-Based and Multidimensional Operationalization and Measurement of Employability." *Human Resource Management 45* (3): pp. 449–76.

Van der Heijden, B. I., and A. B. Bakker. 2011. "Toward a Mediation Model of Employability Enhancement: A Study of Employee–Supervisor Pairs in the Building Sector." *The Career Development Quarterly 59* (3): pp. 232–48.

Van der Heijden, B. I., A. H. De Lange, E. Demerouti, and C. M. Van der Heijde. 2009. "Age Effects on the Employability–Career Success Relationship." *Journal of Vocational Behavior 74* (2): pp. 156–64.

Van Emmerik, I. H., B. Schreurs, N. De Cuyper, I. Jawahar, and M. C. Peeters. 2012. "The Route to Employability: Examining Resources and the Mediating Role of Motivation." *Career Development International 17* (2): pp. 104–19.

Van Harten, J. 2016. "Employable Ever After: Examining the Antecedents and Outcomes of Sustainable Employability in a Hospital Context." Dissertation, Utrecht University, Utrecht, the Netherlands.

Van Harten, J., N. De Cuyper, D. Guest, M. Fugate, E. Knies, and A. Forrier. 2020. "Introduction to Special Issue on HRM and Employability: Mutual Gains or Conflicting Outcomes?" *The International Journal of Human Resource Management 31* (9): pp. 1095–105.

Van Harten, J., E. Knies, and P. Leisink. 2016. "Employer's Investments in Hospital Workers' Employability and Employment Opportunities." *Personnel Review 45* (1): pp. 84–102.

Veld, M., J. Semeijn, and T. Van Vuuren. 2015. "Enhancing Perceived Employability: An Interactionist Perspective on Responsibilities of Organizations and Employees." *Personnel Review 44* (6): pp. 866–82.

Wille, B., F. De Fruyt, and M. Feys. 2013. "Big Five Traits and Intrinsic Success in the New Career Era: A 15-Year Longitudinal Study on Employability and Work–Family Conflict." *Applied Psychology 62* (1): pp. 124–56.

16
Conclusion

Directions for Future Research and Practice

Peter Leisink, Lotte B. Andersen, Christian B. Jacobsen, Eva Knies, Gene A. Brewer, and Wouter Vandenabeele

16.1 Introduction

Previous chapters have focused on specific aspects of the management–public service performance relationship. In this concluding chapter, we zoom out and take stock of what we know as a basis for setting directions for future research and practice. Section 16.2 synthesizes what insights the chapters have provided into our central question, namely how management makes a meaningful contribution to public service performance. We also examine what is known about specific characteristics of the public sector context that play a role in achieving public service performance. Based on the insights gained and the limitations of existing studies, a research agenda is outlined that includes conceptual, theoretical, and methodological issues. In line with this volume's purpose, we also outline implications for public organizations' efforts to create public value.

16.2 What We Know about Management's Contribution to Public Service Performance

Before we can take stock of what is known about the central relationship studied in this volume, we must examine the key concepts involved. We then summarize what we know about how management contributes to public service performance, both directly and indirectly, taking into account the influence of specific characteristics of the public sector context.

16.2.1 Key Concepts

16.2.1.1 Public Service Performance
Public service performance is a multidimensional concept referring to the process and outcomes of public service provision. Boyne's (2002) conceptualization, which

Peter Leisink, Lotte B. Andersen, Christian B. Jacobsen, Eva Knies, Gene A. Brewer, and Wouter Vandenabeele, *Conclusion: Directions for Future Research and Practice* In: *Managing for Public Service Performance: How People and Values Make a Difference*. Edited by: Peter Leisink, Lotte B. Andersen, Gene A. Brewer, Christian B. Jacobsen, Eva Knies, and Wouter Vandenabeele, Oxford University Press (2021). © Peter Leisink, Lotte B. Andersen, Christian B. Jacobsen, Eva Knies, Gene A. Brewer, and Wouter Vandenabeele. DOI: 10.1093/oso/9780192893420.003.0016 involves outputs, efficiency, outcomes/effectiveness, responsiveness, and democratic outcomes, provides a useful starting point for understanding public service performance. Chapter 2 argues that public service performance needs to be understood in relation to different stakeholders who value different collective social outcomes they want to achieve and prioritize different public values in public service provision. We contend that any measure of public service performance should explain which stakeholders' understandings are included, and whether stakeholders' criteria are measured directly or indirectly (i.e. through other sources). Employees are important stakeholders in public service provision, but their interests are included only marginally in existing measures of public service performance. Therefore, the construct of "employee outcomes" should be included in research to complement the "public service performance" concept (as per Brewer and Selden 2000, 689).

Although performance is recognized as a key concern of public management scholars, there is no common framework to guide researchers in their selection of measures despite earlier work on the issue (Boyne et al. 2006). Chapter 2 discusses nine studies illustrating a stakeholder perspective, and it shows that measures vary from the accomplishment of overall official goals to specific aspects of performance such as efficiency. A key observation is that stakeholder interests are typically not made explicit and measured directly. In this respect, Chapters 10 and 13 contribute by paying explicit attention to different stakeholders in their discussion of performance and public values. Chapter 10 argues that diversity management contributes to improving performance outcomes for disadvantaged groups and addressing inequalities in society. It also argues that the two major diversity paradigms are connected to different public values, with the discrimination and fairness perspective relating to equity and social justice, and the synergy perspective relating to organizational effectiveness and responsiveness. Chapter 13 discusses the value conflicts facing public service professionals. These conflicts arise from the differences between the personal and professional values they hold important and the values that are promoted by their organizations, managers, and other stakeholders such as citizens and service users.

Other chapters in Part II of the volume examine (organizational) performance mostly without further specification (Chapters 5, 9, and 11) or emphasize specific aspects of public service performance and/or measure them in specific ways. For instance, Chapter 6 understands performance as meeting the organization's goals and measures this as the percentage of ministerial targets met by central government executive agencies.

What holds for organizational performance also holds for individual job performance. Chapter 14 observes that the heterogeneity of conceptualizations and measures of different types of job performance is immense in the literature on public service performance. Studies focus on different dimensions of individual performance, including in-role and extra-role performance and performance directed toward individuals or society. Studies also use a variety of measures, such as supervisor ratings of employee performance, self-assessed performance, subjective willingness to exert effort, and the number of specific tasks fulfilled. Obviously, this heterogeneity has made it hard to accumulate knowledge. While Chapter 14 argues that there is a need for a uniform conceptualization, it also recognizes that any definition of performance depends on the institutional context because of the value component of performance. The chapter illustrates this point with the telling example of teachers helping children with personal issues. This may or may not be considered performance, depending on what is institutionally appropriate.

16.2.1.2 Employee Outcomes
When chapters in Part II discuss performance, they typically do not include employee outcomes. An exception is Chapter 9 which pays attention to potential trade-offs between organizational performance and employee outcomes. This chapter observes that high performance may well be achieved at a cost to employee well-being when work overload leads to anxiety, stress, burnout, and work–life imbalance, while high-commitment and high-involvement HRM systems may produce employee well-being alongside superior performance.

Chapter 12, which opens Part III of the volume, examines employee well-being following Warr's (1987) definition of the concept as the overall quality of an employee's experience and functioning at work. Well-being is regarded as a multidimensional concept. It involves psychological well-being (focusing on subjective experiences, such as job satisfaction and engagement), physical well-being (referring to bodily health and work-related illnesses, stress, and sick leave), and social well-being (involving interactions among employees and between them and their supervisors and including social support and trust).

Chapter 15 adds a relevant outcome of public organizations' HRM policies, namely employees' employability. Understanding the concept to mean that employees have fair chances in the labor market, Chapter 15 argues that being employable is an important employee outcome with a view to the ongoing changes in the public sector, and that investing in employees' employability is also in the employer's interest. Employability investments can be seen as part of a retention strategy that helps public organizations to match supply and demand in a labor market characterized by shortages of qualified employees. In addition, investing in employees' employability can be seen as public value creation because employers thus contribute to the collective outcome of sustainable employment.

16.2.1.3 Managing
Many dimensions of managing for public service performance are examined in this volume. They include a variety of leadership behaviors: goal-oriented, relations-oriented, non-leader-centered leadership (or expressed in related terms: transformational, transactional, and distributive leadership), and ethical leadership, as well as reputation management, people management, performance management, diversity management, and change management/leadership. Chapter 1 notes that the public management literature features a line of research concentrating on management

systems and another line on leadership. Both are represented in this volume. On the one hand, Chapters 8 and 9, respectively, examine performance management and human resource management systems. On the other hand, Chapters 5, 6, 10, and 11 examine leadership activities generally and diversity and change leadership specifically. However, all chapters pay attention to both management and leadership, thereby integrating different bodies of literature. For instance, Chapter 8 understands performance management as a system that integrates goal-setting activities, performance measurement, and the feedback of performance information into decision-making, and it supplements this with several leadership activities, such as creating learning platforms and facilitating open and purpose-driven dialogue about performance. Likewise, Chapter 10 shows that team diversity as such does not result directly in higher team performance but depends on leadership behaviors to achieve this positive effect. Some chapters, notably Chapters 3, 7, 10, and 15, focus explicitly on people management, involving the implementation of HRM practices and leadership behavior in combination. This resonates with a key point of Chapter 3, which discusses the HRM literature's call for the integration of management and leadership.

Chapter 3 argues that public management studies should not just concentrate on executive or senior public managers but should also study middle and frontline managers who are responsible for managing and supporting street-level bureaucrats and other public service employees. In this volume, Chapters 5 and 8) discuss public managers in general, although the examined types of leadership behavior are mostly related to senior managers. Other chapters make their focus explicit, such as Chapter 6 which concentrates on senior managers; Chapter 10 which pays attention to team leaders; and Chapters 7, 11, and 15 which distinguish explicitly between top managers, on the one hand, and middle and frontline managers, on the other. The value of these chapters is that they cover a range of activities of public managers and relate these to the roles and responsibilities of managers at different hierarchical levels.

16.2.2 The Public Management–Public Service Performance Relationship

The chapters in this volume provide ample evidence for the management–performance relationship that is central to "managing for public service performance." For instance, Chapter 5 concentrates on public managers' goal-oriented, relational, and non-leader-centered leadership and discusses empirical studies that provide support for the contribution each of these leadership behaviors makes to performance. Likewise, Chapter 6 examines senior managers' contribution to meeting the ministerial targets set for executive agencies, and Chapter 8 reviews the contribution performance management makes to performance.

16.2.2.1   Direct and Indirect Relationships

The chapters in Part II of the volume generally concentrate on the direct relationship between public management and public service performance. However, several chapters also report on evidence that supports an indirect relationship. For instance, Chapter 5 reports that recent studies of the leadership–performance relationship provide evidence of the effect of leadership on performance through employees' motivation and organizational commitment, and through employees' organizational citizenship and innovative behaviors. Chapter 9 builds on HRM research on the HRM–performance relationship and supports a multilevel model by including employee attitudes and behaviors as linking mechanisms. Different approaches to the HRM–performance relationship elaborate on employee attitudes and behaviors in different ways, including their abilities and motivation, organizational commitment, public service motivation, and job satisfaction. The chapter finds that the majority of empirical studies of HRM systems in the public sector provide evidence of employee attitudes and behaviors partly mediating the HRM–performance relationship. The chapter concludes that employees are not passive elements in the relationship but dynamic actors who influence the very nature of the relationship.

Chapter 12 opens Part III of the volume, which deals with the mechanisms mediating the management–performance relationship and offers further support for the indirect relationships. Relating to Wright and Nishii's (2013) multilevel model of the management–performance relationship, several chapters discuss employees' individual job behaviors and job performance as an important link in the management–organizational performance chain. Chapter 13 argues that public service professionals, who face multiple public values and public value tensions, take decisions that are, to some extent, guided by the values they personally and professionally hold important. These values impact their job performance and ultimately the extent to which public value is created. Chapter 14, which discusses the relationship of public employees' motivation and their individual performance, holds that individual performance is related to organizational performance but that the strength of this relationship is unclear because many other variables impact organizational performance.

Regarding the antecedents of individual job performance, Chapter 14 concentrates on the contribution of PSM. Based on a comprehensive and systematic review of all relevant empirical studies since 1990, this chapter concludes that a convincing foundation of empirical evidence supports the direct effect of PSM on individual performance. Moreover, this direct effect does not disappear in studies that test for mediating and moderating variables. However, related to the earlier observation of the heterogeneity of measures of performance, it is unknown whether PSM affects different types of performance in different ways. While the results of studies of PSM's effect on in-role performance are mixed, the results of PSM's effect on extra-role performance and organizational citizenship behavior point unequivocally to a positive effect. Finally, Chapter 14 examines the size of PSM's effect on individual performance and concludes that this is relatively small. However, the chapter argues that performance is a complex construct and it is unlikely that any single factor will explain a large amount of variance.

The volume also provides evidence that management contributes to employee outcomes. Chapter 12 discusses studies that corroborate the relationship between supervisors' support and implementation of some HRM practices (e.g. professional development, performance feedback, and financial rewards) and burnout and engagement among public sector employees. Chapter 13 reports on research showing that individuals who experience incompatibility between their own public service values and those promoted by their organization are more likely to report negative well-being attitudes (stress and quit intentions) than positive attitudes (job satisfaction and commitment). Reconciling such value conflicts is seen as a critical leadership task involving ethical or transformational leadership. Chapter 15 discusses studies that provide support for the contribution management makes to employees' employability by implementing training and development practices and stimulating employees' participation in development programs. So when it comes to employee well-being, human resource management systems (Chapter 9), line managers' implementation of HRM practices, and organizational leadership affect a variety of employee outcomes.

16.2.2.2 Contingency Variables

A central feature of this work is the broad approach to the study of "managing for public service performance," which, as Chapter 1 argues, involves both contextual factors that are central to O'Toole and Meier's (2015) theory of the impact of context on public management and public values as institutional features of the public sector context. Chapter 4 elaborates on the public sector context as an institutional environment. This broad approach involves that the chapters in this volume follow O'Toole and Meier (2015) and pay attention to features of the external and internal organizational context, such as the complexity and turbulence of the environment as well as the multiplicity of goals, the degree of centralization, and red tape, which are typical of public organizations. In the institutional perspective, developed by Chapter 4, structural contextual factors are combined with normative and cultural–cognitive features to describe publicness as an institution that, on the one hand, influences public services, but, on the other, is itself reproduced and changed by the actions and behaviors of organizations and individuals. Questions regarding what publicness involves in different public services, what kind of public values are salient, and what their consequences are for public employees, public service performance, and employee outcomes are examined by several chapters.

Focusing on organizational performance, Chapter 5 regards not only senior managers' ability but also their discretion to make decisions and their capacity in allocating resources as variables that determine their impact on organizational performance. Chapter 5 proposes another moderating variable, namely organizational reputation, which is a result of achieving high performance previously and in turn acts as a contingency variable affecting managers' efforts to increase performance. These organizational characteristics are supplemented by the public sector environment's complexity, which, as Chapter 11 suggests, affects management's success in leading organizational change. Chapter 11 regards this complexity as involving the degree of homogeneity and the concentration of stakeholder interests in how the organization operates and performs.

Chapter 9 draws on institutional theory to argue that involvement-HRM and commitment-HRM systems fit the public sector context, but that a high-performance HRM system does not. The basic people–management philosophy underlying the involvement and commitment-HRM systems fits the employee well-being-oriented model of public organizations and their humanist ideals. On the contrary, the high-performance HRM system is based on high management control and low trust, which does not fit the values characteristic of the public sector context. So rather than emphasizing specific variables, Chapter 9 proposes a sort of configurational approach to HRM systems and analyzes their underlying logics in relation to the logic of appropriateness that the authors consider distinctive of the public sector context.

Focusing on individual performance, Chapter 14 discusses several variables that moderate the PSM–individual performance relationship. One of these variables is public managers' transformational leadership. Other variables are the public organization's mission valence and the fit between the employee's and the organization's values. Public values stand out as institutional features that impact the PSM–individual employee performance relationship.

Concentrating on employee well-being, Chapter 12 refers to the generic job demands–resources (JD–R) model and person–environment (P–E) fit model to discuss several variables that impact well-being. Regarding the PSM–employee well-being relationship, Chapter 12 argues that the effect of PSM on employee well-being tends to be positive, but it can also be negative under certain conditions.

16.2.2.3 Conclusion

Overall, the evidence highlights public management's contribution to public service performance and employee well-being. However, this relationship involves multidimensional concepts, different organizational levels, and a vast array of mediating and moderating variables, many of which are not (yet) supported by solid evidence. The systematic study presented in Chapter 14 on the state of the art of the PSM–individual performance relationship stands out as a positive example. That exercise is feasible because it concentrates on a specific, much researched relationship. Even so, the authors note several limitations.

Despite such honest reckoning, motivated by the rigorous nature of scientific inquiry, the evidence reported in this volume indicates that management contributes to organizational performance both directly and indirectly, in many micro-level relationships and on the whole. The indirect mechanisms covered by this work involve public employees' attitudes and behaviors. That is how people, both public managers and employees, make a difference, as our volume's subtitle highlights. From extant studies, we know that public managers contribute indirectly to performance through their influence on, for instance, organizational culture, performance management, management strategy, and rules and red tape (Andersen and Moynihan 2016; Andrews et al. 2012; Brewer and Walker 2010; Gerrish 2015; Walker et al. 2012). The chapters in this volume also provide evidence that management impacts individual job performance and employee outcomes, notably through middle and frontline managers' implementation of HRM practices and their leadership behaviors. There are good theoretical arguments and solid empirical evidence that confirm the influence exerted by the public sector context, including studies that show how public values make a difference.

16.3 Directions for Future Research

The individual chapters have discussed the limitations of existing research and the consequent agenda for future research pertaining to their chapter's topic. Here, we will build on these reflections for an overall discussion of the directions for future research on "managing for public service performance." We will cover several issues, namely the state of different theories in ongoing research, the development of more comprehensive models, the relevance of generic theories and the public sector context, and the call for methodological rigor. We conclude this section with a critical reflection on the relevance of research on "managing for public service performance" in light of public service provision's increasing dependence on networks involving multiple organizations.

16.3.1 From Theoretical Fragmentation Toward an Integrated Theoretical Framework

Section 16.2 summarized the evidence regarding the management–public service performance relationship. An obvious question is: How are these relationships theoretically explained? Chapter 9, which examines the relationship between different HRM systems and organizational performance, observes that studies tend not to expend much effort on elaborating on the underlying theories of the models they use. We agree that theorizing relationships is definitely an issue for the future research agenda.

The chapters in this volume refer to a vast array of theories to explain the specific relationships on which they focus. Going through the chapters, one comes across institutional theory, leadership theory, attribution theory, self-determination theory, motivation crowding theory, social exchange theory, resource-based theory, HRM systems' strength theory, identity theory, and theories underlying the AMO (Ability, Motivation, and Opportunity to perform), JD–R, and P–E fit models. Obviously, these theories are not just alternatives to explain the same phenomenon. Some theories such as institutional theory and resource-based theory are more adequate to deal with macro-level and organizational-level phenomena, while others such as leadership theory, social exchange theory, and attribution theory can more adequately deal with interpersonal phenomena at the micro level. Some of the mentioned theories concern a specific phenomenon such as people's motivations, their likely antecedents, and consequences. Overall, the situation of public management research resembles the field of organization theory. To the question of why there are so many organization theories and why it is so difficult for organization theorists to converge on a common theory, Scherer (2003, 311) answers that the spectrum and variety of topics make it hard, if not impossible, to integrate these into one grand theory.

However, some theories could well complement each other in explaining the same phenomenon. For instance, self-determination theory, social exchange theory, attribution theory, and institutional theory, to name a few, shed different light on behavior in organizational settings. Yet in practice, researchers often have their favorite theories and do not make use of complementary theories to reach a more comprehensive explanation for the phenomenon under study. The consequence is theoretical fragmentation, which thwarts the growth of knowledge. This is not to say that theoretical pluriformity is not worthwhile. On the contrary, theories that offer competing explanations for the same phenomenon––for example, as rational choice theory and institutional theory do in explaining behavior as a result of the pursuit of rational interests or as a result of following appropriate routines and conventions— should be welcomed. Different meta-theoretical perspectives that researchers have in terms of research purposes and methods can also be a source of pluriformity (Scherer 2003), but it does not seem to explain the array of theories we observe in this volume. A situation of theoretical fragmentation rather than of deliberate pluriformity is not fruitful. Therefore, a definite priority on our research agenda is to elaborate more profoundly on the theoretical assumptions of the models used to study certain phenomena, as well as to develop more integrated explanations by making use of complementary theories.

16.3.2 Developing More Comprehensive Models

A variety of issues are relevant for future research on "managing for public service performance" as a multilevel, direct, and indirect relationship that is affected by distinctive public sector context characteristics. We will first reflect on the multidimensional nature of the key concepts involved and then explore more comprehensive models.

Recognizing that the key variables in the management–public service performance relationship are multidimensional concepts, several chapters call for studies that examine the gap in existing research, namely how different dimensions of a construct relate to each other when linked to another variable. Focusing on the independent variable, Chapter 5 calls for more research on the effectiveness of different leadership behaviors independently or in combination. Chapter 11 reiterates this call regarding the effect of different forms of leadership in relation to the implementation of organizational change. Chapter 6 calls for the study of how senior managers' publicness fit and other dimensions of managerial fit moderate each other's effect on organizational performance. Chapter 8 calls for research on how performance management systems can be integrated with various leadership behaviors that shape employees' perceptions and motivation and that facilitate organizational learning.

Focusing on the dependent variable, Chapter 2 emphasizes the need for future research to incorporate multiple stakeholders' views and interests regarding public service performance explicitly. Regarding individual job performance, Chapter 14 argues that we need to study what effects different dimensions of PSM have on specific types of individual performance. Noting that employees' employability is positively related to performance, Chapter 15 suggests that future research examines how different dimensions of performance are affected by employability. Concentrating on employee well-being as the dependent variable, Chapter 12 calls for more research on dimensions that are currently understudied in a public sector context. These involve aspects of psychological well-being such as engagement, absenteeism, resignation, and burnout, and the social well-being dimension involving relations with co-workers and supervisors.

Another type of future research priority concerns the variables linking public management and public service performance. Chapter 9, which studies HRM systems and performance, Chapter 10, which examines diversity management and performance, and Chapter 14, which studies PSM and individual job performance, note the dearth of studies examining the full multilevel chain that links management strategies and systems to individual employees' job performance, work unit, and organizational performance. This multilevel chain is generically theorized by Wright and Nishii (2013), but there are few studies that have attempted to provide empirical evidence in a public sector context.

16.3.3 Attention to the Public Sector Context and the Use of Generic Theories

A prominent issue for future research is the full and systematic study of the impact of the public sector context. This call for future research comes in two forms. First, there are calls for integration of specific public sector variables. This call is clearly motivated by the attempt to develop more comprehensive models, as discussed in Section 16.3.2. For instance, Chapter 7 argues that we need more research on how the conflict between different values affects line managers' people management performance. Chapter 13 adds to this by observing that values are not necessarily explicit and calls for studies that examine what the implications of implicit value conflicts are for employees' job performance and well-being. Other chapters argue that future studies should pay attention to the impact of red tape on employee well-being (Chapter 12), on employee job performance (Chapter 14), and on employees' employability (Chapter 15).

Second, several chapters call for systematic research comparing public, non-profit, and private sector organizations when studying particular phenomena. Chapter 6 does so with regard to the question of how different dimensions of managerial fit, including publicness fit, moderate each other's effects on organizational performance. Chapter 12 encourages scholars to investigate differences in employees' well-being between public, non-profit, and private sectors and within subsectors of the public sector. Likewise, Chapter 15 calls for studies to investigate possible sectoral differences in the factors that are likely to impact employees' employability and its outcomes.

These calls for future research raise the broader question of the validity of the assumptions underlying generic models. Chapter 12 addresses this question as it concludes that the generic job demands–resources model is appropriate for explaining employee well-being in the public sector. The JD–R model can be used to study the effects of public sector employees' job demands and job resources. However, when it comes to operationalizing the generic concepts of job demands and resources, Chapter 12 argues that it is necessary to pay attention to specific variables that the public sector literature considers relevant. Here, the chapter refers to red tape as a hindrance demand and PSM as a resource. In a similar way, Chapter 7 makes use of the generic AMO model to explain individual performance to examine the antecedents of public sector supervisors' people management performance. Chapter 7 uses insights from the public management literature to operationalize the *opportunity* variable in a public sector-specific way by including red tape, which is regarded as a constraint on managerial autonomy. Adding these public sector-specific variables is an example of what Knies et al. (2018a) regard as advanced contextualization that may affect the generalizability of research for other private sector contexts.

However, both Chapters 7 and 12 live up to the requirement set by Knies et al. (2018a) that this kind of contextualization be evidence-based. Chapter 12 discusses empirical studies that show, for instance, that the job resource PSM has contradictory effects, begging the question of what contextual variables can help explain this deviance from the generic model. The chapter suggests that other job demands such as role conflict and role ambiguity also require further study because public sector employees are potentially more prone to these phenomena. This reasoning illustrates the kind of theoretical argument and empirical evidence that Knies et al. (2018a) require to balance rigor and relevance. The public management and organization literature (e.g. Rainey 2014) holds several characteristics of the public sector context as distinctive. Systematic comparative research using generic models can help provide evidence for these theoretical assumptions and help build the argument for contextualizing future research.

16.3.4 Methodological Rigor

While there are concerns about the increasingly tougher requirements for method-ological rigor (Boxall et al. 2007; Knies et al. 2018a), this should not be understood as implying that the methodological rigor of public management research itself is not an issue. Several chapters raise concerns about endogeneity problems related to cross-sectional designs and omitted variables confounding the relationships between independent and dependent variables. Chapter 5 discusses these problems regarding the relationship between management and organizational performance, Chapter 14 regarding the relationship between PSM and individual job performance, and Chapter 12 regarding the relationship between leadership, person–organization (P–O) fit, and employee well-being.

In response to these concerns, future studies are advised to consider several options that contribute to causal analysis. One is to join the recent growth of studies that make use of experimental designs and randomized controlled trials. Bellé's (2013; 2014) studies of the effects of PSM and leadership on job performance stand out as a prime example. Another option is to make use of opportunities for longitudinal research when and where they exist. This is particularly relevant, as Chapter 11 observes, when one wants to study large-scale reforms and the leadership that goes with them, which have their effects in terms of organizational change and public service performance over a long period of time. One example of such a longitudinal study is the study by Day et al. (2016) of the effect of school principals' combination of different leadership strategies on student outcomes.

These suggestions deserve serious consideration. Yet the state of the art in the study of the relationship between PSM and individual performance, which is the most advanced in terms of rigorous research to date, indicates how difficult it would be to apply these suggestions to the field of management–public service performance research. In addition, ethical and practical reasons may make experimental manipu-lation inappropriate or impossible. Discussing this situation with respect to the PSM–performance relationship, Chapter 14 suggests a valid non-experimental alter-native involving meta-analysis and replication studies. The chapter admits that the feasibility of these alternatives is seriously affected by the number of studies available (for meta-analysis) or the need for a concerted effort by multiple teams (in the case of replication through multiple independent studies). Thus, there are no easy solu-tions. For management–public service performance research, the best possible way forward seems to involve improving the rigor of existing research designs by apply-ing the suggestions made for more comprehensive models, by avoiding the use of self-reported performance data or the same data source to measure management and performance (e.g. instead using register data or assessments done by other stakeholders), and by controlling for possible factors that may influence both the independent and dependent variables.

16.3.5 Is Management–Public Service Performance Research Still Relevant?

How relevant is research on "managing for public service performance"? A key reason for questioning its relevance could be the criticism that the management–public service performance relationship is based on assumptions related to the NPM model, which do not fit governance approaches labeled as new public governance (NPG) or public value management (PVM) (Bryson et al. 2014; Osborne 2010; Osborne et al. 2013; Stoker 2006). These NPM assumptions involve the primacy attributed to market-like logics, a preoccupation with performance management and output control, a focus on unit costs, efficiency, and outputs versus the primacy attributed by NPG/PVM to collaborative governance, inter-organizational networks, co-production, and the importance of traditional democratic and constitutional values, as well as new public values such as public service quality, transparency, and accountability.

Focusing on the aspect of the collaboration of multiple actors in the provision of public services, these actors may be organizations, as in the case of the government's public service delivery through private and non-profit organizations or organizations and citizens in co-production (Alford 2009; Alford and O'Flynn 2012; Loeffler and Bovaird 2018). Co-production as seen by Loeffler and Bovaird (2018) goes beyond citizens as service users and involves public organizations working with citizens in discussions about strategic issues such as the prioritization of outcomes and the redesign of services, as well as actions aimed at implementing service–delivery improvements. The reasons for the increased interest in inter-organizational collaboration and co-production are basically the same. These involve the belief that the quality of public decisions and services will benefit from making use of the collective knowledge and experience of organizations and users–citizens, the concerns about the legitimacy of public decisions and the low level of trust in government and public services, and the costs of public service provision which may be affected by pooling resources and citizens' contributions. Another reason for inter-organizational collaboration is that this may be the only way to tackle wicked problems, such as climate change and poverty (Geuijen et al. 2017; Roberts 2000).

In our view, this volume's perspective on "managing for public service performance" remains highly relevant. Its assumptions do not coincide with the NPM model. Our understanding of public service performance emphasizes a plurality of public values and different stakeholders, which is similar to NPG/PVM's emphasis on stakeholders. An essential feature of our perspective is the requirement to make explicit which stakeholders' understandings of public service performance are included and excluded. In addition, public service performance is understood as a multidimensional concept that includes both service performance outcomes and the public values that are considered important for the process of public service provision. This understanding combines the publicness and service approach to public service provision that, according to Osborne et al. (2013), is essential to public management theory in the NPG era.

Future research on managing for public service performance can make a significant contribution to understanding what this means in the context of NPG/PVM. The literature on public value creation in collaborative governance tends to focus on the interaction of government organizations with voluntary organizations, community activists, social entrepreneurs, media, and others and concentrates on deliberation and agreeing on common goals (e.g. Bryson et al. 2017; Lewis 2011). This literature gives less attention to public servants and the issues involved in the joint delivery of public services, although there are multiple issues that require further research. For instance, as Loeffler and Bovaird (2018) argue, achieving the potential advantages of co-production requires specific staff skills, professionals' trust in the ability of service users and communities to co-produce better outcomes, and change management to deal with likely resistance from professionals and managers.

The issues that should feature on the agenda of managing for public service performance in a collaborative governance context have begun to attract attention (e.g. Alford and O'Flynn 2012; Bartelings et al. 2017; Cristofoli et al. 2017; Maccio and Cristofoli 2017; Steijn et al. 2011; Zambrano-Gutiérrez et al. 2017). One issue is the importance of building trust, which may be undermined by public servants not having sufficient autonomy and by typical public sector features such as accountability obligations (Alford and O'Flynn 2012, 128–33). Another issue is the complexity of interactions related to differing interests and levels of knowledge and capability among the network members. Alford and O'Flynn (2012, 203) emphasize the importance of network leaders establishing a shared vision or common purpose while recognizing the differences between the various parties. Several studies provide support for the important role of a network manager. Bartelings et al. (2017) show that the activities performed by a network manager partly fit the managerial roles described by Mintzberg (1973) but differ from traditional managerial work by a set of activities that they label "orchestrational work." This refers to the integration and fine-tuning of activities that are executed by network partners from various organizations to jointly deliver services.

The literature on collaborative governance and public service delivery by organizational networks is rich in the kind of issues that require further research. Managing for public service performance in a collaborative governance context opens up a direction for future research that can build on the insights that our organizational view of "managing for public service performance" has produced and that will extend the present body of knowledge significantly.

16.4 Implications for Public Management Practice

The conclusion that management matters for public service performance and employee well-being in a variety of ways is practically relevant. It indicates that it is worthwhile for public organizations to invest in equipping management with good service provision policies and the conditions to implement these.

Individual chapters have shown the importance of internal management activities, which involve performance management, human resource management, and diversity management, to help public organizations achieve public service performance and employee well-being. Making such contributions requires that performance management and HRM are aligned with the organization's strategic goals and with the underlying human resource philosophy. Chapter 9 argued that public organizations' adherence to humanist ideals and a model employer oriented on employee well-being is not compatible with high-performance management models based on management control and low trust but instead benefits from high-involvement models.

It is important to emphasize that the organization's mission should be the focus of performance management and HRM strategies. The multitude of performance targets and quality standards that have grown over time in the public sector tend to have a life of their own in guiding organizational strategies, but in the end, ticking the box does not mean that the organization's mission will be accomplished and the intended public value will be created (Knies et al. 2018b). Starting from the organization's mission, it is important to establish what employee behaviors are required to achieve the intended outcomes so that the strategies and their implementation by managers can be geared toward those behaviors. For instance, as Chapter 8 illustrates, performance management involves setting relevant goals as well as an implementation approach that motivates employees and stimulates their participation in learning platforms.

Diversity management adds to HRM. Targeted recruitment and selection as well as training, development, and team-building can help create inclusive organizations that support the belongingness and uniqueness of employees. In addition, diversity management practices and leadership are needed to facilitate a productive team diversity, which contributes to the performance outcomes that team diversity can potentially help deliver through its contribution to organizational learning and innovation.

Therefore, senior managers who are responsible for organizational strategy are well advised to ensure that performance management, HRM, and diversity management strategies are aligned with the organization's mission and strategic goals. Senior managers will also need to attend to the creation of the conditions for managers at various levels of the hierarchy to take their crucial role in strategy implementation. These conditions involve, first, that the selection and appointment of managers are made dependent on candidates' leadership competences. It is relevant to make this observation because, as Chapter 7 argues, there is a tendency in public organizations to select the best professional employee without assessing leadership competences or potential. Second, public organizations are advised to invest in leadership development programs. Chapter 5 shows that leadership can be learnt and that leaders benefit from developing several types of leadership behaviors. Third, senior managers have a special responsibility for creating the opportunities for managers at all hierarchical levels to do a good job. These opportunities involve practical facilities such as time and financial budget. It is also important that managers have the autonomy to take decisions and act effectively. This refers to both senior managers (see Chapter 5) and middle and frontline managers (see Chapter 7). The autonomy of public managers in developing and implementing personnel policies is a special case in point. This is often seen as limited due to government directives. However, it is worth scrutinizing the efficacy of rules that internal management has imposed with the objective of management control (Bozeman and Feeney 2011; Van Loon et al. 2016).

Most of what has been observed with the objective of achieving public service performance holds for achieving employee well-being as well. Managers need good HRM policies to support their employees' well-being. Their leadership behaviors are also important as Chapters 3, 7, and 12 argue. Leadership support in itself is one of employees' core job resources that contributes to their well-being. In addition, managers can contribute to employee well-being by paying attention to the balance between job demands and job resources and being aware of the inherent risks of stress and burnout for employees, as Chapter 12 observes. Having resourceful and challenging jobs is also an important factor that contributes to employees' employability (Chapter 15). The different areas of management support for employee well-being underline the importance noted earlier of outlining a clear profile of people management competences to guide the selection and development of public managers.

The presumed shift toward NPG/PVM and the related importance of inter-organizational collaboration and co-production in delivering public services has profound implications for management practice, as we discussed above. One concerns the activities and abilities of managers and public servants who are involved in the joint delivery of public services. Their support by HRM policies requires a reorientation away from the traditional organization view based on internal management control. The implications also concern institutional features of public organizations' *modus operandi* such as their accountability obligations and the related consequences for managerial and professional autonomy. These are difficult to adapt. However, an awareness of the impact that the public sector context has on organizational collaboration would help managers and professionals communicate and collaborate with others involved in the joint delivery of public services.

These implications for managerial practice are not meant as best practice advice. The idea of "best practice" neglects the relevance of context in public policy and management. Rather, this summary of practical implications represents the insights of key factors and mechanisms involved in the delivery of public service that need to be contextualized when they are applied. They are based on both firm evidence from scientific research and on the experience gained by the authors from their involvement in public management practice as advisors. This involvement has enriched our understanding of managing for public service performance, which we hope will contribute to our purpose: improving the delivery of public service and the creation of public value.

References

Alford, J. 2009. *Engaging Public Sector Clients: From Service–Delivery to Co-Production.* Basingstoke: Palgrave Macmillan.

Alford, J., and J. O'Flynn. 2012. *Rethinking Public Service Delivery: Managing with External Providers.* Basingstoke: Palgrave Macmillan.

Andersen, S. C., and D. Moynihan. 2016. "How Leaders Respond to Diversity: The Moderating Role of Organizational Culture on Performance Information Use." *Journal of Public Administration Research and Theory 26* (3): pp. 448–60.

Andrews, R., G. Boyne, J. Law, and R. Walker. 2012. *Strategic Management and Public Service Performance.* Basingstoke: Palgrave Macmillan

Bartelings, J., J. Goedee, J. Raab, and R. Bijl. 2017. "The Nature of Orchestrational Work." *Public Management Review 19* (3): pp. 342–60.

Bellé, N. 2013. "Experimental Evidence on the Relationship between Public Service Motivation and Job Performance." *Public Administration Review 73* (1): pp. 143–53.

Bellé, N. 2014. "Leading to Make a Difference: A Field Experiment on the Performance Effects of Transformational Leadership, Perceived Social Impact, and Public Service Motivation." *Journal of Public Administration Research and Theory 24* (1): pp. 109–36.

Boxall, P., J. Purcell, and P. Wright. 2007. "Human Resource Management: Scope, Analysis, and Significance." In *The Oxford Handbook of Human Resource Management,* edited by P. Boxall, J. Purcell, and P. Wright, pp. 1–16. Oxford: Oxford University Press.

Boyne, G. 2002. "Concepts and Indicators of Local Authority Performance: An Evaluation of the Statutory Frameworks in England and Wales." *Public Money & Management 22* (2): pp. 17–24.

Boyne, G., K. Meier, L. O'Toole, and R. Walker. 2006. *Public Service Performance: Perspectives on Measurement and Management.* Cambridge: Cambridge University Press.

Bozeman, B., and M. Feeney. 2011. *Rules and Red Tape: A Prism for Public Administration Theory and Research.* Armonk, NY: M. E. Sharpe.

Brewer, G., and S. Selden. 2000. "Why Elephants Gallop: Assessing and Predicting Organizational Performance in Federal Agencies." *Journal of Public Administration Research and Theory 10* (4): pp. 685–711.

Brewer, G., and R. Walker. 2010. "The Impact of Red Tape on Governmental Performance: An Empirical Analysis." *Journal of Public Administration Research and Theory 20* (1): pp. 233–57.

Bryson, J., B. Crosby, and L. Bloomberg. 2014. "Public Value Governance: Moving Beyond Traditional Public Administration and the New Public Management." *Public Administration Review 74* (4): pp. 445–56.

Bryson, J., A. Sancino, J. Benington, and E. Sorensen. 2017. "Towards a Multi-Actor Theory of Public Value Co-Creation." *Public Management Review 19* (5): pp. 640–54.

Cristofoli, D., M. Meneguzzo, and N. Riccucci. 2017. "Collaborative Administration: The Management of Successful Networks." *Public Management Review 19* (3): pp. 275–83.

Day, C., Q. Gu, and P. Sammons. 2016. "The Impact of Leadership on Student Outcomes: How Successful School Leaders Use Transformational and Instructional Strategies to Make a Difference." *Educational Administration Quarterly 52* (2): pp. 221–58.

Gerrish, E. 2015. "The Impact of Performance Management on Performance in Public Organizations." *Public Administration Review 76* (1): pp. 48–66.

Geuijen, K., M. Moore, A. Cederquist, R. Ronning, and M. Van Twist. 2017. "Creating Public Value in Global Wicked Problems." *Public Management Review 19* (5): pp. 621–39.

Knies, E., P. Boselie, J. S. Gould-Williams, and W. Vandenabeele. 2018a. "Strategic Human Resource Management and Public Sector Performance: Context Matters." *International Journal of Human Resource Management*, pp. 1–13. https://doi.org/10.10 80/09585192.2017.1407088.

Knies, E., P. Leisink, and S. Kraus-Hoogeveen. 2018b. "Frontline Managers' Contribution to Mission Achievement: A Study of How People Management Affects Thoughtful Care." *Human Service Organizations: Management, Leadership & Governance 42* (2): pp. 166–84.

Lewis, J. 2011. "The Future of Network Governance Research: Strength in Diversity and Synthesis." *Public Administration 89* (4): pp. 1221–34.

Loeffler, E., and T. Bovaird. 2018. "From Participation to Co-Production: Widening and Deepening the Contributions of Citizens to Public Services and Outcomes." In *The Palgrave Handbook of Public Administration and Management in Europe*, edited by E. Ongaro and S. Van Thiel, pp. 403–23. London: Palgrave Macmillan.

Maccio, L., and D. Cristofoli. 2017. "How to Support the Endurance of Long-Term Networks: The Pivotal Role of the Network Manager." *Public Administration 95* (4): pp. 1060–76.

Mintzberg, H. 1973. *The Nature of Managerial Work*. New York: Harper & Row.

Osborne, S. 2010. *The New Public Governance?* London: Routledge.

Osborne, S., Z. Radnor, and G. Nasi. 2013. "A New Theory for Public Service Management? Toward a (Public) Service-Dominant Approach." *American Review of Public Administration 43* (2): pp. 135–58.

O'Toole, L. J., and K. Meier. 2015. "Public Management, Context and Performance: In Quest of a More General Theory." *Journal of Public Administration Research and Theory 25* (1): pp. 237–56.

Rainey, H. 2014. *Understanding Public Management and Organization*. 5th ed. San Francisco, CA: John Wiley & Sons.

Roberts, N. 2000. "Wicked Problems and Network Approaches to Resolution." *International Public Management Review 1* (1): pp. 1–19.

Scherer, A. 2003. "Modes of Explanation in Organization Theory." In *The Oxford Handbook of Organization Theory: Meta-Theoretical Perspectives*, edited by H. Tsoukas and C. Knudsen, pp. 310–44. Oxford: Oxford University Press.

Steijn, B., E.-H. Klijn, and J. Edelenbos. 2011. "Public–Private Partnerships: Added Value by Organizational Form or Management?" *Public Administration 89* (4): pp. 1235–52.

Stoker, G. 2006. "Public Value Management: A New Narrative for Networked Governance?" *American Review of Public Administration 36* (1): pp. 41–57.

Van Loon, N., P. Leisink, E. Knies, and G. Brewer. 2016. "Red Tape: Developing and Validating a New Job-Centered Measure." *Public Administration Review 76* (4): pp. 662–73.

Walker, R., G. Boyne, and G. Brewer. 2012. *Public Management and Performance: Research Directions*. Cambridge: Cambridge University Press.

Warr, P. 1987. *Work, Unemployment, and Mental Health*. Oxford: Clarendon Press.

Wright, P., and L. Nishii. 2013. "Strategic HRM and Organizational Behavior: Integrating Multiple Levels of Analysis." In *HRM and Performance: Achievements and Challenges*, edited by J. Paauwe, D. Guest, and P. Wright, pp. 97–110. Chichester: Wiley.

Zambrano-Gutiérrez, J., A. Rutherford, and S. Nicholson-Crotty. 2017. "Types of Coproduction and Differential Effects on Organizational Performance: Evidence from the New York City School System." *Public Administration 95* (3): pp. 776–90.

Names Index

For the benefit of digital users, indexed terms that span two pages (e.g., 52–53) may, on occasion, appear on only one of those pages.

Subject Index